—Sherwin B. Nuland, M.D., author of
How We Die

Janie Ridder
10·96

"DAZZLING SKILL."
—*The Washington Post*

"CHILLING EVIDENCE."
—*New York Newsday*

"ISSUES OF IMMENSE AND
CONTINUING IMPORTANCE."
—*The New York Times Book Review*

Please turn the page for more extraordinary acclaim. . . .

"A balanced, informative and highly readable account, and a valuable insight into American medical education and practive . . ."

—*The Lancet*

"ROBINS EXAMINES THE CASE . . . WITHOUT BIAS, THOROUGHLY, AND RIGHT THROUGH THE FINAL COURT DECISION."

—*Booklist*

"For more than a decade, the circumstances of Libby's death have been the subject of rumor, suspicion and innuendo. Finally, a tragedy of such epic proportions has found the chronicler it has so long needed . . . [Natalie Robins'] book will bring new reportorial and literary standards to its genre."

—Sherwin B. Nuland, M.D., author of *How We Die*, 1994 National Book Award Winner

"ROBINS' REVELATIONS HERE ARE IMPORTANT, INDEED SHOCKING, but she is most affecting when limning her portrait of gentle, bright, creative Libby . . . Robins does a masterful job."

—*Kirkus Reviews*

"Robins lands squarely on a most interesting question: How can we balance the need of young physicians to assume responsibility for patients against the need of patients to have experienced doctors? . . . *The Girl Who Died Twice* is a thorough recounting of the Libby Zion story. . . ."

—*The New England Journal of Medicine*

" 'WHAT WENT WRONG?' THIS IS THE QUESTION NATALIE ROBINS ASKS IN HER CAREFULLY RESEARCHED AND FINELY CRAFTED BOOK."

—*The Nation*

THE GIRL WHO DIED TWICE

EVERY PATIENT'S NIGHTMARE

THE LIBBY ZION CASE AND THE
HIDDEN HAZARDS OF HOSPITALS

BY NATALIE ROBINS

A DELL BOOK

Published by
Dell Publishing
a division of
Bantam Doubleday Dell Publishing Group, Inc.
1540 Broadway
New York, New York 10036

ISBN 0-440-22267-2

Reprinted by arrangement with Delacorte Press

Printed in the United States of America

Published simultaneously in Canada

August 1996

10 9 8 7 6 5 4 3 2 1

For Diana Trilling,
friend and mentor—
who heard what I couldn't see,
and saw what I couldn't hear.

CONTENTS

"Show him the map, before you travel over the ground."

—Henry J. Bigelow, M.D.,
"Medical Education in America,"
the annual address before the
Massachusetts Medical Society, June 7, 1871

"The art of medicine consists in three things: the disease, the patient and the physician. The patient must combat the disease along with the physician."

—Hippocrates, *Aphorisms*, c. 400 B.C.

"What do you regard as the main principle—the, shall I say the basic idea—which you keep before you when you are exercising the practice of your profession?"

There was a pause while Andrew reflected desperately. At length, feeling he was spoiling all the good effect he had created, he blurted out:—

"I suppose—I suppose I keep telling myself never to take anything for granted."

"Thank you, Doctor Manson."

—A. J. Cronin, *The Citadel*

AUTHOR'S NOTE

I'VE KNOWN SIDNEY and Elsa Zion for over twenty-five years. I know their two sons, Adam and Jed, only slightly, and I met their daughter, Libby, just once. I think it was around 1979 or 1980—she was fourteen or fifteen years old. I can still see her standing very poised in a long patterned cotton dress in the center of a large foyer at The Players' clubhouse, a gathering place for theater people in New York City's Gramercy Park, her curly red hair flowing, her bright eyes ablaze. She was a real presence as she talked animatedly with someone who was basically a stranger—me. She was being more than just polite; I could tell she liked people and was eager to share her delight at being at the party. I've forgotten what the celebration was for—it might have been for her father's first book, *Read All About It!: The Collected Adventures of a Maverick Reporter*, or maybe it was his birthday party. But I'll never forget Libby.

THERE WAS SHOCK and despair everywhere, it seemed, when Libby Zion's death occurred on March 5, 1984. My God, she was an eighteen-year-old college freshman who had barely lived. Dead? How could that be possible? Her obituary in *The New York Times* said simply that she "died of cardiac arrest at New York Hospital after a brief illness." She had entered the hospital the night before with an "earache and fever"—"flu symptoms"—reported the hundreds of national media headlines, news and magazine stories, radio and television shows, editorials, and newspaper columns that later appeared, and kept on appearing for over a decade because her father, Sidney Zion—newspaper columnist, free-lance writer and novelist, legal adviser, deal maker, Broadway character, and man-about-town—was not going to let the world forget how Libby had died. What had gone so horribly wrong that she had entered an emergency room with "a virus that's been going around" and had left the hospital eight hours later in a body bag? Were hospitals no longer safe? Was going to the hospital now a dangerous undertaking? If it could happen to her, it could happen to anyone. Sidney, also a former New Jersey federal prosecutor and ace reporter for *The New York Times*, a man who knew just about everyone worth knowing, concluded that the doctors killed his daughter, and he decided to pursue a course of action that he saw as the only way out of his family's grief. He would use all of his power, all of his connections in New York's highest political, media, and social circles, to achieve justice. Libby Zion's father wanted the doctors involved in her death arrested and charged with murder. And if that failed, he wanted everyone involved in his daughter's death to have their lives marked in such a way that they would never forget their roles in the events of March 4 and 5.

WHEN I DECIDED to write this book, I approached Sidney to ask him what he thought about the idea. I said I wanted to write a balanced account of the circumstances surrounding Libby's death, and would seek the cooperation of New York Hospital. Without hesitating a moment, he said, "I'd love it," and then added, "You have my total okay. It's a great gift to Libby."

Sidney and Elsa later signed an agreement that confirmed their understanding of the book. It spelled out such matters as their granting me the right to depict, portray, and represent Libby's life, their lives, and the life of the Zion family as I saw fit, as well as the right to depict all episodes, exploits, events, incidents, situations, and experiences contained in or associated with Libby's life, and the life of the family. Sidney asked that the published book contain a statement that he and his wife never reviewed nor approved the manuscript. And they haven't.

No member of the Zion family saw any stage of this book, and as far as I know have not read it yet. No member of the Zion family blocked my path at any point during my research. There was one thing I was asked not to mention, and I replied that if I determined it was important to the story I would have to mention it, but otherwise I wouldn't. It's included.

The law firm that first handled the litigation for the malpractice suit filed by the Zion family in 1985, Theodore H. Friedman, P.C., was helpful and gracious, especially Cheryl Bulbach, a free-lance lawyer who worked full-time on the lawsuit from its onset, and later David Bamberger, who joined the firm in 1992. The firm's staff, Barbara Mohan, Angie Guirriero, and Noelle Bernstein, were generous with their time and expertise. No one ever made me feel unwelcome. The same is true of Thomas A. Moore and Judith Livingston of Kramer, Dillof, Tessel, Duffy, & Moore, the firm that took over the Zion case in 1994.

On June 21, 1991, I met with two officials from New York Hospital, Keith C. Thompson, senior vice-president and general counsel, and James Fabian, deputy general counsel and director of risk management, and with two of the hospital's lawyers, Francis P. Bensel and Peter T. Crean, of Martin, Clearwater, & Bell. At this meeting, which I taped, I was told that "the hospital has nothing to hide, and we want to be cooperative." But the officials were wary of me, as evidenced by the first or second question they put on the table: "What other parent, or plaintiff, in a medical malpractice lawsuit has generated this much publicity?" Without doubt, by 1991 the Zion case was practically a legend, and not only had most doctors in America—and abroad—heard about it, but it had already brought about changes in the way hospitals around the world worked.

I understood how they felt. They saw Sidney Zion's quest as a tidal wave out to destroy all of them. They were constantly on the defensive, and didn't like that position at all. They pretended not to see how any of the larger issues in which I was interested—medical education, doctor-patient relations—had anything to do with the case. They didn't understand why I wanted to learn about New York Hospital or why I needed to see how the emergency room operated on a day-to-day basis. They just wanted everything about the Zion case—me included—to go away. Yet they insisted they wanted to cooperate. Nevertheless, my visits to New York Hospital were all "unofficial."

Still, Francis, or "Frank," Bensel, the lead counsel handling the Zion action, patiently answered my questions over the years, and was always courteous and responsive. He even grew to trust me a little, I think, as did his colleague Peter Crean. Luke M. Pittoni, of Heidel, Pittoni, Murphy, & Bach, who entered the case in 1993 as a lawyer for one of the doctors, was always respectful, helpful, and candid.

From 1992 to 1995, I talked to over one hundred medical students, interns, residents, doctors, nurses, and administrators at six medical centers around the country. I learned about many other medical schools and hospitals through extensive correspondence with doctors and officials connected to them. Cornell University Medical College, part of New York Hospital–Cornell Medical Center, was the only medical school, of the more than fifty I queried, to turn down my request to sit in on classes. I was informed that the college does not permit visitors. Later, I was told that Robert Michels, M.D., the dean of the medical school, is positively haunted by the Zion case, and had once quipped, "I can see the headlines: NEW YORK HOSPITAL–CORNELL MEDICAL CENTER THAT KILLED LIBBY ZION DISCOVERS CURE FOR CANCER."

IN A SENSE, the seed for this book was actually planted in 1976, nearly eight years before Libby Zion's death. On December 2 of that year, my daughter Rebecca was born—and died—a victim of human error during an amniocentesis procedure before an emergency cesarean operation at Columbia Presbyterian Medical Center. I mourned for the invisible, because, in fact, I never laid eyes on her. No one thought to place her in my arms at any point. My husband and I, and our then-seven-year-old daughter, who had been born at New York Hospital, grieved over a terrible loss that had no face—or history. During my recuperation in the hospital, I wrote a long series of poems called "Birth Elegy," which were later published in my collection *Eclipse*. "There's nothing left after grief leaves: except the waves that remind us where we've been and why we left and how we can follow grieving to its source: beginning again," said poem "XVI." So in time, we all healed, and we became a family of four again with the birth of our son on July 10, 1978. The doctor whose care I was under when Rebecca died delivered my son.

Oh, I had raged over what had happened to Rebecca. I hated my doctor for calling her a fetus when she was a full-term baby. But it got me thinking about the way doctors often use language either to mask or protect their feelings. At one point, my doctor—or some other doctor—said, "There was vascular trouble," and when I asked what that meant, I was told, "It's a whole syndrome." Well, what it meant was that the pinprick that ruptured my placenta during the amniocentesis test that preceded surgery caused my baby to bleed to death.

I felt bitterness—and shame—for the young doctor who had come into my room to ask "How's your baby doing?" When I replied, "She's dead," he started to argue with me and thought I must be mistaken or suffering from postpartum depression. I remember, though, that he came back the next afternoon to apologize. I also remember being puzzled by his role in my hospital life.

I resented the medical center for putting me on the maternity ward so that when I fell asleep or dozed it was to the noises of newborns crying. I blamed everyone and everything. Yet despite all the things that went wrong and felt wrong, I did not sue my doctor.

I am not stupid, and I am not afraid. I'm very outspoken, sometimes far too much so, and I heard people around me wonder at my sanity in continuing a relationship with the doctor who had brought so much pain into my life. But I had to follow my own feelings, and these feelings told me that my doctor was in agony, too. This man's heart ached. I saw it. And what did he do? Dr. Richard U. Levine talked to me. He talked and talked to me. He may have called every day for a time—I'm not sure—but certainly I remember that weekly calls continued for years. These calls helped me come to terms with my conflicting feelings—not only toward him, but toward doctors in general. Just recently he said to me, "You never asked me how I worked it out." And, indeed, I never had, although I answered, "I assumed you worked it out in your calls to me." "There was much more to it," he said, recalling details from that cold December day that I had either forgotten or had never known. And then he added, "I was your grief counselor. We bonded together."

And so we did.

IT MAY BE that such bonding is the secret to the doctor-patient relationship. A doctor I met during the intense, often enigmatic exploration of my subject told me she thought I was working out my anger over Rebecca by writing this book. No, No, I protested, I worked that out long ago. And that was true. But still, there must have been something lingering that she sensed. I think that what she saw was my bewilderment over, and interest in, Sidney Zion's anger, however different our respective calamities. Why had his anger taken the form it did? How did he sustain years and years of almost warlike conduct that allowed him to strike out at every authority figure in society that defied his objectives?

Side by side with these questions was an impulse not only to examine Libby's life and the life of her family, but to investigate some medical conundrums that my experience with doctors had caused me to think about vaguely, and which, of course, were clarified and made visible as a result of Sidney Zion's historic crusade for justice. My days as a new patient had bewildered me. Who were all these people milling around me? What were their responsibilities? What were mine?

The story I uncovered is not what New York Hospital might want on record, nor is it the story that Sidney Zion told the world.

"Libby and I weren't allowed to tell the truth in our homes," Dale Fox, one of Libby's neighborhood—and closest—friends said to me. "And we wanted the truth to be told."

So in a sad, though not unremarkable way, Libby's death is the beginning of the story, for it enables me to talk about her life as she herself could never talk about it. Thus, as well as the medical story of her death, this is Libby's story. That's it. It's that simple.

Yet what I learned, from official records and through interviews with people who had never spoken out before, and from people who had spoken publicly but told only part of what they knew, doesn't cancel what Libby Zion's father accomplished for American medicine. It is my hope that *The Girl Who Died Twice* explains why.

The details concerning the life and death of Libby Zion are abundant. The truth is more elusive. Family members remember one thing, friends another, and doctors and lawyers yet others. Contradictions and conflicting accounts in many ways define the case, and the story.

Most of the information and dialogue in this book comes from author interviews. In some cases, the information and dialogue comes from pretrial and trial depositions and transcripts, attorney memorandums, school, hospital and doctors' records, letters, newspaper and magazine articles, television and radio programs, and transcripts of New York City and New York State Department of Health and other agencies' hearings, and is so cited in the Source Notes.

Certain people requested pseudonyms or their names were changed to protect their privacy. The pseudonyms are: Jay Eber, Ralph Enders, Paula Este, Barry Fox, Dale Fox, Violet Noss, and Carl Potter.

PART 1

1

I N T H E O R I G I N A L plans of the World War I–vintage building, with its stately marble lobby and inlaid ceiling, the white-walled room in apartment 3B was meant to be a maid's room; it was twelve by twenty feet, right off the small cluttered kitchen. But in the girl's hands, the room had become a cozy, self-contained world that could have been transplanted from San Francisco's Haight-Ashbury to the Upper West Side of Manhattan. It was Libby Zion's haven.

To provide herself with an even cozier retreat, she had built a loft bed in the northwest corner of the little room. On Sunday, March 4, 1984, Libby climbed into her bed.

She was not feeling well.

Three days earlier, on Thursday, March 1, Libby, who suffered from a lifelong fear of dentists, had a decayed eyetooth removed by Dr. Alan Wasserman, a dentist who had begun treating her on February 17.

A first-year student at Bennington College, "Libs"—
her father invented the nickname—had been back home
since January, participating in the school's mandatory two-
month work-study program. Her father, writer Sidney
Zion, had gotten her a salaried job working for Andrew
Stein, who was New York City Council president at the
time.

Libby came to Dr. Wasserman through another doctor,
Kenneth Greenspan, a psychiatrist who specialized in biofeedback, whom she had been seeing since January 1984.
Elsa Zion, Libby's mother, had read about Dr. Greenspan's work in a magazine and decided Libby—and her
father—could benefit from a technique that, among other
things, helps to alleviate stress by "teaching you to
breathe," as Sidney Zion put it. The eight-session program
involved using electronic sensors to measure aspects of the
body's functioning that one might not otherwise be con-
sciously aware of—skin temperature, sweat-gland activity,
brain waves, muscle tension, and breathing patterns. "The
kid loved it," Sidney said. "She wanted me to do it more,
but I didn't have the patience."

On January 19, Libby had told Dr. Greenspan that for
her "entire life" she felt she was "just acting. It's really not
me." He had diagnosed an atypical depression, which he
said was caused by a chemical imbalance. In addition to the
biofeedback treatments, Dr. Greenspan later that month
prescribed to Libby the antidepressant Nardil, a highly
controversial drug because of its side effects; it can lower
blood pressure, for example. Patients on Nardil must pains-
takingly monitor their diets and avoid over fifty types of
food, as well as certain medications, like cold remedies.

Libby's dentist, Dr. Wasserman, remembered that she
"was running against the clock, because she had to get
back to school" on Monday, March 5. But Libby was a

"very good" patient, he said, because she trusted him. "She stayed put in the chair, and didn't jump around." Indeed, they liked each other so much that a very warm relationship quickly developed. "We had a guy we were going to fix her up with—another redhead, another phobic about dentists, too," Dr. Wasserman said. He remembered that she "had cold symptoms when she came in—and not a bad cold, either." It was a "difficult extraction because the tooth was crumbling," but everything went fine, even though "she had some pain. I gave her Percodan—twenty of them. I called her the next day to see how she was doing and she said fine—she had taken one pill and the pain went away."

Elsa said that before Libby went for her dental appointment she had gone to see her pediatrician, Dr. Irene Shapiro, "because she had a nasal drip, and things were not working right in her head." According to Dr. Shapiro, Libby said she had a cold and an earache. However, the pediatrician didn't record any "positive findings" in Libby's chart because she didn't find any infection. In fact, she found no marked redness or fluid in Libby's ears, and noted that Libby's lungs were clear. Libby didn't have a temperature, either, according to Dr. Shapiro. Nevertheless, she prescribed an antibiotic, erythromycin, and also told Libby to take an over-the-counter medicine, Chlortrimeton, for the cold symptoms.

Friday, March 2, was to be Libby's last day at work. For two months she had been doing research for Andrew Stein on drugs and on women's issues. Her fellow employees had planned a going-back-to-school party for her, so Libby went to the office. But she didn't stay long. "I think she felt lousy and came back home, but nothing seemed terribly serious," Sidney said. Elsa got home from work later in the evening and Libby told her she had a fever. "I think it was 101," Elsa said, adding that Libby took her own temperature. She also said "there were no complaints about the tooth. It had to do with the cold." Libby told her mother that she had a sore throat, although by the next day she wasn't complaining about it anymore.

By Saturday, March 3, Elsa said that Libby "felt pretty much the same," and that "she didn't look terribly sick. She looked okay." In fact, Jed Zion, Libby's youngest brother, recalled that he didn't even know his sister was sick that day or the day before. Sidney said that his daughter looked "tired out," and that "it was nothing that overly concerned us." In any case, Libby again took her own temperature and told her mother she was still running a fever. Elsa didn't know whether she ate anything the whole day, but both parents said that they were sure Libby took her antibiotic and antidepressant, plus Tylenol. Later Elsa would not be so sure. She'd say that she didn't know when Libby started taking the Tylenol, because she "wasn't supervising her." She also said that Libby was "entirely" in charge of taking her Nardil. "I had nothing to do with it at all."

Sidney remembered that Libby "seemed more upset." It is possible she was indeed feeling sicker, or it is possible she was upset by a Saturday-morning visit from a longtime boyfriend she had broken up with earlier in the week. The boyfriend, Ralph Enders, described Libby as "sweaty and warm" and said that she "wasn't thinking clearly." He said that "she looked very sick," and told him she "was getting sicker" from taking her antidepressant. But Libby told no one else about that bad reaction.

ON SUNDAY, MARCH 4, the day before she was to return to Bennington, Libby told her mother that she hadn't slept well. Elsa thought that Libby looked about the same as she had for the past few days.

But by the early afternoon, Libby was complaining that she was "burning up inside," so this time Elsa took her temperature, which registered 102. Sidney was on the telephone and said to the caller, "Gee, my kid looks lousy." He later explained that his oldest child looked "nervous" and "jumpy." Elsa gave Libby some alcohol rubs, and tried to cool her down. She also said that she called Dr. Shapiro, who told her to have Libby continue the antibiotic. The doctor also told her, Elsa said, that she was leaving on a vacation and therefore gave her the name of the person who was covering for her. However, Dr. Shapiro later said that she did not speak to Elsa at all that weekend. In fact, the pediatrician said that she was puzzled because she sort of expected to hear from Libby herself and didn't. Accounts of the weekend were to become fraught with such contradictions.

Later on Sunday, Elsa noticed that Libby "was tossing around in her bed," and had "stressful breathing." But by seven, Sidney said, Libby "seemed not to be that bad." She told her mother, "I feel a little better," so the Zions decided to go to a party in the east sixties for a friend who had passed the bar exam. They told Adam, their older son, and Jed to call them if Libby "gets bad or anything." Elsa said, "When we left her, she was calm and things had slightly settled down."

At some point in the early evening, Libby felt well enough to call her paternal grandmother, to whom she was very close, so her grandmother wouldn't worry about her. Adam and Jed had a couple of friends over to watch a Rangers-Penguins hockey game on television. In fact, one of the friends, Sean Pace, said he arrived around five or six and remembered that Libby "wasn't that sick, then, because she asked me to help her move some stereo equipment from the hallway to the back room." Sean said that about three hours later, as they were watching the game, Libby came into the room to ask that the sound be turned down because it was too loud. "I remember she took a shower and came out in one of those towel robes, and she wasn't communicating too well," he said.

At around nine-thirty, Libby was worse. She told Adam, the brother she felt closest to—they were a year apart—that she was afraid, and he did his best to reassure her. It occurred to him that his sister "thought she was going to die." Jed, who was fifteen at the time, remembered that his sister was lying on the floor. "Her condition had deteriorated, and she seemed to be sort of rocking around," he told me. "It was plainly uncommon." Adam said his sister's pupils were dilated, and that she was sweating, and seemed to be breathing irregularly. "She was steaming hot," he said. He lovingly applied a cold cloth to her head and stomach. "It was going hot in seconds. She was moving around. She wouldn't stop," he said. "I blame myself in a lot of ways," he later told me, "because I didn't know *what* to do. I wanted to do something. I just didn't know. I thought maybe if I put her in the bath—an ice bath—that would help."

Adam could see that his sister was not lucid. "She was speaking kind of in a girlish voice, a baby's type of voice," he said. Her appearance "made me very frightened." Sidney would later describe Libby as looking like "half a Mexican jumping bean."

"Religious thoughts came into my mind," Adam later told me. "I swear to you, I don't ever want to see anyone like that. To me I thought I was looking at a death mask."

Sean Pace said that Libby looked extremely ill when the hockey game was over, and that Adam told him it would be best if he left because "he had to call his dad." Libby was in a panic, and had asked for her parents, and Adam said that he reached his father at the party "at five of ten or ten," telling him that Libby was "really bad," and to "please come."

"I'm on my way," Sidney told his son.

This had never happened before, according to Sidney; they had never been called home for medical reasons. Elsa said, "We had no way of knowing what the problem was, how big it was, until we got home." They arrived on West Ninetieth Street at about ten-thirty and "took one look at her and knew she was worse," Elsa went on. Sidney remembered Libby as being out of bed, and in the dining room, although Elsa recalled that her daughter "was in her bedroom, upstairs in the loft. She came down and sort of fell when she came down. She tripped on something, because she was obviously out of control." Adam's memory is of his sister in their parents' bedroom until she left for the hospital. Elsa said that there had been "a screaming scene" when she couldn't find the thermometer. Adam said that whenever his mother is nervous "she gets pissed."

Libby wanted to reach Ralph Enders on the telephone, and had asked Adam to call him. But Ralph wouldn't talk to her, according to Adam. Ralph later said that this wasn't true, and that, in fact, he and Libby had spoken sometime after ten, when she told him her parents were taking her to the hospital. Barry Fox, the brother of one of Libby's closest friends, Dale Fox, was at Ralph's apartment when Adam called, and he talked to Adam. Barry told me he heard "an unbelievable tirade of emotion" in the background. It is not clear precisely what was going on in the Zion household at that time. "Libby was definitely hysterical, and Ralph and Libby definitely played emotional ping-pong with each other," Barry said. Adam recalled that

Libby kept asking, "Why won't he talk to me? Why won't he talk to me?" Barry said that "Ralph thought the call was a play for sympathy, and that Libby was suffering from one of her maladies." Whatever was going on, Libby indeed was suffering.

Elsa said that she didn't observe anything exceptional about Libby's color, "unless she might have been a little flushed," even though Adam said Libby's "skin was red like a sunburn red." However, Elsa did notice that Libby's eyes were dilated, and very strange. "She was very irritated physically," Elsa said, adding that she had never seen her daughter look the way she did.

Libby's "shoulders were moving," and "her eyes were starting to roll around," Sidney said. "That really scared me when I saw that."

So he called his mother's doctor, who was also his doctor, and someone who had seen and spoken to Libby from time to time over the years—a doctor Sidney said he thought of as a family physician, Raymond Sherman. "Not a friend, but a friend enough," Sidney would later say. Dr. Sherman, a 1961 graduate of the Downstate Medical Center of the State University of New York, and a former lieutenant commander in the United States Navy, had first seen Libby on March 18, 1981, and had also referred her to several specialists in an attempt to get to the bottom of chronic gastrointestinal complaints she was experiencing. In 1984, Dr. Sherman was part of a seven-member group practice.

He was a doctor from Sidney's special list, a doctor who had connections to people Sidney knew and respected. "He's more needy than the rest of us," Elsa explained, as to why her husband had such a register.

Sidney had Dr. Sherman's home number and he reached him right away. He recalled that his conversation went something like this: "Ray, she's in bad shape. I don't know what's the matter with her, but I'm worried about her, and I'd like you to take a look at her." He later explained that he had wanted the doctor "to come to the house."

Sidney told Dr. Sherman that Libby "had a fever," was "shaky," and was "jumping up and down." He said that he mentioned that "her eyes were rolling around a little bit," and that he didn't "want her to go through the night like this. I've got to have you see her."

Dr. Sherman, who would later argue that he was told only about a fever and the tooth extraction, told the Zions to take Libby to the emergency room of New York Hospital, that he would have Dr. Maurice Leonard meet them, and, if need be, he would join them there, too. Sidney said that Dr. Sherman told him "it may be a virus going around."

So Libby, who was wearing a T-shirt and underwear, went into her room to put on a pair of jeans while her father went to get the family's blue Oldsmobile Cutlass Sierra for the drive across town to New York Hospital. Cat Stevens's *Tea for the Tillerman* played on her stereo, Adam remembered. It was cool outside, so Elsa brought along Libby's navy-blue down jacket. "She didn't want it on, so I put it around her shoulders."

Adam told me, "I knew how bad it was." He went on, "I went to my room and looked out the window to watch them, and I saw Libby, with her hands in her pockets, walking on the balls of her feet, get into the car, and they drove away."

Both brothers had the same premonition.

"I knew I'd never see her again," Jed said to me.

"I thought I might never see her again," Adam echoed.

"Don't take all those pills," he had said to his sister at

one point that weekend. He didn't know what they were, but he told me, "I kept seeing her take all these pills. Maybe that's what's doing it, I thought. She didn't have the flu or a cough."

As SIDNEY CUT across Eighty-sixth Street on his way to the East Side, he saw his wife and daughter through the rearview mirror, huddled together in the backseat. Elsa was concerned because Libby couldn't sit still. "She didn't want her little coat around her because she was burning up. She kept saying. 'I'm burning up, I'm burning up.' She was in a lot of discomfort." Libby, jumpy and shaking, according to her father, said that she was scared. "We're going to take care of you, and you'll be great," he reassured her. "Don't worry, you're going to the best hospital in the world."

While he parked the car, Elsa and Libby walked into the unimposing emergency room of New York Hospital, at Seventieth Street and York Avenue. Its plain entrance, with a simple red-lettered EMERGENCY sign over sliding doors, incongruously shares a cobblestone courtyard with the more impressive-looking granite Lying-In Hospital, which specializes in the care of women and is part of the New York Hospital–Cornell Medical Center. Surrounding the courtyard are thick ornamental bushes.

Once inside, rows of stretchers can be seen. A lone security guard wearing a uniform and a peaked hat stands by a lectern. Directly across from his post is a bright yellow-and-black warning sign, AUTOMATIC / CAUTION / SLIDING DOORS, and another sign that says PATIENT CARE AREA / EMERGENCY ROOM PERSONNEL ONLY. To the left of the automatic doors is still another sign: AMBULANCE PERSONNEL / TRANSPORT PATIENTS THROUGH DOORS TO NURSES STATION. There is also a large PATIENT'S BILL OF RIGHTS poster on the wall.

There are two moderate-sized waiting rooms to the left of the guard, which are lined with maroon metal-framed chairs with blue plastic upholstery. Paintings of potted flowers and plants, a Caribbean scene, and various museum posters decorate the blue-gray walls. There are several signs: NO SMOKING, NO FOOD PERMITTED IN WAITING AREA, and PATIENTS WILL BE TREATED BASED ON BOTH MEDICAL CONDITION AND TIME OF ARRIVAL. A rack holds such publications as *Gourmet, National Geographic, Colonial Homes,* and *Harvard Magazine.*

When the Zions entered, a television set above a Pepsi machine was turned on, but the few people waiting weren't really paying attention to it. A glass-enclosed cubicle next to the triage unit housed two registration desks, and while Libby, who was very edgy and beginning to hyperventilate, sat on a chair next to her mother, Sidney went up to one of the windows to check in. The time logged on the "emergency pavilion record" was 11:43 P.M. "Fever" was listed as Libby's "reason for admission," and her "major problem."

"I remember doing something, saying 'Where's Dr. Leonard? We were supposed to have this set up,' " Sidney said. "I kicked up a little fuss, I'm sure . . ." Still, "It was at least half an hour before we got in," Elsa remembered.

Sidney remained in the waiting room as an admitting nurse talked briefly to his wife and daughter, and then escorted them through the triage unit, where patients are sorted according to the severity of their injuries. They turned left into a corridor that runs down the center of the emergency room, and were directed into one of the several curtained treatment areas that make up the emergency-room complex. There was a desk between two of these treatment rooms, and the surrounding walls were lined with shelves holding medical supplies. A large green oxygen tank stood at the end of the corridor, near a twenty-by-forty-foot special-trauma area.

The admitting nurse handed Libby a short blue-and-white-print hospital gown, and helped her as she took off her jeans and T-shirt and put it on. Elsa rubbed her daughter's back as Libby rested on the gurney that took up most of the space in the small cubicle. There were very few sounds.

Anne Gallagher, an emergency-room nurse, took Libby's temperature, which registered 102.9, and also began to draw blood. She noticed that Libby was unable to sit still and was bouncing around the gurney. She was shaking, and appeared uncomfortable, the nurse recalled. Gallagher, a registered nurse for nine years, also inserted an intravenous line so she could begin giving Libby 1000 cc of fluid containing protein, salt, sugar, vitamins, and minerals to help regulate her temperature. Shortly afterward, Dr. Maurice Leonard, who had been sitting at the desk and had noticed Libby and her mother walk into the emergency area, entered the room and introduced himself. He had been told by Dr. Sherman, "I know the family," so he was especially keen-eyed. "Dr. Sherman was one of the most popular attendings," he said. "He was also one of the more involved."

"What's going on?" Dr. Leonard asked Libby. "How long have you been sick?" Libby or her mother told him that about five days ago she had an infected tooth removed, and then four days ago a pain in her right ear had begun.

"I remember Dr. Leonard examining her," Elsa said, "and his asking all kinds of questions, and certainly predominantly the questions about 'what is she taking?'"

In fact, Dr. Leonard used a standard technique that varies little from hospital to hospital: he took Libby's full history from both Libby and her mother. Elsa said that she mentioned "everything" Libby had been taking "because she had been sick," and told Dr. Leonard about the "Tylenol, and very specifically the antidepressant stuff, the Nardil, because they had drummed in Libby's head the whole business of conflict of drugs." Elsa thought that Dr. Leonard "was very intelligent, very knowledgeable, and understood all of those things."

Libby told Dr. Leonard that she had been feeling better until earlier that day, when her earache returned, and that she had not taken her antibiotic or her antidepressant that day because she felt so bad. She said that at some point Sunday her temperature had reached 106 degrees, although she hadn't mentioned it to any family member.

"The very first moment I saw her, she was lying there, not moving. She appeared stable," Dr. Leonard said. He took Libby's blood pressure, and when she went from a lying-down to a sitting position, it fell, and her pulse rate rose. Lying down, her pressure was 110/60, which is on the low side, and her pulse was 100, which is normal to mildly high. Sitting up, her pressure was 80/50, which is extremely low, and her pulse was 130, which is quite high; when the admitting nurse had first taken Libby's pulse in the triage unit, it had been exceptionally high, 156. Normal blood pressure for someone Libby's age would have been 120/70, the rate it was when she visited her gynecologist in 1983; in 1982, Dr. Sherman had registered it as 115/80, and in the fall of 1983, a doctor in Vermont had noted it was 120/84. A normal pulse rate would have been anywhere from 60 to as high as 100.

Low blood pressure can be the result of diabetes, anemia, undernourishment, pregnancy, sudden emotion, certain infections, fever, or the use of drugs.

Dr. Leonard examined Libby's eyes, nose, and throat, and found them normal. He noted that her right eardrum was slightly reddened, although one account in the massive files that eventually accumulated about the case referred to it as her left eardrum, possibly because at one point Libby told another doctor that her left ear hurt more than her right one.

Elsa remembered a "fuss about a little bump on Libby's leg," and that Dr. Leonard asked if it was recent. She told him no. Dr. Leonard speculated that the tiny reddish-purple spot on Libby's right leg "might well have been a birthmark" or perhaps a rash "that is sometimes present in infections." Elsa thought "it was like a mole, only it wasn't a mole." She was bewildered by the doctor's interest. "That was the only question that was asked," she mused, "that made it sound like there might be something we should worry about. And I have no idea what it was."

SIDNEY WALKED IN and out of the treatment room, "trying to figure out what was going on," he remembered. He was frantic. At one point, Elsa joined her husband outside. "They were evaluating Libby," she said. All the same, she "didn't get a sense that they were focusing" exclusively on her daughter. "There was no kind of special interest," Elsa believed. "Libby was just another patient," and it was business as usual.

When Libby and Dr. Leonard were momentarily alone, he said that he asked her if she used marijuana. She told him that she frequently did, although not that day. He asked if she took any pills, and she said no. She said that she had not taken aspirin or Tylenol. He asked about "any other medicines" or "any other drugs of abuse" she might have taken, and she said there were none. He asked about cocaine, "whether she injected it, snorted it," and again she answered no. For the ten minutes that Libby and Dr. Leonard spoke together, Libby's agitation continued—the rocking around her brother Jed had witnessed an hour or two earlier, and the shoulder movements that had frightened her father. "She would suddenly move an arm, a leg, sit up, sit down, without any clear reference to any particular pain or symptom," Dr. Leonard said. "Probably the most remarkable component of it was that she was able to stop the purposeless movement almost at will, to answer questions and cooperate with the examination. She had moments when she was calm."

Libby's initial blood count suggested "that there was an inflammatory process going on," according to Dr. Leonard. She had an elevated white-blood-cell count of 18,200. Normal was 8,000 to 12,000. The elevation could have indicated stress, dehydration, or have been a result of her fever; but it also revealed a mild shift to the left—that is, the rapid appearance of immature white cells, usually associated with a bacterial infection. A urinalysis established that there was no evidence of bacterial infection involving the genital-urinary tract. It also confirmed that Libby was dehydrated. A portable one-view chest X ray performed in the emergency room was normal—that is, her lungs appeared clear. There was no sign of any pneumonia, no haziness in her lung tissue.

Libby was subjected to test after test in an attempt to find out the source of her fever. A cardiac exam disclosed "an extra sound commonly present in people who have a fast heart rate with fever." It was not considered a significant finding. During all these tests, Elsa tried to keep her daughter calm. "She kept apologizing for not being able to lie still," her mother said, "and she was sorry because everything kept getting messed up." Libby's breathing was shallow, and Elsa encouraged her to breathe deeper, and to use biofeedback techniques.

The emergency room nurses' flow chart listed Libby's

major problem as fever and chills. Both parents later said that she didn't have chills—or sweating—although others had seen those symptoms over the weekend.

The flow chart mentioned a rash. Was that the tiny mark Dr. Leonard noticed on Libby's leg? These spots, called petechiae, can signal infection or bleeding under the skin. After Libby was admitted, a purplish facial rash was observed, and Libby told one doctor that she developed it that day, and she told another that it had been there for several days. During the long night, multiple reddish skin abrasions would be noticed on her lower extremities by the hospital staff.

"There was no rash on Libby's face while she was in the emergency room," Elsa said firmly. "I think I would have noticed or remembered it." Sidney also said he didn't see one, "or any discoloration," at any time.

The flow chart reported that Libby was having difficulty urinating. Dr. Leonard, as part of his examination, had asked Libby whether she was having any such problems. She told him no. Later, Elsa told me that Libby kept repeating that "I feel like I have to go but I can't." In fact, Elsa said that her "whole head-set actually was that symptom," although the first Elsa actually learned of it was when Libby told her after their arrival in the emergency room. "That was my concern," Elsa said. "I thought Libby was in renal failure, as a matter of fact." Dr. Leonard said that there was never any reference made to him of such a problem at any time, so Libby—or her mother—must have mentioned it only to one of the nurses who helped Libby use the bathroom while she was waiting in the cubicle, and that is how the symptom got listed on the flow chart.

Anne Gallagher, the emergency-room nurse who first drew Libby's blood, said that Libby's agitation was such that "had she been alone, she would not have been able to give a complete medical history on herself." Indeed, during the time Elsa was talking with Sidney out in the waiting area, Libby could not answer Dr. Leonard's questions about why she was moving her body around so much, or whether or not anything hurt. She never complained of pain, just that she was burning up inside, Elsa said. Her face was like a vicious sunburn, Adam had said a few hours earlier. "Can't you give her something to calm her down?" Elsa asked someone. She was told that it was unwise to administer a sedative to a person with a temperature because "the body needs to fight against the fever."

Meanwhile, Sidney continued to pace between the waiting room and the treatment area. He later described his daughter's agitation as "looking like something going on inside of her was doing it," and confessed that he didn't tell the hospital staff about Libby's precise condition at home because "they didn't ask me."

At some point during Libby's slow two-hour evaluation, Sidney heard a nurse say "the fever went up to 103.5," and then he overheard Dr. Leonard talking on the telephone. "I didn't know for certain who he was talking to," Sidney said, "but I heard Dr. Leonard say something about 'she's quite hysterical.' Then I knew he must be talking to Sherman. I said, 'That's that.'" He used one of the three pay phones situated at the north end of the security guard's station to call Dr. Sherman at home a second time. It was now well after one in the morning of Monday, March 5.

Sidney will never forget their conversation. He said that Dr. Sherman spoke very harshly, asking, "Why are you calling me at home? Why didn't you call the service?" Sidney protested, "Don't yell at me . . . hey, wait a minute, I only know you fifteen years," and pleaded, "I'm calling you because I don't know who these people are, and I want you to be here." Dr. Sherman calmed down and apologized, Sidney said, telling him, "Look, I didn't mean to yell at you, but don't you think I know what's going on?" He then told Sidney that he was in touch with Dr. Leonard, and that the doctors in charge of Libby "are the best people there are."

Dr. Sherman remembered the call differently. "I don't remember an apology for something that didn't require an apology," he said, adding that he never became excited. "Why would I criticize him on the second call and not the first?" he asked, acknowledging, however, that he did point out to Sidney, "In general it's a good idea to call the office because that way you get directed to a physician. It's not good medical care to call a doctor at home." In any case, Sidney told Dr. Sherman that he had heard about and was alarmed at Libby's now 103.5 fever, and asked if it was really true. Dr. Sherman told him it was.

"Well, get down here. Let's get this thing going," Sidney urged. He said that Dr. Sherman—who doesn't remember Sidney ever asking him to come to the hospital—reassured him that even though the hospital might keep Libby overnight to run some more tests, the virus she was probably sick from had been around for the last several months, and it wasn't "anything to worry about or I'd be there." He stressed that he'd be available "all night long," and Sidney said he took comfort from the fact that "Ray talked to me as if I was just a jerky Jewish father who was overreacting."

So Sidney Zion, a man who said that he grew up thinking of doctors as gods, was mollified. "I didn't have political figures as heroes; doctors were my heroes," he said.

THERE WAS MORE waiting around for test results.

"What's going on here?" Sidney asked a passing nurse. He was walking back and forth, "trying to get closer in to talk to Leonard," he said. Somebody told him, "Just let everything go on as it is going on." But Sidney felt as if he was being shoved aside. "The attitude was I'm not supposed to be involved in this," he complained. "It seemed to me they were locking me out. I was not happy about what was happening, because I didn't know what was happening."

Dr. Sherman and Dr. Leonard consulted on the telephone three times—once before Libby arrived at New York Hospital, once after Dr. Leonard's examination, and once after some test results became available. Shortly after Sidney's second phone call to Dr. Sherman, he asked Nurse Gallagher how much longer it would take before the doctors decided how to proceed with his daughter. His question went unanswered.

However, during Dr. Leonard's last conversation with Dr. Sherman, a decision had been made to admit Libby for further evaluation of her fever, although it had first been considered that she remain in the ER for an extended period, or be sent home. Dr. Leonard did not believe Libby's condition was critical, but both he and Dr. Sherman were baffled about her strange body movements, and according to Dr. Leonard they "weren't sure how to put that together with her fever." Dr. Sherman said that "it was pretty clear that Libby was going to have to stay in for hydration and diagnostic testing. There wasn't much question in my mind."

That particular Sunday, when Libby Zion became a patient, the only staff member on call—that is, available for night or weekend duty—on the private medical floors was Dr. Luise Weinstein, although there was another staff member on call on the nonprivate, or "service," floors. Dr. Leonard paged Dr. Weinstein, and told her that she had a new admission. They spoke about Libby's history and examination for five or ten minutes. Dr. Leonard also told Dr. Weinstein about his conversations with Dr. Sherman.

Dr. Weinstein told her immediate superior, Dr. Gregg Stone, about her new admission, and they decided to meet in the emergency room. Dr. Stone arrived first. He had been told by Dr. Weinstein only that Libby had a fever, and before he entered the treatment room to see her, he spoke briefly to Dr. Leonard.

In various records, Libby's fever was reported to have been going on anywhere from one to five days. The nurses' record said it had been three days. Sidney believed that her fever began "on Saturday, maybe Sunday," although someone told Dr. Stone that Libby was on day five of the fever.

Dr. Stone spent about a half hour with Libby, and, he said, he was struck by "the gross movements of her head, arms, and legs," which he "sensed" were volitional. "She would go ten or fifteen minutes without anything happening," he said. He also noticed that she had rigors—a rhythmic, involuntary shaking of the upper trunk and jaw—rapid breathing, and marked sweating. Libby told him that she had begun sweating that day. She said that she had a sore throat, that her ears were "full," and that her eyes were "burning." Even though Dr. Stone had a difficult time getting Libby to focus on many of his questions, he did not feel that he was looking at a critically ill patient.

"Miss Zion, why are you acting like this?"

"Because I'm so hot. I'm uncomfortable," Libby replied.

"And then we'd have a conversation," Dr. Stone said, although "when I left the room she slowly started the movements again." Still, he was able to get some history from Libby after he started asking yes-or-no questions. Libby told him that she was not taking any prescription or over-the-counter drugs other than erythromycin, which she was taking four times a day, and Nardil, which she said she hadn't taken since Thursday. She said that she had never used any illicit drugs, including marijuana. Dr. Leonard had already told Dr. Stone that Libby said she used marijuana, but now Dr. Stone wondered if that was actually true. Libby also told Dr. Stone that she occasionally had a drink at a party.

Elsa and Sidney were not with Libby when Dr. Stone began taking her history, because they had already left the emergency room to go to the floor where they were told their daughter would soon be taken.

By 1:45 A.M., Libby was worn out from all the questioning, testing, and probing, and like most new hospital patients, she didn't understand why she was answering so many of the same questions from so many different doctors and nurses.

SOMETIME BEFORE TWO, one of the emergency-room nurses told Dr. Stone that Libby was about to be transported upstairs, so he told Libby he'd continue his examination of her when she got to her floor. He looked at her chest X ray, and reviewed it with a radiologist resident while she was being transferred, and then left the ER so he could arrive in her room before she did.

Nurse Anne Gallagher watched as an aide moved Libby to a stretcher, and it seemed to her that there had been no change in Libby's condition from the time she had first entered the ER. Over two hours had passed.

Dr. Weinstein had been delayed before starting out for the emergency room. As she approached it, she passed a young woman lying on a stretcher in the hallway, and asked the aide if this was Libby Zion; she was told it was. Dr. Weinstein didn't talk to her new patient because she

could see that Libby was about to be taken up in the
elevator. She studied Libby for about twenty seconds, and
watched her trying to sit up on the gurney, moving from
side to side in what she described as a "hyperactive" way.

Dr. Weinstein went upstairs, and talked to Libby for the
first time sometime after two A.M. in room 516, on the fifth
floor of Payson Pavilion, a wing of New York Hospital that
comprises nine floors.

E L S A   S A I D   T H A T she and her husband "got a little lost
along the way" to their daughter's floor. "It took us a while
to find the room," she said. "She was in a room with a lot of
people," Sidney said. "It didn't even look like a room to
me."

When they did arrive, Elsa said that Dr. Weinstein and a
nurse, Myrna Balde, who had been assigned to Libby's
care, were at her bedside. Dr. Stone said in a deposition
that he had reached room 516 before Dr. Weinstein, and
had already completed the rest of his examination by the
time the Zions appeared, although he remained on the
floor to write up his notes. Later he recalled that Elsa Zion
was in the room part of the time he was there.

Sidney said that "everyone seemed very sympathetic,
and acted as if nothing terribly serious was going on" with
Libby. He described Dr. Weinstein as a "kind of sweet-
looking person, in a way."

The patients on Payson 5 had diseases ranging from
phlebitis to AIDS. Libby was in a ward with three other
people; one of her roommates was suffering from lupus, a
debilitating disease that causes swelling in almost every
system in the body. The other patients were either sleeping or dozing when Libby joined them.

A small window behind Libby's bed faced the nurse's
station; a thin beige-pink-and-blue cotton curtain covered

it. A similar curtain encircled her bed, so she would have some privacy. A light over the bed, which was in the front of the room, to the left of the doorway, stayed on all night.

Although Sidney and Elsa never spoke of it, Myrna Balde said that Libby was "throwing herself around the bed" and "cursing" soon after her arrival. "She was saying things like 'fucking this' and 'fucking that.' She was crashing around the bed." The nurse also commented that in taking Libby's history she "could not understand what Libby was saying" because she was "kind of delirious." Although Libby had moments of lucidity, on the whole she was not really communicating well, a symptom her brothers and their friends had observed over five hours earlier. Yet the nursing progress record, following the lead of the emergency pavilion record, had listed Libby's major problem just as a fever. It was a fever not only of unknown origin, but of an unclear duration. Libby's incoherence was never charted.

"They were giving her intravenous, they were getting her set up," Elsa said. "They were doing all the things you have to do when somebody is suddenly an inpatient." She said that she remained by Libby's side much of the time, and tried to keep her still because she was complaining about the IV. In fact, when Libby had first arrived from the emergency room her IV had become disconnected, and Dr. Weinstein had had to replace it.

Sidney sat in a solarium at the end of the corridor, and his wife joined him there from time to time. They agreed with the assessment of the emergency-room nurse, Anne Gallagher, and said that their daughter's condition was "essentially the same as it was downstairs," that is, she was still very agitated and extremely uncomfortable. However, Elsa also felt that Libby answered Dr. Weinstein's questions appropriately, although Dr. Weinstein said that Sidney and Elsa were not present when she took Libby's history from her at 2:20 A.M.; in fact, Dr. Weinstein at first thought that Libby's parents had gone home. But they had only retreated to the lounge.

Sidney believes that he "must have said a few words" to Dr. Weinstein, but agreed that they had "no real conversation." Dr. Weinstein confirmed that there was never any substantial conversation during the time the Zions kept a brief vigil on Payson 5.

Dr. Weinstein referred to Libby as a poor historian, hardly an original complaint. Libby was so ill—and so confused—that at one point she told Dr. Weinstein she had only one brother. Libby also told Dr. Weinstein that she had had a sore throat for four days. Dr. Weinstein said that Libby's throat was "slightly reddened."

"I don't know what kind of history they wanted," Elsa said. "She was suffering a lot for her to concentrate on these detailed questions," she went on. "It seemed to me we answered whatever questions it was that they asked us. I don't know what else they needed other than what medications she was taking. They're so fixed on drug stuff. It's too bad they don't focus on the thing that they're going to do rather than the thing that they're worried about that you've done."

Somehow Dr. Weinstein also received the impression from one of the other doctors that Libby's agitation had lasted all day. The erratic movements were Libby's most puzzling symptom to the doctors, yet it remains unclear how Dr. Weinstein learned what she knew about their possible beginnings.

Libby's bizarre behavior was frustrating to both Drs. Stone and Weinstein. "It was seizurelike," Dr. Weinstein said, although she maintained that "there was definitely a control" to it. When she drew a blood sample from Libby and asked her to remain still, Libby was able to do so, and, Dr. Weinstein went on, "there wasn't a lot of wild flailing." She said that Libby was able to get out of bed to have her blood pressure taken, and could follow directions with ease when she was asked to perform a sensory test involving a cotton swab and a pin. Libby's blood pressure lying down was 110/70, and her pulse was 104. Sitting up, her blood pressure was now 96/60—it was 94/50 when Dr. Stone had taken it—a slight improvement from the ER reading, and her pulse was 120, 10 beats slower than the ER reading.

Soon after Libby's arrival, Dr. Weinstein had to fix her IV line yet again because Libby had ripped the tubing from the hanging bottle. When Dr. Weinstein first discovered the yanked line, she found Libby walking around the room. Her parents were not with her. When Dr. Weinstein asked her why she had climbed out of bed, Libby explained that she just wanted to walk between the beds. Dr. Weinstein, who took Libby by the arm and escorted her back to the narrow bed, said that her patient seemed to be strolling around as a "form of exercise."

PAYSON 5 WAS fairly quiet; after all, it was past two in the morning, and the Zions were the only visitors. "Libby's complaints were now in full force," Elsa said when she described the time she and her husband spent going to and from room 516 and the solarium. What Elsa meant was that during that time, Libby had not once stopped reporting that she felt she was burning up inside. Her complaints were exactly the same as they had been in the ER. "She couldn't urinate," Elsa repeated. In fact, Libby now told Dr. Weinstein about this symptom. According to Elsa, Libby still "couldn't breathe. She wasn't breathing properly," although the charge, or head, nurse on Payson 5, Jerylyn Grismer, said that Libby had no shortness of breath.

The solarium was a large, irregularly shaped gazebolike area. It was meant to cheer up patients and visitors, with its white trellises painted on the walls, its blue wrought-iron garden furniture adorned with pastel-striped plastic cushions, its soft lighting, and its tables displaying the remains of flowers left by former patients. Doors to a nurses' management office and a private nurses' lounge could be seen off to the left. There was a single phone on the right wall, and a television set that played on and on, just like the one in the waiting area of the emergency room. A bank of windows, covered with yellow blinds, overlooked another elegant courtyard and the main entrance of New York Hospital–Cornell Medical Center. A handful of lights from surrounding apartments on York Avenue and Roosevelt Island, along with the lights from the Fifty-ninth Street Bridge, burned gently in the dark sky. It was here Sidney and Elsa sat while awaiting word about Libby's condition.

The histories taken by Drs. Stone and Weinstein said that Libby's temperature had reached 105 before she entered the hospital. Dr. Leonard had been told it was 106. In her confused state, Libby probably said both.

Sidney said he would "drop in the room once in a while and hold Libby's hand or tell her to relax," although neither Dr. Weinstein nor Dr. Stone ever saw him there. Both Sidney and his wife were very worried about Libby's troubled breathing, but Elsa said that neither of them mentioned this to the doctors. Sidney, however, said that he talked to Dr. Stone about it, and was told "it comes with the virus." Dr. Stone said such a conversation never occurred.

The Zions recall that out in the hallway, Dr. Stone asked if Libby "overdramatized" or was "melodramatic," and that they both said no. They also remembered that Dr. Stone told them Libby was acting as if she had a 106 fever when it was only 103, although Dr. Stone denied that he ever asked "anything like that" or ever used the words "overdramatized" or "melodramatic." In any case, Elsa told him, "Libby doesn't have the highest threshold for pain."

Sidney said that Dr. Stone then told him they were testing Libby for meningitis.

"Get Ray Sherman on the phone," Sidney said he asked, " 'cause you can die from that." He said that Dr. Stone—who said that Sidney Zion never made such a demand—told him to stay composed "because everything seems to be okay." The test results came back very shortly, and proved negative.

Dr. Stone said that he spoke to Dr. Sherman about 2:15 A.M., although it could have been closer to 2:45 A.M., according to the Zions. Dr. Sherman agreed with Dr. Stone that Libby's condition was not life-threatening. Dr. Stone said that Elsa told him that the body movements everyone was observing were normal for Libby because she was "an agitated, anxious child with a history of depression." But he also said that Libby's mother told him that while they had seen this kind of movement in the past, it now appeared to be "worse than usual," even though they could not say exactly when the "worse" behavior began. However, Sidney later said that he had never seen Libby move like that before, and in fact had never seen anyone ever move like that. Still, Dr. Weinstein emphasized that the Zions were "not surprised" by their daughter's agitation. "It wasn't a major concern of theirs." Dr. Stone agreed. "They were not extremely concerned about her behavior." It was her fever that was their main concern, he believed.

Shortly before 2:45, Drs. Stone and Weinstein talked over a modest treatment plan for the rest of the night—what Dr. Stone later called "a plan of conservative care." Neither discussed it with the family, and Sidney and Elsa said that they hadn't asked the doctors about one. In any case, the plan that evolved, with the help of Dr. Sherman, was one of observation and hydration.

SIDNEY SAID THAT Dr. Stone told him that he and Elsa should go home, and that perhaps without their hovering Libby might settle down. But Dr. Stone said later that he felt it was important that Libby have people around to offer a "soothing influence." He said that it was the Zions who had asked him if they should stay or if it was all right for them to go home, and he had told them that they could go if they wanted to because Libby seemed to be stable. "I think they were ready to go home," he commented. "I think that's what most parents would feel in the middle of the night." Dr. Weinstein said that "no one told them to leave as far as I know." Nurse Balde agreed. A Zion family friend said that Libby herself might have encouraged her parents to leave, saying, "You don't have to hang around. I'm going to be fine." Such a gesture would have been in keeping with Libby's gift for nurturing. She wanted her parents to get a good night's rest, even if she couldn't.

But Elsa maintained that "Stone clearly said 'you should go home.' " She insisted that "it was clear that they urged us to go home, and that there was no perception of any danger, and that they were in charge. And indeed they were in charge when we left. Everybody was around or dealing with Libby." She was not alone.

Still, Sidney said that he told Dr. Stone that he and his

wife weren't "going anywhere until I talk to Ray Sherman." Dr. Stone replied, Sidney said, that he had just talked to Dr. Sherman, "and that's what he says—that it would probably be better if you don't stay here." Dr. Stone would later say that this was "totally false," and Dr. Sherman would agree. But Sidney said Dr. Stone repeated in so many words what Dr. Sherman had told him when Sidney had called him from the pay phone in the emergency room: "Libby will be fine."

"Well, what's the matter with her?" Elsa then asked Dr. Stone.

"It hasn't been determined yet," he answered.

So Sidney Zion, who likes to say that he listened to doctors because they were his heroes, said he and his wife reluctantly agreed to leave Libby's side.

Around 2:45 A.M., the Zions walked back into room 516 and stood by their daughter, who was awake and sitting up in bed, they said. Dr. Weinstein was there. "Libby was very restless, sitting up and lying down," Dr. Weinstein recalled. Fifteen minutes earlier, Nurse Balde had given Libby some ice water when she had complained of being extremely thirsty. Dr. Weinstein later said that she had taken Libby's temperature around that time, and it had gone down to 102.9 from 103.5, most likely a result of the ice water, which Dr. Weinstein did not know had been administered, or an alcohol rub that had been given to Libby by Nurse Balde sometime between two and two-thirty, although it was not registered on Libby's chart.

"Libby, they say you're going to be fine, and we're going home now," Elsa told her daughter.

"We're leaving because you'll rest easier, and things will be better for you. Dr. Sherman agrees," Sidney said.

"I know, Daddy," Libby replied, and then she added, *"Shloft Gezunt"*—sleep healthily.

"You're in good hands. Don't worry. You'll pick her up in the morning," a nurse advised the Zions on their way out.

But for Elsa Zion the moment of leaving the hospital was forever etched in her memory. Recollecting that moment, Libby's mother accused not herself and her husband of walking away from their daughter, but accused the doctors of walking away from their patient. "It's the whole business of walking away. It's hard to understand what was going on in their minds," she told me, breaking down into sobs. "The minute we were gone they just walked away."

ELSA AND SIDNEY were the only passengers on the elevator to the main floor. The medical center was quiet, "and we didn't see anyone around," Elsa remembered. They walked back toward the emergency room to get to their car, which Sidney had left in the courtyard after learning it wouldn't be towed away during the night. The air was still chilly. "We were trying to convince ourselves that they'd never have sent us home if she wasn't going to be all right," Elsa said. She was tense, and slightly annoyed, not an unusual reaction to anxiety.

Sidney reassured his wife by pointing out that Dr. Sherman had promised that he was "right on top of it," so what could go wrong? "It's one of those things that looks worse than it is," he told her as they turned left out of the dimly lit courtyard and entered Seventieth Street.

Traffic was not heavy and hardly anyone else was out in the middle of the night, although by the time they crossed over to the West Side, some more intrepid New Yorkers could be seen on the sidewalks. "We were so tired and concerned," Elsa said. "I knew in my heart without any doubt that if this was anything serious," Sidney reflected, "that he who I have known for many years—Ray Sherman—would have been there on the spot."

On Broadway at Ninetieth Street, a restaurant's red neon sign—ARGO—that turned off only late at night was dark. Sidney stopped the car in front of their apartment building so his wife could go upstairs while he went to park farther up the block. In a few hours, he would have to move the car again to conform with Monday parking regulations.

Elsa walked across the hushed lobby, and stepped into the waiting elevator. It climbed slowly to the third floor. With a small jolt it stopped, and she moved quickly to unlock the front door of their apartment.

The living room lights were on, and as she walked quietly through the apartment she saw that her sons' bedroom door was closed. Adam and Jed were asleep. Soda cans and empty bags of chips littered the two coffee tables in front of two soft green-and-red-print sofas. She took off her jacket, threw it on one of the brown corduroy-covered chairs in the living room, and went into the kitchen to get two glasses. A two-liter bottle of her husband's favorite scotch, Johnnie Walker Black, was on the counter. She picked it up, took some ice, and returned to the living room just as he came in the front door.

Sidney was sanguine: "I told my wife I felt great." He wasn't going to worry at all. They went home because Libby was "all right." In point of fact, one of the nurses on the floor later said that the Zions were "not unusually upset."

"We had a drink before going to bed, and we talked about when we were going to take Libby back to school," Sidney reflected. "She was due back that very day, but we were sure she'd be home in a few days—so we talked about taking her up to Vermont on Thursday, something like that. One of us would be driving her."

"It was four by the time we got into bed," Elsa said. She rested her head on a pillow and stared at the bookcase next to her, on the wall fronting Broadway; the small clock radio gave off the only light in the room. Her husband was soon asleep.

"While Libby was dying I slept well," Sidney Zion mourned. "It was the last good sleep I ever had."

A T 7 : 4 5 A . M . the phone rang in the apartment that the Zions' friends sometimes good-humoredly described as having the appearance of a college fraternity house. Adam walked into the living room from the spacious bedroom overlooking Ninetieth Street that he shared with his brother Jed; its two wooden beds had originally been built as a bunk bed by an artist who was also a carpenter. Jed was brushing his teeth in the middle bathroom, next to their father's office, a small room decorated like a nineteenth-century professor's study, featuring an art deco dental cabinet that had belonged to Sidney's father, a dentist, which Sidney now used to store manuscripts. Adam answered the phone. "They told me to get my father. It was a male voice."

He walked over to the open door of his parents' hall-way-bathroom-bedroom suite, which is almost like a separate studio apartment, and called out to his father that someone wanted to speak to him.

Sidney picked up the receiver of the telephone on the table next to his bed, and heard Dr. Raymond Sherman's voice. Without waiting for him to speak, he said, "Hi, Ray, how is everything? Is she all right?"

"I was sure he was going to tell me to pick Libby up," Sidney said. But that was not the message.

"It's very bad, very bad," Dr. Sherman said somberly. "Get down here right away."

"How bad is it? Is she going to survive?"

But Dr. Sherman did not answer those questions.

"Just get down here right now, real fast. It's real bad. Something happened real bad."

Sidney hung up the phone and turned to his wife and said, "I think she's gone."

Elsa glared at her husband. "Don't you dare," she said as she got out of bed and hurried to get dressed.

"We've got to get over there right away," Sidney told her. He went into the bathroom to wash up, and when he came out he saw that Elsa was on the phone. "Are you trying to tell me my daughter is dead?" he heard his wife say.

"And then Elsa closed her eyes," he remembered.

What she was hearing was Dr. Luise Weinstein's voice. Dr. Weinstein was telling her "I want you to know we did everything we could for Libby. We couldn't get the fever down. We gave her medication. We gave her ice baths."

After Elsa asked Dr. Weinstein the question her husband had overheard, Dr. Weinstein had answered, "Yes."

"I couldn't really respond to that. She said, 'Are you there?' and I said, 'Yes. I can't believe what you are saying,' and I just hung up," Elsa said. "She never said Libby had died. I realized what she was trying to say to me because she was saying it in the past tense."

Adam, a senior at the New Lincoln School, from which his sister had graduated that past June, was standing in the doorway. Sidney looked at his son. "They did it," he said to him. "They killed your sister." He was crying.

IN A NOTE written at Bennington sometime in November, Libby had reminded herself to "register for voice next term." But there would be no next term, and there would be no voice lessons.

At 7:30 A.M., while her parents slept, and her brothers got ready for their day, Libby Ethel Zion was pronounced dead; her voice was still.

2

THE GIRL WHO was pronounced dead at seven-thirty on Monday morning, March 5, 1984, was born on a crisp fall day late in November 1965. Libby Zion, named after her paternal great-grandmother, who came to America from Lithuania at the turn of the century, weighed in at six pounds, eleven ounces, at Mount Sinai, a thirteen-hundred-bed hospital on Manhattan's Upper East Side.

She had died more or less alone in a large, impersonal hospital room, without her familiar belongings around her. Room 516 was very different from her beloved haven on Ninetieth and Broadway, where "she was into making it a great place to hang out," said her brother Adam, who lived in the room eleven years later.

It hadn't changed much since Libby's death. A gray tweed wall-to-wall rug covered the floor, and three multicolored throw rugs were scattered about. Libby's close neighborhood friend Dale Fox had helped her paint the closet door and the door of a tiny bathroom, off to the left, bright blue. "We were taking care of each other," Dale said.

A bookcase was still filled with some of Libby's books—*The Wealth of Nations, The Prince,* and Cynthia Ozick's *Levitation*—but the edges of the mirror above the dresser were no longer jammed with picture postcards and photographs. There were several ashtrays on a shelf, one with a drawing of horses—to which Libby was allergic. A poster of Mickey Mouse as the Sorcerer's Apprentice in *Fantasia* had been taped to the wall on the right. A photograph of her youngest brother, Jed, eating a cookie still hung in a frame on another wall. Three guitars leaned against the closet door. An arrangement of flat aluminum disks—a good-luck charm—hung next to the light-blue-curtained window that overlooked Broadway.

The centerpiece of the room was the wooden loft, which made the place look like a duplex. A mattress dominated the space. Here Libby had spent most of her time, writing in her journal, doing homework, filling out college applications, sleeping, and talking on the phone to her friends. The phone was on a small ledge attached to the upper wall. "We rigged it up, but it never worked right," Adam said.

The space under the loft had served as a living room. It was where she and her friends listened to music—Cat Stevens, Fleetwood Mac, and the Grateful Dead. Paula Este, a high school friend of Libby's, told me, "We never sat down and ate with the family. We were on our own schedule, and were self-sufficient." Libby's room was always noisy, but no one really complained because the area was far away from the living room and her brothers' and parents' bedrooms. It was a teenage paradise.

"Libby was unique," Dale said. "And that's why we got

along. I mean, I was busy wearing my black-and-pink-striped pants with my weird haircut and my leather jacket, and we accepted each other, and we needed that. God did we need that!"

Libby was known as an adaptable, munificent spirit, although she was not always at ease with that description. "Sometimes I think she was a dreamer," Paula suggested. In a letter to a boyfriend, Libby wrote about herself, "I must be a catch-22. I'm just a mass of contradictions." Still, Dale Fox said, "She mirrored my exact qualities, and that was what was so attractive about her to me. Libby was the kind of girl who would have eaten—let's say she liked chocolate—but she would have eaten vanilla because she thought it had feelings."

"She was not your usual fourteen-year-old," remembered a parent of one of her classmates at the Fieldston School in the Riverdale section of the Bronx. Libby, who first attended Public School 84 in Manhattan, went to the private Cathedral School for junior high, transferring to progressive Fieldston for her freshman and part of her sophomore years, before completing her education at the even more liberal New Lincoln School in Manhattan.

"Libby was a powerful young woman," Dale stressed. "She was highly perceptive and intuitive. She was one of the few people who really encouraged me to think."

She was also very maternal, a quality her friends found gratifying. But she was not happy—and her friends from Fieldston and New Lincoln noticed. "She was doing things that weren't good for her," Paula Este remembered.

This hadn't always been the case. "She was no different than other children in some ways, but she was a little different where brainwork was concerned," her grandmother, Anne Zion, said. "When she was six or seven she was the only kid in New York who knew about Damon Runyon," her father boasted.

It was clear from everyone with whom I spoke that Libby was a gifted child.

As a young girl, Libby often visited her paternal grandparents in Passaic, New Jersey, taking the bus by herself. Once, when she was eight, and a third-grader at P.S. 84, the bus driver forgot her stop, and Libby ended up in Paterson instead of Passaic. The driver tried to make her pay another fare to return to Passaic, but Libby said it wasn't fair because he had forgotten to tell her to get off. She won the argument and rode back free.

"She was a close family kid," Sidney said. Libby trusted her grandmother so much, she could write her from Bennington on November 1 that "my best friend here is my cat." She also confided that she had met a boy she liked better than Ralph Enders, and warned her grandmother not to tell anybody. "That's our secret. Don't even tell Daddy," she wrote, "though I know it's tempting."

When she was about four or five, she printed a note to her "Gram" telling her "I am fine and my poison ivy or whatever it is is much beter and I hope your knee is beter . . ." At six or seven, she wrote her grandmother that she wanted "ballet slippers and new sneakers and a mouse and a diamond ring." For Christmas that year she asked for "ice skates and two fish and they have to be pregnet," and she reminded her grandmother that the mouse she wanted for her birthday should also be "pregnet." Libby was a "free spirit," as her father described her. She was very much a child of the sixties, an admirer of hippie style and form.

But as her teens approached, she changed. She withdrew, and stayed in her room more, but no one thought anything was amiss because her friends were often there with her.

"I think one of the biggest problems for Libby, who had been suffering since she was thirteen," Dr. Greenspan, her psychiatrist, said, "is that she felt she didn't belong." He added that for such people, "life may be a feast, but they are locked out, looking in." Sidney said that his daughter "never looked depressed" around him "because she was always smiling," and his wife pointed out that depressives don't function, and Libby did. But what parent can accurately read a teen-age mind?

Elsa believed Libby would get upset sometimes, "but upset is not the same as depression," and she thought her daughter devoted too much energy to trying to solve her friends' problems. "She had a need to be needed," Dale Fox said. But Elsa would tell Libby that she "had a certain inner strength, and other people tend to feed off you and you should try to remember you are just a young girl."

As time passed, as often as not, Libby began to turn her inner strength against herself.

LIBBY GENERALLY DID well in school, of which Sidney and Elsa were naturally proud. She had always been a voracious reader, and when her grandmother Anne once told her that *Wuthering Heights* was too difficult for an elementary school child to read, Libby finished the entire novel over a weekend visit. Dale said that Libby was the brightest girl she knew.

Yet Libby got only B's and C's at Fieldston, where an English teacher praised "her good ear." But Libby didn't like Fieldston, and so she left in the middle of her sophomore year. Dale said that Libby moved "because she thought geographics would fix her. She didn't understand that it was all inside her. She couldn't have known that."

Paula Este said Libby "would feel angry about things, then depressed. She was frustrated."

After she transferred to New Lincoln in the winter of 1981, there were fewer C's, and more A's and B's. An advanced-placement literature instructor noted on Libby's paper about Thomas Mann that her remarkable ideas had influenced his own. Another paper for a course entitled Disease and Society was praised as "a model of its kind." Over and over, all her high school teachers used such words as "highly articulate," or "impressive and mature" to describe Libby, yet alongside these plaudits were observations that "Libby has been absent nearly half the time." Indeed, during her senior year at New Lincoln, Libby was away from school a total of forty-two days. One friend commented that she couldn't remember being in school with Libby, only out of school with her. Sidney said that the family never received any notification of excessive absences from any of Libby's teachers.

Libby was immediately attracted to Bennington College because, her mother said, she "felt that these were her kind of people." *The Fiske Guide to Colleges* describes Bennington as "a place for those seeking room for creativity, self-expression, and a sixties-like passion for the learning experience . . ." Elsa doesn't remember her daughter applying anywhere else, but surmises that "she must have." Libby's college-board report indicated above-average SAT and achievement-test scores and that she was going to apply to Columbia and the University of California at Santa Cruz. Adam thought that his sister had also applied to the University of Colorado.

For a personal statement required on the Bennington application, Libby had written an essay about a journal she started keeping in her junior year at New Lincoln. A former boyfriend who read parts of it said that it contained "personal recollections and descriptions of friends and their lives." Libby told Bennington that she wrote stories, poetry, and songs in the journal, and "also used it as an emotional outlet, which I had never previously had." She wrote that "it wasn't easy, because not only was I unused to letting my feelings out, but I found that letting them out gave rise to many questions about myself which I had never asked before." Bennington's director of admissions told Libby he was disappointed that she didn't include actual excerpts from the journal "since you do have literary aspirations." Nonetheless, Bennington wanted Libby as much as she wanted them, and they granted her request for financial aid as well.

Even though Libby wrote "Thanks Mom!" on an early draft of her college essay about her journal, Elsa would deny the existence of such a journal, although she conceded that Libby wrote song lyrics in a spiral notebook. Sidney also said that he did not know about a diary or journal, although Jed admitted that his sister had kept a diary "a couple of years before she died," and said he had looked through it but had never actually read it.

So one has to wonder if anything about the journal—it has never been found—caused her parents to deny its existence. Some loose pages I discovered among Libby's school folders resembled journal entries. On a piece of lined paper torn out of a spiral notebook identical to the paper Libby used to write notes at Bennington are these dark and disturbing lines:

"Right now I be the extremely unhappy one. I do not like my position in this household any longer. What is his problem? Or for that matter, what is mine?"

Interspersed on the page are also song lyrics. It is not clear if this haunting line is a lyric, but it might be: "Maybe oneday but it could be Sunday I just might as well throw it

in every way. Might as well, Might as well—whoopee!
Maybe it doesn't matter anymore!"

SIDNEY EDWARD ZION and Elsa Ruth Heister were
an unlikely pair.

He was Orthodox Jewish and she was Catholic, although
"for my mother's sake I had Elsa convert," he said. "It was
clear I wasn't really acceptable," Elsa remarked, "but I
knew it was better to do it." She understood how important it was to her husband, although she pointed out that
"Sidney always says I'm an atheist," which is not true, she
said. "I'm just not religious." However, she added, "If I
was going to defend a religion it would be Judaism. I would
go to war for it." Sidney now considers himself "quasi-
nonobservant"—"a contradiction in terms, but only Jews
are crazy like this," he allowed.

Maxie Teninbaum, a first cousin who was practically
brought up with Sidney—his mother was Sidney's
mother's sister—said the family was "traumatized" at first
because his cousin "was the first in the history of the family to marry out of the faith." But after everyone met Elsa
Heister at "headquarters"—the Zion house in Passaic—
they all agreed, "this girl is great." Indeed, Sidney's
mother told me that her daughter-in-law "is one of the
nicest people I know." One only had to be in their presence for a moment to grasp the exceptionally devoted relationship Elsa and her mother-in-law shared for thirty years.

Elsa Zion is one of six siblings, and Sidney is an only
child. "Every only child is ambivalent," he cautioned.
"You're continually attacked, but I did love it. If you do
one thing wrong, they say, aha! That's it. No other group is
so libeled."

Elsa was raised to be self-sufficient and independent,
and in turn raised her own children the same way. She told

me she never discussed her conversion with her parents and siblings because "I was off living my own life in New York City." In fact, she thinks they never knew about it at all.

She was also taught to be stoic. When she was young and broke her nose playing baseball, the town's only doctor was away, so she had to wait twenty-four hours to have it set. The procedure was done improperly. The steel rod used by the doctor to move the bone into place went too far, causing the bone to become tangled in her sinuses, and years later surgery was required to repair the damage. When I asked her if her family got upset over such medical crises, she said, "There was very little hysteria about anything."

Her husband was raised to be indulged and placated. Sidney said that after his grandmother Ethel Zion looked into his crib and announced that the infant within was a prince, "From that moment on, women spoiled me all my life."

But no one, absolutely no one, I discovered, would spoil him like his mother, Anne. I learned that all of his rebelliousness, temerity, and defiance, all of what turned him into a spirited lawyer, journalist, and crusader, had its roots in the actions of his mother. It was from her that he learned that he didn't have to take no for an answer. "She taught me that you don't accept things that you don't have to, you just don't accept it if somebody in authority tells you you gotta do something. You do not accept that!" His mother, he said, "knew everybody, and they were afraid of her." At her funeral on October 15, 1993, her only son told the congregation, "If you don't know my mother, then you don't know me."

I was struck by the empathic relationship I observed between mother and son during my two visits to Passaic. I was especially touched by a very tender kiss I saw Sidney place on his mother's hand after I remarked that their hands looked alike.

The devotion was more than earned. When Sidney was in the fourth grade and was switched to a new school, one farther from his house on Passaic's Sherman Street, his mother, in a few days, "did a whole lot of things," and "pulled a few political strings," according to her son, so he could stay in his old school. When I asked his mother how she did it, she just smiled and said, "How'd I do it? I did it. I just did it." She would move the earth if it made her son happy. Sidney said, "If I could get out of that, then I knew you could get out of anything!"

ALTHOUGH ELSA AND Sidney Zion were both from small towns, hers, Winthrop, New York, was bounded by farms and Indian reservations and was ten miles from the Canadian border, and his, Passaic, New Jersey, was bounded by factories and stores and was twenty miles from New York City. They both attended local public schools, and Elsa graduated from Bard College in 1956, writing her senior thesis on the idea of self-realization. She also received a master's degree in education from the University of Chicago. Elsa explained that a self-realized person "understood himself and was fully self-accepting and really in control, and therefore outwardly commanding." She also became interested in the theories of David Riesman. *The Lonely Crowd*, which Riesman cowrote, was one of the most influential sociological works of the fifties; in it, the authors introduced *inner-*, *other-*, and *outer-directed* as aspects of human nature.

Sidney graduated from the University of Pennsylvania's Wharton School of finance in 1955, and Yale Law School in 1958. After he was accepted by Yale, his mother wrote him in a letter she never mailed that "I feel you are compensating me for all I've tried to do for you through the years . . . you are so worthy of it all." Sidney had done what "seemed beyond any immigrant's dream," he said, and the whole town of Passaic rallied around him. He even got free haircuts. He was launched.

At Yale, he never took exams on schedule. "I'd always have an excuse. I thought it outrageous that they should tell me when I could take exams," he explained. "Let's pull a 'Sid Zion' went on for years at the law school." When he passed his bar exam, once again Passaic cheered. "That world is gone now. No more," Sidney commented when we visited his hometown.

Elsa is a descendant of Baron John de la Greaux ("Great John") of Chartres, who died in 1790, four years before the first malpractice case in the United States was reported.

Great John's sons, John I and Peter, escaped about a year before the French Revolution in 1789 by smuggling themselves in a barrel aboard a ship bound for Canada (a third son died en route). John II, who became John Grow, was born in 1805 and in 1834 left Canada to settle in the northern New York town of Winthrop, where he became a carpenter.

Sidney is a grandson of Lillian ("Libby" or "Lily") Alper Rudnitsky, a friend of mayors and other Passaic city officials, as well as one of the founders of Congregation B'nai Jacob on Washington Place, and Abram Rudnitsky, a Russian-born peddler who later founded a flourishing produce business. *The North Jersey Herald & News* of Passaic and Clifton called them "pioneer residents." And in 1919, Sidney Zion's grandfather, Abram, was "the first in the family" to try to file a lawsuit against a doctor when his red-haired son, Sammy, died of peritonitis after an appendectomy. "The lawyer laughed at him, and said, 'You can't sue doctors,' " Sidney said. "The doctor had screwed up and didn't know that Sammy's appendix had burst," he went on. So another of Abram Rudnitsky's sons, George, nicknamed "Chicky" because he kept chickens in his backyard, "took a hatchet from his store and was going to kill the doctor." Members of the family walked all over Passaic looking for Uncle Chicky, and a relative finally found him standing behind a dense bush near the doctor's office, and stopped him from committing murder. On a visit to Passaic, I overheard Sidney comment to his mother, "He should have done it," and his mother replied, "He should have."

"Uncle Chicky knew instinctively that *that* was the only way to get doctors, and that a lawsuit wouldn't work because doctors are an outlaw profession," Sidney told me. "It's the only profession outside the law, except if they steal money."

I would think about the seeds that Abram Rudnitsky and Uncle Chicky had planted in the family history, and remember how Sidney had told me that his relationship with doctors had been defined by his childhood physician, Dr. Edward Whelan. "Whelan took care of my whole family, particularly my grandfather. He thought I was named after him—my middle name is Edward. I wasn't, but he thought so," Sidney told me. "I once went to him for a shot of penicillin when I was around seventeen or eighteen, and he wouldn't take any money.

"Well, it turns out that in the early 1920s Whelan needed some money for a building he owned. He asked my mom for five thousand dollars. Her family owned the Passaic-Garfield Fruit and Produce business on the corner of First and Essex Street. She told him she'd give him ten thousand dollars, because if you're asking for five you must need ten! She told him, 'When you have it, you'll give it back.' There was no interest either. And after that, Whelan never charged our family for *anything*—even operations! That's why I trusted doctors. Whelan paid us back, too. I never had a bad moment with a doctor before Libby." However, a longtime friend of the Zions told me that after Sidney's father died of heart disease in 1982, his only child had considered suing the doctor. But a lawsuit was never filed.

ELSA WAS BORN in the town where John Grow had settled, and later in her childhood moved to nearby Brasher Falls, New York; both towns are close to the serene blue-green waters of the St. Lawrence River, the hundred-mile channel that drains the Great Lakes and links the United States and Canada to the ocean. Her mother, Beatrice Grow, was born in Helena, New York, in 1912. Elsa's maternal grandparents were Harry J. and Ella Keenan Grow, whose ancestors were Irish Fitzgeralds. Her father, Robert Heister—"He was as graceful as they come and he could waltz like nobody's business," a friend once wrote about him in a newspaper column—was born in Troy, New York, in 1906, and orphaned at the age of eleven. Elsa told me that her aunts helped him, "But basically he got an athletic scholarship to college and lived a hard, tough life." Robert Heister once wanted to play professional baseball until a shoulder injury "became a problem," his daughter said. He turned to teaching, and eventually became principal of the St. Lawrence Elementary School, and after his retirement in 1966 taught at Potsdam State Teacher's College.

Elsa's parents married in 1932, and for all of her life Beatrice Grow Heister was a homemaker. "My mother was a great, swinging person," her daughter said. "She would tell us wonderful stories about how she used to drink down at the Indian reservation during Prohibition, and her brother used to run booze over the border all the time. It was a wild time." Elsa said that she is more like her mother, and that while everybody loved her father, "he had a dour German side . . . when he was happy he was just funny and wonderful, when he was sour he was a miserable sort that none of us liked." But, she added, he was an early feminist. "He certainly said as women you had to stand alone and be able to take care of yourself. And it was never anybody else's fault—it was your responsibility and you were responsible for yourself and that was it. So it wasn't a bad philosophy as far as survival was concerned."

Sidney's father, Dr. Nathan Zion—"I never noticed he was a great man," Sidney told me—was born in Waterbury, Connecticut, in 1901, and later went to live with relatives in Brooklyn. After graduating first in his class from Stuyvesant High School in 1920, he went to the University of Pennsylvania School of Dental Medicine—class of 1924—because "it's the best one in the country," according to his son, who added that "everybody wanted him." When his father first applied to the dental school he was asked, "Where do you pray?" and his father answered, "I pray at home," Sidney said. "The dean of admissions said they needed the information for social reasons, and my grandmother, who was with my father, told the dean, 'His answer stands.' My grandmother went to a state senator eventually and the law was changed—you couldn't ask that question anymore on applications."

Nathan Zion, who was a first lieutenant in the Army Dental Corps during World War II, when he was forty years old, married Anne Rudnitsky, one of five brothers and sisters, on Christmas Day, 1932. Their only child was born on November 14, 1933.

Sidney told me that when he asked his father why he had joined the Army, his father answered, "I knew one day you'd ask me." So he told his son that he "couldn't handle having an only child think he didn't go to war, but stayed home just to make black-market money like so many in the family did."

I would learn from family documents that Nathan Zion had actually been in the Army reserves since July 22, 1936. But patriotism might not have been Dr. Zion's only reason for going to war. A relative of a now-deceased nurse once employed in one of his several New Jersey offices—he went bankrupt three times—said that the only time Dr. Zion had an income was when he was in the Army. She said that "he never made a living" because he "never had any patients." His wife single-handedly supported the family, and "covered up for him her whole life." Anne Zion worked until the age of eighty, the rabbi said at her funeral.

I asked Sidney's best childhood friend, Paul "Paulie" Nelson, about Dr. Zion. Paulie, once "almost Sidney's shadow," he recalled, lived four blocks from the Zions' house at 141 Sherman Street—a gray house with black shutters—and fondly remembered how Dr. Zion walked the two friends to school every day of the year. Now a dermatologist—he graduated from Jefferson Medical College of Thomas Jefferson University in Philadelphia, and was a resident and chief resident at New York's Bellevue Hospital in the mid-sixties—Dr. Nelson remembered that Dr. Zion "didn't ever seem to be busy, ever," and that he didn't have a big practice. He suggested that "maybe Dr. Zion didn't like private practice. He did his best as an Army doctor."

But Sidney said his father "never cared about money," and "suffered a lot" because people ostracized him for having blacks as patients. He remembered that after his father returned from the war, and the sun porch of their house was turned into an office for him, a delegation from the town complained about Dr. Zion "taking niggers." He said his father threw the head of the delegation down the stairs.

Whatever the reasons for his father's idled career as a dentist, or whatever shortcomings he might have had, Sidney Zion for all of his life chose not to see them. Although others might have treated Nathan Zion as if he didn't exist, his son didn't. But the family struggled, and Sidney, who first and foremost always wanted to please his mother, grew up at her side, where he learned everything he needed to know to get along in the world. Anne Zion poured all her love into her only child, and he blossomed. Her last words to him before her death were that he "sure did" still need her around. He was about to turn sixty.

"Unconditional love was her greatest gift," Sidney said. "They can't hurt you if your mother loves you that much."

SIDNEY LIKES TO boast that his grandmother Libby "went to Socialist meetings in the woods" when she was still living in Lithuania. She had a radical streak. So did his grandfather Abram, who had been a builder of houses before he came to America at the turn of the century. His grandson has a picture of Abram Rudnitsky taken in Paris, but no one in the family knows why the picture was taken or why he went to France. At any rate, it is a junction of sorts between the descendants of Abram Rudnitsky of Lithuania and Baron de la Greux of France.

Medicine began its transformation from its humble origins around the time that Abram Rudnitsky was planning his venture to America. And almost thirty years before his son Chicky would want to kill a doctor, and almost a century before his grandson Sidney would crusade for medical justice, what amounted to a revolution in medicine and medical institutions occurred. Medicine became a major profession only in the first two decades of the twentieth century.

In the time of the ancient Romans, medicine had been considered a lowly occupation, and had remained so for centuries. Through contact with prisoners of war in 265 B.C. the Romans were first introduced to Greek medicine and learned how Hippocrates of Cos saw the patient as an individual whose constitution reacted to disease in its own way. Hippocrates viewed disease as a natural process, one that evolved in logical stages, like the acts of a Greek play. But many of his beliefs were neglected for centuries, causing the role of the doctor to fall into a long darkness. Centuries later, when light radiated once again, Hippocrates would be honored as the patriarch of medicine, and the fifth-century-B.C. ethical oath attributed to him would come to be used by medical school graduates, as it is to this day.

The status of doctors was still very low in the eighteenth century, and they longed to be accepted by the privileged classes. Even by the nineteenth century, most doctors were still not considered part of the aristocracy, and were usually quite poor, although a great deal of medical research, especially experimental research late in the century involving specialized surgeries and diagnostic techniques, was underwritten by their wealthy patients. The all-important stethoscope had been developed in 1816, and nearly two hundred years later many doctors still agree that this instrument, along with a doctor's own common sense and intuition, is often all that is needed to guide them to a sound diagnosis.

Medicine progressed quickly after 1900, and by 1920, soon after the time Sidney Zion's uncle Chicky wielded his hatchet to express his rage at medical error, the United

States was already a competitor in worldwide medical achievement.

NEW YORK HOSPITAL was founded in 1771 by a group of doctors that included George Washington's physician, Samuel Bard, who was at that time on the medical faculty of New York's first medical school, King's College, founded in 1768, which later became the College of Physicians and Surgeons of Columbia University. America's first medical school, Philadelphia's College of Physicks, had opened in 1765, and four years later, in 1769, after an impassioned speech by Dr. Bard on the need for a public hospital in New York, his audience offered him a thousand dollars toward the future construction of one. New York Hospital, the first hospital in the state to train medical students, was chartered two years later.

Since its completion in 1791, the august 1,046-bed hospital has been at the forefront of medical and surgical treatment and research. Along with the Pennsylvania Hospital and Massachusetts General, it was considered one of the three great general hospitals of nineteenth-century America.

In 1912 it conducted the first-ever research on allergies to common foods; in the thirties it founded the state's first blood bank; in the forties it invented infant formula, and also produced the first Pap exam for cervical cancer. Over the decades it added many other firsts to its accomplishments—the first complete burn center in New York and the largest in America—and has attracted a steady flow of both rich and poor patients from all over the world to fill what is now its capacity of forty-one hundred beds in fifteen auxiliary hospitals. New York Hospital–Cornell Medical Center is consistently on every "best" list in the country for medical care and the training of doctors.

Dr. Maurice Leonard, the first doctor to see Libby Zion, came to New York Hospital by way of Yale University and the Albert Einstein College of Medicine of Yeshiva University, where he was a member of the Honorary Medical Society. Dr. Gregg Stone, the second doctor to see Libby, arrived as a magna cum laude graduate of the University of Michigan, and the Johns Hopkins University School of Medicine. Dr. Luise Weinstein, the third doctor to see Libby, was a Phi Beta Kappa and summa cum laude graduate of the University of Rochester and its medical school. All three had chosen, and had been chosen, by New York Hospital because they were, and it was, considered the finest the nation had to offer.

Dr. Raymond Sherman, after graduating from the Downstate Medical College, had done further training at New York's Roosevelt Hospital, and had studied nephrology at Strong Memorial Hospital and Highland Hospital in Rochester, New York. In 1984 he had nearly a thousand patients in his private practice, and had been connected with New York Hospital since 1970. He had the utmost faith in the caliber of the hospital staff.

Dr. Sherman said that he wanted to tell Sidney the truth in person, so "shortly after Libby died," he made his 7:45 A.M. call and told Sidney only that her condition was "extremely serious." Meanwhile, Dr. Weinstein, who thought the Zions already knew about their daughter's death, had telephoned because, as she explained, she "had been the one doctor who had observed this patient over time, and was still involved in her care . . ." No one instructed her to make the call. It was something she wanted to do.

Shortly after he learned of Libby's death from Dr. Weinstein, Sidney called Dr. Sherman to say he had been told Libby had died. He did not mention that he had learned the news from Dr. Weinstein. "What happened?" he said to Dr. Sherman. The doctor's response, Sidney said, was that "if I was there with the ten greatest doctors in the world, we couldn't have saved her."

When Sidney was later asked "What did you do next?" he replied, "I screamed a little bit, cried a lot, and then decided I could not get myself to go to the hospital and see my kid that way. And I didn't. I just couldn't go." He "cursed God," he said, until Jed told him "this is no time for you to lose faith. It's a time to be glad you have faith." His younger son, he said, "straightened him out, very quickly."

Elsa didn't go to New York Hospital either, or call anyone there. "I didn't do any of that," she said.

"I COULDN'T FIND my mother," Sidney said. "She was on her way to work." Meanwhile, I "had plenty to do. I tried not to go crazy and to keep my kids alive . . . I tried to keep everybody from going wild is what I tried to do. I tried to figure out, number one, how I was going to find my mother and how I was going to tell my mother and how I was going to get to New Jersey to do all this. And I wanted the family around to make it as easy as possible."

Someone called cousin Maxie Teninbaum. Someone else called Mary Schilling, a friend of both Zions for over twenty years. She had worked with Elsa for almost twelve years, from 1971 to 1982, at Transworld Feature Syndicate, an international agency that handled literary material and managed photographers and sold their work around the world; at one time it sold the syndication rights for Marvel comics and for all Condé Nast magazines. Transworld had offices in Mexico, Europe, and Japan, and was first owned by Elsa's brother-in-law, and then by Elsa herself, who became its president and CEO in 1980. Elsa traveled all over the globe for her company. The Schillings and the

Zions and all their children usually spent their summer vacations together. "Sidney would come down in the morning," Mary Schilling told me, "and say, 'No one's squeezed my orange juice?' and Libby would scream back, 'What am I? a maid?' " When Elsa was away, Libby often cooked meals for her father.

Sidney called his best friend, Herbert "Herbie" Fisher, whom he had known since their Yale Law School days. Fisher, now a lawyer with Winthrop, Stimson, Putnam, & Roberts, in New York City, came right over, Sidney said. He arrived at 9:00 A.M.

"I started crying, not knowing I was going to," Herbie Fisher said, describing his arrival at the apartment. "We spent the next two or three days together."

From her home in lower Manhattan Mary Schilling called Ruth and Sol Stern, who lived a block away from the Zions, on West Ninety-first Street. Sol Stern, who said Libby was "very much like her father," more so than her brothers were—"Everything came out of her mouth very quickly!" his wife added—had first met Sidney in 1967, when Sol was an assistant managing editor at *Ramparts* magazine. Later his wife, Ruth, a photographer, worked with Elsa at Transworld. "Libby was friends with friends of her parents," Ruth Stern said. She was "very mature," and was always "an equal in a relationship. She'd talk to you straight, and had confidence in what she had to say. She was stunning and warm, 'a red thing.' " Although they grew apart when Libby became a teen-ager, Ruth Stern believes that if she hadn't died they would have gotten close again.

The Sterns arrived after Herbie Fisher. "Elsa was alternately crying and walking around in a daze," Sol Stern said. There was also a sense of obligation in the household. "I expected total hysteria, but everyone seemed to be functioning. They started talking about arrangements."

Over in New Jersey, Maxie Teninbaum planned the funeral. "There was chaos over the plot," he said, "because it belonged to me." But Maxie turned it over to the Zions, "in record time."

"Somebody from the hospital called about an autopsy," Sidney said, "and we didn't even have a choice; of course, being Jewish you could have an argument over it."

But he made no objections.

As the morning progressed, other people started coming in, Sol Stern recalled. Mary Schilling arrived. "I remember getting to the apartment and Elsa was cleaning," she told me. "It reminded me of my mother, because when my brother was wounded in Vietnam, my mother started washing windows." She said that she and Elsa cried together, but that Elsa never really said anything.

Mary Schilling took charge of the phone. "And I remember the first phone call that I received was from the dentist, Dr. Wasserman. How he heard about the death I have no idea. And he was really concerned because he wanted to know if it had something to do with Libby's tooth, and whatever medication he might have prescribed. And I related it back to Sidney." She doesn't remember Sidney's response.

Herbie Fisher drove Sidney to New Jersey to break the news to his mother. Elsa went to her mother-in-law's home, too, but drove out with someone else. When they arrived at Anne Zion's apartment at 80 Passaic Street, Herbie Fisher said that he stayed in the car, "because I didn't think it was appropriate for me to be there when he told her. And then I went up to her apartment five minutes later." He had always been impressed with Sidney's mother, and admired her determination and spirit. This time was no exception. "She was an impressive lady," he told me. "She had a unique relationship with Libby. She grabbed the reality of her death incredibly quickly, but she took the hit."

Sidney said that telling his mother "was as hard as losing Libby." Anne Zion told her son she didn't want to live anymore, and Sidney proposed a suicide pact.

"Then she said, 'No, you have other children,' and she became a mother again," he said.

Herbie Fisher drove Elsa back to New York, and Sidney returned home later in the day, although Mary Schilling thought that he spent the night at his mother's apartment. Sidney doesn't remember what he did, but told me, "I probably did stay there. I can't imagine leaving her alone." At first I thought he was talking about his wife, and then realized he was referring to his mother. In any case, Elsa told me she is sure he returned to New York by the evening.

"Elsa was very concerned about an outfit that Libby could wear," Mary Schilling said. "She knew it was in the cleaner's, but she couldn't find the ticket for it. And of course, I went down to the cleaner's and did the best I could, and I don't know to this day whether they ever found the dress."

"People started coming over at night," Herbie Fisher said. All day friends had called friends or colleagues had called colleagues to circulate the crushing news. The Zions had a wide circle of friends and acquaintances from many different worlds—journalism, book publishing, entertainment, television, sports, city government, the law, society, even the underworld.

The Bennington College community was stunned. They immediately issued a notice to the returning students that said Elsa Zion had telephoned to say "Libby had developed a sudden illness over the weekend, and that after only a few hours in the hospital, had died." Libby's roommate, Katherine Kellogg, told me that although they were all shocked, they were also puzzled, like everyone else. "We never got a straight story."

Libby and Katherine had not become fast friends, despite a shared liking for the Grateful Dead. Libby had written her grandmother Anne that the tension between them "was pretty bad." All the same, Katherine had come to New York on October 11 after Sidney, who nicknamed her Special K, had gotten the girls tickets for a Grateful Dead concert. Katherine thought her roommate was "very talented," although she was worried because she seemed "really depressed and unable to deal with school." After the concert, she stayed overnight on West Ninetieth Street before returning to Bennington the next day. She remembered that there were no parents around.

Libby's neighborhood friends were jolted. Dale Fox's brother, Barry, called her with the news. "What do you mean?" she asked him. At first she could not take in the awful words. It took her years to come to terms with her best friend's death. She called Paula Este right away. Paula was dumbstruck. "For a long time there was an unreal character to Libby's death," Paula said. "I went through denial," and she even imagined that Dale was playing some sort of sick joke on her. Paula had spoken to Libby a month before she died. "I felt that she had found strength within herself for the first time in years, and that maybe, hopefully, the self-destructive force that had been driving her had finally concluded its course," she wrote about Libby in a diary after their last conversation.

HERBIE FISHER SAID that in the first shock of Libby's death, "I don't remember blame." But, he went on, "when the doctor didn't come over, it started building."

Sidney hadn't heard from Ray Sherman since his 7:45 A.M. phone call. He didn't count the one he had made to Dr. Sherman after Dr. Weinstein's call, even though Dr. Sherman said that he had "expressed profound sorrow and condolences" and had told Sidney he felt "terrible." But Dr. Sherman hadn't initiated any further phone calls the day Libby died.

Right before he left for Passaic to break the news to his mother, Sidney decided to call Dr. Sherman a second time. "They had to find him. And he got right on, and I said, 'Ray, look, this is the most terrible tragedy that can ever befall parents.' I said, 'I don't know. Why would I have ever left the hospital? I feel like I am going to have to go out that window.' He said, 'Don't feel like that.' He said, 'Don't you feel anything like that.' I said, 'What was it, what did she die from?' And he said, 'I don't know.' And I said, 'Do you realize what you are saying to me?' I said good-bye, and I hung up."

Sidney added a postscript to this testimony. He said, "Oh, before I hung up Ray said to 'come and pick up her belongings,' cold as that. That's the way he puts it. I said good-bye. That was it . . ."

He told Herbie Fisher that he felt Dr. Sherman was being standoffish, and too careful about what he said. Arthur S. Freese, M.D., argues in his book *Managing Your Doctor* that "doctors don't always consider the effect of what they say, and often speak bluntly, leaving the patient stunned and missing half the information."

Was Dr. Sherman too stunned himself to assume a sufficiently compassionate position? Was he angry—over the circumstances of his role and the tragic consequences? "I was clearly stunned," he admitted. "I was not angry. I was upset at myself."

"Dr. Sherman handled it badly," Herbie Fisher told me. "That conversation developed into the tornado the Zion case became." Dr. Sherman believes, however, that no matter what he might have said to Sidney, "the outcome would have been the same."

3

"ALL REPORTING IS to get people to say what they wouldn't say," Sidney Zion once said.

He has been a lot of places since he burst on the New York scene in 1963 to become a reporter for the *New York Post*, after a two-year stint as an assistant United States attorney in New Jersey. He told a journalist that he "knew too much" in that job, and realized that he "could end up either governor of the state or in jail."

"A press card, unlike a lawyer's license—or anything else—provided a front-row seat to the lively doings of the world," he subsequently wrote. "It was an entrée to everything, including the shadows. And when you got the story, you didn't go home and tell your wife and friends, you printed it, right out there for all to read, and under your own byline. What could be better than that?" Between 1963 and 1984, the year Libby died, he had been a metropolitan legal correspondent for *The New York Times*. He had founded a muckraking magazine called *Scanlan's Monthly*, with Warren Hinckle, a writer and editor; it lasted only eight issues despite wide backing that included a three-thousand-dollar investment from his mother. He had written columns for the now-defunct *Soho Weekly News*, as well as for *New York* magazine, *The New York Times Magazine*, and the *New York Post*, and had become a part owner of Broadway Joe's Steak House. He had also won an Overseas Press Club award for a *New York Times Magazine* piece called "The Untold Story of the Mid-East Peace Talks," and in the winter of 1982 had published a collection of his articles, *Read All About It: The Collected Adventures of a Maverick Reporter*. He had even found the time, and the need, to become a member of the New York State Bar Association.

His hometown newspaper, *The Record*, noted that he "sounds like a character out of Ring Lardner, his favorite author," and that "he talks like Sylvester Stallone in *Rocky*." It described him as a "Runyonesque character" who "resembles Phil Silvers as the sergeant in the 1950s television series *Sgt. Bilko*." No one leaves Sidney's presence without recognizing that he or she has met a unique man. He is known as an inveterate storyteller. Mary Schilling said "there was always something happening in that household." Sidney, a tumultuous charmer, quickly makes friends, especially with the mighty and moneyed, stars and soon-to-be-stars. "Elsa has always enjoyed her life with Sidney," Mary Schilling said: being a very private person from a small town, she is convinced that she "probably wouldn't have done anything much with her life if it hadn't been for someone like Sidney."

Sidney has had a lifelong fascination with mobsters; like them, he "thinks everything is fixable," says a colleague. He was once under contract to a publisher to write a non-fiction book about Jewish gangsters—Meyer Lansky,

"Bugsy" Siegel, "Legs" Diamond—and despite a mass of powerful material, he was never able to complete the project. None of his friends ever understood why. Years later, he called upon that trove to write a series of essays to accompany a pictorial history called *Loyalty and Betrayal: The Story of the American Mob*, published in 1994.

Another central passion is Israel, but Sidney was not able to complete a contracted book on that subject either. He had also once signed a contract to write a book about *The New York Times*, to be called *Against the Times*, but he was talked out of it by a friend who convinced him that he needed the paper more than the paper needed him.

In 1988, he published the "autobiography" of Roy Cohn; "Organized by my hand but in his voice," he explained. Although Sidney had detested the red-baiting Senator Joseph McCarthy, for whom Roy Cohn was chief counsel, he had been fascinated with Cohn—"an only child, too"—ever since covering a 1964 trial in which Cohn was one of the defendants. Roy Cohn, Sidney said in an interview in the New York *Daily News*, "lived in a world of contracts, deals, markers," a world that also interested Sidney. He had begun a novel about that world the year of Libby's death, and he told a newspaper interviewer that Libby had been editing it. But after she died, he said, he "tried to write, but I just sat there. It was insane. Then I did another hundred or hundred and fifty pages, but then I ran out of money and the Roy Cohn book came up."

One colleague said that Sidney "only gets things done when the guillotine is about to fall." Many people believe he should never have left *The New York Times* in 1969 to start *Scanlan's Monthly*. The magazine—rebellious and ahead of its time—was named after John Scanlan, a rambunctious pig farmer the editors overheard being toasted by some Irishmen in a bar because they were so glad he was dead and gone from the world. Although *Scanlan's* carried colorful articles on subjects ranging from dirty kitchens in New York restaurants to J. Edgar Hoover, it ran out of money. The editors wanted total editorial control, and believed the only way they could accomplish this was by not "chasing the advertising dollar."

Sidney reports in *Read All About It* that Abe Rosenthal, then the *Times*'s executive editor, told him, "There was no limit to where you could have gone on *The New York Times*. I don't understand it, why did you leave?" Although he writes that his five years with the *Times*—he called it "the Goddess"—made him feel like "a kid on a carousel," this was not the total truth. Elsa said that "all he ever did was complain about it," and she told him, "If every day you go to work and every day you come home from work and all you do is bitch about it, well, it's time to get the hell out of there."

Sidney also writes that Arthur Gelb, then managing editor, told him, "You always wanted to cover the Supreme Court. If you stayed, Abe would have given it to you, but you didn't have patience."

Some of his associates agreed about his lack of patience, and went even further and said he also didn't like having to report to an authority—any authority. Another colleague said that Sidney Zion was the most self-destructive person he had ever known.

After *Scanlan's Monthly* failed, Sidney became a free-lance writer. He would never again work for anybody on a regular basis. He would work for others, but on his terms. Only his terms.

And then, Elsa said, the "blacklisting" came, a period lasting several years when her husband was locked out of the print medium. Many people believe that the events surrounding the blacklisting may be the real reason his career never went where it should have gone.

In 1971, *The New York Times* published articles based on the top-secret Pentagon Papers about American involvement in Southeast Asia. The highly controversial publication was a dazzling journalistic coup—as well as a significant historical coup, for the papers uncovered an extensive trail of government deception and treachery. Their exposure led to the beginning of the end of direct United States involvement in the Vietnam War a year later.

The acquisition of the Pentagon Papers brought about the kind of headlines Sidney would have killed for. He longed to be part of the story, for it contained elements of everything that stirred him: power, dominance, intrigue, and justice.

But he wasn't part of the story. He wasn't even on a newspaper staff anymore.

So Sidney decided to find out who had leaked the papers to Neil Sheehan, the *Times* reporter responsible for the front-page exclusive. Sidney later explained that "my mission was to find out who he or she was before anyone else—for no other reason than to show the people at the *Times*, my old buddies, that I could do it."

SIDNEY KNEW SOURCES, he knew a lot of sources, and he knew how to reach them, but he couldn't find anyone to print the name he eventually came up with of the person who had leaked the Pentagon Papers to Neil Sheehan. "Daddy, you can tell it to me," first-grader Libby had offered.

Sources are a journalist's mainstay, and there's an unwritten rule among editors and others not to delve into them if the reporter has integrity, a trait Neil Sheehan possessed in abundance. So what Sidney was doing to the

Times reporter was breaking a trust—a trust between Sheehan and his source, and a trust between Sheehan and his editors. But Sidney decided to follow his own rules of conduct. He went on *The Barry Gray Show* and announced to its radio audience that Daniel Ellsberg, a political activist who had formulated defense-policy studies while working at the Rand Corporation, was the person who had leaked the papers to Neil Sheehan.

Sidney Zion tattled. He broke the journalists' code. Yet he steadfastly maintained that if he had been working for a newspaper at the time, he would have received awards for his "scoop." Later, however, he wrote candidly that "as an outsider—albeit temporarily, between engagements—I was considered an immoral bastard," and he agreed he "looked like a scoundrel." For the first time in his life, he said, his father offered him some advice, and even traveled to New York to give it to him. Dr. Zion told his son that he wanted him to defend himself, and said that unless he did, "they're going to leave you for dead." And so Sidney followed his father's advice, and wrote an article on why he did what he did. But the only place he could get it published was *Woman's Wear Daily*, an unusual place for such a defense to appear. Nevertheless, Sidney allowed that "the piece began the long process of saving my ass," thus conceding, though only in a whisper, really, that he had been ill-advised to do what he did.

But a maverick forever lives in his soul. Victor Navasky, the publisher and editorial director of *The Nation* magazine, the author of several distinguished books, and someone who has known Sidney since their Yale days together and was a pallbearer at Libby's funeral, told me that "it's one of Sidney's most interesting contradictions, that he's such a religious person and leads the freest life of all the people I know." Navasky added that although Sidney "may care about a career in a conventional sense, his whole persona is anticareer." When he was at the *Times*, "like so many of us, he cared too much about getting his name in print, but went out of his way to make enemies," Navasky said. My husband, Christopher Lehmann-Haupt, daily book reviewer for the *Times* since 1969, also knows Sidney from their Yale days, although he went to its drama school. He told me that "Sidney gets locked into one view of things and doesn't allow for any alternate views that are just as plausible. He doesn't wait to see what happens, and doesn't allow for other interpretations of events."

In 1993, Sidney was fired as a columnist for *The New York Observer*, partly, he says, because he wrote about an angry confrontation with the poet Maya Angelou at a private party in the Hamptons, which ended with all the guests walking out and Angelou calling Sidney "a bald-headed Jew in midlife crisis." It was another typical encounter for Sidney, yet he could possibly have saved his job, or at least still have been able to write an occasional column, if he had not, as he himself confessed to me, told his young editor at the *Observer* that she was "yuppie scum," "a piece of shit," and then hung up on her. "I don't control myself in these situations," he told me. He lost his job, but remained an antihero, what someone once toasted him as being best at.

"They don't want my voice anymore, and it's a real political thing," he said. He threatened "to get" Arthur Carter, the *Observer*'s publisher. "I'm already finding out stuff about him," he bragged, although nothing ever came of this. He went on television, appearing on Connie Chung's *Eye to Eye* in a segment on male bashing, where he announced that he was fired from the *Observer* because he was a member of the "group most hated today," the white male.

Nora Ephron, the writer and movie director, who has

known Sidney since the early sixties when they worked
together at the *New York Post*, said that because "he has
such a great voice," she wishes he would take it more
"seriously." She also echoes the view of many people
when she added that "whatever you ask him about, it's
always what nobody else thinks." And, she said, "because
his mind is so weird and interesting, he's never on the
mark. He's never exact, he's always got an angle."

In 1992, a new magazine at the time, *Cigar Aficionado*,
commissioned a piece because Sidney famously smokes
Macanudo cigars, but its publisher ended up rejecting it,
Sidney told me, because it encouraged the flouting of no-
smoking rules. Sidney vigorously believes that health reports about secondary smoke are a hoax, and that anyone
who doesn't let him smoke is a fascist. But Sidney Zion
could usually find a place to fit in, and eventually sold his
cigar article to *Penthouse* magazine.

In 1993 he undertook a weekly column for the *New York
Post* while also trying to sell a new novel. He wanted to get
a contract based on an outline only, and didn't want to have
to write any of it if it wasn't going to sell. "I know he can
do a great novel because nobody's got a better handle on a
kind of Jewish mob novel," his greatest supporter, Elsa,
said. "There ought to be prisons for writers. Forced exile."

But no publisher would take a chance on just an outline.
He still had to pay some dues if he was going to try fiction,
and he didn't want to, so the novel floundered. Instead, he
put together a collection of some of his old and more recent
columns and articles, often a guaranteed formula to raise
cash.

Yet he couldn't find a mainstream publisher. So he went
to Lyle Stuart, a rebel publisher in the same tradition as his
newest author. *Trust Your Mother But Cut the Cards* was published in 1993.

He went on a massive campaign to put his second collection on the best-seller lists. If Molly Ivins could do it with her columns, then so could he, he said. He found a restaurateur to underwrite a big publication party. He got himself mentioned in a lot of gossip columns, and he asked for and received a highly sought-after bookstore window display. He pressured Christopher Lehmann-Haupt for a daily book review, and when he didn't get one, he stopped returning his old friend's telephone calls. When he learned through connections that his book was to be one of the six or seven books on the "In Short" page in the Sunday *New York Times Book Review*, he arranged to have the paragraph—a favorable paragraph—upgraded to a longer, separate review. The resulting piece turned out to be negative. Somehow it never appeared.

The book received some praise. *The National Review* applauded Sidney for vividly evoking "the old New York saloon life, when Broadway produced tunes you could whistle," and a "guy could call a woman columnist a 'right broad' without getting slapped . . ." But *Trust Your Mother But Cut the Cards* didn't make any best-seller lists.

Fortunately, Elsa, a major financial contributor to the household throughout her marriage, has no illusions about a writer's life, and understands why her husband "laughs about the fact that even the biggest dummies he knows make three times more money than he does." But "it doesn't really matter," she said, "He never cared about money, and he certainly has a better life than most people I know, so if you can get away with it, I guess it's okay." Still, she worries about the future. "You just pray you're somehow going to get it together before your time runs out for all of this. It's terrifying to think about your old age, so you don't think about it." Elsa sold Transworld Feature

Syndicate in the early eighties for a substantial amount of money, and works in city government.

Now writing a weekly column for *The New York Daily News*, Sidney is wistful about the life of a journalist. "Reporters aren't what they used to be," he said to me. "I got all my best stories late at night. You don't see reporters anymore. They're invisible."

Or "in AA," he added.

IN HIS BOOK *Read All About It*, Sidney Zion records that in his exaltation over his Pentagon Papers "scoop" he told then-six-year-old Libby, "This is the biggest story I've ever had." It was the beginning of such shared confidences between father and daughter. "The kid edited my leads from age eleven or twelve; I'd pass them through her before I'd go on with a column, a magazine piece, a book, even a letter to the enemy," he wrote in a tribute to her. "She also edited my ties," he once said. "She was around me when she wasn't around, and I still feel that way."

Libby was a sixth-grader at the Cathedral School when she became her father's editor. "If she didn't like the lead, she'd smile and kiss me on the head," Sidney explained. "If she liked it, she'd nod."

She worshiped him, and identified with him, because they were so much alike. "She was closer to me than anybody in the world," Sidney commented. "She was my confidante. She was my buddy."

Dale Fox said, "Libby and I believed our fathers to be infallible." When Libby was sixteen, she boasted to a friend that "Daddy told me today that Trump bought the *Daily News*, and he's *definitely* editor-in-chief!!! As long as the union deals go through, it's in the bag. So we'll know *positively* by Tuesday, March 30 . . ."

But as those things often go, it never happened.

Dale felt that because Libby "took a lot of other people's pain on as her responsibility," she became too preoccupied trying to figure out their difficulties. This was especially true with her father. "She was a caretaker," Dale said.

Although Libby and her father argued a lot, Paula Este said, they did so, she felt, because they were both "stubborn." What teen-ager has not followed the exact same scenario? And like typical teen-agers, the girls would talk for hours "about family and other matters," said Dale. But Libby had a particular burden. She was worried that her father drank too much. "She actually did talk about that," Dale said. "She'd say, he's drunk again, and we used to make jokes about it, because things were so much worse in my house."

Sidney was aware that his daughter worried about his drinking, and even said so to friends. He had liked her watching out for him. "She loved her dad very much," Dale said. But even though Libby thought of him as unerring, sometimes he seemed the exact opposite, and Dale remarked bluntly, "I know that Libby also felt her father was completely fucked-up."

She was in a bind.

"There were no boundaries in the household," Dale reflected, "and because of that, Libby might not have known where one person starts and the other one begins. It's very confusing."

After all, if her father was out of line, even out of control at times, Libby had to wonder if it would happen to her, too, or already had.

Dale Fox is the relative of an alcoholic, and herself a recovering alcoholic and drug addict. She explained that "a drinking problem doesn't make someone a bad person, it just means that he's got a disease. None of us asks for this bloody thing. And an alcoholic cannot be emotionally available. It's just not what happens. When you have an alcoholic living in the house, the child grows up with this insane need—this instant scream of need—in their head at all times. I'm talking about me, but I'm also talking about Libby." Dale sighed. "Libby was so enmeshed with her entire family—and always in that room. Everything was always in that room."

A T E I G H T P . M . on Monday night, Libby Zion's body was removed from New York Hospital and taken by a brown van to the Manhattan morgue, which is housed at 520 First Avenue, on the northeast corner of Thirtieth Street, in a bland fifties cement-and-glass office building with decorative blue steel trim, next door to the New York University School of Medicine. The medical examiner's office explains that the law requires it to investigate "deaths of persons dying from criminal violence, by accident, by suicide, when unattended by two physicians, or in any suspicious or unusual manner."

The mortuary van parked in a basement-level garage that also served as the building's trash collection point. A dozen or more Dumpsters lined the grimy quarters. Four large signs repeated the same message: PLEASE DO NOT THROW LOOSE CLOTH OR BLOODY SHEETS ON THE DUMPSTERS. A single sign next to the gray entrance doors declared ANYONE DELIVERING OR REMOVING A BODY IS REQUIRED TO SIGN IN AND OUT OF THE REGISTER.

The driver of the mortuary van turned in Libby's papers to an office just inside the doorway, past a security guard, and was assigned a number. Libby, encased in a black body bag, was put on a dented metal gurney and wheeled into the morgue, a large foul-smelling area with soiled blue-tile walls. Her body was placed in one of 126 metal refrigerator compartments that preserve flesh at a temperature just above freezing.

The autopsy at nine A.M. the next morning, March 6, did not get off to a good start. As Libby's cold body lay on one of the eight metal tables in the operating room, there were already contradictions in her preliminary postmortem records.

For a start, there was the information given to the New York County medical examiner's office by two employees of New York City Council President Andrew Stein's office, who had identified Libby's body for Sidney and Elsa the day before. They had said she had no known medical problems, which was not the case, and that no known medicines had been taken, which was also not the case. Properly, they had mentioned the oral surgery, but had not characterized her illness adequately, calling it the "flu."

An autopsy is a systematic study meant to determine the cause of death, and while a cursory overview given at a routine identification is not all that important when one considers that five doctors are generally present at an autopsy to explore specifics, nevertheless, any kind of overview, at the very least, sets a tone. No one knew why Libby died, so every piece of information received had to be dependable because every clue could help determine a cause. Ideally, the doctors and the family are in a quest together.

While Sidney's shock and horror could explain his reluctance to identify his daughter's body himself, his or his wife's presence at that procedure—or his just being available at the hospital at some point—might have set in motion something meaningful. And, even though Libby had been an intern in Andrew Stein's office, why send two outsiders? Why not a relative or a close friend? In fact, a spokesperson for the medical examiner's office said that it is highly unusual for anyone other than a family member or close friend to do the identifying. It would almost seem that from the beginning, Sidney Zion did not want to know how his daughter died.

The autopsy took about an hour and a half. Afterward, Dr. Jon Pearl, the associate chief medical examiner in charge, reported that "pending further study," the cause of Libby's death was "bilateral bronchopneumonia," a swelling of the lungs that can be caused by either a virus or a bacteria. Dr. Elliot Gross, the chief medical examiner, later elaborated, and suggested that Libby died of "hemorrhagic pneumonia," which is ordinarily associated with bacterial infection. He said that the disease was extensive, but gave no further details; it was later established that the hemorrhaging was most likely the result of extensive resuscitation efforts.

A bacterial infection is caused by a one-celled microorganism that often lives in colonies in organic matter, and is sometimes beneficial to its host, but can also multiply and produce powerful toxins that damage the body's cells. A Gram's stain—the test used to identify the presence of bacteria—from Libby's lung tissue showed negative. Cultures were also taken from her lungs. Three different microorganisms later grew out: *Streptococcus viridans*, *Enterococcus*, and a few yeast colonies, or fungi. These findings were not ordinary. *Streptococcus viridans* is usually found in the mouth, throat, and skin, and is frequently a contaminant, that is, a microorganism that penetrates a previously uninfected area. *Enterococcus* rarely causes pneumonia, and is also often a contaminant. It is likely that the fungi, too, was another contaminant that came from the marijuana which Libby told Dr. Leonard she smoked. Marijuana is made from the leaves and top of the hemp plant, *Cannabis sativa*, which contains more than four hundred chemicals.

Extended pot smoking can do great harm to the body's immune system, making the lungs susceptible to infection. While it is possible that the Gram's staining was done improperly by the medical examiner's office, or that the erythromycin Libby was given by Dr. Shapiro might have masked any other bacterial growth, experts for New York Hospital would ultimately assert—and experts for the Zions would agree, at least until 1995—that Libby did not have any infectious bacteria in her lungs at all.

Unlike bacteria, a virus is a disease-causing microorganism that is not able to reproduce on its own, but instead invades the body's cells and takes over—like the common cold, or AIDS. Did Libby have a virus after all? Her autopsy did not determine any significant pathology, or origin of such a disease. Although Libby's tracheobronchial system was inflamed, the amount of pneumonia actually found in her lungs was much too small to have caused her death; and the actual cellular changes associated with pneumonia were extremely weak. Indeed, Dr. Pearl, who inspected her lungs during the autopsy, said that only 10 percent of her lungs was affected.

The autopsy had been uncomplicated. Libby's eyelids "showed areas of redness and drying" and her lower extremities showed "reddish blotches." These were the odd rashes some people noticed. Dr. Weinstein later said that she had seen scratches and abrasions on Libby's arms. "There was little inflammation" where her lower left molar had been removed the week before, on March 1. No infection was found anywhere in her eardrum or surrounding tissues. However, Libby's liver had "congestion," which was consistent with an acute toxic reaction from a substance.

Samples of Libby's blood, bile, brain, liver, stomach,

lungs, and urine were stored in a large refrigerator in the operating room, and later sent for toxicological study.

THE DEATH OF a child is a catastrophe, pure and simple. How does a parent come to terms with such a tragedy? Where does the parent begin? How does the parent hold on, especially if there are other children to be cared for? How can someone go to the depths of a despair that feels like forever, and then be expected routinely to surface and go on with daily living?

Sidney was "cut in half by this," Herbie Fisher said, yet he could still function with all his powers and skills and become "a one-man communications team" who would begin to turn Libby's death into a campaign for the kind of justice he felt he deserved. "Grief and rage are not a defeat for him," said a longtime family friend. Sidney would speak out at hearings, in print, on radio and television. He would have a lot to say, but he would say none of it directly to Dr. Raymond Sherman or any of the other doctors involved in his daughter's care. In his mind, all, and especially Dr. Sherman, had violated an old French proverb: The presence of the doctor is the first part of the cure.

Mary Schilling said that she thinks "Sidney was angry almost from the beginning." It was as if a desire for revenge came before a feeling of loss, because he had the presence of mind to call two very influential connections the day Libby died. "I know I spoke to Ted right away, quick. He was an old friend," Sidney said. Theodore Friedman, a well-known malpractice lawyer, would eventually be asked to handle the case against New York Hospital, Dr. Sherman, Dr. Stone, Dr. Weinstein, and Dr. Leonard.

Sidney also called Andrew Stein, New York City Council president, who, in time, would become an important ally. "He was a friend of mine. I called him. He was one of my first calls," Sidney said. The medical examiner's records indicate that between March 6 and May 11, 1984, Stein made eight calls to that office.

Two years before Libby's death, Sidney had taken a trip to Israel with Stein to introduce him to "generals, and all the people Sidney knew," Elsa told me. "And of course, Sidney wanted to go to write stories. He had extensive connections in the government at that time."

In a letter from Tel Aviv to Libby, Adam, and Jed, Sidney wrote frankly and humorously about his wayfaring friend: "Andy Stein insisted on taking more goddamn pictures. He kept posing next to a tank, with soldiers, without soldiers. They gave him a helmet and a flak jacket and a rifle; click, click, click. And the rockets are getting louder, closer. Suddenly there's a big bang and the soldiers instinctively back away, it couldn't have been more than a couple of hundred feet away, the PLO blast. I'm too dumb to get scared, but when I see the soldiers blink, I decide not to be a perfect asshole. 'Out of here,' I say. Andy says one more time. He doesn't like the idea of a Brooks Brothers shirt under his flak jacket. He takes off the shirt, puts the flak back and again click, click. I turn away—I guess that's when his toupee came off in the helmet because then I heard the soldiers laughing—and I say to our guide: 'I don't intend to die on any fucking green line. I want to die in New York City at age ninety-four with a bottle of Johnnie Black at the ready and a twenty-two-year-old blonde lying next to me.' I think that's when I must have thought about writing you. Because I should have said I wanted my great-grandchildren next to me. Only you know I'd prefer the blonde."

For most of his life, Sidney was also famous for the "groupies" that followed him, as if he were a rock star. It was preposterous, and comic, and part of what Victor Navasky meant by his friend leading the freest life of all the people he knew. Fortunately, "Elsa can be sophisticated enough to deal with it all," Mary Schilling said. And, "His mother could have said something like 'if you ever do anything—you'll get your knees broken.' "

Sidney seems larger than life sometimes, so when any of his "lady friends," as they were called, showed up with him places, or even in his own home, people accepted it as part of who he is. "He belongs to a fading school of males that need constant reassurance," a friend says.

Mary Schilling said that as more and more people crowded into the apartment on West Ninetieth Street the night of Libby's death, and talked to Sidney, his anger grew, because each person "triggered something that he hadn't thought about at the time." She remembered that Elsa was "totally numb."

One of the mourners who showed up was Dr. Kenneth Greenspan, the psychiatrist who treated Libby with biofeedback and Nardil. Sidney introduced him to the relatives, friends, and colleagues gathered in his house as "the doctor who gave my girl a month of happiness." Later, Dr. Greenspan told me that Libby "was clearly like a different person" for that "one whole month. An alive, vibrant person. It was like someone being born again."

At one point during the evening, Sidney took Dr. Greenspan aside to ask if he knew what happened to Libby. Dr. Greenspan told him that he didn't. "Sidney let me know he could understand God taking his daughter, but not the mistakes of another man," Dr. Greenspan said.

"The whole thrust of her treatment was her moving on," Dr. Greenspan told me. "There was not much focus on the past; the present and the future is what she focused on. She was finished when she died, but she would have dropped in on her school vacations, to check in," he went on. "She was given some exercises to use. She didn't need the machines so much." Dr. Greenspan said that once Sidney "lost her, he moved into another place—on the attack, so to speak. He didn't wait for the doctor-patient relationship to try to heal things."

The theme "went from grief to business in two days," Herbie Fisher said. "Two days become very long." In addition, because of Sidney's nature and temperament, the evenings had the feeling of social occasions. Adam, who said that when he first woke up on Monday morning, he sensed his sister was dead, was particularly unhinged by the atmosphere. "There were a hundred people over," he told me. "I couldn't believe a party was going on."

DR. SHERMAN HADN'T called the Zions on the day of Libby's funeral, Wednesday, March 7—nor did he attend the funeral—and Sidney was more embittered than ever. Dr. Sherman "never came to my house," and "didn't talk to me for three months," he said.

However, Dr. Sherman—who explained that "in general my colleagues and I don't attend funerals of patients"—said that just a few days after Libby's death he gave Sidney a preliminary autopsy report that he had received from a pathology resident, Dr. Karen Jahre, who had obtained it from the medical examiner's office. This is the report that had first suggested pneumonia.

Elsa said Dr. Sherman had called her around the same time to tell her that "they could find nothing that would indicate why Libby died," because "there were no abnormalities of any vital organs." She reported that he had also told her that the small amount of pneumonia found was "not enough to kill a young person."

In *Talking with Patients,* Brian Bird, M.D., writes, "The

patient's understanding of words may be remarkably different from the doctor's meaning of them, and in the final analysis it is not what the doctor says that is important—it is what the patient thinks he says that counts."

One of the most compelling reasons for having a long-term relationship with a doctor is that both the doctor and the patient learn to read each other, and to anticipate problem areas. There has to be give-and-take in the relationship. It has to be a fairly equal relationship, too; that is, the doctor cannot diminish the patient by using distancing language—jargon—nor can the doctor infantilize the patient through attitude. The patient, in turn, must not expect a doctor to be a mind reader, a spiritual healer, or a miracle worker. The patient must ply the doctor with questions, ideas, suggestions—anything that can contribute to better communication and a better diagnosis.

What exactly was the relationship between Sidney Zion and Dr. Raymond Sherman? Why weren't they able to transcend the early acrimony that often develops as a form of shell shock? What was Dr. Sherman's relationship with Libby and her other doctors? What was Libby's relationship with Dr. Sherman and her other doctors?

The actual relationship at that time of Sidney and Libby to Raymond Sherman is somewhat ambiguous. Sidney was not only a patient of Dr. Sherman's, he was also his friend, or so Sidney felt. Dr. Sherman considered Sidney only an acquaintance. "He was not a personal friend," Dr. Sherman said. "He never came to my house and I never went to his house." But Sidney maintained that they were "closer than a doctor would be normally to his patients." Indeed, they were frequently thrown together at parties and family events because of Sidney's close friendship with Dr. Sherman's brother-in-law, Victor Temkin. Temkin, a former publishing executive who now does consulting work in Los Angeles, was one of the very few people Sidney might listen to for writing advice. In fact, Temkin was often the only person Sidney would listen to besides his mother.

Sidney's mother and Victor Temkin's mother were old friends and confidantes, and had used Dr. Sherman as their internist long before Sidney became his patient. Dr. Sherman's home phone number had come to Sidney from Temkin, who had thought the operative connection was their mothers. Indeed, Sidney often pointed out that he and Dr. Sherman were close "because he took care of my mother." Sidney agreed that he and Dr. Sherman talked quite often on the phone, mostly about his mother. Yet he also said that "Libby talked to Ray more than I did. Ray would tell Libby, 'Don't bother coming in, we can do it on the phone.'" Dr. Sherman made it clear that he had never given Sidney his home phone number, and did not know how he had got it until his brother-in-law confessed later.

Victor Temkin said that Ray Sherman wasn't on call the weekend Libby entered New York Hospital, and he has felt guilty for involving his brother-in-law in a situation of which he might ordinarily not have been part, especially since Temkin believed, at the time, that Dr. Sherman wasn't really Libby's doctor. He was surprised Libby had also been a patient.

In the Zion family, although Dr. Sherman was considered Sidney's own special doctor, whenever there were serious health concerns with any family member, Dr. Sherman was consulted, as he had been the night Libby was taken to New York Hospital. Dr. Sherman said that he had seen Elsa as a patient one time.

In 1981, after Libby had complained of stomach pain, her father had sent her to Dr. Sherman, who had offered medication, and sent her to several specialists. Dr. Sherman even consulted with Libby's gynecologist about her problems, and they had come up with the diagnosis of irritable bowel syndrome, which was treated with medication. But no one seemed to recognize that because the colon is partially controlled by the central nervous system, Libby's irritable bowel syndrome could have been caused by any number of drugs she was already taking.

Dr. Sherman had prescribed various drugs to Libby—or noted in his records that other doctors had given them to her—from age fifteen on: Tagamet, used for ulcers and various other stomach ailments; Bentyl, an antispasmodic; Anaprox, an anti-inflammatory; Donnatal, used for insomnia, anxiety, and bladder or digestive spasms; Darvocet, a painkiller; Librax, used for muscle spasms and nervousness; Motrin, a pain reliever, especially for inflammations and difficult menstruations; Actifed, to reduce allergic symptoms; tetracycline, a treatment used for bacterial infections; and the tranquilizer Valium. Libby had received many prescriptions from other doctors as well, not noted in Dr. Sherman's records: Butazolidin and Indocin, anti-inflammatories; Robaxin, a muscle relaxant; Tylenol with codeine, a narcotic analgesic; two more antibiotics, doxycycline and ampicillin; sulfa, used for urinary-tract and other infections; Atarax, an antihistamine; and Dalmane, a tranquilizer.

Dr. Sherman had actually only examined Libby twice, the first time in 1981, and the second in 1982. All the rest of their contacts were by telephone. "I examined her when I thought she needed to be examined," Dr. Sherman explained. "I really felt we knew what to do without actually bringing her in."

By 1984, Libby had a choice of at least six other doctors in addition to Dr. Sherman to whom she could go for her drug prescriptions, and she rarely bothered to keep her various doctors informed as to what she was taking or how much. In addition to her pediatrician and gynecologist, there were the specialists she was referred to by Dr. Sherman, as well as school physicians.

It never dawned on Dr. Sherman that Libby might be overdoing drugs. He simply didn't know her well enough. "She didn't tell me how bad things were," Dr. Sherman said. He was also unaware of the very existence of Libby's pediatrician, whom, as it turned out, she had visited a few days before her death.

It was even whispered among people who knew both Dr. Sherman and Sidney Zion that Raymond Sherman had no desire to be the family's doctor. But it was a relationship from which he couldn't easily extricate himself.

DR. BRIAN BIRD writes in *Talking with Patients:* "On the opposite side, the physician should make absolutely certain what the patient's words mean." Nothing should be taken for granted.

And perhaps what the patient thinks the doctor *doesn't* say is what counts, as well. At the hospital, did Sidney and Elsa understand what they were asked or told? Did Libby? In her illness, was Libby perhaps still a caretaker, guarding her family from her symptoms? Sidney said that Libby hardly ever complained to him about her pain. "I don't think she wanted to upset me too much about those things."

4

THE DAY OF Libby's funeral, Wednesday, March 7, was bitterly cold. In the apartment on West Ninetieth Street, letters and telegrams of condolence poured in. They included messages from Mayor Ed Koch, former mayor John V. Lindsay, gossip columnist Liz Smith, political columnist Anthony Lewis, Roy Cohn, humorist Calvin Trillin. These notes did what they were supposed to do: they brought comfort to the shattered Zion family.

Frank Sinatra sent an extravagant bouquet of garden and exotic flowers to Anne Zion's small apartment in Passaic, where later there would be a postfuneral gathering of family and friends. It was the centerpiece of the occasion.

Sidney had met Frank Sinatra four years earlier at the home of a mutual acquaintance, and they had become friends. A year after their meeting, Sidney had written a cover story for *The New York Times Magazine* in which Sinatra was prominently featured. The theme of the piece was that the old tunes were coming back. "Between the rock and the hard disco the melody began to slip back in" was its opening—vintage Sidney Zion.

Frank Sinatra understood markers. "Read all about it is the best advice I can give about *Read All About It,*" he wrote for his friend's book jacket, and he endorsed Sidney's novel, *Markers*, as "worldly, warm and wise," and said that "if it were a song it would be Rodgers and Hart."

Right after Libby's funeral, he invited Sidney and Elsa to rest and recuperate at his home in Palm Springs, California. This trip would become the subject of much gossip and envy—Sidney Zion staying with Ol' Blue Eyes himself.

Libby was fifteen years old at the time her father wrote the Sinatra story, and she got into the piece, too, when her father described a bagels-and-cream-cheese breakfast party she was having for a dozen kids. He wrote, "The radio is on, but they're not listening because it's not 'their' music." He had asked them if they knew who was singing, and he described how they all looked at Libby, who knew, but didn't say. Then he wrote, "I've got a bunch of very bright kids in my apartment, and when they don't know the voices of Crosby and Astaire, I can't call it anything less than cultural genocide."

Also vintage Zion.

The service for Libby was held in the Sanctuary of Abraham and Sarah, a sprawling white building that houses marble-plated, above-ground burial sites in the middle of the New Cedar Park Cemetery on Forrest Avenue in Paramus, New Jersey. Its distinctive architecture and baronial entrance with four pillars and a circular driveway is in stark contrast to the rural green acres surrounding it.

More than a hundred mourners walked across the sanctuary's brown tweed rugs, and those who arrived early enough found seats in the rows of light-colored wooden benches that faced a simple pulpit backed by a large modern purple-blue-and-maroon menorah hanging on the wall. An everlasting flame flickered dimly. As the benches filled up, people stood in the back or sat on stairs leading to a balcony on the second level. Some mourners leaned against the balcony's railing.

A rabbi known by the family conducted the brief service, and there was only one speaker. Nora Ephron said that when Sidney stood up at the funeral, "I remember feeling I'm going to go to pieces. I'm not going to be able to bear the pain of this . . . and then, of course, he was great. He was charming and wonderful." Another friend added that "*it was all about Sidney!* It was all about how he got Libby to listen to Sinatra, and to admit that Sinatra was good. Yet the talk still gave you a sense of Libby in a wonderful way, even though it was always about himself."

Sidney doesn't recall exactly what he spoke about, but he told me he did remember that he told the story of hearing Libby listening to Billie Holiday and Bessie Smith, "and she said to me, 'you can only go so far with rock and roll.' "

"Music was always part of everybody's life," Elsa said. As a child, Elsa was in the glee club, played the piano, played the bass drum in the school band, and was even offered a scholarship to the Crane College of Music. "My father's family was very musical," she continued. "His father was a violinist and repaired violins as well." She said her husband's side of the family had musical talent, but she thinks there wasn't "much of an opportunity" to express it. "Libby had a beautiful singing voice, and Adam plays the guitar very well and sings well, and Jed sings well, but he gave up the guitar," she told me. No one has "spectacular" ability, she acknowledged, but they were "good."

Libby's voice was highly praised by voice teachers at both New Lincoln and Bennington, although a guitar teacher she took lessons from for a while during high school admitted that he "didn't see any future in music for her." He added that "she had a desire to do well, but the truth was she didn't focus," and he said that she often came to her lessons "stoned." A jazz workshop instructor at New Lincoln wrote that "we did not see much of Libby this year," yet he praised her excellence as a lead vocalist. Libby's voice teacher at the school said she finished all her work, although she missed her performance in the senior assembly. Absent but doing fine work was Libby's leitmotif, and this theme enabled her to remain free of the rules and regulations her father said she never liked. But her high school adviser had been concerned, and criticized this "blithe approach to her work," and cautioned that she seemed unconcerned about the consequences of her actions.

Still, she continued her music, and during what would be her only semester at Bennington, she became known as "the guitar-playing one." Elizabeth Saltzman, an editor at *Vanity Fair* magazine, as well as a highly visible New York personality—"Ms. Moment," the *Daily News* called her in 1993—was a friend of Libby's at Bennington, although she dropped out after two months. But she said that Libby "loved her music class; I remember her always not wanting to be late for that." Libby's roommate, Katherine Kellogg, remembered overhearing a phone conversation Libby was having with her grandmother Anne: "But Gramma, I know I'm a good writer, but I want to be a singer. I want to sing like Frank Sinatra."

"She was happy with her music," Elsa remembered. "She had a beautiful singing voice," Katherine reiterated. Libby herself wrote the official evaluation of her fall voice class, analyzing that "although I have not been able to do any singing so far this term due to having a cold for a month, I have learned a lot about singing just by listening to others sing . . . it taught me how to listen better; in other words, what to listen for, and how to isolate both the good things and the bad things in singing techniques."

Elsa said that "Sidney and I had already tried to find people for Libby to talk to, so she could understand how this music world worked and whether she had any chance of even pursuing it. We found out that it didn't have anything to do with talent, it had everything to do with desire—that if you really wanted it hard enough, and you pushed hard enough, you'd get it." After being told by a teacher that her voice was golden, Libby even gave "a little concert" at Bennington, Elsa recalled. But Libby told her mother that she had been "humiliated," because she had panicked and had forgotten the words to her song. "Interestingly enough," Elsa pointed out, "she didn't seem to be really distraught about that. She somehow could laugh about it." Libby often showed such resilience. It was the trait that her friends had always found irresistible.

At seventeen and eighteen, Libby almost seemed an average teen-ager searching for a calling.

But certain of the paths she had chosen to find herself were more dangerous than the average teen-ager would take. I eventually learned how endlessly depressed she was, and how isolated and tormented she felt. I learned that even though she made an impact at Bennington in her brief time there, she was, in fact, hardly ever present. She'd return to New York every Thursday for a long weekend, and she was there once for a full week. "Her parents didn't know," Katherine Kellogg told me. "She went to New York to be with Ralph Enders. I'd cover for her a lot, and say she was in the library." In fact, after the weekend Katherine came to New York for the Grateful Dead concert, Libby stayed on in New York, although her parents thought she had returned to Bennington with Katherine. Once Katherine slipped, and told Anne Zion that her granddaughter was in New York. Libby was furious. "Libby never dealt straight with her parents," Katherine said. So Elsa and Sidney, while aware that "it was very difficult for her to make transitions of any kind," as her mother described it, did not really know just how unhappy Libby was, or the extent of the secret life she was living. Adam, however, said that he knew that his sister came home every weekend. "Libby missed a lot of school," Katherine said. "She'd lie about not having classes."

Libby's adviser, Richard Tristman, wrote in his fall 1983 report that the term was indecisive because Libby had a medical excuse, although he also said that he had the sense she was doing fairly well. The exact nature of her term-long medical excuse is not spelled out anywhere in her college records, although a comment by a history professor refers to "a series of misadventures" that prevented Libby from writing the first paper of the term.

Richard Tristman also explained that he had "caught sight—I think—of a bit of frenzy. Perhaps even aside from medical distractions, Libby has needed a bit more academic composure." Later, he would say that she seemed "cranky," and that he got the feeling her life was problematic. He would have liked to have helped her, but he believed that members of the faculty have "no right to police student lives. I'm a professor, not a psychologist."

Libby began to see a counselor early into the term, although her adviser was not aware of that. He said that their contact was mostly "on the humorous side, both being New York Jews," and that he didn't see her that much. Indeed, no one at Bennington saw Libby that much.

"The biggest single problem was that she wasn't eighteen, couldn't go with the other kids to the local bars," Elsa said, "so she would be left alone in the dormitory."

"There was only one bar on campus," Katherine Kellogg said. "It sold beer and wine, and was very strict about IDs, and anyway, Libby didn't drink." "She couldn't, it bothered her stomach," her mother agreed.

Elsa's notion of the recreational life at Bennington was not accurate. I have been told by other people that bars do not play that central a part in the life of the student body. Many of the undergraduates stay on campus all the time. "Every Friday night, a different dorm hosts a party," one former student said. Students could also go to a nearby diner, and downtown Bennington was only four miles away. There were movies and shopping, and naturally there was always hiking, camping, or skiing. After all, Bennington is situated between the Taconic Mountains of the southwestern part of Vermont and the Green Mountains, which extend down the center of the state from the Canadian border to the Massachusetts line.

According to Katherine, Libby would "either be in the room, or in New York." She didn't even go to meals very often. "She ate a lot of soup," which she heated on a hot plate, Katherine said, explaining that a friend with a car would often take her roommate to a local supermarket.

To finance her clandestine trips to New York, Libby sold drugs at college. One of her classmates thinks it was "just pot" she sold, but confessed that she was a little naïve "back then," and said "Libby might have sold other drugs as well," although she only saw her smoke pot. But this acquaintance said, "I don't know. There were a lot of drugs on campus." Dale Fox said that some of the people

Libby traveled around with sold drugs, "So of course she was doing sidelines, I would think. How could she not? I mean you're in the business, it becomes second nature."

When Libby was on campus, generally just on Tuesdays and Wednesdays, she spent much of her time smoking pot. She coughed a lot from the amount she smoked, her roommate said, adding that she wasn't aware of any other drug use, except for Valium, assorted antibiotics, and possibly "Maalox and ulcer medicine." "I thought of her more as a pot smoker," Katherine observed. It was "almost universal with that generation," Libby's adviser remarked. In fact, in 1983, marijuana was the most popular illegal drug in America.

Nevertheless, on the margin of a list that included such reminders as "Pick up laundry and fold, etc.," "Get *The Wealth of Nations, Antony and Cleopatra,* (read them)," "Eat, find a ride to the bus station," and "Read 'Tonio Kroger,' write paper [for] Belitt," Libby wrote "Snow!" which is a street name for cocaine. Adam Zion said that an intimate friend of Libby's told him that she used cocaine at Bennington, and "was completely addicted to it."

"I was always finding people I didn't know in her room," a housemate of Libby's said. She remembered that Libby once had all her money stolen—her monthly allowance of ninety dollars from her parents, as well as her cash from drug deals—which meant that she had no money with which to sneak into New York. Libby had called her parents in a panic. "Obviously there was a thief on campus who was watching things," Elsa recalled. "Libby hadn't drawn her curtain and she had put her money in what she thought was a safe place." Elsa told her daughter to calm down, to borrow twenty dollars from a classmate, and that more money would be sent immediately.

"She had a lot of trouble functioning," Katherine said.

"She was sometimes manic, too. She'd be very verbal or way down. She seemed manic-depressive to me." Once another resident of Kilpatrick House, where Libby and Katherine lived, came into their room and told Katherine that Libby was acting very strangely, that she was sitting on the floor right outside the door—"just sitting there, staring into space." Her roommate had no idea how long Libby might have been that way, but everyone thought it was very peculiar. They were worried.

Because of her "depression," Libby skipped classes. "She'd get up, call Ralph Enders, have breakfast, and call Ralph again," Katherine said. It was a miserable existence.

But Libby persisted. She tried to make college work for her.

She even adopted a cat from the ASPCA. "She poured a lot of love into that cat," Elizabeth Saltzman said. She named it Killer and told her parents it was a stray she had found. It was also a point of contention between Katherine and Libby, because Katherine was allergic to cats; but she didn't make much of a fuss because she thought the cat might "mellow Libby out." She didn't know that Libby too was allergic to cats. Libby would take Killer with her to New York. "It would sleep on her neck in a little scarf. She'd give it Valium so it wouldn't get upset by the bus trip," Elizabeth Saltzman remembered.

Libby tried to keep up with her college work despite her absences. "Circumstances beyond Libby's control have compelled her absence from five of our class meetings, and an injury to her hand and wrist has held up all three papers assigned . . ." reported Ben Belitt, her literature professor. The injury to her hand and wrist had happened Libby's first weekend at school. "Libby had a fight with Ralph on the phone," Katherine said, "and afterwards she put her hand through a glass door."

Libby did tell her parents about the incident. Her father even mentioned it in the tribute he later wrote about her. In this tribute, Sidney praised his daughter's taste and honesty, especially the way she would cross things out of his articles because there was "no sentiment permitted in the old man's leads. And no overwriting." But, he said, "it gave her trouble now and then, this taste and honesty. It gave her trouble with teachers here and there, with friends, with boys. The Libby-smile would disappear when it happened, she'd stomp around the apartment, break some dishes. Once at Bennington College, she put her hand through a window. But always the laughs brought her back. Don't worry, Daddy, I can handle it . . ."

And she often did.

In his next evaluation, Ben Belitt reported that "the task called 'Herculean' at midterm—the make-up of papers (six) requiring a double labor of written work due before and after midterm—has been successfully accomplished, with hardly a moment to spare or a second plea for extension." He called her papers "firmly reasoned," "perceptive," and "done with praiseworthy specificity and verve." The term has been "unexpectedly retrieved," he said.

It was nothing short of miraculous.

During high school, Libby had written a boyfriend that "writing feels good," and as she wrote in her college essay, her journal offered her a means to express her emotions: "To lay beside you, my love still sleeping now / to tell sweet lies one last time and sing good night / to lay me down," ended one of her melancholy song lyrics.

Speaking not of her own daughter, but of a young acquaintance who had recently committed suicide, Elsa later mistakenly said that "people who are depressed and who have chronic depression hide it very well, and there's very little ability for anybody else to do anything about it." And then, speaking of Libby, she later said, "And if it—the depression—was there, the only guy who ever came into contact with it was that guy whose name I can't remember anymore. The biofeedback guy."

"Sleep is a dream, wake is a dance—an illusion of love," Libby wrote at Bennington with the kind of incoherence perhaps not unexpected in a sensitive adolescent. "And when it all comes down to you—well, is it all that matters? Is it the reality or the illusion which draws you down till the time is come to make it somehow on the straws that still remain?"

ALTHOUGH ONE OF Sidney Zion's publishers called him the "most controversial columnist in America," his wife said of her husband, "When it comes to tough emotional things, he will back right off it."

This is especially true of Libby's drug use.

Neither parent ever mentioned anything about it—even as a remote possibility—to any doctor. In later depositions, both parents swore that their daughter did not use drugs. Sidney said Libby once told him she had tried marijuana, emphasizing to him, he said, that "I'm not on anything, Daddy." Elsa said that her husband "objects to any kind of drugs," and "would never have tolerated their use." She also said that Libby had told her that only "off-the-wall kids" used drugs.

For parents to see only what they want to see is certainly not uncommon. Dale Fox believed that the Zions "pulled a shade over" Libby's drug use, just as her own parents did with her. "A parent does not want to think that about their child," she said, "because what does that say about them?"

Libby began using drugs at fourteen. So did Dale Fox.

"I probably turned her on, I mean, I'm sure I gave her quaaludes," Dale confessed. "Some people experiment with drugs and leave it," she went on. "They grow up and it's over."

Libby never had a chance to grow up and find that out.

"We were all very unhappy kids," Dale said. Their unhappiness in high school went beyond the normal teen-age struggle for independence or the usual teen-age escapades; their unhappiness saw black light when the sun came out.

"Libby was always unhappy and miserable and in pain—physical, emotional, spiritual," Dale said. "I used to try to cheer her up and make her laugh and keep her mind off her pain, and also give her drugs."

Libby's unhappiness ultimately sought solace in endless drug taking—not as mere experimentation or thrill seeking, but in a serious, habitual way that blotted out problems that could not be faced or even articulated. "I feel like I can't escape it, or whatever it is that's bothering me which I want to escape from," Libby wrote in a letter to a boyfriend when she was sixteen. "I just haven't figured out yet what I want to run from. But whatever it is, it's catching up—quickly."

The friends smoked marijuana, used amphetamines—"yellow jackets" and "black beauties"—opiates, barbiturates, antidepressants, tranquilizers, LSD, cocaine. There was plenty of alcohol, too, but this would seem not to have been one of Libby's means of escape. Libby hardly drank, because of her stomach problems. "The closer I get to touching my feelings, the more nervous and neurotic I get," Libby wrote in the same letter to her friend.

"We used to sit in her room when we were fifteen and trip our brains out," Dale Fox said. Something else that Dale told me was disturbing. She said Libby got "a lot of mixed messages" from her parents, and it seemed to Dale that "Sidney and Elsa were never home. Those guys went out to more events than anybody I knew. That's why I loved it there. It was like a little drug haven. You couldn't do drugs in your own home, so you could go to their house. I couldn't believe what we got away with there. It blew my mind," she said, adding that of course the Zions loved all their children, she doesn't doubt it for a moment, yet she believed "Libby was ignored. I think she suffered terrible neglect—the type of neglect that you cannot pinpoint."

"We'd drop acid in that room all the time," Dale said. "It was like an open house in there, twenty-four hours a day." Libby's house was "more like a dormitory" than a home, because hardly anyone ever questioned what they were doing. "I think Libby just eased into the background and faded away into the woodwork," Dale said, speaking of the family dynamics. Often, Dale would sleep over, and in the morning she and Libby "used to wake up and do coke."

Libby would then go to school.

Libby found it easy to get good grades and stay high at the same time. A former Fieldston student, who believed that "kids in New York always do things earlier than kids in other places," said that "pot was not a big thing," indeed was only looked upon as dangerous if it was used as a "crutch." Libby used it as a crutch. Even though Dale Fox faults Libby's "bleeding-heart liberal" private schools for not picking up on the severity of her situation, the other student said that it was easy to go to classes stoned because it never showed. Cocaine use never showed, either.

Libby wrote a boyfriend, "I went to school, but I split early. Couldn't deal with waiting for three hours for math class." In another letter, Libby berated herself for misspelling words "that never used to give me problems." She recalled that she had won a spelling bee in the eighth grade, and explained, "Then again, I didn't smoke so much pot in eighth grade, and I had never done any other drugs either. Back then, I was generally considered the smartest girl in the school. That's probably why I went to Fieldston. It's also exactly why I left. Figure it out yourself."

From the age of fourteen on, Libby and her friends comforted one another. "She was really trapped, so we were like each other's escape hatch," Dale said. And the refuge they found in Libby's room, where they were on their own, made them feel safe.

The group even had its own language. "Just some goofy thing kids do," Dale said. She and her brother, Barry, made up most of the words, and Libby joined in. One of Libby's favorites was the word for happy things, *jernt*, which Dale said had no connection to the word *joint*, for pot, even though, she went on, "we were like the drug crowd. That's what we did." In fact, Dale said she herself was a major drug dealer during her high school years.

"As long as I was on drugs, I was protected," Dale said. "Libby was just very good to me. She gave me her version of love, which was to allow me to stay there. I believe her friendship saved my life."

At fourteen, Libby actually recognized that she had the habit of responding to her problems by getting sick. She told a boyfriend that she associated her spastic colon and irritable bowel syndrome with being depressed. She also told him she was taking Elavil, an antidepressant. No record exists of how or where Libby obtained that medication.

Paula Este said that Libby, who "was more unhappy than the average teen-ager," also "tended to describe things in extremes," and she was worried because Libby was unable to find a middle ground. Dale said that "Libby was always in physical pain. She had more physical problems for a young kid than anyone I knew." From the age of thirteen on, Libby suffered from hives, migraine headaches, tooth pains, clamped jaw, irritable bowl syndrome, premenstrual syndrome, insomnia, nightmares, depression, stress, anxiety, depersonalization, plus assorted sports injuries—torn ligaments, sprains, and broken bones she sustained, particularly playing soccer at Cathedral and Fieldston. And all her life, Libby was a little overweight. "Kid's fat," her mother called it. "The pediatrician told me once that redheads are much more sensitive and fragile, and life is going to be more complicated. Every time she had a cold, it became a big cold, and it was clear she had a lower threshold of pain," Elsa explained.

"I got so tired hearing about her physical problems," Dale admitted. "I thought there was something really wrong with her at a certain point—emotionally—to me it sounded like she should have been hospitalized for the rest of her life the way she was talking."

Yet Libby was able to find friends that shared and understood her frustrations. "We connected at such a core level," Dale pointed out. "I know that Libby felt a thousand years old in her heart. I'm sure she did. I know I did. I felt far too old for my age. We were like ancient disappointments. Thousand-year-old disappointments—in fourteen-year-old girls. It doesn't make sense. It shouldn't be that way."

As a young teen-ager, Libby began waking up too early in the morning. She had trouble falling asleep at night. She had hives. She had pains in her eyes. She had trouble with her teeth.

Dr. Irene Shapiro, Libby's pediatrician, did her best to help.

A graduate of New York University and its School of

Medicine in the early forties, Dr. Shapiro did her residency at Mount Sinai, where Libby was born. She treated her infections and colds, sent her for tests and X rays, and prescribed Robaxin, a muscle relaxer.

When Libby was sixteen, Dr. Raymond Sherman was brought into the picture to help, and as Libby's complaints grew, Dr. Sherman suggested various specialists. In late March of 1981, Libby visited Dr. George Stassa, a gastro-enterologist, and the tests he performed showed a normal esophagus, no evidence of an ulcer, and a normal small bowel. Dr. Sherman also had Libby undergo a pelvic ultra-sound and an abdominal sonogram in 1983; both tests were normal. On May 5, 1981, Dr. Sherman suggested that Libby see a colon specialist. Two weeks later, Dr. Howard Goldin wrote to Dr. Sherman that Libby most likely had "an irritable colon variant." He suggested dietary changes. In 1983, Libby saw Dr. Goldin again, when he performed both a barium enema, which showed a normal colon, and a sigmoidoscopy, which had to be terminated because Libby had not done the necessary preparations for the test. She was to return the next day, but never did.

According to Dr. John Lyden, an orthopedic surgeon, his hospital colleague, Dr. Sherman, sent Libby to see him on January 25, 1984, just six weeks before her death, because in a telephone call she complained that she had a sore shoulder. Dr. Lyden said that Dr. Sherman asked him to determine whether Libby's pains were real or not.

Dr. Sherman has no written record of any such conversation. In fact, he maintains that he sent Libby to Dr. Lyden for "real pain." Sidney said that he was never aware that Dr. Sherman had referred Libby to Dr. Lyden. "I don't know who he is."

Dr. Lyden, a 1965 graduate of Columbia University's College of Physicians and Surgeons, did his graduate surgical training at Roosevelt Hospital from 1965 to 1967, and had further orthopedic training at the Hospital for Special Surgery, part of the New York Hospital–Cornell Medical Center, where he joined the staff in 1969. In 1972 he received a fellowship in hand surgery. Dr. Lyden reported that Libby, who was "agitated, mobile, and evasive," told him she had "aching pain in both shoulders," and that it had started when she was "rolled over by a large rubber ball" when she was thirteen years old. She had never reported this to Dr. Sherman.

Dr. Lyden recalled that Libby was "a little vague on the details," and told him that "many physicians" had evaluated her, although she would not disclose their names. He said that she mentioned that she had recently seen a doctor who gave her Indocin, an anti-inflammatory drug, but that she had only taken it for two days. She said the only additional medications she had received were Darvon and Robaxin; but, he said, he believed there were others. "I knew or presumed she was lying at the time," he went on. Libby also told Dr. Lyden that she had migraine headaches, a spastic colon, and was taking biofeedback treatments "to control her bodily problems."

Dale Fox's brother, Barry, said, "Once a kid sees all she has to do is cry or whine a bit—once it became obvious to Libby she could get drugs, either for physical or psychological problems—her complaints became overblown." Dr. Sherman used the word "pain" twenty-two times in his five-page record on Libby. There is "abdominal pain," "intestinal pain," "pain persists all day," "pain radiates to back." These records clearly indicate that he knew he was dealing with a patient with a serious problem. "I was fooled by this woman in terms of her drug use," Dr. Sherman later told me. "I didn't believe at the time it was imaginary pain, but I think it could have been a manifestation of stress."

Dr. Lyden sent Libby for X rays of her neck and both shoulders. An hour later she returned to his office, and he told her the X rays were normal, and that he could find no underlying cause for her discomfort. He had noticed that her joints were "loose," so he suggested that she try some mild exercises. But, he said, Libby became very annoyed when she learned he was not going to prescribe any new medications to her. "To the best of my recollection she wanted a narcotic, either a codeine or Percocet, Percodan type of thing," he said. He remembered that she was "sophisticated about medication."

Dr. Lyden decided Libby was "severely disturbed on an emotional basis," and just looking for drugs, and that therefore he "had nothing to offer her." He did not bill her, later explaining that "if the patient was upset with me, and this patient was very upset with me, I found it less troublesome not to bill them." He called Dr. Sherman immediately, told him all his impressions, including his judgment that her pains were not real. He was very explicit. He also sent Dr. Sherman an official, written report, which did not reflect the dramatic descriptions he used orally, although he later told the New York State Board for Professional Medical Conduct in 1988 that the words "emotional, quite mobile," used in his report, are code words for "crazy." After reading a transcript of the hearing, Sidney Zion told the same board that Dr. Lyden's testimony was "vicious." He said angrily that "he tried to make her out a cokie."

Dr. Sherman later said that he did not remember whether or not he had spoken to Dr. Lyden after Libby's visit to the surgeon, although he did recall Dr. Lyden's written report. All the same, Dr. Sherman said he did not consider Libby emotionally disturbed, although she was sometimes "anxious," and "under stress." She told him she had "occasional nightmares." Dr. Sherman later told me, "I never heard Dr. Lyden say this is an emotionally sick girl."

Yet at least some of Libby's pains were plainly, as Dr. Lyden testified in a deposition, psychosomatic. Dr. Greenspan, her psychiatrist, said the pressure she complained about in her stomach was "psychological pressure."

"I am going through massive amounts of pain right now," Libby wrote in a letter in 1982. "I don't think that my stomach could hurt more even if it wanted to."

She kept medicating herself.

A pattern developed, and she was caught in a vicious cycle. For drug abusers, there is always one crisis after another, which covers up the real crisis, dealing with the drug problem.

Barry Fox said that in Libby's mind, all her complaints were legitimate, "because she was being prescribed." But eventually, "she overdramatized. It was well-known that she overdramatized," he said.

Is that what everyone believed?

At Bennington, Libby had frequent colds. On October 4, 1983, she asked the infirmary for cough syrup, and she was given Robitussin. The next day she still complained of her symptoms, and Actifed was added to her regimen. By the third day, when she said that her cough was still not better, and that she was having difficulty sleeping, she was given Robitussin with codeine. Eleven days later, on October 17, she was back for more Actifed. On November 1, she wrote her grandmother Anne that "at last I don't have a cold anymore," but three days later, on November 4, she was requesting more Actifed, "for allergy symptoms." On November 22, her last visit to the Bennington infirmary, she again requested Actifed.

Did Libby have just colds? Was she suffering from allergy to pollen, horses, and cats? Or were her symptoms related to something else? Cold symptoms and nasal congestion are common side effects of cocaine use. In addition, cocaine's high is such that it enables the people using the drug to perform the sort of "Herculean" task Libby had performed in finishing six extraordinary term papers in a very short amount of time.

Dr. Shapiro, Libby's pediatrician, had not known Libby was on Nardil. "She did not tell me," Dr. Shapiro said. She had not even known Libby was seeing a psychiatrist. She had not known Libby was taking Valium or Dalmane. She had never seen Libby "anxious," "hysterical," or "uncooperative." She had never thought that Libby was troubled. None of her regular doctors did, it seemed.

Dale Fox said that because everything "looked so good" on the surface, no one knew. Libby always tried to put up a good front. Perhaps she was trying to put up a good front in the emergency room, and even at the end, when her parents left her in the hospital.

LIKE A LOT of adolescents, Libby wanted constantly to test herself and her surroundings, and usually ended up in that never-never land of looking and acting like a woman while still feeling and understanding like a little girl. She was the first in her crowd of friends to have a major love interest—an older man who lived in her neighborhood, according to Dale, who was shocked by the relationship. "We were both rebels without a clue," she said, adding, "but at fourteen she's going to this guy? Where's her childhood? There is no childhood. She had no childhood."

Libby's choices bothered her friends. "Libby was look-

ing for something to get out of herself—to get out of her
home, so she channeled all her passion into Ralph," Dale
said. Barry added, "She was escaping, maybe to give herself a break from overachieving." Libby once wrote in a
letter that "I'm sleeping okay, now. And in fact, too much.
But that's okay—escapism in sleep is cool . . ."

The Foxes and some of the other neighborhood teen-
agers, along with some of Libby's school friends, like Paula
Este, would discuss Libby and Ralph all the time. "We'd
say, 'What is she doing?' He was a control freak and so
abusive," Paula said. She believed that Ralph, a college
dropout, "possessed" Libby. "She dressed the way he
wanted, she listened to the music he wanted," she said.

Libby had another boyfriend for a while, whom her
friends didn't like either: Carl Potter. Dale said she didn't
like the way Carl and Ralph talked to Libby. "I didn't like
what they said, I just didn't like the whole deal. And I felt
that Libby was not in reality at all. Neither was I." Libby
had met both boys around 1980, when she was fifteen. She
dated Carl for about a year and a half, until they became
just friends. They were at Bennington together, although
he entered a semester before she did. Theirs was an intense and unsettling relationship, climaxed by Libby's saving him from a drug overdose.

Barry Fox said that Libby "got involved in a situation
over her head" with Ralph. "She shouldn't have had to
worry about a domineering guy. Ralph was intent on having Libby think Ralph thoughts. She was in a wife role
with Ralph, and it's a lot for an eighteen-year-old kid to
handle. She couldn't be Ralph's emotional crutch when
she was partly crippled herself."

Libby had two abortions during her last year of life, one
in February 1983, and one in the fall, when she was at
Bennington.

Elsa told me how Ralph Enders, "vibrating with anger," had "spilled out" the news to her when she helped Libby move some of her belongings—"her bicycle, her guitar"— from his apartment the month before she died. Libby and Ralph had "a huge fight," she said, and Libby had called for help, telling her mother, "I've got to break it off, but I can't do it by myself." Elsa said that Libby "was obviously, clearly, deeply upset, and I said, 'Come home immediately.' Both Sidney and I said to her, you are in this situation that you cannot deal with, nor are you capable of dealing with." Elsa said that Libby told her "I wanted to tell you about the abortions, and I was going to tell you, but I didn't."

Elsa told me, "Maybe five years down the pike we could have worked that out and decided why she had such bad taste in men. It was clearly a pattern that should not have been repeated." Barry agrees. "Ralph was robbing her of herself in a lot of ways. But it was a phase she was going through. She would have gone on to bigger and better things. I'm certain of it."

"And I think she was getting there," her mother said quietly.

In a brief time, "she made important moves," Dr. Greenspan said. "She broke up with her boyfriend. She got closer to her parents, especially her father, and she decided to go back to school."

Libby had thought about not returning to Bennington for the spring semester "because she couldn't cope with depression," Dr. Greenspan explained. "I'm very practical," he reflected. "I want to do the most good I can in a short time. She belonged back at school, not in New York."

AT SIXTEEN, LIBBY had written her friend Carl that "my brain is in a lot of confusion at the present moment,

due to increased amounts of a certain powder entering it."
It was *C-fernt*, Libby's made-up word for cocaine. She also
wrote him that she had used so much pot and cocaine that
she had her "first accident coming up to my loft—I bashed
the shit out of my knee." She said she had thrown up after
doing "a line" with two friends. This could be more
C-fernt, or possibly heroin. Dale Fox said that "people have
told me she was trying it."

On March 22, 1982, Libby indicated in a letter to Carl
that even though she had a fever of 102 degrees, and had
been "throwing up for three days," she had used cocaine.
In fact, she said that she had waited "all weekend long" for
the shipment to come through. She told him that she
"couldn't even taste the coke" because her "sinuses were
so fucked up," but, nevertheless, despite "the flu," she
was feeling "extremely festive."

In another letter, dated the next day, March 23, Libby
wrote, "I feel as if I'm falling apart faster every day." Falling apart or not, Libby kept up with her work at New
Lincoln, where she was in the eleventh grade. Although
she was out of school for eighteen days, and late fifteen
times, her work was "excellent." She was praised by her
English teacher for working "particularly well with such
matters as the complexities of structure, irony, and paradox
in *Catch-22*." Although another teacher said that her work
was "too often diluted by absences and by a propensity to
distraction by personal concerns," he was "most impressed" by her "handling" of "contradictions and confu-
sions innate in human nature." What happened in other
people's lives was easy for her to deal with. It was her own
reality that was difficult.

On April 9, 1982, she wrote Carl that "my family is kind
of falling apart, and I can't deal with it. So much is going
on, but none of it is good."

What was she talking about here? Her grandfather Dr. Nathan Zion died that month. Her father had temporarily given up journalism and was one year into being part owner—and main host—of Broadway Joe's Steak House. Elsa's brother-in-law had put up most of the money for the venture, and tensions were running high over how to make the restaurant work. Elsa had sold Transworld Features Syndicate, and was not working. Things were in flux.

That month Libby sang in her school's art festival. She picked something she considered hers, Fleetwood Mac's "Gold Dust Woman." She had written Carl earlier that "the words say so much more than you could possibly imagine."

Two weeks before the arts festival she had written him that she had remained "straight" for five days—no drugs at all, "except for energy pills, which don't count." She also wrote him a welcome observation. "Dealing with life is easier when you're straight," she said.

But she was not able to sustain the feeling for long.

ALTHOUGH LIBBY HAD some counseling at Bennington, there was no formal treatment for her problems until she began seeing Dr. Kenneth Greenspan in January 1984. Dr. Greenspan is a 1963 graduate of the Albert Einstein College of Medicine of Yeshiva University, and did fellowships and residencies at Boston City Hospital, Yale–New Haven Hospital, and Columbia Presbyterian Medical Center.

For five years, since the age of thirteen, Libby had self-medicated the atypical depression—mood swings—he later diagnosed. Libby told Dr. Greenspan that she got "dizzy," and didn't "feel her body." She told him that she felt "spaced out and unreal," and that the only time those feelings went away was when she smoked pot. She told him that she had nightmares about people turning into monsters and that the nightmares made her feel as if she "was melting away."

Dr. Greenspan testified in a deposition that marijuana was the best therapy for depression Libby could have found without a physician, but that after she came under his care, he wanted her to stop. However, he agreed that she could continue smoking it "if she feels that she needs it."

All through high school and during her semester at Bennington, Libby was a very heavy pot smoker. She rolled it into cigarettes, or often used a pipe. "I practically got stoned living next door to her," Elizabeth Saltzman commented. "The pot she smoked was high-quality and strong," Barry Fox said. "She smoked it to the point of incoherency."

Elsa told me Dr. Greenspan "called to ask our permission for Libby to use it if she got too stressed out, and we said, 'Yes, of course,' if she absolutely felt she had to."

Marijuana can relax the mind and body, but it can also produce mood swings, an issue Dr. Greenspan did not address.

Dr. Greenspan said Libby's atypical depression "manifested itself in stress-related disorders." He never performed a physical examination, although he took blood tests that indicated she had a chemical imbalance responsible for the depression. She was attached to a "thermocenter," and skin electrodes were taped to her "forehead muscle." In her first session her temperature and muscle were monitored to see if she was relaxing. Dr. Greenspan gave her audiotapes to use at home for fifteen minutes twice a week. These tapes focused on her breathing: "Focus on the left nostril, feel the air flowing in and out . . ." By her second visit, Libby had "warmed up" two degrees and "diminished her stress by 50 percent." He checked her inner- and lower-leg temperatures. He put her on Nardil.

On January 24, less than two months before she died, Libby told Dr. Greenspan that she "thinks about suicide." But she struggled, and fought back. "She became aware that there were parts in her that she had forgotten about," Dr. Greenspan said. Two years earlier she had written that very same thought in a letter to Carl Potter: "I'm beginning to feel as though I'm discovering parts of me that I never knew existed. Well, I knew they existed—it's just that I buried them so far under the surface of myself that I lost touch with them. And now that they're coming out, I feel really confused . . ."

She was "unbelievably improved," Dr. Greenspan said.

Libby told her mother that biofeedback was "wonderful."

"It has a spillover effect," Elsa told me. "It's 'I now control myself, therefore I am in control.' So I thought nothing but good could come from something like that. But it never got a chance to fulfill itself. The question mark in all of this, of course, is, would the depression stop?"

BARRY FOX SAW a lot of Libby during the last year of her life. During the fall and early winter, when she was sneaking out of Bennington to be with Ralph in New York, he saw her every day. They all smoked a great deal of pot, and did cocaine and "some mushrooms," but he said, "no one was a big coke addict. No one was sitting around snorting coke all the time." He said that after a member of Ralph's family died from a heroin-and-quaalude overdose, "all the drugs went out the window." But there were still plenty left, it seemed. And Libby always shared her ample supply of prescription drugs.

They'd sit around and listen to music, watch television, eat junk food, and often go on bike rides together, to Coney Island and over the George Washington Bridge into New Jersey, which Libby called the "swamp."

"Libby's heart and body were strong," Barry said. "She was fit," he believed, despite her constant drug use.

Sidney is deeply embarrassed about his daughter's private life, and Elsa said that although she "can deal with those things, he can't." She tried to explain why. She said her husband is someone "who had not the slightest awareness of what a little teen-aged girl—what her life was all about. So he would have no way of understanding what was going on." This was not said critically. She said he never really had the opportunity to understand because there were only "those few months that we had really begun to deal with what was going on with her." Elsa was referring to the biofeedback sessions with Dr. Greenspan that her husband also attended. "He liked to be hooked up so he could understand what she was going through," Dr. Greenspan told me. He said that Libby and her father weren't as close "as they could be because Libby was depressed and that kept her from getting closer. But they were getting closer. She loved her father very much."

There is no disputing that. "They were doing this thing together and it was working well for them," Elsa said. "And then it was gone. It was there and then it was gone."

"I'd say, 'Who gives a shit?' I'm going to die before I'm eighteen anyway. We all said that," Dale Fox confessed.

But Dale's despair at fourteen translated into survival. She believes she lived solely because she had a stronger constitution than Libby did. "I survived two bouts of endocarditis—when a microorganism eats away your heart valve." Dale was told she'd have to be in the hospital for six weeks, but she left after three. A year later, she said, her doctor "could not believe that I did not need to have open-heart surgery; he couldn't believe that I wasn't going to die."

I asked Elsa if she thought marijuana was the only drug Libby used. Her answer surprised me.

"Oh, she may very well have done whatever, I don't know, cocaine, right? Because I don't really know. But I know she didn't do uppers and downers."

When I asked her how she knew that, she told me sternly, "I just know she didn't."

But she also said that Dr. Greenspan knew Libby had "done drugs," and that "it was clear" that she "wasn't going to do them anymore." Saying this, it was as if she were telling me that so long as anybody knew, it was all right.

ELSA SAID THAT she had several more phone conversations with Dr. Raymond Sherman shortly after Libby's death. In one he told her that a trace of marijuana had been found in Libby's body.

"You are trying to set me up," she reacted, because, she said, she knew it "wasn't true."

During another conversation, he told her that a trace of cocaine had been found.

She did not respond.

Dr. Sherman also called and spoke to Sidney again about the final written version of Libby's autopsy report. In that conversation, according to Dr. Sherman, he revealed to Sidney that Libby "had some cocaine in her nose."

Sidney brushed this aside, said Dr. Sherman. "She didn't use cocaine."

* * *

L I B B Y   Z I O N ,   N E W York Hospital History No. 171-03-32, was placed in a concrete, steel-reinforced crypt in the middle section, third from the top, on the first level of the Sanctuary of Abraham and Sarah.

"I couldn't put her in the ground," Elsa told me.

PART 2

5

Sidney and Elsa Zion did not realize that in any teaching hospital, that is, a hospital affiliated with a medical school, as New York Hospital is with Cornell University Medical College, the patient travels on two converging avenues. On Sunday, March 4, 1984, Libby was both a teaching case and a treatment case.

Dr. Leonard and Dr. Sherman had made what Dr. Leonard called a joint decision to admit Libby to the hospital, but all the same, from that moment she was under the control of the house staff—the doctors-in-training who ran the day-to-day functions of the institution. It made no real difference that Libby had a private doctor. Dr. Sherman, the attending doctor—that is, the senior doctor accountable for her—was out of the picture. "The attending was someone you talked to an hour a day," Dr. Leonard said.

In the seventeenth and most of the eighteenth centuries, when the hospital as an institution was first evolving in France, American doctors-to-be apprenticed to reputable physicians and did what is now called by trainees and others *scut* work. They'd mix drugs, wash bottles, run errands, and hardly ever see patients. Some of their mentors had studied medicine in Europe.

In 1885, twenty years after the emergence of the modern American university, requirements for admittance to some medical schools were lower than they were for a competent high school, and the course work, which consisted only of going to lectures, lasted for a mere eight months. Students automatically received an M.D. degree even if their academic records were inferior. Some students then became hospital trainees, but the majority just put up a shingle and opened an office.

In 1890, the term *resident* was first used at Johns Hopkins University—Dr. Gregg Stone's medical school. The trainees, or residents, would actually reside in the hospital, and they could train there as long as they wanted to, that is, until they felt ready to go off on their own. The precedent for residents living outside the hospital began after World War II. In 1995, many doctors sometimes wished things could go back to the earlier model.

By 1900, the house staff—the residents-in-training—had become, at least in New York, the de facto staff of every hospital. This is true to this day. In 1990, Dr. Raymond Sherman testified that "the house staff at New York Hospital played an important part in the team effort of evaluating every patient."

But many residents feel that they are at hospitals just to be free labor, since Medicaid and Medicare pay the hospitals for their services—for taking care of the elderly, and uninsured or low-income patients who cannot afford a private doctor. Medicare gives teaching hospitals educational grants—in 1994 it was one hundred thousand dollars each year per resident—for training doctors. In 1984, residents were the largest group of employees at New York Hospital.

In time, residents everywhere would begin to question their actual educational role, and patients would begin to question the role of residents in their treatment. There would be talk of residents controlling hospitals, dispensing medications they did not fully understand, making decisions they were unsure of, and being afraid to ask for help.

In 1904 still only 50 percent of medical school graduates in America went on to an internship the first year after medical school, but it almost didn't matter, because the training that did exist then for postgraduate work was for the most part unsupervised. The majority of people I talked to felt that poor supervision is still the case today. In fact, I discovered that this aspect of a doctor's education is the most controversial issue still to be resolved.

Part of the controversy involved an area usually kept private but often linked to the question of supervision: namely, mistakes. Dr. David Hilfiker comments on this sensitive issue in his book *Healing the Wounds*. He writes that doctors "cannot bear to face their mistakes directly. We either deny the misfortune altogether or blame the patient, the nurse, the laboratory, other physicians, the system, fate—anything to avoid our own guilt." A doctor who uses the name Dr. X writes in his book, *Intern,* of the fact that residents "will inadvertently kill the patient who might otherwise have lived, through stupidity, or blundering, or blind inexperience . . ."; that it is "the price that [people] collectively have always had to pay for the privilege of having well-trained and competent physicians. Dreadful and frightening as this seems, it is true."

I discovered that most doctors need permission to admit errors. They need some sort of sanction, and without it, they react arrogantly, defensively, or silently to their own mistakes or the mistakes of other doctors because, as Dr. X writes, "every doctor is haunted by the knowledge that next time it could so easily be me."

THE FLEXNER REPORT, published in 1910, was a graphic exposé of 155 American medical schools, and led to reforms in medical education in America not only in terms of more stringent requirements for admission, but also in terms of a stronger, more rigorous curriculum. It produced "an immediate and profound sensation," according to its author, Abraham Flexner, a prominent educator. The report, which advocated four years of schooling, two of them in clinical training, made instant headlines, and newspaper editorials enthusiastically endorsed its conclusions. Only three medical schools were given clean bills of health— Johns Hopkins, Harvard, and Western Reserve, now Case Western Reserve.

It quickly became clear that the other 152 schools had some hard work to do. The Flexner report forced them to reorganize, although some doctors today would say that they moved in the wrong direction by stressing science over humanity, even though Abraham Flexner himself opposed such an emphasis.

Still, Dr. Bertrand Bell, distinguished university professor at the Albert Einstein College of Medicine of Yeshiva University in New York City—Dr. Maurice Leonard's alma mater—believes that the Flexner report "turned medicine into a science," and that "most of the time you don't need science" because "medicine is not a science in itself. Medicine has to do with healing." Dr. Bell, who found himself embroiled in a very public political struggle stemming from his role as chairman of the committee that created regulations concerning resident working conditions, which went into effect in 1989, believes that "you can't be a healer and a scientist." What he means is that if a doctor focuses strictly on the technical aspect of an illness, important underlying signs and symptoms could be overlooked.

Not much about postgraduate training changed for decades, although in the twenties the American Medical Association, which had been created in 1847, further transformed medical schools by recommending specialist education. This was a significant change, but one that a lot of people would later decide contributed to some of the problems in medicine, particularly those involving the doctor-patient relationship. With so many different doctors involved in a patient's care, who was in charge?

The idea for specialists actually had ancient roots. Some pharaohs had one doctor who was "keeper of the drugs," and another who was "shepherd of the anus." An ancestor of Tutankhamen, King of Egypt in the fourteenth century B.C., had one doctor for his left eye and another for his right eye.

I would later begin to fear that, metaphorically speaking, Libby Zion, by the age of eighteen, might have had one doctor who looked into her left eye and one doctor who looked into her right eye, and no one, no one at all, who looked at them both at the same time.

EVERYTHING, *EVERYTHING* THAT medical students learn is geared to the day their graduate medical education begins, and they join the house staff of one of the 1,647 teaching institutions in America.

Dr. Luise Weinstein joined the house staff of New York Hospital on June 20, 1983, nine months before she heard the name Libby Zion. She was a PGY-1, or postgraduate year-one, the rank that used to be called intern, which many hospitals still use even though the term was officially changed in 1975. In 1984 New York Hospital continued to call PGY-1 an internship.

June 20 was the first of a two-day orientation. Out of one thousand applicants, the thirty-six interns chosen that year by the department of medicine of New York Hospital–Cornell Medical Center, at a salary of $23,935, attended informal discussions concerning their responsibilities and duties, received their work schedules, copies of the graduate staff manual, and were taken on a grand tour of the complex. There were approximately ninety-eight interns participating in orientations from eighteen other departments, such as anesthesiology, ophthalmology, pediatrics, pathology, psychiatry, and surgery. Interns in the Department of Medicine would learn to care for a wide range of clinical problems involved in internal medicine.

The affiliation between Cornell University Medical College and New York Hospital began in 1910, following the example of Columbia University's College of Physicians and Surgeons' alliance with New York City's Presbyterian Hospital, so the medical school could have "complete and permanent control of the hospital staff and of the facilities for clinical teaching."

From the time of Dr. Weinstein's first rotation to Memorial Sloan-Kettering Cancer Center, one of the top ten hospitals in America according to *U.S. News & World Report*, where she spent six weeks admitting patients and caring for them, Dr. Weinstein was recognized as a *mole*, housestaff slang for an extremely solid, serious student doctor. In the mid-seventies, as an undergraduate at the University of Rochester, she was a gifted student, graduating summa cum laude, and a member of Phi Beta Kappa in 1978. Before she entered the University of Rochester School of Medicine and Dentistry, from which she graduated with honors in 1983, she took a year off, working as a methods analyst for the Saks Corporation in New York City.

In mid-August of 1983, Dr. Weinstein, whose coworkers applauded her skill and "quiet dignity," rotated to the Payson 4 intensive care unit in New York Hospital, where she worked for a month before joining the neurology service on Payson 6 and F-6 East.

After neurology, Dr. Weinstein spent a month on renal service, where, for the first time, she met Dr. Raymond Sherman; he had come to lecture on kidney function. She then helped out in the emergency room for one week. There was no formal rotation there for PGY-1s.

In mid-November, Dr. Weinstein was assigned to the general medical service in Baker Pavilion, which has four floors for private patients, and often employs fewer residents than the other medical sections. It is the place where the rich and the famous usually go for their hospital care. In January, Dr. Weinstein worked on Whitney 2, 3, and 4 caring for patients.

She started at Payson 3 and F-3 East in February, after a week's vacation, and remained on that assignment until the end of March. On Sunday, March 4, she was "the intern on call," which meant that she remained in the hospital overnight, an obligation she carried out every third night. Dr. Weinstein worked between 95 and 110 hours a week.

When she went to bed around midnight on Saturday evening, March 3, in her apartment close to New York Hospital, she had no idea that when she woke up at eight the next morning, the rest of the weekend would change her life forever.

She arrived at New York Hospital at nine, two hours later than the usual resident starting time. The more relaxed Sunday hours were one of the few luxuries the hospi-

tal offered to interns and residents—there were no morning rounds on that day. Dr. Weinstein was especially
grateful for the extra time since she was the only intern on
call that day and night on the private medical floors—Payson 3 and F-3 East—and in addition to her own patients
she was responsible for the patients usually covered by the
other two trainees on the floors. It is customary on Sundays
for all teaching hospitals to be so understaffed. During the
week, a house-staff medical team at New York Hospital
usually comprises three interns and one resident. Dr.
Gregg Stone was the supervising resident.

Immediately after her arrival on Payson 3, Dr. Weinstein
read the sign-out sheets of the previous intern to learn
about any problems with the forty patients she would now
be in charge of; later, she made rounds to see them. During
these rounds she talked to all her patients and in many
cases gleaned new information from them. At eleven-thirty
she checked the orders for tests to make sure they had
been sent to the laboratory, and then drew blood for some
additional tests needed by some of the patients.

In the early afternoon she and Dr. Stone went on
"chart" rounds, that is, they discussed every patient's
chart—and then she monitored a new patient who was
having a cardiac catheterization, the injection of dye into
the coronary arteries to find out if there is any blockage.
She stayed with this patient until six-thirty P.M. Between
then and nine-fifteen, when she unwound a bit and had
pizza in a conference room on Payson 4, Dr. Weinstein
wrote notes and resolved myriad problems on Payson 3.
After her meal, her first of the day, she discussed her new
cardiac patient with a fellow, marking down some of his
suggestions in the order book.

The order book is the most crucial link between the
resident and the patient, for it contains all the things to be

done for the patient while he or she is in the hospital. The order book was once called the doctor's order book, and then the vital signs book, which was incorporated in the medical records book, and was usually kept in a loose-leaf binder. It is now all consolidated into a computer in most hospitals. But whatever its physical form, the order book is the key to everything that happens in the hospital experience of a patient. What's done to patients is what's in the order book, and it's done by interns and residents.

After evaluating some other matters on Payson 3 and F-3 East, Dr. Weinstein spoke to the assistant chief resident, Dr. Martin Carr, about new admissions. Dr. Carr was a 1978 graduate of Brown University and a 1981 graduate of Brown University's medical school. A PGY-4 and senior assistant resident in charge of the house staff that evening, as well as head of the cardiac resuscitation team, he evaluated the current situation with the intern he considered "better than average." Afterward, Dr. Weinstein studied charts and wrote up special orders received from certain attending doctors.

At one in the morning Dr. Maurice Leonard, who had been contacted by Dr. Raymond Sherman, called her from the emergency room to say she had a new patient who would have to "board" on Payson 5 because there were no other beds available. This meant that although the patient might be a private medical patient, he or she would have to occupy one of the twenty-nine beds on a service floor, where patients did not have private doctors. Resident slang also considers the term *boarder* to mean "usually unwelcome."

Dr. Weinstein was supposed to be working only on Payson 3 and F-3 East, a section abutting Payson; both share the same main corridor, and are, according to Dr. Weinstein, "a city-block away" from Payson 5.

Dr. Weinstein called Dr. Stone to tell him about Libby
Zion, who, like all the other patients she was taking care of
that night, would be her responsibility. She was the principal doctor, the one to be called by the nurses if problems
arose. She was the one who would make the life-or-death
decisions. She was the one who would make the difference. It wouldn't really matter if Libby had her own doctor. "The intern is the one who writes orders and is involved in the minute-to-minute care of the patient," Dr.
Gregg Stone said.

On the night of March 4, 1984, Dr. Weinstein, who had
been working practically nonstop for sixteen hours, was in
charge. It was her *call*, or judgment call, and it was what
some doctors call a *closed order book*, the best-kept secret in
hospitals, and the dirtiest little secret in medical education.
The closed order book meant that Dr. Weinstein, alone, as
the intern caring for Libby, wrote the orders to be followed
by the nursing staff. It meant that she could write orders
without obtaining permission from anyone. Although her
supervisor, Dr. Stone, could and did make suggestions
about her patients, even he was not required to superin-
tend her orders when they were written. This was how one
learned to be a doctor. Dr. Sherman, who later said that he
considered Libby's symptoms "easy to handle," had
turned her care over to the house staff for the night. Dr.
Weinstein, who would receive her medical license on July
30, 1984, four months after Libby's death, was on her own,
because unless she did it herself, it wasn't real medicine. It
didn't matter that Dr. Leonard recommended one thing, or
Dr. Stone another, or Dr. Sherman a third. She listened.
She listened well, because she was an excellent student.
But it was now she who decided what to do, collating the
information she received from the patient and from her

colleagues, even though while she was in charge of Libby's care she was still an unlicensed physician.

"Residents here write orders for nurses and they dispense the medicine," explained an intern at the University of California, San Francisco School of Medicine. "Attendings do not see orders."

From California to New York, all across America, the closed order book, and the lack of minute-to-minute supervision of interns it encouraged, was the law of the land.

BOTH DR. MAURICE Leonard and Dr. Gregg Stone had been out of medical school for less than two years; since their graduations they had been on the house staff of New York Hospital. As JARs—junior assistant residents, or PGY-2s—they were still students, albeit licensed physicians earning $25,990 a year. Now, however, their duties also involved teaching. They had to guide and nurture the PGY-1s, just as the PGY-1s guided and nurtured the third- and fourth-year medical students—the *drones*. The PGY-2s also had to independently take histories and conduct physical examinations on the patients of the interns. They then had to discuss in detail all aspects of the illness and recommend courses of treatment. In addition, they were responsible for their own patients, who had been assigned to them by the chief resident. These were most often, although not always, patients who did not have private doctors.

PGY-2s were part of the team of residents running the hospital, including the emergency room and the intensive care units. On Sunday, March 4, 1984, Dr. Leonard's official assignment was to be in charge of internal medicine management in the emergency room—that is, to run the place, although surgical, psychiatric, and pediatric residents were close by. Nevertheless, Dr. Leonard was the sole house-staff physician on full-time duty there—the *twit in the pit*, as his fellow residents around the country sometimes called that assignment.

Before Libby Zion's death, the Greater New York Hospital Association, whose members include every hospital in the city, had ruled that attending doctors should also be present in emergency rooms along with the residents. There was one hospital that disagreed.

It was New York Hospital.

At the suggestion of a doctor I met in my travels across the country, I read a book called *The Student Physician*, published almost forty years ago. In a chapter called "The Cornell Program," the authors describe a concept that is still followed, to varying degrees, not only at New York Hospital but at all teaching hospitals: "Responsibility for patients is the most effective way for the student to learn wisdom in patient management and gain the ability to think through a clinical problem. It also motivates him to read about the clinical entities he encounters so that he may better help the patient, thus stimulating more intensive study of scientific medicine."

Of the 459 residents at New York Hospital–Cornell Medical Center in 1983–84, approximately 134 were PGY-1s. There were approximately 120 PGY-2s, and the rest were PGY-3s, PGY-4s, PGY-5s, and PGY-6+'s. The fourth-, fifth-, and sixth-year residents were clinical or research fellows. The chief resident, a position that carries a great deal of power and responsibility, was a PGY-7, Dr. Joseph Ruggiero. He was on call every other night, taking turns with the assistant chief resident, Dr. Carr. Dr. Ruggiero is a 1977 graduate of the New York University School of Medicine, did his residency at New York Hospital from 1977 to 1980, and was a fellow in the departments of hematology and oncology for three years before assuming the job of chief resident. He was in charge of the house staff, and reported directly to the physician-in-chief, Dr. R. Gordon Douglas.

The residents and fellows were spread around the medical center in eighteen different areas. In the department of medicine, where Drs. Sherman, Leonard, Stone, and Weinstein worked, there were fifty-four PGY-2 and PGY-3s.

Dr. Leonard had been assigned to the emergency room on February 27, and on Sunday, March 4, he began work at 8 P.M. He would finish his twelve-hour shift at 8:00 A.M. on Monday. There was no emergency-room residency at the hospital; the emergency room was run by the department of surgery. In fact, the hospital had only recently been assigned to receive city ambulances. When Dr. Leonard began work the night Libby Zion became a *hit*, which was slang among the house staff for a newly admitted patient, he had never been on emergency-room duty before—except as a medical student.

Dr. Leonard said that he asked Libby innumerable questions, although he admitted that "I'm only human and I sometimes forget to write things down." So certain responses are not in the record, for instance the findings of Libby's brain and nerve examination, which showed normal functioning. In addition, he went to see if Libby had any previous records at the hospital, and he located the results of the specialized tests that Dr. Sherman had overseen in 1981 and 1983.

Even though Elsa said that she told Dr. Leonard that Libby had been taking Tylenol as well as erythromycin and Nardil, the emergency-room chart did not mention it. Under "meds taking" were only two drugs: the erythromycin and the Nardil. There was also no mention of the Chlor-Trimeton Dr. Irene Shapiro had suggested Libby take four days earlier. There was no mention of the Percodan that had been prescribed for the pain of Libby's tooth extraction on Thursday. There was no mention of any other medication she might have used in the recent past. No one even told Dr. Leonard about the biofeedback treatments. In fact, under "History—Physical Findings," "no depression" is listed, even though Dr. Leonard knew Libby was using an antidepressant, Nardil.

Although Dr. Leonard was troubled by Libby's erratic motions, which he described as "writhing . . . not writhing, but turning side to side," he speculated that Libby could have some sort of viral syndrome. "At times she was calm, and lying still, and then there would be jumping up," he said. "She was like a light switch." He tested her stool for blood and the results were negative. He also did a pelvic exam, which was normal. He was concerned about toxic shock syndrome, or some other condition that could be causing her fever. He decided to hold antibiotics "for a while," since no bacteria were found anywhere.

Dr. Leonard is sure that he did not use the word *hysterical* when he spoke to Dr. Sherman. "It is not a word I usually use," he said, adding that he did not, in fact, believe that Libby *was* hysterical. "I need to listen to your lungs," he told Libby. "And she'd stop her movements. I told her, 'Stay still while I look into your eyes,' and she could do this. We had no explanation for her whole presentation," he explained.

But he did believe she was improving. After all, her pulse was 156 when she first arrived in the ER, and eventually it went down to 100. And her 106 temperature at home, which put her at grave risk—any temperature over 104 is considered dangerous—was at a somewhat safer level in the hospital. It was 102.9 when Libby first came in, and then rose to 103.5, dropping back to 102.9 on Payson 5. He said that he and Dr. Sherman never considered the intensive care unit, or ICU, because Libby was "stable." She wasn't having any cardiac problems, and she didn't require any special drugs.

So Dr. Leonard wondered if Libby's agitation might have a psychological component, and felt that Dr. Sherman was concerned about this aspect, too.

Was Libby what some residents call a *crock*, a candidate for *psychoceramic* medicine, terms used to ridicule psychiatry?

While the Zions waited in the ER, Drs. Sherman and Leonard debated over the phone about whether or not Libby could have a common cold, a urinary-tract infection, or meningitis. They spoke of the possibility of drug use. Dr. Leonard said that "the drug reaction that we were most concerned about was with Nardil," and said that they discussed whether "she may have taken something, and that, in and of itself, or in interaction with Nardil, may have been causing some of the symptoms we were seeing." Dr. Leonard said that they "mentioned pain medicines, cold tablets, cocaine, any pills, things like that." However, New York Hospital at that time was not able to do a middle-of-the-night drug screen.

Dr. Leonard did not ask Dr. Sherman to come to the hospital at any point. "It would be very unusual for an attending to come down," he said, and in Libby's case there was absolutely no indication that it was necessary. Indeed, Dr. Leonard said that they both believed that Libby was exaggerating her symptoms. "Dr. Sherman would see her routinely the next morning," he said. Dr. Stone, who saw Libby after Dr. Leonard did, said that he didn't think Libby was exaggerating her symptoms. Later, Dr. Sherman said, "exaggeration is not a word I would have used then, or now."

Dr. Stone had arrived on Payson 3 from his apartment

across the street at the same time as Dr. Weinstein that
Sunday morning. Although they were both on call, he was
allowed to go home when he had completed all his necessary work. If Dr. Stone's presence was needed again he
could be reached by beeper, or the hospital operators could
reach him by phone in a matter of seconds, and he could be
back on any floor in the hospital in "less than five minutes."

But interns rarely disturbed PGY-2s, just as PGY-2s
rarely disturbed the fellows or the chief resident or the
attending physician. Unless there was a *train wreck*—a full-
blown medical disaster—the second-year residents could
count on several hours of undisturbed sleep.

Dr. Weinstein remained in the hospital, and while there
were on-call rooms with cots set aside for interns to sleep
on the patient floors, she rarely did. There were no on-call
rooms for PGY-2s. In general, she usually got about forty to
fifty hours of sleep a week. On Sunday, March 4, she had
found time to rest, but had not slept. She said that at three
in the morning she was in her "usual state of health," and
that at six-thirty in the morning she felt the same way. She
had work to do, and did it. Thirty-eight hours on call was
the longest stretch she had mastered. Neither she nor any
of the other residents had ever been told, nor was there any
hospital policy on, the maximum number of hours they
should work. So they worked until they felt that the job
was done. That was how good doctors were made.

"House-staff training is a sequence of graded responsibility," Dr. Daniel Federman, dean for medical education
at the Harvard Medical School, told me. The Green Book,
or the American Medical Association's *Graduate Medical
Education Directory*, adds that "residents must be supervised by teaching staff in such a way" that they "assume
progressively increased responsibility for patient care ac-

cording to their level of training, their ability, and their experience."

But I discovered that it is precisely this aspect of supervision that is so often overlooked. Although Dr. Sherman said he had spoken to the emergency-room resident "numerous times" on Sunday, March 4, he did not know how much experience Dr. Leonard had in an emergency room, and did not know that as a resident he was spending his first week in "the pit." Dr. Sherman couldn't recall "specifically" how much he had worked with Dr. Stone, but said "at his level of training, New York Hospital house doctors have had a lot of experience dealing with fevers." Dr. Sherman also said that although he had spoken to Dr. Weinstein previously, and he believed she had done a history and physical examination on one of his private patients before the night of March 4, still he did not know anything "specifically" about her experience.

How then could Dr. Sherman determine whether or not Dr. Leonard, Dr. Stone, or Dr. Weinstein were ready to assume a certain level of responsibility in accordance with the standards of the American Medical Association?

The answer is he didn't have to, because this sort of supervision has rarely been taken seriously, and the roles of residents have almost always been taken for granted.

The residents have "almost total care" for patients in university-run hospitals, Dr. Bertrand Bell said. "The closed order book is universal in graduate medicine," and "it's not unique to New York Hospital. It's all over—New York, Houston, New Orleans, Boston—all academic institutions." Dr. Rosemary Fisher, director of the house staff at Yale–New Haven Hospital, said, "We try to keep the closed order book system."

Everyone did.

Dr. Homer Boushey, the chief of medical services, and

codirector of the residency-training program of the University of California, San Francisco School of Medicine, told me, "We discourage attendings from writing orders." At Yale, "PGY-1s and up can write orders whenever they want, and they don't have to be countersigned," Alexandra Boer, a fourth-year medical student, told me. At Yale, as well as at Columbia and most other institutions, resident orders are discussed but not countersigned. In some places, the attending or chief resident is supposed to either write a note in or countersign the order book within twenty-four hours, but in actual fact this is not done.

Attending doctors are allowed to write orders, but often choose not to in order to give the intern or resident an opportunity to learn. The lines of authority can be blurred, which seems to be what happened with Libby Zion. Dr. Sherman let Dr. Stone and Dr. Weinstein make decisions that he could have made, but didn't, because of New York Hospital's emphasis on the importance of young doctors learning to take responsibility for their patients with the closed order book.

A former state health department official commented that Dr. Sherman actually had "no choice" because New York Hospital is so especially geared to teaching. "Once the patient is given over to floor care, the attending is forced to give over the care to the house staff." And once this happens, the attending has practically no influence. "Residents have their own agendas," a doctor told me.

"It's like throwing yourself into hell," said Elsa Zion.

DR. STONE, WHO was on call every third night, and had supervisory responsibility for eighty patients on two floors, said that drugs were high on his list when he was first told about Libby Zion's symptoms, and in a deposition he said that he "first thought cocaine," but then realized that it was unusual for the drug to cause a fever for four or five days, which was his understanding of the duration of Libby's fever. Indeed, his list of eight "differential" diagnoses placed "drug reaction" at number seven, although later Dr. Stone emphasized defensively that the order is a rough one. "The working diagnosis is based on the facts you have at the time," he said, "what you think the illness is going to be. It's your best guess."

He said that he brought up the subject of illicit drugs with Libby's parents, but Elsa and Sidney remember no such discussion. Dr. Stone recalled that the Zions "were a little surprised I asked." He said that "they certainly conveyed to me that their daughter was never the type that would ever be doing illicit drugs."

He brought up the subject with Libby two times.

"Libby, we really have to know. Have you used any amphetamines, any cocaine?" He said that he also asked her about barbiturates, angel dust, and heroin, as well.

"No."

"I had no reason to doubt her," he said. Dr. Weinstein wondered if Libby was having withdrawal from barbiturates or "a stimulant of the cocaine family." She also thought that the agitation was similar to patients she had taken care of who had "OD'd on prescriptions," although later she would say that Libby didn't seem to be having an "acute" drug reaction. At one point when she was alone with Libby, Dr. Weinstein also told her that she really needed to know what she had taken that night, and Dr. Weinstein said she wouldn't tell anyone. But Libby told Dr. Weinstein that she hadn't taken anything. Nothing at all. Dr. Weinstein believed her. Nevertheless, both residents understood that, as Dr. Weinstein said, "it's difficult for patients to reveal that kind of information."

Dr. Stone said that the Zions told him that they didn't

know what medications their daughter was using; they knew she was on Nardil, but not what dose or when she had last taken it. "They had very little knowledge of the prescription drugs," he said. Dr. Stone ruled out any neurological process, a urinary-tract infection, meningitis, and toxic shock syndrome, although he considered that Libby might have some animal-carrying infection like rabies or encephalitis because she had said she had both a cat and a dog. There had been Killer, the cat at Bennington, and the Zion family owned what Elsa called "a completely neurotic" poodle named Pierre. Libby had told Dr. Weinstein only about her cat.

Dr. Weinstein believed Libby showed signs and symptoms of some infection, too, and said that Libby had admitted to her that she had pain on urination that had been "going and coming." The intern noticed "a moderate amount" of urine in the bed pan, although Libby's output of fluid was never carefully monitored. When Dr. Weinstein took Libby's blood pressure sitting up it was 96/60. When Dr. Stone had taken it a little earlier, it had been 94/50, also a slight improvement from what it was in the ER. Her temperature was still 103.5, as taken by Nurse Balde.

Dr. Stone had ruled out pneumonia, though Dr. Weinstein would still consider it a possible underlying cause. "There was absolutely nothing wrong with this patient's pulmonary system," Dr. Stone said. "There was no indication of a problem with oxygenation."

"I have to talk to you," Dr. Stone said to Libby several times. "She'd say, 'Okay, okay,' and answer my questions," although sometimes "she'd look at me and say nothing."

Dr. Weinstein said that Dr. Stone thought Libby's agitation and restlessness were from "psychological overload."

Later, Dr. Stone went to great pains to argue that he had

used the word "overlay" rather than "overload," explaining to me that "overload means too much, and overlay means everyone has a certain sort of psychological makeup, and certain people respond to illness differently than others." Still, Dr. Stone said that Dr. Sherman agreed that Libby's bewildering body movements were "a psychological response." He said that he "went through every concept" of his examination summary over the telephone to Dr. Sherman.

In his "Note," or summary, Dr. Stone wrote: "I suspect this is just a viral syndrome with hysterical symptoms." The words *hysterical symptoms* are not a common medical expression, and indeed many doctors would later try to explain that the words were chosen to characterize Libby's motor activity, and were not meant to be any kind of diagnosis. "It means the best indication is that it's going to turn out to be a viral infection," Dr. Stone said. He stressed that his use of the word *hysterical* was not pejorative. "It's a way to describe a series of behaviors," Dr. Weinstein maintained.

I recalled a phrase from *The House of God*, a comic novel about residents in a fictitious hospital, written by Samuel Shem, M.D. Some medical students I met at the University of California in San Francisco told me to educate myself by reading it. The residents in the book sometimes offered their patients "bedrest until complications."

Was this the treatment plan for Libby?

Not exactly.

Dr. Weinstein, who was the person responsible for her care, decided to use Tylenol to control Libby's fever; Dr. Stone had suggested one tablet every three hours, but Dr. Weinstein rejected that suggestion and changed it to one every four hours.

It was her prerogative to do so. Dr. Stone had also suggested the use of a cooling blanket to treat Libby's fever. But Dr. Weinstein decided this was not necessary. "We had anticipated from the intervention of fluid, Tylenol, and rest that the patient would improve," Dr. Weinstein said.

Demerol had also been discussed, and according to Dr. Stone, Dr. Sherman told him it was "a good idea." But Dr. Sherman said that Demerol was not brought up. "Dr. Sherman wanted to use a low dose," Dr. Stone recalled, adding that "it was one of many things we talked about. We probably talked about Demerol for seven seconds. Dr. Sherman just doesn't remember." Dr. Sherman, in keeping with the routine of a closed-order-book system, replied that "it's not something you expect a house officer to say. Dr. Stone probably felt he told me, or should have. We recall this differently." Dr. Sherman added that during a conversation he subsequently had with Dr. Weinstein, she indicated that she did not think the suggestion had come from him.

In any case, Dr. Weinstein, who would later testify that Dr. Stone was present when she wrote the orders for Libby, decided to use a subtherapeutic—a below-standard treatment—dose of 25 mg of the narcotic analgesic Demerol to help control Libby's "horrific" body movements and contortions, although New York Hospital would insist that the drug was used only to reduce her rigors, or severe chills. "I never use the stuff like that," Dr. Sherman said later.

WHILE ELSA AND Sidney were preparing for bed in the early hours of Sunday, March 4, 1984, their daughter was wide awake. She yanked out her intravenous line again, and Dr. Weinstein replaced it. Libby was still very uncomfortable, a word her mother used when describing the last time she and her husband saw Libby. Indeed, a nurse later said that Libby had remained uncomfortable most of the time she was a patient on Payson 5.

Dr. Stone had left Payson 5 at around 3:00 A.M., had seen some other patients, and had then gone across the street to his apartment on York Avenue, where he could be reached by beeper or phone.

The hospital record indicates that at around three-thirty A.M., Myrna Balde, a registered nurse for more than seventeen years, gave Libby the Demerol Dr. Weinstein had ordered to help calm her. Nurse Balde had come on duty at eleven-thirty P.M. and would remain on Payson 5 until seven-thirty in the morning, responsible for the care of fifteen patients. In order to obtain the Demerol, she had gone to her superior, Nurse Jerylyn Grismer, for the keys to the cabinet where narcotics were stored. Nurse Grismer was a 1983 graduate of the Wagner College School of Nursing on Staten Island, and despite her inexperience, she was the head nurse on Payson 5. But Nurse Balde was the only person involved in Libby's hospital care who knew that Demerol was contraindicated with Nardil, though she said that at the time she hadn't read Libby's emergency-room sheet and therefore didn't realize Libby was taking the drug. She said that she *had* questioned Dr. Weinstein about Demerol, but only asked about the uncommonly small dose. "Dr. Weinstein said 'I want her to have 25 mg,' and that was all she said," Nurse Balde recalled.

At four A.M., one of the nurses drew aside the curtain covering the small window that looked into Libby's ward. Dr. Weinstein was sitting at the nurse's station writing up her notes. She listed Libby's diagnosis as "fever," and her condition as "fair." Shortly afterward, Dr. Weinstein herself checked on Libby and discovered that her IV line was out again. To prevent her from dislodging it yet another time, Dr. Weinstein fastened gauze around Libby's right arm. Libby remained restless, although she "seemed to have fewer of the more exaggerated movements," Dr. Weinstein said. "I spoke to Libby, hoping to calm her down." The intern also thought that turning down the lights might help quiet Libby. But Nurse Balde said that Libby's extreme agitation "was going on for a great part of the night." In fact, she said that "at four-fifteen she was doing the same thing that she was doing when she came in."

After finishing up her logging, Dr. Weinstein returned to Payson 3 to look in on her patients there. One of them had had a sudden loss of consciousness earlier in the evening, and several others had been running high fevers. She had a very busy night ahead of her, even though most of the patients she was responsible for were sleeping, and only four to six were awake.

Five or ten minutes after her departure from Libby's floor, Nurse Balde asked Nurse Grismer to telephone Dr. Weinstein to request that she come back to see Libby because her condition "was getting worse," and she was getting "more and more excitable." Nurse Balde later explained that at first she thought Libby was more restless, but then realized that because there wasn't anyone to stay with Libby after Dr. Weinstein left, it seemed to her as if she were worse, but she was actually just the same as when she first arrived on the floor. Libby seemed to do better with people around her, but there wasn't anyone who could remain constantly at her side. Around the time that Sidney and Elsa had left, Nurse Balde had noted in her record that Libby was becoming increasingly restless. "Libby didn't make sense," Nurse Balde said. She was kicking and swearing, " 'this fucking this, and this fucking that.' " Nurse Balde was perplexed by Libby's behavior, because "usually a patient with a fever is listless, and she was very active. I didn't know what to think." Dr. Wein-stein said that her "sense was that the agitation was persist-ing, and not getting worse."

The other patients in Libby's room were upset by the commotion, particularly by all the swearing. Nurse Balde, who attended to them, as well as to Libby, said that they were concerned about so many lights being on, and "were getting anxious." They couldn't sleep. Nurse Balde told them that Libby was a new arrival, and that things would calm down soon. Although one of Libby's hospital mates said she didn't "remember any noises," or remember "anything out of the ordinary," the other two patients in room 516 did. One, who died a few months after Libby, reported to her son that "she heard noises, possibly even screams," and the other patient told her daughter that what happened that night "made her afraid of hospitals." This patient, who died in 1986, told her daughter that she thought Libby "had been on drugs."

Shortly after four-fifteen, Nurse Grismer called Dr. Weinstein and suggested that perhaps Libby ought to be restrained in some way. Nurse Grismer herself had ob-served Libby pulling her covers off, trying to remove her hospital gown, and attempting to climb over the side rails of the bed. Libby also knocked some items off her bedside table.

Nurse Grismer said that at one point she and Nurse Balde "had to stand on opposite sides of the bed in an attempt to prevent Libby from getting out." She said that when she asked Libby if there was anything wrong or what could be done to make her more comfortable, Libby did not answer and she made no change in the way she was moving. Nurse Balde recalled that Libby could often an-swer rationally, but then she would return to her "kicking and cursing."

Dr. Weinstein instructed that Libby be bound in a Posey bedjacket, a mesh and broadcloth vest restraint that wraps around the chest and back, leaving the limbs free. Nurse Balde told me that it is not unusual to order restraints. "We thought it was a fever, and she was agitated, and that was it. Nobody expected her to die."

Nurse Grismer said that Libby was able to sit up on her own, and cooperate, although "she had to be asked several times to put her arms through the vest before she would obey." After the Posey was secured, one of the nurses raised the bed to around forty-five degrees.

Despite the vest, Libby was still thrashing, so nurses Balde and Grismer decided to tie her wrists and ankles to the corners of the bed. They did not discuss their decision with Dr. Weinstein, who later said that she "did not think that it was appropriate to have put Libby in four-point restraints."

They decided first to tether only Libby's wrists to the bed.

Nurse Balde said that after they did that, Libby attempted to free her arms.

Nurse Grismer said that five minutes later, when Libby "began throwing her hips and legs over her head, almost putting her feet through the plate-glass window," they then tied her ankles to the bed.

Although Libby was unable to kick anymore, she still continued to try to move her legs and her head. Nurse Grismer called Dr. Weinstein a second time, and asked her to come up and give Libby a sedative drug because the restraints were not working.

Dr. Weinstein said that since she had just seen Libby about fifteen minutes earlier—there would later be much debate on just how much time had elapsed—and that because there seemed to be no change in Libby's behavior, she felt that she didn't have 'to return to Payson 5. Nurse Balde, who said she also called Dr. Weinstein on her own, although Dr. Weinstein would later say this was not true, remembered that Dr. Weinstein insisted that she "knew what was going on," and said she "had another patient admitted and that's why she couldn't come back."

It is standard hospital procedure that the first thing a nurse does when in doubt about anything concerning a patient is to call a doctor. "But she didn't come," Nurse Balde later told me.

In Nurse Grismer's second phone conversation, Dr. Weinstein asked if there were any changes in Libby's appearance and respiration. Nurse Grismer told her that there were none, so Dr. Weinstein ordered 1 mg of an antipsychotic tranquilizer, Haldol, to be given to Libby intramuscularly.

At some point before Nurse Grismer called Dr. Weinstein the second time, she spoke to Susan Myerson, the night nursing supervisor responsible for the entire medical department. Nurse Myerson, a registered nurse since 1947, had peeked in at Libby several times during the night. She said that Libby was moving very actively when she saw her. She also said that New York Hospital's use of restraints was "an everyday occurrence."

At four-thirty A.M., Nurse Grismer told Libby she was going to give her a shot that would help her relax, but Libby did not acknowledge her presence, or react to the needle. Nurse Balde said that Libby fell asleep about twenty minutes after the injection. At five A.M. Nurse Grismer checked on Libby, and saw that she was sleeping peacefully. Nurse Grismer reported that Libby's "color was pink," her breathing "even and unwavering," and "her skin temperature not overly cool or overly warm."

I learned that the use of Haldol in Libby's circumstances—or presumed circumstances—is so routine that it is one of the few drugs that has been incorporated into resident slang. It's known as *vitamin H.* "Let's give some vitamin H" is the black humor used when a student doctor thinks a patient is incapable of self-control.

At five-thirty Nurse Balde changed Libby's IV bottle, and observed that Libby's breathing was "regular" and her color "good." She also discovered that her restraints had been removed. She did not make any notation in Libby's chart about their absence, and said she did not know who removed them. Just who did has remained a mystery, although later Nurse Balde, who testified in a deposition that Libby was "fighting" her restraints, told me, "Maybe I did, but I don't remember," adding that usually when her patients "calm down, I take them off. Who likes to be tied?"

NURSE BALDE SAID that at six A.M. she gave Libby two Tylenol tablets, first waking her, and then helping her sit up so she could swallow the pills with some water. She said that Libby was flushed, and that she could tell from the touch of her skin that she had a fever, although she didn't think it was "that high." Libby's breathing was regular. The Zions would wonder whether Tylenol had actually been given to their daughter, because it was not marked in the proper box on her chart.

Nurse's aide Bronte McKend, who had worked at New York Hospital for ten years, began her rounds at six to take the temperatures of the patients on Payson 5 she was responsible for. She reached Libby's bedside at six-thirty.

Later, the Zions would say that this was the first time that their daughter's temperature had been taken in over three and a half hours, despite the fact that the reason for her admission had been her fever. Nevertheless, Dr. Weinstein had not left orders to have Libby's temperature taken more than every four hours. Nurse Balde believed it was the proper interval.

Ms. McKend talked to Libby, but later could not remember if Libby replied. She tried to take a rectal temperature, but couldn't because Libby was "tossing her head and her hands and kicking her feet." She also tried to take an oral temperature, but Libby would not open her mouth. So she took Libby's temperature by putting the electronic probe in her armpit, and holding her arm in place. Generally an axillary, or armpit, reading is one degree lower than an oral reading, and two degrees lower than a rectal one.

Bronte McKend found that Libby's temperature was either 105.8 or 107.6—both numbers are recorded. Nurse Balde said in an interview with me that it was 106. The Zions later said it was 108, in which case Libby's internal temperature would have been 110 if the reading had been taken rectally.

She was burning to death.

The nurse's aide raced to tell Nurse Grismer, who immediately called Dr. Weinstein. The intern told the nurses to apply cold compresses, and to order a cooling blanket from the pavilion manager.

The nurses collected buckets of ice from the machine on the floor, took some towels to make compresses, and rushed to Libby's bedside to apply them.

Nurse Balde noticed that Libby was "drowsy" but could follow commands "to some extent." She said that Libby was able to move when "we asked her to turn in order to sponge her back." Nurse Grismer said that Libby looked "pale." But Susan Myerson said she could not remember if Libby was conscious or not. Nurse Balde said that after sponging Libby down, she "left the room temporarily," and when she came back Libby was "unresponsive."

Soon Libby's color turned gray, and her respiratory rate lessened. Her pulse became "thready": abnormal, somewhat rapid, and weak.

And then it was gone. There was no pulse at all.

Libby's heart had stopped beating.

It was 6:40 A.M. Nurse Grismer applied cardiopulmonary resuscitation and called the cardiac-arrest team, because she knew that Libby Zion would die in four minutes if her heart did not begin to beat again.

Nurse Balde rushed to grab the "crash cart" near her station, which contained emergency equipment—sutures, suction devices, surgical instruments, sponges. When she went back to Libby's room, she saw Dr. David Palet, an intern who was assigned to Payson 5 but not to Libby's care. He had been asleep in an on-call room on the floor. Later, Dr. Weinstein said that he told her he had first been assigned to Libby, but the order was changed. Dr. Palet would challenge this. Nevertheless, he was the first doctor to arrive after the "code"—a special signal used so patients and visitors won't be alarmed—was called. He was followed by the assistant chief resident and head of the cardiac-arrest team that night, Dr. Carr.

Meanwhile, at F-3 East, Dr. Weinstein was sitting at the charting area. "I had just come from being with a patient," she said. She hadn't heeded Nurse Grismer's telephone call right away, but instead put away what she was doing and then lingered to collect her notes, ophthalmoscope, reflex hammer, tuning fork, sterile pins, and gauze, until she heard the arrest code over the hospital intercom: "Cardiac team, Payson 5, cardiac team, Payson 5." "I ran up the stairs," she said.

Dr. Carr and his team of more than a dozen doctors and nurses, including Dr. Weinstein—Dr. Stone was not summoned—tried for fifty-five minutes to revive Libby, who had no heart rhythm at all during her code. They used lifesaving techniques and equipment like intubation, defibrillation, and a breathing bag. They used lifesaving medications. They tried calcium chloride, epinephrine, and sodium bicarbonate in order to get her heart beating, and they tried Narcan, which is used to reverse the effects of narcotics. "We tried everything," Nurse Balde told me. "It really hurt me." She and Nurse Grismer wept at their patient's side. "It shocked us. We didn't expect this. It really bothered me because I have kids, too."

Dr. Weinstein, who had helped in attaching an electrocardiogram to Libby, called Dr. Sherman and told him that Libby had gone "flat line."

"What do you mean?" Dr. Sherman asked.

"She's had a cardiac arrest," Dr. Weinstein said.

An attendant cleaned up, disposing of fluids and sheets of paper that had collected at Libby's bedside.

6

SOMETIME DURING THE morning of March 5, Dr. Luise Weinstein reported Libby's death to the medical examiner's office. Such a call to launch an official autopsy is routinely made after an "unexplained death," especially when the patient dies quickly, Dr. Sherman said.

Since the thirteenth century, autopsies have served medicine by revealing the body's secrets; the procedure is also used by first-year medical students, who dissect an actual human being in their anatomy class.

Dr. Weinstein told the medical examiner that a possible cause of Libby's death was a pulmonary embolism—the blockage of a large vein in the lung by a blood clot or air. She also filled out a statement of particulars for the medical examiner, and noted in it that arterial blood gases—tests to measure the amount of oxygen and carbon dioxide in her arteries—done on Libby when she was close to death indicated that Libby had hypoxemia, or an abnormal lack of oxygen in her blood, "despite intubation and the use of 100 percent oxygen."

Libby's troubled breathing, as well as her low blood pressure in the emergency room, could have been an early indication of the seriousness of her illness. But an analysis of her blood gases was not done at that time; if it had been, it, too, might have clearly indicated to the residents that Libby was experiencing, among other things, a drug reaction. However, Dr. Carr, the assistant chief resident in charge of Libby's resuscitation, later said that he felt that the blood taken at Libby's code was from a vein and not an artery. If his feelings are correct, then the conclusion of hypoxemia might be in error.

Although the toxicology laboratory received Libby's samples on the day of her funeral, Wednesday, March 7, not until May 8 did Dr. Milton L. Bastos, director of the laboratory, sign a report concerning his findings. No mention was made of marijuana, but a positive reading for cocaine "considerably stronger than a borderline one" was discovered by a technique called radioimmunoassay, or RIA, in a sample of Libby's blood taken at the hospital.

The lab had received two bottles of Libby's antemortem blood from New York Hospital, and the blood had been diluted in a ten-to-one ratio with a medium used to culture bacteria. The labels on both bottles are puzzling. Bottle number one was dated February 29, five days before Libby had entered the hospital, and bottle number two was undated (and was never used for analysis). New York Hospital at first said that the February 29 date reflected when the culture medium was prepared, but later said it might have been a clerical error. However, questions would abound. Was it really Libby's blood? If not, whose blood was it? Controversy would arise about the medium used in the test—had it been first tested to determine its components—soy and beef heart broth, preservatives, and a white-blood-cell inhibitor? Sidney Zion would charge that these substances interfered with the RIA test and mimicked cocaine.

Cocaine was not found by the medical examiner in a sample of Libby's blood collected at the autopsy. Although cocaine quickly metabolizes, it remains in the blood for four to six hours, or even longer, depending on the dose; the RIA test can detect its reasonably stable metabolite, benzoylecgonine, for up to forty-eight hours after drug use. Cocaine is the only substance that produces benzoylecgonine.

Libby's hospital, or antemortem, blood was drawn shortly after 11:43 P.M. on March 4, and shortly after 2 A.M., March 5. The autopsy, or postmortem, blood was drawn sometime after 9:00 A.M. on March 6.

Although Libby's boyfriend, Ralph Enders, denied any involvement with drugs, both Dale Fox and Paula Este told me that he had in the past sometimes supplied Libby with cocaine, which she used frequently, and marijuana, which, along with Valium, were her drugs of choice. Libby always managed to have a prescription for Valium, which is called "dry alcohol" because the effects are similar. Although Ralph Enders was never charged with drug dealing, he received immunity from any such charges when he testified before the grand jury in 1986. He stated that immunity was forced on him by the district attorney's office.

Could Ralph have brought Libby some cocaine on Saturday, March 3? Or earlier in the week? They had met each other at the beginning of the week in Riverside Park, near Libby's home. Was it possible that she had used cocaine over the weekend, Friday or Saturday, or, more specifically, on Sunday, March 4, between the time Adam's friend, Sean, had helped her move her stereo at five or six P.M., when he said that she didn't seem that sick, and three hours later, at eight or nine, when he said she "wasn't communicating too well"? Had she used some cocaine before or after taking all the pills her brother Adam spoke of? At around nine-thirty, Libby's eyes were dilated, according to Adam, who told me that his sister was "really, really sick" at that time.

The medical examiner's report also said that a trace of cocaine—actually benzoylecgonine—was detected by RIA in Libby's nose. Most medical examiners take nasal swabs during the autopsy of an unusual death.

Cocaine can be discovered in the nasal passage for up to three hours after use. Ralph Enders and Carl Potter testified in depositions that they often saw Libby snort cocaine, and Ralph testified she had a "hole burned through her nose," although no such hole was found by any of the residents or on autopsy. Ralph also said that Libby often had nosebleeds as a result of her cocaine use.

In cocaine testing, a confirmation test to check for false positives is usually done by a process called gas chromatography; however, in 1984 this test only detected whole cocaine and not its metabolite, benzoylecgonine. Dr. Lorenzo Galante, assistant chief toxicologist in the medical examiner's office since 1984, said that the RIA test is one of the most highly sensitive tests available in his office. Dr. Galante said that the gas chromatography test was used as a general screen for basic drugs rather than as a confirmatory test for benzoylecgonine, and that is why it was not used to confirm the findings in Libby's blood sample. The better RIA test was proof enough.

The medical examiner's office was unable to confirm its cocaine nasal finding because there was insufficient nasal material available. But, as a grand jury report prepared a few years later explained: "Since cocaine is rapidly broken down by the body into its metabolite, the RIA reading alone is 'presumptive' evidence of the presence of cocaine."

On May 17, 1984, Dr. Raymond Sherman received a phone call from the chief medical examiner, Dr. Elliot Gross, who told him that the final report on Libby would include the fact that a "small amount of cocaine" was found in her nose, and "unconfirmed elsewhere."

LIBBY ZION HAD over thirty symptoms before she entered New York Hospital on March 4. Yet when I asked Elsa Zion to go over exactly what Libby's symptoms were that night, she said, "She was running a high temperature, and had been for a long time—many hours—and was burning up inside. I mean that was the whole thing."

But it wasn't.

And Elsa acknowledged as much when I brought up the subject still another time. She added that not only could Libby not sit still, but she was beginning to hyperventilate in the emergency room, "so it was clear."

What was clear?

Among other things, including fever, hyperventilation can be triggered by depression or anxiety. Elsa told me she thought Libby's "breathing problem was because she was in pain."

She told me, "All their questions would immediately concentrate on what medications have you been taking, what's going on with you? Why is your temperature so high? And we said she had her tooth extracted. She had a cold."

But was that all?

According to the records I read and the people I talked to, the complete list of Libby's symptoms or complaints included the following: high fever; flushed face; chills; rigors; sweating; body aches, especially in the back; joint aches; muscle soreness; earaches; sore throat; nasal drip; a sensation of burning up inside; burning in the eyes; eyes rolling around; dilated pupils; an inability to stay still; head moving from side to side; flailing of shoulders, arms, and legs; shallow breathing; slight to extreme incoherence; confusion; delirium; a babyish-sounding voice; a violet-colored rash on face and eyelids; a reddish-purple mark on right leg; multiple skin abrasions; painful urination; difficulty in urinating; dehydration; low blood pressure; rapid pulse; thirst; and increased white-blood count. Also, Ralph Enders said that Libby complained of a slight headache when he visited her on Saturday.

The mind wants to block out upsetting incidents, but still, I had to wonder if reality sometimes is too overwhelming to be denied. After all, what about Adam's and Jed's intense reactions to their sister? How in the world did absolutely no one else see, in Adam's words, Libby's "death mask"?

Why didn't other people see what Libby's brothers had seen? Sidney Zion, when later questioned at a deposition on whether he had asked Adam and Jed upon arriving home from the party "how their sister's condition had changed, if at all, as they saw it," had replied, "I didn't have to ask them because I just saw it."

What did he see? Did he see what his sons saw?

What exactly did he communicate to Dr. Sherman?

What did the residents at New York Hospital see?

What was communicated by them to Dr. Sherman?

"The impression that was conveyed to me was that Libby was awake, responsive, oriented," Dr. Sherman later said.

When I eventually began to learn something about drugs and medications, I found it odd that an important clue was missed, and that no one, not a single person, acknowledged that Libby's body movements—her agitation—would be volitional if, say, she had used a drug that affected her central nervous system. A drug like an amphetamine affects the user's brain and not the limbs, and therefore body movements such as Libby's could be controlled. I would come to understand that some of Libby's other symptoms also might have been misunderstood—her difficulty in breathing and problems with urination might have been the result of a drug reaction.

Dr. Sherman later agreed that some sort of drug could have produced Libby's agitation, but he acknowledged that possibility far too late. He said that he and the residents really believed Libby's denial of drug use. "We really believed the family, too," he told me. "I told the house staff these people are reliable. We got taken by the patient."

I kept picturing Libby taking "all those pills" over the weekend of March 3. What were they? Did she know? Dale Fox told me that drug abusers don't give a second thought to mixing drugs; she said, "Do you know how many times I drank and did heroin when I had been taking a prescribed medication for an illness?" She reminded me that "Libby had a weak constitution. I mean, she wasn't healthy to begin with. She had never been as long as I've known her." It was Dale's opinion that people with weak constitutions "can't handle the kind of beating" Libby might have been receiving from the drugs she was using.

On Thursday, March 1, 1984, Libby filled prescriptions from her dentist, Dr. Wasserman, for twenty Percodan, and from Dr. Greenspan for two hundred Nardil and thirty Valium. Between October 1983 and February 10, 1984, she had received prescriptions for seventy Valium from Dr. Sherman. Although Dr. Sherman prescribed other drugs to

Libby, according to the New York State Board for Professional Medical Conduct, which did not cite a complete listing, Dr. Sherman had issued seven prescriptions for Libby between December 21, 1982, and February 10, 1984—five for Valium and two for Darvocet.

Dr. Greenspan had briefly given Libby another kind of antidepressant, Tofranil, but she hadn't liked its effect on her system. In addition, on February 17, 1984, he gave her a prescription for thirty tablets of Dalmane, a drug not unlike Valium that is used to treat tension, muscle spasms, convulsions, and insomnia. Two weeks later, on March 1, he prescribed the thirty Valium to Libby, and the two hundred Nardil for her to take to Bennington.

"Libby had Valium *all the time*," Barry Fox said. "She was always able to get another script for it." Dale Fox confirmed this. "We'd, like, swap drugs—I'll trade you some 'blow' for a Valium—because I loved Valium." Ralph Enders claimed that there was an unmarked vial containing two to three hundred Valium in Elsa and Sidney's medicine cabinet, and he reported that Libby freely borrowed those pills. "This is totally true," Dale said. "Oh yes! She used to give us her dad's Fiorinal and Valium. They had drugs in the house." No one ever noticed any pills were missing, she said, because "nobody seemed to be paying attention, so why would they know?" Ralph claimed that Libby once told him that her parents used to give her Valium "to calm her down or put her to sleep" when she was a little girl. Jed testified in a deposition that he knew his sister used Valium and amphetamines "recreationally." Indeed, Sidney confessed to me that he himself had used cocaine recreationally in the seventies. "Everyone did it, it was fun," he admitted, adding that "we didn't know the dangers of cocaine then, that it can do tissue damage." But, he added, "everyone would take a snort, and someone would say to me, here try it. But I used to say, 'I get no kick from cocaine.' "

An official in the Manhattan district attorney's office told me that during Libby's one term at Bennington, she filled drug prescriptions for tranquilizers and painkillers from "three or four different doctors" at more than one Vermont pharmacy. In 1984, triplicate forms to regulate drug use and prevent misuse and abuse were not required by law. "Libby Zion was a multiple drug user," the official said. Or, as Barry Fox bluntly put it, "The shit Libby was doing that was fucking her up in the fall and winter of '83 and '84 were all prescribed to her. They all have residual side effects that go on for a year." Throughout high school Libby "had all these prescriptions," and "had them legally," Paula Este concurred, so Libby "didn't have to do all these drugs illegally," even though some of those she used were illicit. Libby was able to pick and choose from any number of drugs already in her possession, or within easy reach. Mary Schilling, the Zion family friend, told me "there's lots of prescription drugs in the Zion household," and various other friends of the family, who wish to remain anonymous, often remarked to me about the assortment of medications they would see lined up in the kitchen and elsewhere when they visited: cough medicines, antihistamines, anti-inflammatories, antispasmodics, ulcer medications, muscle relaxants, adrenergics, barbiturates, tranquilizers, narcotic analgesics, amphetamines. These friends could not understand the necessity for an array that seemed to be so much more than most people had.

Ralph Enders described how, when he visited Libby on Saturday, March 3, Elsa "brought in a trayful of between fifteen and twenty pills" that he was told were vitamins, which Libby took "all at once." But Elsa, who said that Libby took charge of her own medications, suggested to me that Ralph is mixed up, and remembered "that incident happened long before." She also said "it was a joke. Everybody's got pills, but they were all kept in this one place in the kitchen. I had allergy pills. I had vitamins. I brought in bottles—the whole tray—to Libby and said, 'Take your pick.' I mean, I was not feeding my child pills. It was a joke."

I remembered a conversation with Dale Fox about Ralph Enders. "I don't buy anything he says," she said. "I don't believe the boy has one iota of integrity in him." Ralph Enders did not answer any of my letters, but I believe Dale, not only because of her forthrightness but because of her love and respect for Libby.

On March 1, 1984, Libby also filled the prescription from Dr. Irene Shapiro for the antibiotic erythromycin. Two weeks earlier, she had filled the prescription from Dr. Greenspan for thirty Dalmane, basically a sleeping pill. Two months earlier she had filled prescriptions for two other antibiotics, tetracycline and doxycycline.

So during the last two months of her life, Libby had at least eight prescriptions filled for herself. Were these perhaps the pills that Adam saw his sister taking the weekend she died?

She was also using Tylenol, Motrin, and Chlor-Trimeton. On autopsy, a trace of acetaminophen, the fever-reducing and pain-relieving drug found in such over-the-counter drugs as Bromo-Seltzer, Dristan, and Tylenol, was found in the contents of her stomach. Libby had also been given Tylenol tablets in the hospital.

Pheniramine derivative, found in Chlor-Trimeton, was detected by two tests.

Besides the detection of cocaine in her hospital blood by RIA, salicylates were detected in Libby's hospital and autopsy blood. Salicylates are the common analgesic, anti-inflammatory drug found in such aspirin products as Bayer aspirin, Anacin, and Bufferin. It is also an ingredient of Percodan. Later it would be said that there was such an abundance of salicylates found that Libby might also have taken plain aspirin at home in an effort to lower her raging fever herself.

Between March 1 and March 4, Libby consumed at least fifteen of the twenty Percodan tablets prescribed to her, and she lied to her dentist, Dr. Wasserman, on Friday, March 2, when she told him that she had only needed to take one. She had taken many more than just that one single Percodan. "She said she'd call back if there were any problems," Dr. Wasserman said. "But she didn't call. Monday morning. Bingo. She's gone."

Dr. Wasserman knew Libby was on Nardil, and during our interview he showed me the front cover of the manila file holding her records, which had the medication spelled out in large, red block letters. Yet a mystery remains. Percodan, which he prescribed to Libby for the pain of her tooth extraction, is contraindicated with Nardil. He did not show me Libby's records, but later I would see them through another channel. Nowhere was Nardil mentioned. The top right corner of her chart had a space for "Medical Alert," but it was blank. The only mention of Nardil was on the outside cover, not inside, where the record was kept. This practice is common. Still, did he really know about the contraindication with Nardil on March 1 as he claimed, or did he find out later?

When Libby went to see her pediatrician on March 1, Elsa had told her to tell Dr. Shapiro that she was on Nardil, but she didn't. The Chlor-Trimeton Dr. Shapiro recommended is also contraindicated with Nardil.

The effects of the antidepressant Nardil can last for up to fourteen days. Even if the patient stops taking it, the body continues to react as if it is still receiving that medication. The biofeedback technician's records for "February 30"—which was actually March 1—had noted that Libby was on "a painkiller." Libby had told Dr. Greenspan's technician that she was "still waking in the middle of the night—4:00 A.M.—and unable to go back to sleep even after reduction of medication." The technician never reported this exchange directly to Dr. Greenspan, who later testified in a deposition that he did not know what medication Libby had been talking about.

Nardil? Dalmane? Valium? Percodan? Unknown others? What was Libby taking and how much of each?

How much was a "reduction of medication"?

The *Physicians' Desk Reference*, the guide to medications that all doctors and hospitals use, warns doctors that "patients' estimates of the quantity of a drug ingested are notoriously unreliable."

Finding a correct dose of Nardil can take from four to six weeks. Libby had begun taking it on January 27, 1984. During the last week of February, which would have been her fifth week on the medication, when she said she stopped taking it "for several days," she did so because it was evidently having a bad effect on her. As she told Ralph, it was making her sick. It would have made no sense for her to have stopped for any other reason, especially since she had said she felt so much better on it, and Dr. Greenspan recorded in his notes that she had "no serious depression" while she was taking it. *"It was like someone being born again."*

If Libby had ingested cocaine over the weekend of March 3, or earlier, the Nardil effect could have reduced, or slowed down, the cocaine metabolism—the breaking down of its ingredients—thus increasing the risk of cocaine toxicity. Indeed, New York Hospital would suggest that it was

possible that after an initial snort of cocaine, the arteries in
Libby's nasal passages constricted and then opened up periodically throughout her hospital stay, causing a waxing
and waning of her symptoms. Dr. Greenspan said that the
combination of cocaine and Nardil produces "the worst
disaster on mankind." It is like ingesting a poison pill.

Chlor-Trimeton, which Dr. Shapiro had recommended,
and which Libby took regularly anyway—along with another antihistamine, Actifed—for ongoing allergy and cold
symptoms has an increased antihistamine effect when
combined with Nardil or even with Nardil's aftereffect.
This interaction could have contributed to Libby's agitation, rapid heartbeat, difficult urination, fever, and confusion.

Both Valium and Percodan taken in excess and combined with Nardil, or the up-to-fourteen-day aftermath of
it, can cause sweating, hypotension, hyperpyrexia (exceptionally high fever), and death. When Elsa Zion learned of
Percodan's contraindication to Nardil, she allowed that
perhaps that is what "kicked off" Libby's "reaction." She
did not elucidate.

There is another precaution to be taken with Nardil.
Caution is recommended if any kind of surgery or dental
treatment or emergency treatment is required. One doctor
not known to the family wrote in a letter of sympathy to
Sidney that Nardil made Libby a "pharmacological booby
trap, ready to explode when the proper minor stimulus
occurred."

Valium and Dalmane are depressants of the central nervous system. If Libby had taken too much of either—
together or alone—some of the symptoms that she had
over the weekend and in the hospital might have been the
result: slurred speech, clumsiness or unsteadiness, difficulty in breathing, uncontrolled movements of the body,

including the eyes, low blood pressure, problems with urination, skin rash, and increased thirst.

If Valium and Dalmane are combined with erythromycin, the liver may not metabolize them efficiently, and the concentration of these drugs will rise, possibly leading to a decrease in alertness and a fall in blood pressure.

Valium or Dalmane combined with cocaine lessens the effect of the tranquilizers. If Libby was experiencing a cocaine reaction the following symptoms—all of which she had—would be present: chills, confusion, anxiety, severe restlessness, sweating, and dilated pupils. In fact, Dr. Lewis Goldfrank, the director of emergency medicine at Bellevue and New York University hospitals, told the New York State Board for Professional Medical Conduct that "it is not uncommon for patients who deny using cocaine to present to the emergency room exactly like this."

It is also possible that Libby might have combined marijuana and cocaine, a highly dangerous fusion. Dr. Greenspan, and the Zions, had, of course, condoned Libby's continued use of marijuana. The drug was not found on autopsy, although later a toxicologist would say it had been present in Libby's body but was not reported.

If Libby was on an incorrect dose of Nardil, it is even possible that Valium or Dalmane could have increased her depression, since those drugs are "downers." She might have taken more than the necessary amount of Percodan because it is an opiate. Percodan is often used with marijuana and amphetamines to increase the euphoria even more.

Why did Libby say the Nardil was making her sick?

Why did she stop taking it?

"This woman had a lot of pain," Dr. Greenspan said, "a lot of days and a lot of nights until she took Nardil. And then for the first time ever she had total relief and was almost totally relieved from the pain. I don't understand why she would want to stop it."

I thought about something that Dale Fox told me. "There's one thing drug addicts know, and that's what drugs they're taking." So if Libby did know exactly what she was taking, could she have taken "all those pills" because she couldn't face the prospect of returning to college on Monday? After all, although she had broken up with Ralph, she was still seeing him and still pining for him. She felt lost and abandoned. She herself, for whatever reasons, had seemingly abandoned Nardil, a way out of depression, and was back to self-medicating herself with an assortment of drugs. Was she in despair?

I remembered the song lyric Libby had written in her journal: *"Maybe oneday but it could be Sunday I just might as well throw it in every way. Might as well. Might as well— whoopee! Maybe it doesn't matter anymore!"*

"Maybe she didn't have a strong will to live," Dale said. "That's what I often think about."

ON MAY 18, 1984, Dr. Jon Pearl, the associate medical examiner, announced that "acute pneumonitis" had killed Libby Zion. Acute pneumonitis, an inflammation of the lungs, can be caused by a virus, organic dusts or molds, or a reaction to chemicals. There would be no further mention of a bacterial infection until 1995, eleven years later.

That same day, May 18, Dr. Pearl also wrote to the Department of Health's Division of Vital Records, and included a "complete amendment" to Libby's certificate of death. It now said "acute pneumonitis four days following dental extraction and in the course of treatment with erythromycin. Hyperpyrexia and sudden collapse shortly following injection of meperidine and haloperidol while in re-

straint for toxic agitation. History of therapeutic
phenelzine injection. Unclassified."

Hyperpyrexia is an extremely high temperature often
caused by an infection.

Meperidine is a narcotic painkiller found in Demerol,
the first drug—25 mg of it—given to Libby by Dr. Weinstein. No evidence of this drug was found in Libby's body.

Haloperidol is found in the antipsychotic Haldol, and is
the second drug given to Libby by Dr. Weinstein. No evidence of this drug was found in Libby's postmortem tests,
because she was only given 1 mg.

Nardil was not found in postmortem tests either, which
would verify Libby's statement to Drs. Leonard, Stone,
and Weinstein that she had not taken her antidepressant
"for several days."

Haldol and Demerol, *given together*, are contraindicated
in a patient using Nardil, and Libby was given those *after*
her admission to New York Hospital. It is within the realm
of possibility that those two drugs could have been the last
straw for her overworked central nervous system, especially since Demerol alone is contraindicated with Nardil,
although there is no known case of an interaction with such
a low dose as Libby was given. But the use of Haldol alone
is undesirable in a patient with a fever, since it can elevate
the temperature even more. Had she "exploded" from
these "minor stimuli"? In his May 17, 1984, phone call to
Dr. Sherman, the medical examiner told him that "sudden
death occurs in people in restraint under Haldol."

An official in the Manhattan district attorney's office
said that "Libby Zion wasn't honest about her drug history. If she had disclosed it at the hospital, her illness
might have been treated differently." All the residents
agreed. Still, one might add: What held the doctors back
from more prudent monitoring since they all suspected

drug use, and since symptoms of it were evident? Why didn't they act?

In *Becoming a Doctor*, Melvin Konner, M.D., writes, "It is often said that 85 percent of the information needed to make a diagnosis is in the history, with most of the rest coming from tests."

Drs. Leonard, Weinstein, and Stone knew only about erythromycin, Nardil, and marijuana. They knew nothing about the Percodan, Valium, Dalmane, cocaine, or anything else. Dr. Stone told the New York State Board for Professional Medical Conduct that if he had had a strong suspicion that Libby was abusing drugs or if anyone had told him of any past history of drug use, he would have placed her in the intensive care unit, where she would have been observed around the clock. New York Hospital did not have a drug detoxification unit.

But Dr. Sherman knew not only about Libby's use of Valium, since he gave her a prescription for it, he also knew she had used amphetamines. His records reveal that on her first visit in 1981 she had told him she smoked an "occasional" joint. On her second visit, on March 10, 1982, he recorded "taking amphetamines—has stopped this now." He said that he believed her.

Still, Dr. Sherman had another reason for caution: his conversations with Dr. John Lyden, the orthopedic surgeon he had sent Libby to six weeks before her death. Dr. Lyden had believed that Libby was not only severely disturbed, but had come to him strictly looking for drugs.

But Dr. Sherman never knew of his patient's Nardil use up until her hospitalization. Neither Libby nor her parents had ever told him.

Too much Nardil or the wrong dose can cause a skin rash, slurred speech, confusion, restlessness, hyperactive reflexes, rapid heartbeat, low blood pressure, troubled breathing, sweating, and fever, all symptoms Libby displayed at home and in the emergency room. Fever alone is often an indication that the amount of Nardil needs adjustment. Even though the autopsy finding eliminated the possibility of a Nardil overdose, it would have been prudent for Dr. Sherman to have been apprised in the very beginning of Libby's use of it. It would also have been prudent for the Zions to have been asked by Dr. Sherman if there were any new medications Libby was using, or it would have been prudent for someone in the family to have kept Dr. Sherman up-to-date.

One of Libby's symptoms in the emergency room had been difficult urination, a complaint serious enough for her mother to speculate about possible renal failure. In addition, Libby had told Dr. Greenspan on January 19 that she had a "uterine infection."

The worry and anguish involved in rushing a child to an emergency room understandably can blur a parent's mind, but at some point, especially after three hours of waiting around, doesn't some careful thinking emerge, just as a second wind often does? No information was volunteered about Libby's two abortions to any of the doctors. The hospital should have been told these facts, especially in the light of Libby's urinary complaint. With her weak constitution, as Dale Fox called Libby's state of health, every medical detail should have been made available to the staff. Although both Zions said that they didn't know anything about the abortions—Sidney charged during his deposition that the hospital's lawyers were asking about them in order to slander Libby and "blame the victim"—such is not the case, of course. Elsa knew.

* * *

WHY DID DR. Jon Pearl use the term *toxic agitation* in
describing Libby's condition in the hospital in the amendment to her death certificate?

What led him to use that expression, an expression that
can imply that Libby's agitation was drug-induced? Dr.
Sherman later speculated that Dr. Pearl "might have been
struggling for a way to explain what happened," and that
the words provided "a way of working around cocaine."

A laboratory work sheet from the medical examiner's
office indicated that benzoylecgonine was discovered in
Libby's urine. Benzoylecgonine is the cocaine by-product
most commonly found in urine drug testing. There is no
reference to this discovery in any official report, most likely
because there are three question marks next to its mention
on the work sheet. Indeed, I learned that work sheets usually incorporate both the clear-cut findings and the suspi-
cions of various laboratory assistants, and are considered
"interim results." But I also learned that there are degrees
of suspicion, as well as degrees of what constitutes an interim result. The presence of salicylates is also flagged with
a question mark—albeit a single one—on the work sheet.
Nevertheless, unlike the benzoylecgonine suspicion in
Libby's urine, salicylates is included in the official report.
Benzoylecgonine was also detected in Libby's bile, but the
amount was considered too low to report as a positive finding. Later, a toxicologist said that "scientifically" there was
cocaine in her bile, and that, in fact, the bile is tested only
when there is a prior indication of cocaine either in the
blood or urine. This toxicologist also believed that Libby
had ingested up to 100 mg of cocaine anywhere from just
before she died to twelve to sixteen hours before her
death.

Did Dr. Pearl's description of *toxic agitation* come from
the work sheets? From a confidential conversation with Dr.

Sherman, or one of the residents? "I have no idea where it came from," Dr. Sherman said. Neither did Dr. Stone, who saw the words for the first time in court.

Although *toxic agitation* is certainly accurate, this description is used nowhere on Libby's hospital records and charts, and she certainly wasn't treated for it.

She was treated for a *viral syndrome with hysterical symptoms,* and the reason given for placing her in restraints was not *toxic agitation,* as Dr. Pearl wrote in the death certificate amendment, but protection from injury because she was thrashing around hysterically. Later, a grand jury report would state that the use of those restraints could have contributed to her death.

Why were restraints put on a dying girl?

Restraints are easily misused. They must be initiated in response to a *patient's* needs rather than in response to the doctor's fears or a shortage of suitable resources. A patient in restraints is at risk, among other things, for hypotension—or low blood pressure, which Libby already had. Restrained patients need very close observation, especially in the beginning, with vital signs checked *every five minutes.*

The *hysterical symptoms* that Dr. Stone had written in his "Note" was a medical determination, whether he meant it to be or not. The pattern that began in the emergency room with Dr. Leonard wondering if perhaps Libby's agitation had a psychological component to it, and went on to Dr. Stone's mention of "psychological overload"—or "overlay"—and Dr. Sherman's accord with that view, was set in motion, and passed along to Dr. Weinstein. Although the residents might have had the best intentions in the world, nevertheless that night Libby had become just another *brainiac,* a word used by the house staff to describe the erratic behavior of a child with a high fever.

Even though Dr. Stone's expression *hysterical symptoms*

wasn't exactly resident slang, still it was very close to it. It seemed to fall into a curious zone that exists between medical slang and medical terminology. The expression was a code. It was a code designed to send a clear message to everyone who received it: This is just an out-of-control girl with a virus.

Yet Adam Zion later admitted to me, "They didn't say she was hysterical for nothing. They might have misdiagnosed her, but she was pretty incoherent. She wasn't really formulating sentences. Her movements were pretty wild."

ADAM ASKED ME, "What's the real story? Is New York Hospital a sane place to go if it's generally understood that you're rolling the dice on a Sunday night? I guess she had so many problems—she had some colon problems at one point, and she always seemed to be having one sinus thing or another. Maybe they just thought, hey look, man, she's a hypochondriac—and there's nothing really wrong with her . . . They said she was hysterical. She looked pretty nuts to me, I mean, at that point she was, like, out of it." Later, he told me that "in my heart of hearts what I think killed her was the fact that they four-cornered her. It haunts me a lot at night. She was crucified in the fucking bed."

There is something else that is haunting.

If *toxic agitation* had actually been Libby's diagnosis the night she entered the hospital, she might have been viewed as a drug case, and survived.

DR. SHERMAN CALLED Dr. Elliot Gross, the chief medical examiner, sometime in June to check on the progress of the toxicology report, and learned that the final account would also include the information that cocaine was found "by one method" in Libby's blood from New York Hospital. Dr. Gross told Dr. Sherman that he planned an investigation of the findings. He did not elaborate, and he never reported anything more about the presence of cocaine to Dr. Sherman, although the final toxicological report did mention that cocaine was found in Libby's hospital blood, but not in the blood collected at her autopsy, and also reported that a trace of the drug was found on a nasal swab.

LATER, PAUL ROONEY, an attorney working with Dr. Weinstein, called the medical examiner's office to question a statement that was written on one of the pages he had received from them. The statement said Libby Zion had a "history of drug abuse," and Mr. Rooney wanted to know where this information originated.

A memo from the medical examiner's office about Rooney's call indicates that its "records do not show such information."

So where did the information come from?

A March 9, 1984, Division of Laboratories report from the medical examiner's office had typed on it: "The deceased had a history of a drug abuser (amphetamines and marijuana)."

Where did *that* come from?

New York Hospital's lawyers said that they had no idea where the information originated. Dr. Sherman, however, admitted that the information about amphetamines and marijuana must have come from his records. "Someone must have called me," but, once again he said, "it's a conversation that I just can't recall."

In any case, the report was written four days after Libby's death, but the information in it appears nowhere in Libby's hospital records, death certificate, or autopsy report.

The Division of Laboratories report is typed and unsigned. Why is it unsigned? There are some handwritten notes on it. One says "phenelzine"—the generic name for Nardil—and is underlined, and below that it says "Rush for Dr. Gross, also Dr. Pearl." There is also a handwritten sentence that is only partially legible. It appears to say: "On 3/16/84 at 7:30 I received from Dr. [illegible—with a word like *Zion*, and an unclear reference to two or three] bottles of culture medium for blood, containing [the next few words or numbers are undecipherable and then it ends] of blood."

Less than a year later, a panel of lawyers and medical consultants would report to then Mayor Edward I. Koch on a "poisoned atmosphere" in the medical examiner's office, and describe it as a place "plagued by mutual mistrust and factionalism." Libby Zion's autopsy and toxicology studies would be caught in the middle and would never be satisfactorily resolved because of ongoing allegations of improper actions by both the medical examiner's office and the Zions' lawyers. New York Hospital would say that Libby's toxicological reports were the result of "sloppy work compounded by pressure on the medical examiner" by Sidney Zion.

ON FATHER'S DAY, Sunday, June 17, 1984, Sidney Zion said that he received a "bizarre" phone call from Dr. Sherman, who greeted him by saying "Hello, this is Ray Sherman of New York Hospital."

"How are you?" Dr. Sherman asked, Sidney remembered.

"I'm not very well," Sidney said he answered. He said that Dr. Sherman "laughed in some kind of funny way," before telling him that he had received the medical examiner's report and that it contained "no surprises."

He mentioned the cocaine, Sidney recalled, "but only

Libby at Bennington, fall 1983. © 1995 KATHERINE H. KELLOGG

(above) and (right) Libby and her cat, Killer, photographed by her roommate at Bennington, fall 1983. © 1995 KATHERINE H. KELLOGG

The main entrance to New York Hospital–Cornell Medical Center.
COURTESY OF COURT TV.

Sidney Zion in front of New York Hospital. COURTESY OF COURT TV.

Dr. Raymond Sherman, Libby Zion's attending doctor, on the stand during *Zion* v. *New York Hospital*. COURTESY OF COURT TV.

Sidney and Elsa Zion listen to the testimony of Dr. Sherman COURTESY OF COURT TV.

Dr. Maurice Leonard, the PGY-2 in charge of the emergency room on the night Libby Zion was taken to New York Hospital.
COURTESY OF COURT TV.

Dr. Gregg Stone, who was the PGY-2 on duty the night Libby Zion became a patient. COURTESY OF COURT TV.

Dr. Luise Weinstein, who was the intern in charge of Libby Zion's care. COURTESY OF COURT TV.

Sidney Zion testifying on January 30, 1995. COURTESY OF COURT TV.

At the end of testimony about her daughter's condition, Elsa Zion breaks down. COURTESY OF COURT TV.

New York Hospital lawyers Peter Crean, Frank Bensel, and Luke Pittoni entering the Supreme Court building during *Zion* v. *New York Hospital*. COURTESY OF COURT TV.

Plaintiff attorney Tom Moore. Judge Elliott Wilk, who presided at the malpractice trial, is in the background. COURTESY OF COURT TV.

Adam, Elsa, and Sidney Zion listen to the verdict being read on February 6, 1995. Jed Zion was not present. COURTESY OF COURT TV.

in order to upset me," and then that Libby's death had been "a fluke."

"A fluke?" Sidney said he responded.

"Yes," Dr. Sherman said, Sidney recalled.

"If that's your idea of a fluke, I don't know what to say to you," Sidney said he replied.

Sidney remembered that he and Dr. Sherman argued about the emergency-room staff, and that Dr. Sherman said "they are really good people."

Sidney said that he brought up the matter of putting restraints on Libby, something he had learned about recently, and "Dr. Sherman changed the subject."

"I know your lawyers have served some papers, and I want to help," Dr. Sherman told Sidney, Sidney recalled. These were some preliminary papers sent before the actual malpractice lawsuit was initiated. Dr. Sherman then asked who was being sued, Sidney said.

"No decisions have been made," Sidney said he calmly told him.

Later, Dr. Sherman would say that he could not remember using the word *fluke* to Sidney or talking about the emergency room and restraints. "This is not reality," he said of the Father's Day conversation. He didn't even realize, he said, that it *was* Father's Day; for him it was just another Sunday he was working.

Also sometime that month, Sidney asked New York District Attorney Robert Morgenthau to prosecute Libby's doctors on charges of criminally negligent homicide. He told the *San Francisco Examiner*, which reported that he wanted "the doctor or doctors responsible to go to jail," that he would be "committing a sin in any religion" if he failed to accomplish this. "Sidney's very comfortable in the role of disarming the mighty," said Nancy Weber, a former coworker at the *New York Post*. "It's his habit of mind."

* * *

SIDNEY'S LAWYER AT the time, Ted Friedman, who was still a year away from filing a suit on behalf of his client, maintained that the "unconfirmed positive cocaine finding was simply a laboratory error."

On August 27, 1984, a highly unusual supplementary report was issued by the toxicological lab and signed by Dr. Milton Bastos, the director of the toxicology laboratory. It stated that the same blood samples used in the May 8 report were retested and found to be negative for cocaine. This report became part of the earlier so-called final toxicological report.

In mid-April, Dr. Leslie Lukash, who was the medical examiner of Nassau County, and Dr. Thomas Manning, a toxicologist on Dr. Lukash's staff, had been hired by Ted Friedman, at Sidney's request, to carry out the follow-up testing.

A handwritten note initialed by someone in the medical examiner's office on a letter Ted Friedman wrote to the office on August 2 authorizing Drs. Lukash and Manning to look at Libby's autopsy materials says that "slides and specimens were reviewed in histology and toxicology by Drs. Manning and Lukash." But Friedman's office explained that before the doctors could actually make arrangements to do the retesting, Dr. Bastos informed them—as well as Dr. Gross, the chief medical examiner—that it had already been done and was negative.

Dr. Manning later said that Dr. Bastos himself indeed did the testing while Dr. Manning and Dr. Lukash were at Bastos's lab. It is likely that Dr. Bastos, who is no longer alive, performed the retest himself to avoid second-guessing by outside experts, or to be sure that the Manhattan office didn't look foolish or complicit in some kind of cover-up.

Dr. Manning testified in a deposition that the "prime purpose" for his wanting to look at the samples had to do with the original cocaine finding, and that when the second test performed by Dr. Bastos came out negative, there was no need to proceed further because "we got a negative result, which was the important thing."

It had been, in fact, their mission.

Still, Dr. Manning also testified that "the swab testing was positive." New York Hospital later charged that the medical examiner was pressured to add the phrase "not enough material for confirmation" to the final toxicological report to play down the positive result, even though some experts maintain that nasal swabs cannot actually be confirmed because of the nature of the testing.

IN THE LETTER from Israel that Sidney wrote to his children in 1982, he spoke of death and dying. He told them, "I mention death only to tell you what I learned about life . . . And here's what I learned, it's all I know. Never let anybody dominate your life." He told his children that "I've been saying it to you by action since you were in the cribs . . . Never let anybody dominate your life. Never let anybody dominate your life. Never let anybody dominate your life. If you forget it you'll break my heart . . ."

In March 1984, Sidney Zion, with a broken heart, entered the most important combat of his life. The cocaine findings in Libby's body would become the subject of much debate, so much so that Sidney would do battle with them for over a decade, hand-in-hand with his quest to change the working conditions of residents in America's hospitals.

As he told the New York State Board for Professional Medical Conduct in 1988, "I was informed that the cause

of death was the doctors. That's the cause of death." He
said that "almost immediately after we left the hospital
they abandoned my kid . . . nobody took care of her anymore except to execute her . . . I learned that they gave
her Demerol, which the physicians handbook says you do
not give against Nardil, that when she began writhing
around, trying to break loose or whatever, trying to get out
of that bed, Luise Weinstein refused to come down and see
her and ordered a bed thing put around her, a restraint put
on her, without examining her; that when Libby broke that
restraint Luise Weinstein was called again and coldly ordered another one, another restraint. I think there were
two restraints that were broken. Luise Weinstein still refused to come down and see the kid, ordered her hands
and her feet tied to the bedpost and then had her hit with a
drug called Haldol, and Luise Weinstein never saw her
again until they put in the code.

"It is my definition of a murder," Sidney Zion said.

"I am led to understand that Dr. Gregg Stone took off
and never saw her again. I learned from all this that there
was a great conspiracy to get rid of us, throw us out of that
hospital so they could get rid of Libby and pay no more
attention to her. That's what I learned," he went on in a
fiery speech to those present at the state board's hearing.

"I learned that they decided that she was a hysteric, a
crazy kid, and they didn't give a goddamn whether she
died; that they let her die there like a dog and worse than a
dog."

Sidney Zion was not going to allow his life—or his
daughter's death—to be dominated by toxicological reports.

Never let anybody dominate your life.

Never.

Never.

Never.

7

I'M NOT SURE what doctor-patient relations has to do with the Libby Zion case," many doctors said to me. Sometimes they'd add, "There was no doctor-patient relation" in her case, not recognizing that they had just made an important point.

Although one could argue that Libby was not Dr. Sherman's regular patient, and that, in fact, he had no idea she was depressed and using a strong antidepressant, or was a drug abuser, still, he had agreed to act as her doctor when he directed her to the emergency room on March 4, 1984. Dr. Sherman said that Sidney Zion did not communicate the complexity of her problems that night. "I didn't know how serious it was from Zion's description," he argued. Although Sidney said he used emphatic language—from her "eyes are rolling around" to "she's acting like half a Mexican jumping bean"—Dr. Sherman insisted that they never discussed agitation of any kind, or that Libby's eyes were rolling around in a peculiar manner.

Later, Dr. Stone said, "If we had heard a little more clearly—or actually if we had heard at all—that Libby had this low-grade illness which was sort of percolating along at home, then, boom, all of a sudden when the parents were out of sight that she had gotten so dramatically worse—that would have painted a different picture. The picture we were given was more of just a gradual deterioration."

Sidney Zion saw one thing.

Elsa Zion saw another thing.

Adam Zion, a third, and Jed Zion, a fourth.

How did Libby herself perceive her problem?

What did Raymond Sherman see filtered through the telephone? Most of his contact with Libby had been by telephone, and it may have seemed normal to him once again to be treating her at that distance. After all, his attitude could have been that he was being a Good Samaritan just by giving her access to his eminent hospital. Dr. Bertrand Bell, Distinguished University Professor at Albert Einstein, said that what Dr. Sherman was doing was what any attending would have done because "emergency rooms do the work of attending doctors."

Do eighteen-year-olds have particular medical needs? After all, although they are able to vote and serve in the military, in the eyes of many they are still children.

I asked many doctors whether an eighteen-year-old should go to the family internist or continue with a pediatrician, most of whom are trained in adolescent medicine. The answers I received were evenly divided.

Dr. Andrew Zweifler is a professor of internal medicine at the University of Michigan Medical Center, where Libby's case was discussed in his "Introduction to the Patient" course "in the nature of a cautionary tale." He said that "teen-agers have special needs, and not all physicians are good at working with them." Dr. Kurt Hirschorn, head of the department of pediatrics at Mount Sinai Medical Center, the hospital where Libby was born, pointed out that the American Academy of Pediatrics recommends that a person remain under the care of a pediatrician until the age of twenty-one.

Dr. Robert Glickman is the medical director of Boston's Beth Israel Hospital, affiliated with the Harvard Medical School, and was a witness on behalf of Dr. Weinstein and Dr. Stone at their professional medical conduct hearings, as well as a star witness for New York Hospital at the Zion malpractice trial. Nevertheless, he commented to me that what happened in the Libby Zion case was "a systems failure."

A systems failure.

Dr. Hirschorn said that because her history wasn't readily available, "people were guessing. Libby Zion didn't have continuity of care."

''THE RESIDENTS IN charge of Libby Zion were in the wrong place at the wrong time—this would have happened to anybody," is how Dr. Gregg Stone positions himself and his colleagues during the time when they left themselves exposed to a malpractice suit.

C.Y.A. has never been a curriculum option in any medical institution, but it has been for years, and continues to be, especially in the aftermath of Libby's case, one of the most talked-about subjects in corridors, on-call rooms, cafeterias, empty conference rooms, or anywhere in which medical students and residents cluster.

C.Y.A.

Resident slang for *cover your ass.* Medically, a defensive technique, usually intended to ward off malpractice threats, of which the earliest known case occurred in 1374, when an English surgeon was sued for negligent treatment of a patient's hand. Although the patient lost, his case created the first definition of malpractice—if a patient is harmed by negligence or not cured in a reasonable time, the doctor is liable.

The first year of medical school varies from school to school, but in general the focus is on the basic sciences, preclinical studies such as anatomy, biochemistry, microbiology, or neurology. During the second year, basic medical knowledge is taught—organ systems, pathology, pharmacology, physical diagnosis—and most students believe this is their most important year. For instance, that year Dr. Weinstein learned about monoamine-oxidase (MAO) inhibitors like Nardil, and antipsychotics like Haldol. She never formally studied them again.

The third and fourth years of medical school—called clerkships—are spent learning about medicine in a clinical setting. Medical students are such a familiar sight in teaching hospitals, and have become so useful to the house staff, that many patients don't know that they are students. Dr. Leonard said that when he was in medical school, fourth-year students "were actually responsible for patients admitted to service," or the nonprivate section of the hospital. In fact, fourth-year medical students in such situations are called sub-interns. Of course, most patients don't realize that the residents treating them are only trainees, even though postgraduate year-twos, or PGY-2s, and up have their medical licenses.

Every medical school has its own style and rhythm. Some offer first-year students courses traditionally not taught until the second or third year. Others stress small seminars, or will introduce clinical training earlier than usual.

The doctors involved in Libby Zion's care went to many different medical schools. Downstate Medical College, now the State University of New York Health Science Center at Brooklyn College of Medicine, where Dr. Sherman studied, was founded in 1860, and encourages a basically uniform curriculum for every student. The Albert Einstein College of Medicine of Yeshiva University, a privately endowed school located in the Bronx in New York City, from which Dr. Leonard graduated, is a progressive school that emphasizes small classes and permits numerous course options. Johns Hopkins University School of Medicine, Dr. Stone's alma mater, "the single most potent influence ever" on medical study, offers a rigorous scientific education in conjunction with a flexible clinical experience. Dr. Stone spent 60 percent of his time as a medical student in a hospital setting. The University of Rochester School of Medicine and Dentistry, which Dr. Weinstein attended, was founded in 1920, and was one of the first to incorporate school and hospital. It combines an innovative curriculum with early patient contact. In the early 1970s it initiated a program at allied Strong Memorial Hospital, where special "night float" interns worked at night, giving the regular intern time off to sleep; this system would enter the mainstream after Libby Zion's death. Dr. Sherman had done a six-month residency in nephrology at Strong in the sixties; at that time he was on call every other night and every other weekend.

There are 123 medical schools in the United States, 3 in Puerto Rico, and 16 in Canada. No matter how different their approaches, the goal of all of these institutions is to prepare students to become residents.

In 1992 and 1993, I visited six medical centers in California, Connecticut, Massachusetts, New York, and Pennsylvania, in order to talk to students, interns, residents, deans, attending doctors, nurses, and directors of residency programs. In five places I also attended classes and meetings.

What I discovered was very simple, and perhaps somewhat unexpected: medical schools, their faculty, and students are in excellent condition, and have been for many years, and are not the source of what is amiss in medical education. In the long run, the distinctions among medical schools make very little difference. But problems do arise in the later years, when the medical schools work with hospitals. This has been true for decades.

On the whole, the students were wiser and more worldly than I expected them to be; I suppose that I thought I would chiefly meet up with narrow-minded, overbearing science majors. But this was not the case. They were smart, sophisticated, and down-to-earth. The men were anything but stereotypically arrogant. A first-year student at the University of California, San Francisco School of Medicine, told me he became a doctor "to satisfy" his "helper aspect." Others had similar views, sometimes expressed more in terms of performing a specific service. The women were strong and caring. Several deans remarked to me that the large ratio of women now in medical school made for a more civilized atmosphere.

Although medical students receive, in the words of Dr. Daniel D. Federman, dean for medical education at Harvard Medical School, "the longest and most demanding training of any professionals," those I met were not self-important or imperious. Dr. Robert Gifford, associate dean for education and student affairs at Yale University School of Medicine, said the applicants today seem brighter than earlier generations. "Many students have done other things," Dr. Gifford said, "and are older. They make better doctors."

The faculty members I met were more open and more questioning than I had anticipated. I had had images of egotists reluctant to share information, but what I discovered were modest sages eager to teach, and, more important, eager to grow. Of course, the very word *doctor* has its roots in the Latin *docere*, which means teach.

According to the Association of American Medical Colleges, approximately 117 medical schools in the United States and Canada require that their students take a class on doctor-patient relations. Twenty-five years ago no such courses were taught. Ten years ago many schools offered such classes. In the 1990s, there's hardly a medical school without one.

Marshall A. Lichtman, M.D., the dean of the University of Rochester School of Medicine and Dentistry, Dr. Weinstein's alma mater, believes that such courses are not only vital, but "set a tone" for the student's future approach to patients. "What happens in the privacy of a room between doctor and patient is not always translated accurately afterwards," Dr. Lichtman said, adding that "many times a doctor may do his utmost to send a message to a patient, but the message received is different from the one that the doctor thought he or she was sending. This works in the other direction as well."

Medical students are learning in all sorts of ways to communicate better with their patients, and most of all they are learning to listen more carefully.

After an enterprising doctor-patient class for first-year students at the University of Pennsylvania School of Medicine, Dr. Gail Morrison, associate dean for clinical education, asked for volunteers to stay behind to discuss ways to improve the course for the next year. It was the last lecture of the series, and Dr. Morrison wanted to be sure the students were receiving what they needed or needed what they were receiving. The lecture that day was "Tough Patients," by Dr. James L. Stinnett, a professor of psychiatry, and it was hard to see how it could have been improved upon.

In a lighter vein, right before the lecture, some students had sung "Happy Birthday" to a classmate. "We never used to sing 'Happy Birthday,' that's a good change," Dr. Stinnett commented to the class. Such a seemingly innocuous celebration would not have been possible in the early eighties.

The very serious topic of Dr. Stinnett's lecture in and of itself reflected a new sensibility: the willingness of medical schools to discuss awkward subjects, in this case, hostility toward patients. Over and over I had heard people comment that the doctors at New York Hospital had either been intimidated by Sidney Zion's attitude or put off by it altogether. In any case, Dr. Stinnett explained to his students that "no matter how saintly you are, you will end up disliking" certain patients. These patients, he explained, could range from those who are offensive, pushy, or destructive to those who avoid dealing with their illnesses. But, he went on, doctors have to accept not only feeling uncomfortable in these situations, but also that they are part of whatever is happening with any patient, and therefore have to strive to understand the behavior even of difficult ones. But, Dr. Stinnett emphasized, doctors also had to set limits. "Doctors don't like to be punitive," he said, "but they live in the real world." Later, a medical student told me, "With patients you don't like, the medical care is the same, but not the emotional support."

Dr. Herbert Pardes, dean of the faculty of medicine at the Columbia University College of Physicians and Surgeons, told the 148 students of the class of 1997 that they would be making less money than doctors ever did before, but no one indicated that this was of pressing concern. "We're not in this for the money," one student told me. Dr. Pardes also told the students they would be sharing patient responsibility more—with nurses, for instance. Most of the students saw this not as further bureaucratic entanglement, but as an opportunity to provide more for their patients and themselves because of the wider support system. Dr. Linda Lewis, the dean of students at the College of Physicians and Surgeons, told the same students that they had moved beyond "the competition to get into medical school," and that they would now be helping one another. I got the impression that compassion was replacing competition among students everywhere, another change from the way things had been a decade or more ago. Dr. Lewis also told the group that "75 percent of what we teach you is probably wrong," a statement meant not only to illustrate the rapid changes taking place in research, but also to let the students know that doctors are fallible, something most people still have a hard time accepting. I discovered that this point of view is not the taboo subject it once was in medical schools.

Students were encouraged to be candid and plainspoken, particularly in the doctor-patient classes I attended. "You will talk about things that seem irrelevant but later shed light on the situation," Dr. Connie Park told a class at the College of Physicians and Surgeons that was learning how to talk to an AIDS patient. "It takes some time to sense and understand subtle innuendos from patients that may have enormous meaning," Dr. Fredric Burg, vice dean for education at the University of Pennsylvania School of Medicine, told me. "It's not easy to be a good listener. It takes complex skills."

Dr. Rita Charon, director of the "Introduction to the Patient" course at the College of Physicians and Surgeons,

told the members of her "Literature and Medicine" seminar that as doctors they needed to use both their intellects
and their hearts. "Do both," she urged, "but not at the
same time. One can contaminate the other." Dr. Charon
stressed to her third-year students that doctors must explain clearly and thoroughly. To help them explore their
feelings about patients, as well as to learn as much as possible about the patients, Dr. Charon invented "parallel"
charts: her students are encouraged to keep a chart or record of their own private thoughts about the patients along
with the regular chart. Such parallel charts bring to the
surface ideas and feelings with which the student might
not normally be in touch because of the frenetic routine of
hospital life. Dr. Charon's students also read Virginia
Woolf, William Carlos Williams, James Joyce, and others to
search for ways to increase their listening skills. After reading a chapter from Toni Morrison's *Sula*, one student told
the class that Morrison's depiction of a certain character
had strongly influenced the way she perceived an unruly
patient.

Medical students, I learned, are slowly being inched
along to let go of or let up on becoming "the mother or
father figure caring for people, or curing them," as Dr.
Fredric Burg put it, even though, he went on, "some of the
magic of medicine may have been in that hierarchical kind
of relationship with patients." Indeed, a doctor at Stanford
University believes that "when you knock people off ped-
estals, they don't want to be in charge anymore, and they
don't take responsibility."

"It used to be paternal, but it's gone now," a second-
year student at Columbia's College of Physicians and Surgeons told me.

Even by 1988, four years after Libby's death, an article
in *The New England Journal of Medicine* declared that "the

heroic image of the physician is fading." But the doctor at Stanford warned, "Medicine is a calling. Most doctors today see it only as a job."

Dr. Gregg Stone added, "People started on-call every night initially, and then every other night, and then every third, and then every fourth, and now every fifth in a lot of places. I think over the years we are losing something in medicine by being less committed to it. I think our patients have a little less confidence in us, and I don't think working less is the answer."

The students at the schools I visited understood that patients had to learn to share responsibility with their doctors. Dr. Fredric Burg believes that when a doctor brings the patient and family in "as partners," he is "more likely to have a better outcome."

But certainly in the instance of Libby Zion the groundwork for such partnership had never been laid. When she was admitted to New York Hospital, neither the doctors nor the parents were fully in possession of the information that was required for Libby's proper treatment, nor was Libby herself able to participate effectively in her treatment. "Deny, deny, deny," Dr. Sherman commented. "The hint is in my chart." And so, by the time the Zions entered the ER, a mode of behavior not conducive to partnership had long been entrenched.

A T   7 : 3 0   A . M . on Monday, March 5, 1984, Dr. Joseph Ruggiero, the chief resident, arrived at New York Hospital to take over from the assistant chief resident, Dr. Martin Carr, who had been on call Sunday night. It was Dr. Carr who kept the list of which medical team was next in line to receive a new admission. Dr. Ruggiero said that he was supposed to conduct "a teaching exercise called morning report," but the residents were not at their usual meeting place, the medical library. "They came in late, and I inquired what had held them up, and they told me there had been a cardiac arrest on one of the medical floors," he recalled. Dr. Ruggiero then spoke to Dr. Carr, who told him "the rough outlines" of what had happened to Libby Zion.

After Dr. Ruggiero finished with morning report, he read Libby's medical record, and checked the *Physicians' Desk Reference* for Nardil. He had not known about its contraindication with Demerol. Neither had Dr. Carr. Like most other residents, they had studied pharmacology in their second year of medical school, and that had been the extent of their formal instruction on the subject.

Later in the morning of March 5, Dr. Ruggiero spoke to Dr. Stone, Dr. Weinstein, and Dr. Sherman, who had once been a chief resident himself, at Highland Hospital in Rochester, New York. Dr. Ruggiero also consulted with Dr. Marcus Reidenberg, the head of New York Hospital's department of pharmacology, about Nardil. He asked if there were any tests available that could detect a Nardil reaction. "I found out there was no way to track this down," Dr. Ruggiero said.

Dr. Ruggiero then conferred with the physician-in-chief of the hospital, Dr. R. Gordon Douglas, Jr. Dr. Douglas, like Dr. Ruggiero, was intimately familiar with his surroundings, because not only was he a 1959 graduate of Cornell University Medical College, but he had also done two years of residency training at New York Hospital, where, at that time, he was on call every other night. Dr. Douglas had also done a third year of residency at Johns Hopkins, and had returned to New York Hospital in 1963 to become the chief resident in the department of medicine. He had also done further training at the National Institutes of Health, and was the author and editor of two definitive textbooks on infectious diseases, his specialty. Dr. Douglas, who believed there was a "psychological nature" to Libby's flailing, said that although Demerol was "acceptable therapy" for her fine tremors, she should not have received it. Nevertheless, he did not think the drug had anything to do with Libby's death because of the small amount she had been given.

Over the next few weeks after Libby Zion's death, the physician-in-chief himself spoke to the residents. Dr. Douglas asked Dr. Leonard about Libby's negative chest X ray in the emergency room, especially in the light of the pneumonia findings, however small, on autopsy. Experts later testified before a grand jury that an X ray might not show pneumonia in a patient as severely dehydrated as Libby was that night.

Dr. Douglas questioned Dr. Weinstein about the use of restraints, and she told him she was afraid Libby would injure herself, especially with the IV needle. Dr. Weinstein also told him that she could tell in her phone conversation with Nurse Grismer that Libby's agitation had not increased, and that was why she didn't think she had to return to Payson 5 to see for herself. Furthermore, she said that she didn't believe that Libby's temperature was going to go up. They also discussed Libby's rash, and Dr. Weinstein told Dr. Douglas she had wondered if Libby had acute lupus erythematosus. She also told him she wondered about toxic shock syndrome, which would later be Dr. Douglas's "favorite cause of death." Dr. Stone had all but eliminated it as a likely diagnosis when he had examined Libby.

Dr. Douglas said that toxic shock syndrome "accounts for most or all of the findings" at the autopsy, and described it as "essentially an influenza A virus." He said he couldn't prove it, but it was "as strong as anything else," even illicit drugs, as a reason for Libby's death. In fact, he stated that toxic shock syndrome was a diagnosis that was reached as part of the quality-assurance review, that is, the postmortem evaluation of Libby's medical care.

Although Dr. Douglas said there were "bizarre and un- usual" reactions to cocaine that could lead to sudden death, it was not his most likely diagnosis. He believed that Libby had toxic shock syndrome when she first showed up in the emergency room of New York Hospital. He was the only person to hold that belief, not an unusual position for any single doctor when faced with a mul- tifaceted mystery.

He also agreed with some of the residents that Libby had "improved somewhat during the six hours or so of observation" on Payson 5.

"When did she stop improving and start dying?" an examiner from the New York State Board for Professional Medical Conduct later asked Dr. Douglas.

"Not until 6:30 A.M."

"So, up until 6:30 A.M. she was improving?"

"That's correct."

"What happened at 6:30 A.M. that made her stop improv- ing, do you have any idea?"

"I don't think anybody knows the answer to that ques- tion," Dr. Douglas replied.

Later, when I pressed Elsa Zion and asked what she thought had happened to her daughter, she said, "Medi- cally, it's impossible to even imagine."

But Elsa was able to step back and look at the impossi- ble. "It's true," she told me, "that the only evidence of drugs was the medications that we had said. Maybe they decided she was a . . . that in fact this was a drug case. But if in fact it was a drug case, they didn't do anything! They did nothing at all. How did they let her lie there with a fever going up constantly? Where was the panic button? At what point did they consider this was a crisis, that they might actually not be dealing with an hysterical child, and actually be dealing with somebody who was dying?"

DR. DOUGLAS SAID that Dr. Stone did not use the word *hysterical* in their postmortem conversation about Libby. The word appeared only in Dr. Stone's note.

Later, the New York State Board for Professional Medical Conduct would point out that Dr. Stone had listed separately and underlined his controversial *viral syndrome with hysterical symptoms* phrase, thus indicating by its separation from other possible diagnoses that this, in his view, was the correct one.

Dr. Sherman said that he had never heard the word *hysterical* used in his phone conversations with Dr. Stone, although he acknowledged that the word has "relatively specific psychiatric features." He said that it was his understanding that Libby was "anxious" and "upset" by her illness, and that her agitation "was one way in which she was reacting to it."

In accordance with hospital procedure, Dr. Stone, as the PGY-2 supervisor of Dr. Weinstein, had handled all the communication with Dr. Sherman. It was rare that an intern spoke directly to an attending. Dr. Stone passed along Dr. Sherman's responses to Dr. Weinstein, who, because she decided to treat Libby with restraints and psychotropic drugs, made the final decision to go along with a psychological view of Libby's illness that had begun in the emergency room.

Ira Hoffman, M.D., associate chief of medicine at Lenox Hill Hospital, who reviewed Libby's case for the New York State Department of Health, and who would later find himself involved in a trying political battle between his hospital and New York Hospital, said that " 'viral syndrome with hysterical symptoms' tells the staff that this patient is not seriously ill and can wait until the next day for further workup, that nothing more is needed." Dr. Bertrand Bell thinks that Dr. Sherman "didn't know what was going on, and said, 'Admit her.' " Dr. Bell also believes that the house staff thought Libby was "a faker."

Most of the residents I talked to agreed.

Dr. Steve Thornquist, a resident at Yale who was the 1992–93 chair of the American Medical Association's Resident Committee, told me that Dr. Stone's phrase made Libby "sound like a crazy person," and it reminded him of another phrase residents use: *supratentorial disease*, which means "all in the head."

Most of the private language that doctors use among themselves is meant to break the tension of whatever situation is causing them discomfort. Morbid humor often gets doctors through the most horrendous events. It's a perfectly healthy coping mechanism that people in many other occupations also use, and it only becomes a problem when it evolves into a weapon.

The retreat into banter begins early in the training of doctors. A second-year medical student told me, "When something bothers me I'll make sarcastic jokes. It reflects that I have some idealism that has been wounded."

Doctors *catch* a newborn; a *pushy* patient—that is, a patient in the second stage of labor—*poops* a baby. A patient is *buzzed* with radiation. Physicians don't consult other physicians, they *insult* other physicians. The private language of physicians sounds harsh to laypeople. It is intended to separate doctor and patient.

It has been said that ever since the invention of the stethoscope, the distance between the patient and the doctor began to grow. Doctors used to put their ears directly on their patients' chests. But no more. Over time, doctors began to leave the bedside altogether—at least symbolically—as house calls ended, and specialists took over.

Euphemisms also get doctors through terrible experiences. Patients will be said to have *terminal living, to have checked out, crumped, dwindled, gone sour.* They are also said to have shown the *Q sign*—the tongue is hanging out of the side of an open mouth—to be *imminent,* or to have a *negative outcome.*

Die is not an easy word for doctors to use.

There are many words used that sound judgmental. For instance, the word *deny,* as in "the patient denies the use of illegal drugs," seems to imply "refuses to acknowledge" rather than "declares untrue." The patient *claims,* as in "the patient claims to have taken her medicine," seems to suggest that no fact has been established; it leaves the question open. The patient *fails,* as in "the patient fails to respond to the drug," is a statement with a moralizing implication. Ruth L. Fishbach, a Ph.D. member of the department of social medicine and the division of medical ethics at Harvard Medical School, who teaches doctor-patient relations to first-year students, said, "The drug failed the patient. Don't blame the victim." Dr. Fishbach also cited the word *complain,* as in "the patient complains," which she believes should be "the patient is reporting," not complaining.

But resident slang not only offers a resident relief from stress, it also provides insight into the resident's state of mind. Sometimes the words can be a disguise for weariness or hostility. A fourth-year Yale medical student said that often the language that develops "reflects that people are tired." A third-year medical student at Columbia's College of Physicians and Surgeons admitted that sometimes the "trivializing" that house officers engage in can be "upsetting" to hear. Another third-year medical student at Columbia told me that outsiders "are not meant to understand" medical language. "We don't want them to understand it," he said.

THE CHIEF RESIDENT, Dr. Joseph Ruggiero, said that he tried to understand Libby's "perplexing" behavior. "Both Luise and Gregg told me the gross motor movements seemed controllable to them." He learned from Dr. Stone, who he believed was "an extremely bright resident" with "good clinical judgment," that Libby's fine tremor had contributed to her fever. "Luise was my intern for a year," Dr. Ruggiero said. "The chief resident gets to know his interns very well. Never once in twelve months did anyone, resident or nurse, ever complain to me about anything Luise ever did." He said that she did "a very thorough physical" on Libby, and "had carefully written up a differential diagnosis and a treatment plan." He explained that "generally the intern and resident share responsibility for the patient, but the physician on the scene most of the time is the intern." In accordance with accepted custom, the least experienced member of the house staff is in charge. This rite is observed nationwide.

Nurse Grismer said that Dr. David Palet, a 1983 graduate of the Medical College of Pennsylvania, had observed Libby through the glass partition in the nurse's station, saw her struggling, and suggested that she call Dr. Weinstein at once. But Dr. Palet said that he could not recall any such discussion, and that he had been asleep anywhere from two to four hours in Payson 5's on-call room, which was about fifty feet from the nurse's station. He said that he did not wake up until he heard the code for Libby.

Although there would later be much debate about Dr. Palet's role, he was simply following hospital hierarchy by remaining detached from Libby's care while she was boarding on his floor. Dr. Weinstein was in charge of Libby, not Dr. Palet, and he could not break rank by interfering or seeming to judge another intern's decisions, although according to Nurse Grismer he had, by offering an unsolicited opinion about Libby.

Although Dr. Stone said that Dr. Sherman, as the attending doctor, had the ultimate responsibility for Libby, this was not true in practice while she was in the hospital. If Libby had lived, Dr. Sherman might have assumed that responsibility the next day when he joined the residents on their morning rounds. But on Sunday night, March 4, the responsibility was Dr. Luise Weinstein's, not Dr. Sherman's. Even Dr. Stone was not required to remain on the scene, according to Dr. Ruggiero.

Dr. Douglas later spoke about the teaching hospital's "team approach to care," but emphasized that the attending doctor most definitely is the boss. I would find this more legalistically than literally true.

Still, the PGY-1 at the University of California, San Francisco School of Medicine, who had told me that "attendings don't see orders," also said that "they are on the scene all the time, and we ask them, if we have a question, and we often do." When I sat for an extended time in a chart room at Moffitt/Long Hospital in San Francisco, I was struck by the number of conferences the residents had with both the nursing staff and more senior doctors. Nevertheless, "attendings do not see orders" was most definitely the rule everywhere I went.

Dr. Douglas said, speaking of Dr. Stone, that he had done "a good workup" on Libby, and that "he communicated his information to Dr. Weinstein and Dr. Sherman. That's his role." By confirming Dr. Stone's role as a supervisor/intermediary, Dr. Douglas also affirmed Dr. Weinstein's role as the hands-on doctor in charge. Since Dr. Weinstein was on the premises, and Dr. Sherman, the attending, was not, that made her boss for the night.

In fact, in a dramatic exchange at his deposition, Dr. Douglas said that Dr. Sherman was not even apprised of the intended administration of Demerol to Libby, thus corroborating Dr. Sherman's own position. Adding to his accusations of Dr. Sherman's inadequate care of Libby, Sidney would come to believe that the Demerol was solely responsible for his daughter's death because of its contraindication with Nardil. Indeed, the medical examiner himself told Dr. Sherman on May 17, 1984, "that the bottom line was there was a reaction between Nardil and Demerol."

"In the normal course of events, one might not ask the attending physician every little detailed order," Dr. Douglas said. What he left out is that New York Hospital encourages its PGY-1s and PGY-2s to order on their own and discourages attendings from interfering with this "effective way" for residents "to learn wisdom in patient management."

Those outside the medical profession who know about the closed order book commonly assume it exists only where the patients cannot afford private medical care, and long ago they decided that making such a patient a teaching case was better than giving the patient no care at all. But the closed order book doesn't exist only in clinics, but everywhere, in private hospitals as well as public institutions. As Dr. Bell puts it, it is like a "separate culture."

It took me time to discover the conventions and practices of this culture.

There are degrees of the closed order book. At its most extreme, the attending doctor is mandated by the hospital not to write orders on his own patients. A former official of the New York State Department of Health told me that at this extreme, a nurse cannot act until an intern or resident has signed the order book, even if the attending has signed it. According to this official, the intern or resident can make all the decisions whether or not the attending agrees, "so you have interns telling attendings what to do." This form of the closed order book was a "model" at select New York hospitals, including New York Hospital. But, the official added, it probably doesn't go on any longer.

The official may be wrong.

Referring to the Demerol and Haldol given to Libby in the hospital, Dr. Sherman made clear that the house staff "had the latitude to use these medications." The interns and residents had this "latitude" because of the closed order book, which has existed from the turn of the century. Yet the closed order book, and its varying degrees of application, it might be pointed out, is treated as a trade secret so dark that many doctors I interviewed said they hadn't ever heard the term used, although they described the essence of what they had never heard precisely, and defended its use as indispensable in medical education.

Others, like Dr. Bertrand Bell, whose commission created new resident regulations in 1989 that, among other things, limited a resident's hours to eighty per week, and who delights in referring to himself as a PGY-40, are ardent opponents of the closed order book because it leaves residents unsupervised, and "no one takes responsibility." The closed order book encourages resident-run hospitals. Dr. Bell, a 1955 graduate of the State University of New York at Buffalo School of Medicine, who did his postgraduate training at the two public hospitals affiliated with the Albert Einstein College of Medicine of Yeshiva University in New York, cautioned me that doctors were "going to wonder" how I knew about the closed order book.

This is precisely what happened.

At first, when I used the term *closed order book* in a way that implied I was being critical, I often received either blank stares or guarded responses. Later, if I mentioned the term with sufficient casualness, I received a spontaneous reply, replete with fact and detail.

It was as if I had accidentally pressed a hidden code. Whatever the response, I couldn't fail to recognize that there was something about the closed order book that made my attention to it indiscreet. Many people in medicine are reticent about revealing to those outside the profession information that carries the weight of tradition. It was inevitable that to such people I seemed to be intruding into areas where I didn't belong, areas that could be easily misunderstood. But I also saw that I had touched on something not only very deeply ingrained in medical practice, but also of so sensitive a nature that the mere mention of its name by a nonprofessional threatened its existence.

Yet the closed order book is legitimatized by its inclusion in the Green Book—the American Medical Association's *Graduate Medical Education Directory*. On page 42, under *C*, "The Curriculum and the Teaching Program in Internal Medicine," it clearly states: ". . . Residents should write all orders for patients under their care."

Why all the secrecy? Here it is in black and white in the *Graduate Medical Education Directory*.

I soon began to understand that the secrecy was hiding lack of supervision of what was once meant to be a carefully supervised teaching tool. But the closed order book had become something different, something that had nothing to do with education at all, but everything to do with the new realities of medicine—sicker and poorer patients, increased service needs, staff deficiencies, insurance and other financial concerns, and the knowledge that residents are being trained at the expense of patients.

"Hospitals need internship labor," a resident told me, and that is why so many institutions are fearful of any health-care plan or government spending cuts that limit the number of internships and residencies in teaching hospitals across America.

8

AFTER CONDUCTING HIS investigation into Libby's death, Dr. Joseph Ruggiero concluded that her "fever and agitation when she came in may have been due to an interaction between the Nardil and something she ingested prior to her admission." He said that his feeling about this was overwhelming, and in retrospect, he would have put a drug reaction "up near the top" of possible diagnoses. He believed that all of her symptoms "were present before the Demerol was given."

No one asked his opinion when it mattered.

Interns are commonly taught to tough it out. A fourth-year medical student told me residents say, "If you don't wake me up, it's 'honors' for you."

The biggest strains facing residents are time pressures and sleep deprivation. A fourth-year medical student at the University of California, San Francisco, said, "You hear two questions in the morning: 'How many *hits* [admissions] did you get?' and 'How much sleep did you get?' "

A third stress factor confronting interns and residents is hunger. Simple hunger.

Interns and residents rarely have time to eat. In an effort to alleviate this, food is usually served at every conference, meeting, or lecture they attend. In 1989, the physician-in-chief of New York Hospital, Dr. R. Gordon Douglas, told a meeting of the chiefs of various departments of medicines in the United States that getting New York Hospital to pay for house-staff meals at night "had a greater impact on morale than anything else we've done."

Lack of adequate supervision is a fourth and very major stress factor, and until 1984 was not acknowledged as a hardship for a doctor-in-training.

I asked an intern, "What is your greatest fear?"

Without hesitating, she answered, "That I will kill a patient."

Everywhere I went I heard the importance of supervision repeated more frequently than anything else by deans, professors, and directors of residency programs. Almost everyone agreed that more and better supervision of interns and residents was a good thing.

"There has to be enough supervision on the floor, and the resident has to be willing to say, 'I don't know,' " said Dr. Rosemary Fisher, director of the house-staff program at Yale University School of Medicine. Dr. Fredric Burg, vice dean for education at the University of Pennsylvania School of Medicine, explained that "part of learning is knowing your limits."

When Dr. Rita Charon answered a question in her seminar "Introduction to the Patient" at Columbia University's College of Physicians and Surgeons by saying, "I don't know," the effect in the room was palpably electric. With

that simple statement, she had freed her students to become doctors of the twenty-first century, and to accept the
limits of their knowledge.

For decades, residents were taught to face their problems on their own. It was a sign of weakness to ask for help.
This lesson still lingers, and the medical students and residents I met, in contrast to their seniors, were divided on
the issue of supervision. Interns and residents are often
uneasy about the depth of their medical knowledge, yet at
the same time they need to conceal, or at the very least
control, this nervousness for the sake of their patients. But
I also discovered that it was becoming a sign of strength to
admit not knowing. "One of the greatest skills is knowing
what your limits are," said a fourth-year medical student at
Yale, echoing Dr. Burg's comments. As another medical
student put it to me, "You can't be oversupervised."

Still, most residents picked the program in which they
wanted to work largely based on the amount of responsibility it permitted them. One resident told me, "Some people
don't like to be supervised."

"Residents don't want to go where they can't be the
one to write orders," Dr. Rosemary Fisher said. But there
are places where faculty members not only supervise the
residents, but also reject the closed order book. Some medical trainees like it that way.

Joseph Tenenbaum, M.D., an attending cardiologist at
Columbia Presbyterian Medical Center, is known by his
medical students as "a doctor's doctor" even though he
does not allow them to take charge. He orders all the drugs
for his patients. "The residents follow my orders," Dr.
Tenenbaum said, conceding that the order book "causes
the most tension between house staff and attendings."

I learned that such tensions are a throwback; during the
nineteenth century, fear by attendings of conflicts between

themselves and the house staff was one of the reasons there were few internships until the beginning of the twentieth century.

A medical student told me that he felt having a prudent role model was far more important to his education then being given the opportunity to have total—and un-supervised—care for hospital patients. Indeed, John L. Clowe, a past president of the American Medical Association, said, "Role models speak much louder than books, papers, or courses."

FOR INTERNS AND residents, February and March are the dreary, waiting-around months. Waiting for winter to be over, waiting for spring. These are the months when resentment, anger, or depression are most likely to show themselves with a vengeance.

Their year begins in July, and after seven or eight months they are well into their routines, but are a little stir-crazy, a little surly, even a little bored. "They're tired," and "it feels like it will never end," Dr. Rita Charon said. As an American Institute of Stress survey reported, the first year of residency training ranks fifth among the ten most stressful jobs in America. "There's a downslope in winter," declared Dr. Richard I. Kopelman, director of house-staff training at New England Medical Center.

In a few months, at every level there will be a change of status. The PGY-1 will be getting off the bottom rung, and stepping up to run things. The PGY-2 will go on to specialty training and fellowships.

It's not uncommon for residents to experience mood swings, to go from elation to self-doubt. One doctor referred to "the loss of social skills that happens after you've been working all night."

Interns are particularly vulnerable. After all, they are in

what used to be referred to as the fifth year of medical school. Suddenly they are being pushed to cope on their own with anxious, suffering patients, or difficult, hostile ones. They live under the weight of seasoned maxims: "A young doctor means a new graveyard," says a German proverb.

One of the closest parallels to the doctors' situation, according to Dr. Rita Charon, is that of the police force. Both doctors and policemen are "at risk," encounter "life-and-death decisions, and make decisions as agents of society." In *Learning Clinical Reasoning*, Dr. Jerome P. Kassirer and Dr. Richard I. Kopelman comment: "Clinicians and detectives have much in common. Both deal with problems that may have subtle and well-hidden solutions." Dr. Rita Charon continues: "Both are often reviled from a training point of view." She said that "the task of the police academy is not unlike that of the medical school. The recruits learn law and interpersonal skills. You prepare them as well as you can with cognitive skills, then you put them on the street with a gun and a badge." She added, "Cops say rookies make us honest," and doctors say "medical students keep us human." In terms of supervision, both doctors and policemen are "always making balanced judgments."

Less supervision invites problems. As Dr. Lewis Goldfrank, director of emergency medicine at Bellevue Hospital–New York University Medical Center, said on behalf of the New York State Board for Professional Medical Conduct's inquiry into Libby Zion's death, "Inexperienced people can't always recognize when they need help."

Residents are also prone to what Dr. David Hilfiker in *Healing the Wounds* called the worst kind of mistake, "a failure of will." Here, "the doctor knows the right thing to do but doesn't do it because he is distracted or pressured or exhausted."

Could this have happened to Dr. Weinstein?

At hearings later called by the New York State Board for Professional Medical Conduct, the disciplinary wing of the New York State Department of Health, which hears all charges investigated by the department and has the power to revoke medical licenses, Dr. Weinstein admitted that she was not involved in any emergencies and could have gone to see Libby when first called by Nurse Grismer.

One might wonder whether she was simply fed up with this patient, a patient in the *outfield*, two floors away? A patient who was just a girl acting hysterical.

"Libby Zion was treated as an adversary." This was the opinion of a resident in California as he contemplated the case.

Another doctor, also not of the New York Hospital staff, suggested that because Dr. Weinstein didn't have any training in emergency medicine, she "hadn't ever seen a case like Libby's." Still another doctor thought that Dr. Weinstein might have been "operating on autopilot."

The most recent Green Book of the American Medical Association specifies that interns, or PGY-1s, in internal medicine—fresh medical school graduates—should be responsible "on average" for four to six new patients "per admitting day," and for the "ongoing" care of eight to twelve patients.

In 1984, New York Hospital's manual for residents mandated ten patients as the average load for an intern, so Luise Weinstein, with forty patients, was pushing the limits of anyone's endurance. Indeed, a resident at Yale–New Haven Hospital later told me that ten patients is considered too many. "If you get ten patients, you've been *staked*," the resident said. By that definition, Luise Wein-

stein had not only been staked but was being burned at the
stake on Sunday, March 4.

Did Dr. Weinstein make an *EJ*—an error of judgment—
an act common enough to have earned a place in resident
slang? Several doctors and program directors to whom I
spoke even suggested that perhaps Dr. Weinstein had
been envious that Libby was in bed, where she herself
would have so much wished to be. "Patients are a good
target for taking out your frustrations," a medical student
confessed to me. Or could Dr. Weinstein simply have believed the nurses would take care of Libby for her?

Residents speak of patients as having been *buffed*, by
which they mean "made to look better," or *turfed*, by
which they mean "got rid of." Any resident, especially one
working in the dead of night on a chilly weekend in early
March, might ask or be asked this question: Was Libby
Zion *buffed* and *turfed* until morning?

To make matters worse, Libby might have been treated
as a *cheap case*—resident slang for an easy case to figure out
and diagnose. After all, her attending doctor didn't seem to
be very worried about her. "She was a private patient, a
college student from a prosperous Upper West Side family,
and she was written off," someone close to the state's investigation of her death told me. "It was one out of a
million that someone like Libby Zion had a terminal disease."

JUST TWENTY DAYS after Libby's death, one of the
residents involved in her treatment was implicated in another malpractice case, along with an intern and a medical
student, although no charges were ever brought against
either of them. The story has never been told, not because
of any confidentiality agreement, but because the family
involved in the case wishes to have what happened to

them remain private. "It was a long time ago. It's over," the patient's daughter told me.

The case was responsible for a major change in hospital procedure, yet no one anywhere heard anything about it. If the case had been widely publicized, there is little doubt the public would have been caught up in its furor, and the public would not have let go, not only because of the circumstances involved, but because it revealed a new threat to patients everywhere as furtive and sensitive as that of the closed order book: medical students playing doctor— for real.

Besides dramatizing that medical students are routinely being given responsibilities beyond their abilities, the case concerns the compelling issue of "Do Not Resuscitate," or "DNR," orders, which means that heroic actions are not to be taken—that is, a code is not to be called—when certain terminally ill patients experience heart stoppage or are unable to breathe. The case also reveals a contempt for the elderly that defies comprehension. "There's discrimination against the elderly," said the patient's daughter, in terse understatement.

The case is on record in papers housed in the basement of the Supreme Court building in lower Manhattan. These papers are readily available to the public for the asking. But to ask for them, the public would have to know of their existence.

My own informant about the case wishes to remain anonymous. This is the case, my informant said, that should have been the Zion case.

On Thursday, March 15, 1984, eighty-eight-year-old Violet Noss was taken to New York Hospital's emergency room after her live-in home aide noticed a change in her mental functioning. She was admitted to the hospital with a diagnosis of pneumonia by the emergency-room resident.

The intern on call was Dr. David Pearlman, and the PGY-2 on call was Dr. Gregg Stone.

"This was another being in the wrong place at the wrong time," Dr. Stone said. "It was no more a big deal than anything else that happens every day in the hospital. Medicine is constantly evolving in the way you take care of patients."

Dr. Raymond Hochman, Violet Noss's private doctor, was away, and so Dr. Jerrold Lieberman, who was covering for him, took over as the attending of record. Dr. Hochman resumed care for Mrs. Noss four days later, on Monday, March 19. He was pleased that her respiratory condition had steadily improved, but perplexed that her mental condition had not. Mrs. Noss was in a "state of distress" that Dr. Hochman believed was being exacerbated by the hospital environment. Still, her all-around condition was not "life threatening," and, in fact, she was scheduled to be discharged from the hospital a week later, on Tuesday, March 27.

Over the weekend of March 24–25, another attending, Dr. John Brown, covered for Dr. Hochman. Dr. Brown reported that Mrs. Noss was continuing to improve. She was a feisty lady.

On Sunday, March 25, besides the intern on call on Violet Noss's floor, there was also a fourth-year medical student, or *drone*, William Mayo-Smith, involved in Mrs. Noss's care. Drones, also called sub-interns, are supposed to be very closely supervised by interns and residents, although often they are not.

It is no surprise to find drones on the medical floors; after all, the fourth year of medical school is spent entirely in a clinical setting. What is surprising is the degree to which they practice medicine—not just in New York—but everywhere in the country. They are not simply observing, they are not simply assisting nurses, interns, and residents, they are playing doctor. Third-year students—called clerks—are participating too, because many medical schools combine the third and fourth years. For instance, at the University of California at Los Angeles, the last two years are almost identical: 94 weeks of clinical clerkships.

So in reality, a drone could be a third- or fourth-year medical student, and patients do not know that persons out of college only two years, who have had only two or three years of medical classes and lectures, could be making clinical decisions on their behalf as part of their student education.

The third and fourth year can differ from medical school to medical school, and the length and number of required clinical clerkships vary. At the University of South Alabama College of Medicine in Mobile, fourth-year students have twelve rotations that last four weeks each, and third-year students have just six rotations. The University of Pennsylvania School of Medicine is designed in three stages. Intense clinical training is stage three, and begins the last half of the second year. The fourth year at the University of Virginia School of Medicine is elective, and students can work in hospitals from Alaska to South America, or can do research, or can take graduate courses. At Tufts University School of Medicine in Massachusetts, the third and fourth year differ only in the type of rotations offered to the students.

According to the *Medical School Admission Requirements Bulletin,* published by the Association of American Medical Colleges, at Cornell University Medical College "the third-year medical student functions as an important member of a clinical team composed of residents and attending staff in the affiliated hospitals of the medical center." During the fourth year, students "begin to function effectively in the physician's role, and sharpen their clinical skills in preparation for residency training." Indeed, Dr. Luise Weinstein testified at the Zion trial that medical students are a strong "part of the team." Dr. Stone told me that "there's no real difference between interns and sub-interns. In many cases it's a matter of a few weeks or months before the sub-intern starts an internship." Dr. Maurice Leonard added, "Sub-interns are basically interns at Cornell," although he said that the team requires two sub-interns to replace one intern.

Very aggressive medical students are called *animals* by the house staff because often they start a procedure on a patient slowly and prudently, and as they gain confidence in their ability, they begin to perform the task like an "animal." Such animals are roaming American hospitals caring for patients.

The Association of American Colleges bulletin on medical school requirements states, "When feasible, students are provided the opportunity to follow their patients before and after discharge from the hospital in ambulatory care settings."

What exactly does *feasible* mean here, and who determines when something is feasible?

Is *feasible* one of those words the medical establishment uses that Dr. Bertrand Bell calls "wiggle" words? "They speak a different language called 'medicalese,'" Dr. Bell said.

The bulletin continues, "Lectures and seminars augment the bedside learning provided during patient visits, so-called 'rounds,' with teaching physicians." But one sub-intern said that such rounds are often more of a performance than anything else.

Although medical students are not supposed to write in the order book, many do, especially in "the wards," or service areas that house mostly nonprivate patients, the same sub-intern added. The system easily allows students to function as doctors, and just as interns and residents are supposed to have their orders co-signed, but don't, this inevitably happens with third- and fourth-year medical students as well. "I never have my notes co-signed," a sub-intern boasted.

A third-year medical student at Yale told me that sub-interns there "take on some responsibility, and come up with a treatment plan." Yale is strict about not letting sub-interns write orders, although community hospitals are sometimes more lenient. As Dr. Rosemary Fisher, director of house-staff training at Yale, admitted, "We have sub-interns acting as interns." Dr. Rita Charon of Columbia agreed. "An intern is not all that different from a fourth-year medical student," she said.

A fourth-year medical student at the University of California, San Francisco, told me that "no one checks up" when sub-interns write prescriptions, although another fourth-year student countered, "It's only simple orders they'll let by," and that for the most part "orders have to be carried out by M.D.'s."

The physician-in-chief of New York Hospital, Dr. R. Gordon Douglas, said that sub-interns "are supervised in a different fashion than interns" so that it is "highly unlikely" that sub-interns could act as interns. But because interns are so loosely supervised, it is not an overstatement to assume that sub-interns are too. Dr. Bertrand Bell said that "sub-interns are a hidden part of the hidden closed order book."

And patients know absolutely nothing about any of this.

The fourth year is meant to be an intense learning year, but as one fourth-year medical student declared, "It's a rarity to have time to learn, because you are so busy with patients." Interns and residents like having the students around, because in addition to everything else, their presence often allows for some needed sleep. The residents especially like *scut-monkeys*, the students who are not only good at the dirty work but like to do it.

The general protocol is to refer to a sub-intern as "Doctor." Alexandra Boer, a fourth-year Yale medical student, said she is presented to a new patient with the introduction "This is Dr. Boer. She is a doctor-in-training." A sub-intern is not introduced as a medical student, she said, because "sometimes patients don't take you seriously." Indeed, another fourth-year student told me that "although it's scary to be called *Doctor*," it's also humiliating to be told, "Oh, you're just a medical student?" by patients. So most sub-interns fudge the issue. A third-year student confessed, "At the beginning of the year I remember thinking, we're now part of the medical community, but we know nothing." Another third-year student asked an instructor, "How do you figure out what your responsibilities are?"

On Sunday, March 25, 1984, Violet Noss's second weekend in New York Hospital, David Pearlman was again the intern on call, and Dr. Gregg Stone was his PGY-2 supervisor. Around four in the afternoon, Violet Noss's grandson, Jay Eber, M.D., a former classmate of Dr. Pearlman's at the Albert Einstein College of Medicine, stopped in to see her. Dr. Eber, then also an intern himself in New York City, walked over to his grandmother's bedside to give her a kiss.

"How are you feeling?" he asked her. She did not answer.

"That's strange," her aide told Dr. Eber, "she was absolutely fine a moment ago."

Jay Eber checked his grandmother. Her skin was warm to his touch, and her color was good, but she was unresponsive. He quickly judged that she had suffered a pulmonary arrest, and he immediately began to perform CPR. He also managed to alert a passing nurse, identified himself as a doctor, and told her to call a code. A few seconds later, several more nurses, along with Dr. Pearlman, rushed to Mrs. Noss's bedside.

Dr. Eber said that he was told to "get the hell out of the room." He was startled, but nevertheless retreated to the doorway so as not to interfere with the emergency measures he believed were about to be administered to his grandmother. He watched a team of medical personnel swarm around her bed. But something was wrong. Something was very wrong. No one was continuing the CPR he had begun. No one was checking his grandmother's pulse. No one was even touching her. He then realized no equipment had been brought into the room. None at all. There was no crash cart. No intravenous lines. No electric shock. What was going on? His grandmother's color was still good. She might die if they didn't get to work right away. She could be saved only if they'd start code procedures immediately. But there was silence. A deep and ugly silence.

Was it possible that the medical team was *C.T.D.*? Was the team simply *circling the drain*, watching for death to arrive in an old lady who had *the dwindles*, that is, was *fading away*?

A moment later, Dr. Eber was told by two nurses that the code on his grandmother had been "called off." He was flabbergasted. He told Dr. Pearlman to take another look and he'd see that his grandmother was capable of being resuscitated. Dr. Eber begged Dr. Pearlman—four times—to save his grandmother's life before it was too late; she was drowning from fluid in her lungs. Later it would be determined that her sodium was low, which had compromised her kidneys' ability to regulate fluids, and that was the only thing wrong. Finally, Dr. Pearlman told Dr. Eber that he was under "orders" not to give the patient emergency care because she had DNR status, a decision that had been made "earlier in the week."

But the family knew nothing about any such decision.

Neither did her attending doctor or backup attending doctors.

Who had made a decision to end the life of Violet Noss, an elderly woman who had not been in critical condition?

"The decision had been conveyed to me by Dr. Stone," Dr. David Pearlman first explained, adding that he learned of it on rounds the first morning he met Mrs. Noss, on Friday, March 16. Dr. Pearlman later told Dr. Joseph Ruggiero, the chief resident, that he was told Mrs. Noss was DNR by the sub-intern, and not by Dr. Stone. Incredibly, fourth-year medical student William Mayo-Smith became "responsible," to use the chief resident's word, for Violet Noss's care after Dr. David Pearlman "signed out," something interns don't ordinarily do when they are on call. Yet this seems to be what happened, and as a result New York Hospital thereby authorized a medical student to be Violet Noss's primary physician. "Theoretically, an intern could sign out to a sub-intern," Dr. Maurice Leonard later told me.

"The fact that a sub-intern was involved in this case had nothing to do with the crucial issues," Dr. Stone believed. "The DNR decision was made by the covering physician for the main attending," he argued. "The attending didn't know anything about it because the covering attending didn't tell him." But Dr. Raymond Hochman testified to the New York State Department of Health, which investigated the case, that it was "inconceivable" that the physician covering for him when Mrs. Noss was admitted, Dr. Jerrold Lieberman, would take the liberty of saying don't resuscitate another doctor's patient. However, Dr. Stone would insist that "the determination for code status was made by Dr. Lieberman, and passed on by me to the sub-intern, appropriately, and then passed on appropriately by the sub-intern to the intern, Dr. Pearlman." Dr. Lieberman said he did not issue a DNR order on Violet Noss.

After Dr. Pearlman ordered Jay Eber out of the area, he described how he "closed the curtain and felt for Mrs. Noss's pulse, and looked to see if she had spontaneous respirations." He said that she had neither, so he "shook her to attempt to arouse her, and after finding her unarousable," not breathing, and without any pulse, he determined she was dead. It was 4:07 P.M. on Sunday, March 25, 1984.

His exact words were that he "found her dead."

He then told the medical team to leave the room because Violet Noss was gone.

Why hadn't the intern tried to save Violet Noss?

He acknowledged that earlier in the day he had been told by the sub-intern (or possibly, he said, by his immediate supervisor, Dr. Stone) that Mrs. Noss had improved, and that the most probable reason for her improvement was that she had been suctioned the night before—that is, fluid had been pumped from her lungs.

But Dr. Ruggiero said that Dr. Pearlman also told him that Violet Noss "had not been doing so well." This, of course, contradicts what the medical student William Mayo-Smith presumably told Dr. Pearlman about her improvement. The tragic result of this "systematic failure of communication," as it was called in court by the Noss family lawyers, caused a patient who had shown improvement in the minds of at least three doctors to be left to die, to not be resuscitated, to be "floor-coded"—a phrase used by the hospital as a euphemism for DNR.

The words DNR had never appeared in her chart.

All that appeared was a red circle drawn around her name ("the circle of death," the lawyers charged) in the interns' sign-out sheets.

"It was just that for convenience, code statuses were kept on a piece of paper," Dr. Stone explained. "They were transferred from doctor to doctor. It was very convenient to carry this piece of paper in your pocket." These informal notes are not the same as the order book. In the case of Violet Noss, these sign-out sheets were destroyed by New York Hospital; the family's lawyers accused the hospital of having done this intentionally, which the hospital denied.

At the time of Mrs. Noss's death, New York Hospital had no definition of "floor code," and astonishingly, according to the family's lawyers, there was a procedure at New York Hospital that actually prevented anyone outside from finding out that a floor code or DNR order had been issued with respect to a patient. "That information," the family lawyers said, "was hidden, was secreted in pieces of paper passed for convenience from resident to resident"—the sign-out sheets.

"There was no intention to ever keep it secret," Dr. Stone said. "It wasn't secret. It's just the way it was done."

There was a policy, in fact, of not writing *DNR* on a chart. There was no paper trail.

It was also hospital policy, according to the complaint filed by Noss family lawyers against New York Hospital, and Drs. Hochman and Lieberman, as third-party defendants, "to systematically deny emergency treatment to certain selected patients, without their consent or the consent of their family members." The lawyers claimed that they had information that this policy "was motivated by the desire to maximize . . . profits by eliminating at the earliest possible moment low-paying, long-term patients, particularly the elderly, which the hospital denied. Margaret Eber, the daughter of Violet Noss and the mother of Dr. Jay Eber, who accepted a settlement before the case went to trial, said, "It's a terrible injustice what happens to an elderly patient."

The New York State Department of Health investigation of the case was never made public.

Dr. Stone said, "This whole case was a non-issue." But, he conceded, "they changed the convention to make it a little more solid so mistakes couldn't be made."

Dr. Stone also said that after the Violet Noss case became a matter of contention, but before code statuses were changed and put "on a blackboard or a master system somewhere," Dr. Douglas, New York Hospital's physician-in-chief, called him into his office to discuss the case. Dr. Douglas testified that no notes were kept of the hospital's own investigation of the death of Violet Noss. "I remember one quote of Dr. Douglas's in particular," Dr. Stone said of their meeting, " 'Welcome to the world of adult nastiness.' "

RESIDENT SLANG IS full of cruel terms for the elderly. A *gomer* is a frail and aged patient, and the word is an acronym for "Get Out Of My Emergency Room." A female gomer is often ridiculed with *gomere*, pronounced "gomare." An *"L.O.L. in N.A.D."* is not an exotic disease, but a "little old lady in no acute distress."

New York Hospital had agreed that Dr. Lieberman told Dr. Stone that Mrs. Noss was to be floor-coded, even though both Dr. Lieberman and Dr. Hochman said this was an out-and-out lie. They never, ever, had a conversation with the house staff that Violet Noss should not, in an emergency, be resuscitated. Indeed, on the morning of Vi-

olet Noss's death, Dr. John Brown, who had covered for
Dr. Hochman over the second weekend, had examined
Mrs. Noss and concluded that she was continuing to improve. Dr. Brown said that in 1984, New York Hospital had
no written or oral policy regarding the assignment of DNR
status. On the other hand, Dr. Douglas, the hospital's physician-in-chief, said that the DNR system was so "inflexible" that a floor code order "could not be rescinded by a
house physician on duty even in the face of a plea for help
from a present and responsible family member." Dr. Jay
Eber was forbidden to save his grandmother.

In fact, not only was the DNR system inflexible, but it
was ill-defined. According to Dr. Douglas it meant "simple
measures may be done, such as suctioning, external stimu-
lation, and perhaps a couple of attempts at mouth-to-
mouth." Dr. Ruggiero maintained that a floor code "basically meant that a patient would receive full supportive
measures and full medical treatment on the medical floor,
but that this would not include chest massage or artificial
ventilation or transfer to an intensive care unit. But full
measures short of that would be pursued." The patient
could receive antibiotics, fluids, suctioning, blood transfu-
sions, but not mouth-to-mouth resuscitation, which was
considered "artificial."

The New York State Department of Health later developed evidence that the resident, Gregg Stone, and the
fourth-year medical student, William Mayo-Smith, maintained Violet Noss on DNR status "purely on their own
feeling." Dr. Raymond Hochman, Violet Noss's private
physician, agreed with the state department of health, and
did not see any other way the trainees could have come by
that decision. "It's totally not true," Dr. Stone said. Neither he nor William Mayo-Smith received any disciplinary
action. Still the family's lawyer commented, "New York

Hospital was a headless hospital. The head didn't know what the hands were doing. That is no way to run a major hospital."

It was a hospital in which medical students, not yet doctors, seemed to do pretty much as they pleased.

In his book *Becoming a Doctor*, Melvin Konner, M.D., describes "a medical student's code." The code, he says, means that the decision of whether or not to restore the life of an elderly patient is a matter only between the student "and God." Although no legal determination could be made where Violet Noss's DNR status originated, all the available evidence appeared to indicate it was just such a concealed code.

Unquestionably it is difficult to achieve a balance between enough supervision and the independence necessary for a medical student's, intern's, or resident's growth in professionalism. This is especially true during a time when medicine is in transition because of so many uncertainties, ranging from patients' choices of doctors to state-of-the-art therapies to health-insurance decisions to changing patient populations.

I came to understand that no matter how many outside uncertainties there were, and there were many, the key to the problem of balance, most especially with interns and residents, lay within the closed order book.

The closed order book—and all it represented—had to be confronted by doctors and their patients.

"No law says an attending can't write orders, but everything gets funneled through the house staff," said Dr. Joseph Hayes, vice chairman of medicine in charge of the residency program at New York Hospital–Cornell Medical Center, in my only official interview with a doctor at the medical center.

Many doctors downplayed the realities of the closed-order-book system, which Dr. Bertrand Bell has called "one of the most pernicious and telling pieces of evidence of the sickness in the graduate-medical-education system." Yes, residents wrote orders, but because of the required note or countersignature by a chief resident or attending within twenty-four hours, there weren't many difficulties. Yes, residents wrote orders, but they "had to run them by" the chief resident or attending first, a doctor said. But one resident told me, repeating what so many others said, "You never check with the attending, you don't have to," thus confirming how ineffectual certain edicts are.

A lot can happen within twenty-four hours. Libby Zion died within twenty-four hours. Countless other patients have become sicker within twenty-four hours, and many others have died. Attending doctors often excuse residents who did not "run orders by" them by rationalizing that it was an admirable measure of their initiative, or that it was too late for them to be disturbed, or even that the patient would have died anyway.

Dr. Fredric Burg of the University of Pennsylvania School of Medicine told me that the practice of un-supervised order writing—he has never heard of the term *closed order book*—"has been discussed in medical circles as an issue and as a problem." He said that the issue is "What is the level of supervision by attendings?"

Dr. Rosemary Fisher of Yale told me, "When supervision is not adequate, and when the people involved have ego problems," the care of the patient is bound to be threatened. Errors will inevitably ensue.

Many doctors agreed with what Dr. Burg believes, that the number of mistakes that result from interns and residents writing orders is minimal, and that "attendings are just as likely to make mistakes." Dr. Burg commented that "the errors are usually in the area of 'I might have approached this in another way.' "

Nevertheless, a study made in Texas the year before Libby Zion died showed that PGY-1s made clinical errors 15.6 percent of the time, and PGY-2s and up 13.1 percent of the time. The incidence of errors in diagnosis alone was 40 percent "or more." These are "the facts of life in medical training to which many if not most patients admitted to medical school–affiliated hospitals must submit," caution the authors of *Medicine on Trial*.

Another study of 22,112 patients admitted by on-call interns in a teaching hospital in Minnesota from 1980 to 1987 found "that patients admitted during the night were more likely to die in the hospital than were patients admitted during the day." The report suggested that "expert supervision might be less available to interns during the night, a concern raised in the Libby Zion case." Residents are more overworked and tired at night, especially those in internal-medicine programs. Also, certain services are usually not available at night, and there are often fewer nurses around.

Dr. Bertrand Bell said that when he was in training, doctors lived in the neighborhood, and supervision was not as much of a problem. "Responsibility for the patient has disappeared," he lamented. "It is partly because of specialization, and partly because doctors have moved away from the cities."

Over and over I would be told that today most attendings leave the hospital by five in the afternoon and don't return until the morning, and that they rarely appear on weekends. The only medical service where supervision seemed to be extremely strict was surgery. Dr. R. Gordon Douglas said that at New York Hospital, the surgical residents either go along with the chief's orders, "or you don't go to the operating room." A very simple formula.

Dr. Stephen R. Smith, associate dean for education at the division of biology and medicine of Brown University, where Dr. Martin Carr attended medical school, said, "The Libby Zion situation was bound to happen given the working conditions under which residents function." These conditions are properly a major concern to everyone in the health-care industry, but have overshadowed the more central question of supervision.

Dr. Joseph Hayes, vice-chairman of medicine in charge of resident training at New York Hospital, said that he prefers to call supervision "education, although there is an element of supervision. It's graduate education, and it gradually gets better." Later, Dr. Weinstein countered that "supervision is not synonymous with teaching." Ironically, a resident told me that New York Hospital–Cornell Medical Center, although "prestigious," is not considered a great residency because there are too many private patients and too many interfering attending doctors. "It harms education because the hospital serves private patients," the resident said.

Although Dr. Bertrand Bell recognizes that "residency programs, as graduate education, should be run by educators," he pointed out that supervision by attending doctors is the only way to avoid "resident-run hospitals." However, Dr. Homer Boushey, of the University of California, San Francisco School of Medicine, said, "Our third-year residents are sharper than the overwhelming number of doctors elsewhere," and many other doctors share his sentiments. But does "sharper" substitute for experience?

Dr. Daniel D. Federman, dean for medical education at Harvard Medical School, told me that "if the resident checked every order with the attending, it would slow down independence."

But what is wrong with slowing down independence? Would lack of independence change the way an intern or resident looked at a particular case? Would it critically affect his or her decision-making process? Is there something inherently undermining about being under close supervision?

There should be "a balanced level of supervision," Dr. Federman said. "Ultimately, doctors are going to function alone: when you go into a doctor's office you don't expect to find a group, and would be unsettled if you did," he said. "The independence to which I refer is the readiness of the physician to be in that capacity and yet still to know when he or she needs help, i.e., consultations. The function of the faculty during that time is to provide what I call 'alert hovering,' not unlike what a mother bird does when the offspring are learning to fly. The function of each program is to make progressive and continually refined judgments about which trainees are ready, on the basis of demonstrated performance, to move closer to independence."

Alert hovering.

Although that would be the answer that came closest to addressing a solution to the problem of the closed order book and its cultivation of inadequate supervision, perhaps the issue should be how teaching hospitals can eliminate the closed order book altogether, and how graduate medical education would then be best pursued without it.

And what about patients?

The patients, who know next to nothing about the rank or experience of the residents caring for them, or even what a resident really is, naturally don't have the slightest inkling that there is a closed order book, or a supervision problem. Patients must be educated, too, so that they can participate in the solution to a problem that is every patient's nightmare, and literally a matter of life and death.

What if a patient refused to be cared for by a resident?

One doctor told me that such a patient would be called "difficult," and would be told, "If you want to come to this hospital, that's the way the education system works. If you don't want the closed order book, you'd have to go to some small community hospital." Yet as more and more small community hospitals get swallowed up by large teaching medical centers to ease their economic burdens, the closed order book could become even more entrenched everywhere, and even more camouflaged and hidden.

"There are certain things by tradition which are done in medicine in house-staff training programs throughout the country," Dr. Raymond Sherman said.

Tradition. As T. S. Eliot wrote, "Tradition by itself is not enough."

PART 3

9

THE FIRST REPORTED malpractice case in America was filed in 1794, when a man sued his wife's doctor for causing her death during an operation. A jury awarded the man damages; the amount is not known. Other lawsuits soon followed, and the first malpractice "crisis"—a period when litigation flooded the courts—came about in the mid–nineteenth century. This crisis passed after the Civil War ended in 1865, and there were no further ones until the 1920s, when the insurance companies came on board and offered malpractice insurance to doctors. From that time on, malpractice crises have been cyclical. Claims were infrequent into the 1950s, and began to be filed with more frequency in the mid-sixties. John Giunther, author of *The Malpractitioners*, suggests that the cycles have to do with "social phenomena," and that lawsuits are "a by-product of medical progress." He argues that because doctors cannot control social phenomena, and can only "interact" with these forces, improving the "performance" of doctors would have practically no effect on malpractice claims.

Angela Holder, a lawyer and a member of the Yale University School of Medicine's faculty, who directs the physicians'-responsibility course, told me that her job in teaching students about malpractice "is to keep them from getting scared to death." Although it is "no longer open season," and there are now fewer cases, medical students are still worried. There are financial concerns, too. Some doctors pay more than a hundred thousand dollars annually for malpractice insurance, and the question of who should end up paying those costs—the doctors or the patients—continues. In the mid-eighties, the Harvard Study Group brought up the idea of no-fault insurance, an idea that is still ahead of its time. In 1993, Hillary Rodham Clinton promised a "serious proposal to curb malpractice problems," a blueprint that could include the arbitration of claims and caps on awards for damages.

The Harvard Medical Practice Study of 1987, still the most comprehensive study on malpractice, determined that between 2,967 and 3,888 malpractice claims were filed in New York State in 1984, yet the study estimated that eight times as many patients endured an injury from negligence as filed a malpractice claim. The Eastern Region Alliance of American Insurers reported that in 1985, one doctor in four was sued, and that 60 percent of these suits were found to lack merit. In 1977 it was one doctor in nine, and in 1975 it was one doctor in fifteen.

According to *Consumer Reports*, the rate of malpractice claims declined after 1985. The most probable reason is that many doctors began practicing defensive medicine, what most patients still call overtesting. At any rate, as doctors and patients face the twenty-first century, malpractice claims remain in a downswing, although some people fear there's a lot of malpractice happening that no one is dealing with. Americans suffer more injuries in hospitals than they do when working, according to the Harvard Medical Practice Study.

"Absolute perfection is not possible in medicine," a doctor told me. "Physicians who say they have not made a mistake are not telling the truth."

Medical students may know this, but they are still frightened.

Professional negligence is the underpinning of all malpractice lawsuits. "Even the most qualified doctors are frequently sued," an internist at New York Hospital said. In fact, credentials have never mattered. All that matters in a malpractice suit are four things that patients must prove about their doctors: first, that they owed the patient a lawful obligation, that is, that a doctor-patient relationship really existed; second, that the doctor (or hospital, in some cases) did not follow accepted professional standards; third, that the doctor (or hospital) caused the injury or death; and fourth, that the patient experienced harm as a result of what the doctor or hospital did.

A doctor at New York Hospital said that the medical profession works hard to rid itself of "incompetent practitioners." A year after Libby Zion's death, the *New England Journal of Medicine* estimated that anywhere from 20,000 to 75,000 of the 502,000 physicians in America were incompetent. This extraordinarily variable estimate was determined by the Federation of State Medical Boards, an association made up of representatives from the individual state boards that issue licenses and dispense discipline. According to the *Journal*, the statistical variation was caused by differences among the states in reporting procedures, by the percentages of doctors-in-training, and by the number of doctors licensed but not practicing.

How is incompetence measured, and what exactly does it mean to professionals and nonprofessionals, since the word can have such different meanings?

The American Heritage Dictionary offers three definitions: "1. Not qualified in legal terms: a defendant who was incompetent to stand trial. 2. Inadequate for or unsuited to a particular purpose or application. 3. Devoid of those qualities requisite for effective conduct or action."

A patient might say a doctor is incompetent according to the second definition, if, for instance, the doctor doesn't understand, or take seriously, a certain symptom, thus prompting the patient to take the case to a second doctor who treats the symptom appropriately. Is the first doctor an "incompetent practitioner"? Yes, according to the patient, but no, according to the medical profession, which might only answer yes if the third definition were used.

Doctors cannot be held liable for *EJs*—errors of judgment. Doctors cannot be held liable for choosing a treatment option that is not successful; doctors only have an obligation to use their best judgment, and are not liable if the hoped-for result is not achieved when they use their best judgment. An incorrect diagnosis does not necessarily signal negligence.

Malpractice has evolved from its earliest definition that a doctor is liable if a patient is harmed by negligence, or not cured in a reasonable time. Nowadays malpractice arises when the performance of doctors "falls short of the accepted standards of their profession," according to Carolyn Lavecchia, a lawyer and registered nurse and an authority on the subject. She explains in the book *A Doctor's Prescription* that it is important to understand that "standard of care is a duty of reasonable care and does not require the highest possible degree of care—only ordinary and reasonable care under the circumstances." Proof of a breach of the standard of care usually requires expert testimony, and the burden of proof rests with the patient, who must show that against this standard a surgical procedure, for example, was negligent, or anesthesia was administered improperly, or a treatment was inadequate, or a drug was administered incorrectly, or a consultation was not sought, or a birth injury was preventable, or a psychotic episode was not anticipated.

Many patients and consumer groups say that doctors don't report other doctors. Doctors say that they don't want to become policemen.

And as for interns and residents, over and over I was told there was an unwritten code not to point a finger at another resident. "You cover for people if you see something wrong. You don't become a tattletale," a resident told me. "You never rat on another resident." It is the canon everywhere.

BY THE END OF July 1984, four months after Libby Zion's death, the buzz in legal circles was that New York Hospital wasn't worried about a malpractice suit, because her case was "defensible." It was whispered in the corridors of the hospital that "the treatment may have been poor," but it would be argued that Libby "killed herself." It was murmured in medical circles that the hospital planned to exploit the cocaine findings in the autopsy report. They would claim that her high temperature—and death—were caused by the interaction of cocaine with Nardil. The overall strategy, in other words, would be to make Libby the defendant for her life in the fast lane rather than the doctors for what they did or didn't do in New York Hospital the night she died.

The battle lines were drawn.

Sidney Zion's lawyers had already begun arming their

wrongful-death suit with expert witnesses who would attempt to prove why the doctors were guilty of gross negligence. And on July 17, 1985, the formal complaint was finally served on the hospital, Dr. Raymond Sherman, Dr. Maurice Leonard, Dr. Luise Weinstein, and "Dr. John Doe." The Zions could not recall the name of the fourth doctor—Dr. Gregg Stone—who treated their daughter at New York Hospital, and the hospital chose not to release it to them at that time.

Eventually his name was released, and "Sidney E. Zion, as Administrator of the estate of Libby Zion, deceased, Plaintiff, against The New York Hospital, Raymond Sherman, M.D., Maurice Leonard, M.D., Luise Weinstein, M.D., and Gregg Stone, M.D., Defendants, Index No. 15353/85," which would become known as *Zion* v. *New York Hospital*, would drag on for a decade in the Supreme Court of the State of New York, and be presided over by a succession of judges because of the time it took to bring the case to trial.

Meanwhile, Sidney had been pressing friends and colleagues to write letters urging the district attorney to probe his daughter's death, and had gotten friends and colleagues in the media to write about the social need for a grand jury to be convened to hear the case. By August 26, 1985, he was successful in his yearlong attempt to have the Manhattan district attorney's office consider an indictment of the doctors. "We are looking into it," the office of D.A. Robert Morgenthau announced.

"I'm not suggesting the doctors were sadistic in wanting to kill my kid," Sidney said, and he understood that "they didn't mean it," but he charged that if "a reckless driver jumps a light, and kills somebody, he didn't mean it either, but he can get indicted." Why should doctors be immune from prosecution? Sidney wanted to know.

Medicine would never be the same again if a grand jury indicted the doctors. It would be a radical step. As Jerry Nachman wrote in the *New York Post*, "Nothing like that had ever happened in the annals of American law." Doctors had never been "arrested, indicted, prosecuted as simple cold killers." But it was precisely what Sidney Zion wanted, because he was entirely convinced that the doctors had committed a crime. "They are white-coat criminals," he said.

A September 15, 1985, editorial in *The National Law Journal* essentially agreed, saying, "The medical profession is letting doctors get away with murder—too often, in the literal sense."

The pressure was on.

A few months later, *New York Times* columnist Tom Wicker wrote, "Charges of criminal negligence, if forthcoming in the Zion case, might open the way to more useful public scrutiny."

"I don't care about the civil case," Sidney said. "I care about the criminal case. I want the people who did this to be made to answer for it, not some insurance company."

"I put an incredible amount of time in the case," District Attorney Robert Morgenthau said about his decision to convene a grand jury to hear the charges. A grand jury, made up of between sixteen and twenty-three citizens, hears the evidence and sanctions an indictment when it is satisfied a trial is warranted. In writing a report, the grand jury fulfills a secondary, investigative, function. The rules that guide grand juries are not the same as those that guide trial juries. The public is forbidden to attend the proceedings, witnesses can be forced to testify, the defense is not permitted to call witnesses, and the prosecutor is under no obligation to offer both sides of the case.

The grand jury began its work on May 5, 1986, and held

twenty-four sessions over the next six months. Twenty-two
witnesses testified—doctors and nurses put forward by the
hospital, experts retained by the Zions, experts put forward
by the district attorney's office, and Libby's friends, among
others.

IN 1984, ONLY 25 out of New York State's approximately 40,000 doctors had their licenses suspended or revoked. Utah was the state with the most doctors disciplined, but it revoked or suspended the licenses of only 3
percent of them. The year before, in 1983, the District of
Columbia brought no serious disciplinary actions at all
against the 18,000 doctors practicing there. In fact, that
year there were only 563 disciplinary actions against America's more than 389,000 doctors. In general, the charges
against these practitioners involved alcohol, drug or sexual
abuse, and fraud.

"If doctors had the fear, they'd act differently. Doctors
can't and shouldn't police themselves. No other profession
gets away with it," Sidney said.

And he kept on saying it.

Never let anybody dominate your life, he had written to his
children two years earlier. After Libby's death, he would
keep asking himself why he had left the hospital; it had
been the first time he had ever listened to somebody, and
he shouldn't have, he said.

A Harvard Medical Practice Study, which had sampled
and screened the hospital records of 31,429 patients in
fifty-one New York hospitals in 1984, found that 28 percent
sustained an injury as a result of malpractice. In addition,
of the 2.7 million patients hospitalized in New York in
1984, "medical injury contributed at least in part to the
deaths of more than 13,000."

"My goal is to break the madness going on," Sidney said. "I knew I had to plot a military crusade."

And he did. He raged and wept and talked. "With Zion's media connections, he maintained spin control over much of the coverage of the case," *M.D.* magazine would later note.

He went once again on *The Barry Gray Show,* as he had done when he wanted to broadcast who leaked the Pentagon Papers to *The New York Times.* He told Barry Gray and his audience that New York Hospital had "murdered" Libby. He told the *San Francisco Examiner* that the hospital had given his daughter "killer drugs." He told the American Humanities Association that Libby had been "executed." Over and over he referred to Libby's murderers and executioners. His agony and furor brought audiences to tears, and often indignation. On *Face the Nation,* he told Leslie Stahl that the doctors' white coats "should not immunize them from prosecution." He told a Rutgers University–PBS symposium on medical care that doctors "should be prosecuted for inhuman mistakes," but, no, not for "human mistakes." He could accept human mistakes. But what had happened to his daughter was inhuman. She had been ignored, abandoned, and left to die "in a killing field."

New York Hospital tried to fight back.

They claimed that Sidney had asked his good friend, Andrew Stein, then president of the New York City Council, to pressure the medical examiner's office to keep cocaine out of Libby's final toxicological report. Sidney countered that he had only wanted Andy Stein to find out "if we can goose it up a little and not wait for a long bureaucratic process," and that his friend "didn't ask them any specifics" about the final report.

Sidney believed New York Hospital was "stonewalling"

him, and he was frustrated because he couldn't get information about Libby "right away." He said, "It was the
worst kind of situation to be in, especially when I knew
that I am supposed to have influence and be somebody in
this town." He felt as if he were being "jerked around,"
and added, "Imagine what happens to the average guy."
He insisted that he had asked Andrew Stein to intervene
only because he wanted to know what happened to Libby.
"You hear about these things—infections—raging through
bodies and nothing can be done," Sidney said. He could
not accept Dr. Sherman's "I don't know" when he had
asked him what Libby died from. The phrase echoed in his
head. It was unacceptable.

ALTHOUGH DR. JOSEPH Ruggiero took notes, there
is no written report of the inquiry he undertook at New
York Hospital, because as the physician-in-chief, Dr.
Douglas, stated, "It was not our policy at that time to do
so." *Our* refers to New York Hospital's department of medicine. When asked in a pretrial deposition if the department had a policy that specifically said such reports could
not be put into writing, Dr. Douglas answered, "I think of
it as the other way around. We didn't have a policy that said
it should be in writing." Dr. Ruggiero later said that he
didn't know what happened to his notes, that is, whether
or not they were thrown out.

Dr. Douglas said that he asked Dr. Ruggiero to under-
take the hospital's official quality-assurance review of
Libby's death. A quality-assurance review is, Dr. Douglas
said, "an ongoing process that monitors and evaluates the
quality of medical care." However, Dr. Ruggiero had already begun the investigation as part of his standard duties
when Dr. Douglas made his request, and so Dr. Ruggiero's
regular morning report and the quality-assurance review

called for by the physician-in-chief merged into the same account. This is not an unimportant detail, because New York Hospital later correctly stated that quality-assurance reviews could not be used in court because of the education law of the State of New York that guarantees confidentiality to doctors-in-training in exchange for a complete no-holds-barred evaluation. Sidney's lawyers at the time argued that because the review was part of the standard morning report it was subject to disclosure. Both sides have validity, because, as Dr. David Thompson, the chief executive officer of New York Hospital, said, there was no formal quality-assurance committee in March 1984. One would be formed later. There were five other committees that provided quality-assurance functions.

Sidney's lawyers would later charge that New York Hospital called "everything that occurred there quality assurance," because it wouldn't allow its doctors to be questioned about the investigation. "There was no attempt to cover anything up," Dr. Sherman insisted.

But the most important element in the dispute would almost be lost, the fact that there was never a written record of New York Hospital's internal review of the circumstances surrounding Libby Zion's death.

ALTHOUGH ANGELA HOLDER, the lawyer who teaches physician responsibility at Yale's medical school, told me that "in a teaching hospital, mistakes are not silenced, they're discussed," there was no *M & M* (Morbidity and Mortality) held at New York Hospital on Libby's death. The term *M & M* is resident slang for the weekly conference each medical department in teaching hospitals nationwide conducts for recent deaths, unusual cases, or mistakes. Dr. Ruggiero explained that at New York Hospital the *M & M* is "a teaching conference" concerning pa-

tients "who died in the hospital" and had autopsies there.
He said that perhaps because Libby's autopsy was performed not by the hospital, but by the medical examiner's
office, there was no official *M & M* held on her case.

Indeed, Dr. Sherman said, "I can't recall ever having an
M & M when the autopsy was not done at the hospital
because the nature of the *M & M* is your own pathologists
do the exam and present their findings."

At the *M & M* conference held during the week of
March 12, 1984, on another case, Libby's death was, however, a subject of much discussion by some senior doctors,
who reproached Dr. Stone and Dr. Weinstein for her death,
although Dr. Sherman later claimed there were "absolutely
no reprimands." In time, Dr. Douglas would instruct Dr.
Stone and Dr. Weinstein that they should not have used
Demerol in Libby's instance. Dr. Sherman communicated
a similar opinion to Dr. Weinstein. She replied, "I know."

IN EARLY SEPTEMBER 1984, New York Hospital
asked the medical examiner for a sample of Libby's lung
tissue in order to find out whether she could have had
acute viral influenza. Dr. John T. Ellis, pathologist-in-chief
of the hospital, told Dr. Elliot Gross, the chief medical
examiner, that tests were newly available to screen for influenza A and B, and he said the results would be sent to
the medical examiner's office, along with duplicate slides
for use in the autopsy report, which still had not been
finalized. But because of the pending litigation, Sidney
would not give his approval for the release of the required
tissue, and so a test was never done—by either side, nor by
the medical examiner's office.

Over that summer, Sidney had learned about the injection of Demerol, and that it was contraindicated to Nardil.
He felt that he had found the smoking gun he was looking

for and he didn't need any other primary reason for Libby's death, even though no evidence of Demerol was found in her body. As far as he was concerned, he had caught New York Hospital red-handed with what he regarded as the murder weapon.

But he knew he had to do something about the cocaine findings, about which it was said he was deeply ashamed. He insisted there was no cocaine; New York Hospital had fabricated it, he claimed. Later, Ralph Enders testified that Elsa called him to ask that he tell the grand jury that Libby "had never used cocaine." He refused.

"Lies were spread about my kid," Sidney condemned. "They said she was a junkie." He said that the hospital was blaming the victim. "It's an outrage," he cried. He said that the evidence of cocaine was a laboratory error. Interferences in the blood culture medium could have caused a false positive, which many experts would concede. A positive reading for cocaine could be "cross reactivity" with other drugs like Lidocaine, used in cardiac resuscitation, or Novocain, the anesthetic used by dentists. These had structures and activities like cocaine, although neither contained the metabolite benzoylecgonine, only found in cocaine.

But in any case, Lidocaine was never used on Libby during her code, and the Novocain she had received from the dentist for her extraction on March 1 would not have been in her system seventy-two or ninety-six hours later. The positive radioimmunoassay, or RIA, finding of cocaine could also have resulted from an elevated level of the brain substance serotonin, Sidney's lawyer at the time said. Nardil, alone or combined with other drugs, raises the serotonin level, and an expert witness later suggested that Libby went into serotonin syndrome, a constellation of symptoms including muscle movements, confusion, and high fever, which contributed to her death.

New York Hospital cried foul on the August 27, 1984, retesting initiated by Sidney's lawyers and supervised by Dr. Leslie Lukash and Dr. Thomas Manning that achieved a negative cocaine finding. The hospital said that the test was "totally meaningless," and had been done under "questionable circumstances." In fact, the hospital's lawyers charged that everything involved in Libby's post-mortem reports was "negotiated," and that Dr. Pearl and Dr. Gross, both of the medical examiner's office, "agreed on the language to be used" because of pressure from Sidney Zion.

Nevertheless, since the final toxicological report on Libby included both the positive and the negative findings, in the eyes of many people that amounted to the canceling out of cocaine. It wouldn't matter that both the negative and positive results were determined by the same RIA technique. It wouldn't even matter that a grand jury report would quote an unnamed toxicologist from the medical examiner's office as having said that the "most probable explanation" for the negative reading was that cocaine's metabolite, benzoylecgonine, "an inherently unstable substance, had been broken down over time by chemicals in the culture medium used to dilute the blood." Sidney, who would now no longer dispute whether the blood sample was really his daughter's or question the culture medium present—that is, until 1995, when the subject came up again—said that Dr. Sherman agreed with him that one positive test and one negative test "doesn't mean anything." Dr. Sherman said at the time that he didn't know if cocaine "played a role" in Libby's death, but that he believed that her high temperature caused her cardio-respiratory arrest.

In a letter that Dr. Lukash wrote to Sidney's lawyers, he explained that he and Dr. Manning had had a little talk with Dr. Milton Bastos, the head of the toxicology lab at the Manhattan medical examiner's office. He said they had "brought to Dr. Bastos's attention that the presence of cocaine by RIA should not be reported unless it is confirmed . . ." Not be reported at all? Even the United States Armed Forces, which require that RIA tests be confirmed by gas chromatography—which can now catch benzoylecgonine as well as pure cocaine—report unconfirmed positive cocaine results by RIA as "cocaine not confirmed."

Over time, the positive RIA cocaine finding in Libby's blood would be deemed negative by various forensic experts because there was less than a microgram present in the sample tested. Although they might be following the letter of the law, however, this was not necessarily an admission that cocaine was absent from her blood. Even the reported negative urine and bile findings would not mean the absence of cocaine. Experts would later explain that salicylates could have masked the cocaine in Libby's urine, and that the cut-off point for determining a negative or positive reading was "arbitrary," and often simply an "administrative" decision.

New York Hospital and Sidney also clashed over the nasal swab that had detected "a small amount" of cocaine. Libby's autopsy records did not contain a clear-cut chain of custody for this swab; the autopsy work-sheet form that noted what samples were being tested included a space for *nasal swab* to be checked off, but it wasn't. The only things marked were blood, bile, urine, gastric contents, brain, liver, and lungs. (The work sheet also marked that cremation of Libby's body was authorized by the medical examiner's office. It was not, and Libby had been buried, not cremated.) However, the actual handwritten work sheet mentions "swabs trace cocaine," and the typed toxicological report dated May 6, 1984, lists under "Samples Collected at the Autopsy": "Swabs: trace of cocaine detected by (RIA)—not enough material for confirmation by (TLC)," or thin-layer chromatography, actually a less sensitive test than RIA.

At first, New York Hospital said that the swabs "disappeared" sometime in 1985. In a pretrial deposition, Dr. Manning testified that he was told by Dr. Bastos that "they discard the swab after it's tested." Sidney claimed that someone in the medical examiner's office had suggested that there had never been any swabs to begin with, even though years later the associate chief medical examiner, Dr. Jon Pearl, would sign an affidavit saying that a nasal swab sample had been taken from Libby's body.

When I later asked Sidney how he thought cocaine got into Libby's nose and blood, the two positives mentioned in the report, he answered, "I don't know. It's a mystery how it got there. It wasn't even a false positive—there wasn't any cocaine."

"Why would the medical examiner make it up?" I asked.

"Somebody can do a lot of things," he told me. "Who asked the medical examiner to do the tests?"

"I'm sure it's routine," I said.

"Well, maybe," he replied, adding, "Whoever wrote *cocaine* on the report was very careless. The medical examiner left it on. He should have crossed it out."

As Sidney continued his campaign against the doctors, New York Hospital said that it would defend itself in court—not in the press or on television. "They are mad as hell because I am getting publicity," Sidney countered. He accused the hospital of being paranoid. He said that the hospital believed that somebody on his side "moved" Libby's blood. He said that the hospital believed there had been "tampering" with the evidence. Indeed, some of Libby's blood, urine, and tissue samples were lost in 1985, and this loss would not be discovered for four years. "This is shocking to me," Sidney told me.

ONE YEAR AFTER Libby's death, Sidney began to spin out of control. He told *The Barry Gray Show* that Libby seemed to be getting a little better when he and his wife left the hospital for the night; later, he told the New York State Board for Professional Medical Conduct that Libby looked "a little worse" when he and his wife left her. During a television appearance in Cupertino, California, he told the audience that the Demerol given to Libby was not only contraindicated with the Nardil she was taking, but was also contraindicated with the pneumonia "they didn't pick up."

Most of the news stories, articles, television and radio shows, and forums about Libby's death listed her symptoms when she entered the hospital as "earache and fever." There was rarely any mention of any of the other symptoms. Every now and then in his many media appearances, Sidney referred to her dilating eyes or her jumpiness, but the main focus, increasingly, as the years went by, became her earache, her fever. It wasn't that he or anyone else was withholding information, it was more that Sidney's version of the truth had naturally become everyone else's. Most people had, of course, no way of knowing about other symptoms. The larger issues involved in Libby's death took on a life of their own, and over time the actual facts of the case became less and less important. Most people assumed that any malpractice aspects of the case had been resolved years ago or simply forgot that such a facet ever existed.

"If I didn't make a fuss, no one would do anything at all," Sidney Zion said. "I want to make it public how totally dangerous it is to go to the hospital."

And he made a fuss, a fuss that would begin to transform the training of doctors.

But a relative said worriedly, "I don't see how what he's doing can be for Libby. She's dead. It seems to be a question of trading attacks in the newspaper. Sidney wants to prove he's right. He's entirely convinced that he's right. It's as if he has to carry out some vendetta."

10

ELSA ZION BEGAN working as a special assistant to Andrew Stein two years after Libby's death. In time, Sidney suggested to the city council president that he hold public hearings on the subjects that Sidney was raising around the country. On January 21, 1986, Andrew Stein chaired the first of three public forums. He introduced the topic, "Medical Malpractice," by reminding the audience that although he had the "highest regard" for the medical profession, and believed that most doctors are "extremely caring and competent," nevertheless he was troubled by a "conservative" estimate that at that time there were twenty thousand incompetent doctors in the United States. He said that he wanted to give malpractice victims a chance to be heard.

It was the right time for such an airing. Medicine had grown to mammoth proportions, especially since the nineteen seventies. There were new technologies and new specialties and new diseases and new cures that were over-whelming the profession, and would continue to do.

But the training of doctors had not fundamentally changed for decades. It was inevitable that there would be problems, problems in accountability as well as in educa-tion. And if the problems weren't addressed, they'd grow. The Libby Zion case was "the symbol of problems that had existed in any hospital," Dr. Robert Gifford, associate dean for education and student affairs at Yale University School of Medicine, told me. Dr. Rita Charon of Columbia University's College of Physicians and Surgeons said, "The Libby Zion case helped us come to conclusions and actions. There's a price we have been paying for brutal training. Doctors are mortals."

Andrew Stein warned that according to Ralph Nader's Health Research Group, there were approximately two hundred thousand Americans who received injuries or died as a result of negligence each year. (Nearly a decade later, the number of Americans who died annually as a result of malpractice was put at around eighty thousand by a Har-vard University study, and the total who died annually as a result of "medical accidents" was a hundred and fifty thou-sand.)

Stein called eleven witnesses to his hearing, including Arnold Relman, M.D., then the editor of the *New England Journal of Medicine*, who spoke of the inadequacy of the licensing procedure and the need for periodic reexamina-tion of doctors. New York mayor Rudolph Giuliani, then the United States attorney for the Southern District of New York, was also a witness, and said that "the medical profession has gotten more immunity than is helpful to it," and that "the system for removing licenses is a disaster." Andrew Stein cited New York as having "one of the poorest records for medical discipline."

Sidney Zion also appeared at this first hearing. "I sent them a daughter with a fever," he said. "They sent back a girl in a box." Columnist Nat Hentoff later wrote in *The Village Voice* that "there would have been no hearing by Andrew Stein had it not been for Sidney Zion . . . The story cannot be told too often because each time it awakens legislators, journalists, and everyone else . . ."

Stein had invited Dr. David Thompson, the chief executive officer of New York Hospital, to testify at the hearing, but he didn't appear. A week earlier, on January 15, Stein received a letter from Frank Bensel, a lawyer for the hospital, saying it would be "inappropriate" for Dr. Thompson to appear. Bensel wrote that "while everyone can readily understand the grief of a parent at the loss of a child, Mr. Zion has chosen to manifest his grief by reckless and malicious attacks on the physicians who took care of his daughter." He ended by writing, "It is unfortunate that Mr. Zion with his unique access to public forums is in a position to gain such widespread publicity for his uninformed invective, and we can only convey our concern that your hearing might simply become another forum for that purpose."

On March 3, 1986, Andrew Stein chaired another hearing; this time the topic was "How Safe Are Our Hospitals?" No one from New York Hospital appeared. Among the nine witnesses was John Cardinal O'Connor, who spoke of "grave moral issues" as he invoked the anniversary of Libby's death "two years ago tomorrow."

No teaching hospital across the country is immune from house-staff mishaps, and generally such information is kept under wraps. But sometimes the information gets out, through confidential sources, or even occasionally through official channels.

At Stein's hearing on the safety of hospitals, problems that occurred in New York City at Columbia Presbyterian

Medical Center and Harlem Hospital Center were aired. In 1984, two very ill children were sent home from the pediatric emergency room at Columbia Presbyterian after being treated by an intern and a resident who did not consult supervising physicians. One of the children, a six-year-old boy, was then referred to Harlem Hospital Center for follow-up care; he died en route from undiagnosed meningitis. The other child reentered Columbia Presbyterian and died of acute gastroenteritis. Columbia Presbyterian Medical Center now has full-time emergency-room attending doctors.

It was also revealed at Stein's hearing that at an unnamed voluntary hospital an elderly patient became infested with maggots in the mouth and nostril area "due to inadequate medical and nursing care," and that at another unnamed voluntary hospital a patient died after receiving a wrong IV injection from an intern. A witness at the hearing, Dr. David Sparks, the deputy director for health care standards for the New York State Department of Health, explained that "the syringe used by the intern was unmarked and unlabeled. He proceeded to give the injection without inquiring or verifying the contents or dosage."

Other publicized incidents had taken place at Bellevue Hospital Center, where a patient with a broken nose was given "inappropriate" anesthesia and ended up brain-dead, and another patient was given ten times the normal dose of a heart medication, and died; at St. Luke's–Roosevelt Hospital Center, where a patient with a torn tendon died from an "anesthesia mishap"—the tube had been placed in his esophagus instead of in his trachea; at Lenox Hill Hospital, where a resident gave an oral medicine intravenously, causing the patient's death; and at Beth Israel Medical Center, where a patient died after a resident punctured his arteries in two separate places while attempting to insert a catheter in a vein. Such incidents continue to occur. In August 1991, at Kings County Hospital, Yankel Rosenbaum, a Hasidic scholar attacked during racial violence in the Crown Heights section of Brooklyn, died because an emergency-room PGY-2 resident did not notice that he had a fatal stab wound in his back.

At no time during Andrew Stein's hearings—or any others—were the issues framed with a proper name. There was talk of medical incompetence, negligence, sleep deprivation, long working hours, and poor supervision of the house staff, but the words *closed order book* were never spoken. They weren't spoken because those three words—three words that encourage residents to run hospitals—are the words that hide behind all the other words, and have ever since Sidney Zion began to break the silence on the other topics.

"The big sin is if an attending writes orders," a doctor told me.

But the big sin is actually when unpracticed interns and residents write orders, a protocol that discourages them from asking for help on everything else related to their patients' care and well-being.

THE STEIN HEARINGS contributed to public awareness of essential matters that needed to be aired, and also created a public opportunity for the city council president. A month after his first hearing, he wrote an op-ed piece for *The New York Times* accusing doctors of "killing and maiming thousands of patients every year." At a meeting later in the year, he was privy to a conversation that included Dr. David Thompson, the chief executive officer of New York Hospital, who earlier would not appear as a witness at Stein's hearing. Dr. Thompson told Stein that he thought Libby might have died from something called Thucydides

syndrome, which is an influenza A virus complicated by
toxic shock emanating from the respiratory tract.

It was passed on to Sidney that by 1986 New York Hospital had an attending doctor on duty in the emergency
room at all times, and every department at the hospital had
a quality-control committee. Two years after Libby's
death, some problems were quietly being addressed at
New York Hospital.

But quietly was not what Sidney Zion had in mind.

"Doctors live in their own world," he told me. He felt
betrayed, and wondered whether his daughter had, too.
"What I can't help thinking is if Libby thought while she
was lying there fighting for her life—she fought so hard she
broke the straitjacket—that her father abandoned her," he
said in an interview to the *San Francisco Examiner*.

"He never got over that he left her," said Dr. Paul
Nelson, Sidney's childhood friend. He was crazed with
guilt. He couldn't get the image of Libby struggling out of
his mind.

ON NOVEMBER 20, 1986, the fourth grand jury for
the April–May term in and for the county of New York filed
a report "concerning the care and treatment of a patient
and the supervision of interns and residents at a hospital in
New York County." Although Libby Zion and New York
Hospital were unnamed, this report was the result of District Attorney Robert Morgenthau's long investigation into
the circumstances of her death at that hospital. The Supreme Court of the state of New York accepted the report
as public record on December 31, 1986. In the annals of
medicine, it was the first time that such a report was ever
issued.

Two weeks later, *The New York Times* quoted District
Attorney Morgenthau as saying "there was insufficient evi-

dence, especially regarding the cause of death, upon which to base an indictment." The penal code contains this description of criminal negligence, which Sidney wanted the doctors charged with: "The risk must be of such a nature and degree that the failure to perceive it constitutes gross deviation from the standard of care that a reasonable person would observe in the situation."

Although the doctors involved in Libby's care were not ever charged with a crime, the district attorney explained that the grand jury had denounced New York Hospital, called "a level-one Manhattan hospital" in the report, and the doctors, also unnamed, for the "medically deficient" care and treatment, and had asked that new rules be created at teaching hospitals. "Evidence showed that junior interns were making life-and-death decisions without any supervision," the district attorney emphasized at a press conference. "This has to be changed."

The report was a skillful document that outlined major problems: "A hospital is not the place for recently graduated doctors to grow and develop in isolation; rather, it is a place where the learning process should continue under strict supervision."

It faulted hospitals for interpreting "inadequate and ill-defined laws" to mean that residents could act alone and unsupervised.

It demanded "corrective legislation."

It faulted hospitals for overworking residents.

It asked that hospitals limit the "consecutive working hours" of house staff.

It criticized hospitals for not having PGY-3s (or above) in emergency rooms.

It stressed that PGY-1s and PGY-2s should have "in-person" supervision by attendings or PGY-3s.

It recommended that a study be initiated on the possibility that hospitals "implement a computerized system of checking for contraindicated drugs."

It called for clear-cut legislation for medical hospitals (as opposed to psychiatric hospitals, which already had strict regulations) regarding the use of restraints. When Libby had been placed in restraints, New York Hospital had no guidelines governing their use. None at all. The grand jury reported that it learned that restraints are used "quite often" at New York Hospital, and suggested that they were used on Libby as a "quick solution" to the problem of controlling her.

Although the grand jury could not determine why Libby died, they offered some hypotheses:

The amount of pneumonia found on autopsy was too small to be "the sole cause of death of an eighteen-year-old woman."

Her death could have been related to the contraindication of Nardil and Demerol, although the tests used on autopsy "were not sensitive enough to detect therapeutic doses of Demerol, Haldol, or Nardil."

The use of restraints "could have caused a rise in temperature" as Libby struggled with them; in fact, "the elevated temperature itself could have been the cause of death." In addition, it was "possible that while restrained she aspirated body secretions into her lungs," which could have caused or exacerbated the pneumonia found.

As for cocaine as a cause of death, the members of the grand jury said they were uncertain about its role, if any, in her death. They did say, "Assuming, however, that the patient had a cocaine reaction, the emergency room assessment was woefully incomplete." Indeed, they might also have added, but didn't, that if Libby had suffered from a cocaine overdose, there was, in fact, no specific treatment for that available at New York Hospital in March 1984.

The grand jury was aware of at least eight of Libby's prescriptions—Nardil, erythromycin, tetracycline, doxycycline, Tofranil, Dalmane, Valium, and Percodan—as well as Chlor-Trimeton, the over-the-counter antihistamine. It noted that Nardil could have interacted with the Percodan or the antihistamine. "Knowing that the patient might have taken all three drugs would have been a valuable aid in formulating a diagnosis," the report stated, pointing out that "the possibility that the patient's symptoms were related to a drug reaction or interaction was a recurring conclusion reached by all the physicians who testified." In fact, the report continued, "the evidence in this case raises the possibility that this patient may have died from a drug interaction."

The grand jury also commented that "a physician suspecting a drug reaction should not rule out that possibility merely because a patient denies having used drugs." Libby did not have to die, they concluded, because "both conditions—pneumonia and a cocaine reaction—are treatable." The implication of the report was clear: Libby Zion could have been saved.

Several doctors told me that if Libby entered New York Hospital with a drug reaction, she might have recovered if the residents hadn't added Demerol, Haldol, and the restraints to her already overburdened system.

Yes, they say, New York Hospital and its doctors had contributed to Libby's death, but they did not kill her.

Neither did they save her, however.

They were unable to save her because they were ignorant of her drug abuse. They had no way of knowing of it except through Libby herself or her parents. "For whatever reason, she didn't tell us," Dr. Stone said. She had kept her secret life a secret to the very end, and the residents didn't recognize the death mask she presented.

"It's a funny thing about people who have done drugs," Libby's neighborhood friend Dale Fox told me, "we've been around the block, but we're children. We don't know anything." According to *The Mayo Clinic Family Health Book*, "An addiction may be considered to be the compulsive and continued use of a drug." At the point Libby was brought to the emergency room, she was too distraught and sick to help herself, and she was not recognized as the child she still was, and a possible drug addict.

Adam later said that Ralph Enders once told him that Libby "was completely addicted to cocaine." But, Adam said, "I never saw her doing it." Yet he mused, "I always wondered if it were true," finally adding that "I've heard a lot, and it makes me think that it might be true."

"There's no doubt about it being a tragedy," Robert Morgenthau said, "but she lied about her drug use. With drug users, reactions are unpredictable, and often fatal."

But, as Sidney Zion was willing to admit only many years after Libby's death, "if you suspect drugs, you don't listen to a kid if she says she's not on drugs." This statement may reveal his dawning awareness about drug use, but its point was to add to his indictment of New York Hospital.

TWO MONTHS LATER, in January 1987, the *New England Journal of Medicine* wrote that the grand jury report "was, in effect, an indictment of American graduate medical education." Victor Navasky commented that "what Morgenthau did was extraordinary. He didn't owe Sidney a dime. Contrary, it was probably the other way around." A newspaper editorial referred to the report's "chilling" revelations about "trainee doctors who often work up to thirty-six hours at a stretch as a rite of passage." Another applauded the grand jury for revealing that overworked and undersupervised residents existed all over New York State, and not just in New York City. Soon the public would come to understand that the very same system was in place all around the country, and, in fact, all around the globe.

Although he was satisfied with the grand jury report, Sidney told the *New York Post* on January 12 that "there should have been an indictment. That there wasn't one is a terrible mistake on Morgenthau's part." He told *New York Newsday* that "there was enough evidence. My daughter was executed through medical negligence." Later he said that if the district attorney "had done that one act"—had brought in an indictment—"it would have changed the world forever." He added that "it's not true the D.A. couldn't pinpoint the cause of Libby's death and that's why he didn't indict. Morgenthau decided not to indict because of pressure from doctors."

But Robert Morgenthau is an intrepid public official known for his fearlessness. Manhattan D.A. since 1975, and before that United States Attorney for the Southern District of New York for nine years, Morgenthau didn't fail to indict the doctors because of pressure, but because, as he said, "you deal with the hospital—the system. You don't indict young doctors. The system was wrong. You shouldn't have interns on seventy-two-hour shifts, with no training, no supervision." He said that he had explained all that to Sidney. "I told him he should be concerned about hospitals." The district attorney remembered that Sidney said to him, "I want to make sure this doesn't happen again," and Morgenthau reiterated to him that the report recommended that new rules be instituted at teaching hospitals. "He refuses to recognize that," Robert Morgenthau sighed, adding, "but Sidney thinks whatever Sidney wants to think."

Dr. Bertrand Bell, a fierce opponent of the closed order

book, doesn't place the blame for Libby's death on the residents either. "The responsible person was that attending doctor," he charged. He described Dr. Weinstein as part of the hospital's subculture.

Sidney would become convinced that his friend Victor Temkin, Dr. Sherman's brother-in-law, who had once worked for Robert Morgenthau, went to the District Attorney, accompanied by his mother. "The grand jury report hardly said anything about Sherman," Sidney said. Temkin said such a claim is outlandish. "None of this is true," he groaned. "It's madness." Temkin tried to talk to Sidney, who was dismissive. "He got embarrassed over all this, so we broke it off," is how Sidney explains the end of one of his closest friendships. But for Sidney Zion, it is said, one is not on his side unless one is against all other sides as well.

ON JANUARY 14, 1987, officials at New York Hospital spoke out to the media. "Many of the grand jury's conclusions cannot be objectively supported and are inherently inconsistent." The hospital immediately released a four-page press release that outlined its full position. As in the grand jury report, Libby was not mentioned by name, but those in the know recognized who the hospital was talking about when it wrote "perhaps the tragic death of the young person involved here will teach all concerned of the danger of illicit drugs such as cocaine and, indeed, of the risks in the use and concealment of usage of a vast range of drugs, licit and illicit." The press release also made reference to the cocaine deaths of athletes Len Bias and Don Rogers, which had occurred in the past year.

Sidney was livid, and fired back with a charge of libel, and intentional infliction of emotional distress. He paid no attention to what he had written in *Read All About It:* "I don't believe in libel laws. I think they violate the First

Amendment." His libel claim was also against Frank Bensel, the hospital's lawyer who had not only written to Andrew Stein about Sidney's "reckless and malicious attacks," but had also written a similar letter to the producers of *60 Minutes*, who were planning a segment on the circumstances of Libby's death, to be aired in February 1987. Sidney's lawyers at the time tried to persuade him not to "fight a multifront war," and said a libel case was "unproductive." They even went so far as to decide among themselves that "someone must say no" to him, and "not be overwhelmed by his grief to do anything he requests." But as always Sidney would not take no for an answer, and a suit was filed. Judge Harold Baer, Jr., dismissed it, saying that the hospital's statements, as well as Bensel's letters, were attempts by New York Hospital to defend itself, which it had a legal right to do, and that the letters did not "hold Mr. Zion up to contempt or promote an evil opinion of him." However, the judge acknowledged that the press release was "troublesome," because it did not "make it plain where the facts recited in the grand jury report ended and where the hospital's interpretations, contentions, and hypotheses began."

Yet New York Hospital became bolder, and even hinted privately, unbeknownst to Sidney, that Libby might have brought cocaine to the hospital with her, and used it while she was a patient there. A person close to the investigation admitted that "it's within the realm of possibility that Libby brought it to the hospital." But such a claim would never be proved.

With the passage of time, Sidney too became yet bolder. He began to blame Robert Morgenthau for the fact that the cocaine issue wouldn't disappear. He said that the Manhattan district attorney "destroyed the grand jury with cocaine." He said he knew that some of Libby's former boyfriends had testified that she had used the drug. He felt betrayed again because he maintained that the district attorney "looked me straight in the eye and said cocaine has nothing to do with this case." Privately he called Morgenthau a "psychopath," and a "danger to society." "Morgenthau campaigned against your kid," he said a source told him. "Bob Morgenthau allowed New York Hospital to have a say in the grand jury. That's unprecedented," Sidney declared.

Later, Sidney said another source told him that the district attorney "tried to intervene" in the case against Dr. Luise Weinstein.

When I asked Sidney why he thought Morgenthau would want to intervene, especially since he had attempted to bring an indictment, Sidney answered, "Well, maybe because of the system. Maybe he felt sorry for them?" Ever the conspiracy theorist, he also suggested that the district attorney "might have done it as a contract" for Dr. Weinstein's lawyer. He said that New York Hospital could go full-steam-ahead with their cocaine theory because the doctors weren't indicted; "they're making up a story because they know no one is there to punish them. There is nothing to fear now."

"He's living in his own world," Robert Morgenthau said calmly. "He's unrealistic. He's got to have a devil. Sidney Zion had a tremendous sense of guilt."

I pressed Sidney on the issue of whether his daughter had ever used cocaine. "What if the charge that she had used cocaine was true?" I asked him in 1993.

"It's not true," he answered me irritably. "There's no way there was cocaine. It's like saying I'm black."

When I still pressed on, he once more assumed the prosecutor's role. He began to question how the hospital could "take this ugly shot" about Libby's cocaine use.

"They are admitting it was there, and that they ignored it and let her die. They can't have it both ways. If it was cocaine, why didn't they fix it?"

New York Hospital "is betting everything on cocaine," he declared. "I'm upset. Bob Morgenthau gave them that issue."

THE GRAND JURY report led to the immediate formation of a New York State Department of Health advisory panel on emergency services, which later became known as the Bell Commission, after its chairman, Dr. Bertrand Bell. By June 1987, the panel had made some preliminary recommendations, such as limiting the hours of residents to twelve per day in emergency care, and sixteen per day on other services. Finally, in 1989, on July 1, the day residents traditionally begin their training, new regulations involving major reforms were adopted in New York State, the first state to ever institute such rules. Sidney told a newspaper reporter, "If the death of one kid can destroy a system, then the system was already destroyed."

The leading reforms were as follows: nonsurgical house staff should not work more than eighty hours per week, averaged over a four-week period.

Residents should work no more than twenty-four consecutive hours.

Scheduled rotations should be separated by at least eight nonworking hours and one twenty-four-hour period of nonworking time each week.

Residents should be supervised by attending physicians twenty-four hours a day.

Auxiliary services—aides and technicians—should be available so the house staff isn't overburdened with *scut* work, resident slang for everyday, routine chores.

These regulations, alternately called the Libby Zion

regulations, the Bell regulations, or the 405 regulations (the name favored by most people, even Libby's father—although in 1995 he started calling them "the Libby Laws"), are not actual laws, and hospitals can't be charged with criminal liability if they don't comply with them. There is no established policing policy, and countless New York State institutions ignore the rules altogether. "The regulations have the force of law," Sidney stressed, "but no one is willing to close down hospitals if they don't comply. And there's no money to do it. There should be money to enforce the regulations. Congress should enact a law."

Nevertheless, the American Medical Association's Green Book—the *Graduate Medical Education Directory*—now incorporates the regulations in the section on internal-medicine residencies. The establishment has acknowledged that the old system is dead.

But it wasn't easy.

In 1987, the AMA created a new division, a subsection on residents. Steve Thornquist, M.D., a Yale resident, and the chairman in 1992–93, said residents wanted to find a way to work with "the voice of medicine"—the AMA—even though it's very traditional, and "doesn't want to rapidly change things." However, Dr. Thornquist said they are more and more receptive to the concerns of residents, even though it took three years of "significant lobbying to bring them around to seeing that the medical environment is not the same anymore."

Some hospitals around the country have formed house-staff unions, although under 10 percent of all residents are unionized. The Committee on Interns and Residents is a union of residents working in public hospitals in New York, New Jersey, Massachusetts, Maryland, and the District of Columbia, and has been in existence for over twenty years. Unions are not popular in the private sector. The American

Hospital Association opposes them; its position is that residents are primarily students, and not employees. Bruce Elwell, an organizer for the committee, said that most of New York's private hospitals don't even allow union organizers on the premises. They are banned. "They don't like how we look, or how we act," Elwell said, adding that "we'd have to be ready to bloody places to get recognized." Still, he said that "in most medical specialties, there is an attempt to reduce hours."

"My one solace is that at least it wasn't all in vain," Sidney said at the time the new regulations went into effect. The New York State health commissioner, Dr. David Axelrod, said the rules "relate not just to Libby Zion but to a whole host of 'Libby Zions,' many of whom did not die, but who may have suffered because of the limited ability of the house staff to respond."

During 1987, do-not-resuscitate guidelines were finally and firmly established in New York State as a result of Violet Noss's unnecessary death in 1984. Until that time there had been no state *or* federal regulations. Violet Noss's daughter said that this was the only good thing to come of her mother's death.

On September 25, 1987, *The New York Times* reported that "medical students at New York State's teaching hospitals would be barred from performing clinical procedures without close supervision by a physician, under new rules being proposed by the State Health Department." The article did not mention the Violet Noss case, but the loss of Violet Noss was everywhere in it. The new regulations were intended to avert "life-threatening mistakes" by unsupervised third- and fourth-year medical students. It was suggested that medical students be limited to such tasks as taking medical histories, drawing blood, giving electrocardiograms, or carrying out physical examinations. These proposals were the first by any state to define the areas of responsibilities of medical students in hospitals.

But in actuality the regulations have never been spelled out specifically, with the exception of one sentence stating that "medical students, in the course of their educational examinations, may take patient histories, perform complete physical examinations and enter findings in the medical record of the patient with the approval of the patient's attending physician." But the rules, which are actually a subsection of the 405 section, are also full of vague generalizations like "medical students may be assigned and directed to provide additional patient care services under the direct in-person supervision of an attending or authorized postgraduate trainee." Wiggle words.

Dr. Alfred Gelhorn, director of medical affairs for the New York State Department of Health, and a former member of the Bell Commission, recognizes that "hospitals are not good in education now," and says "that's where the work needs to be done" regarding medical student responsibilities. "There needs to be better coordination between medical schools and hospitals," he said, adding that "much of medical education bears little resemblance to life after medical school."

I would think about Sidney's belief that if he didn't "make a fuss, no one would do anything at all."

Who is shouting for medical students to stop playing doctor and to start learning how to be doctors?

How many Violet Nosses have there been since 1984?

11

S IDNEY HAD WANTED to set up a living memorial to Libby, so a year after her death he decided to establish a fellowship in her honor. "A year to go and do something creative, that's what she would have liked," he told the *Yale Daily News*. He and a board made up of members of the Yale faculty chose the winners of a five-thousand-dollar nonacademic grant; the first recipient spent a year in China "taking verbal snapshots" as a free-lance journalist, and the next—actually the next three—used the money to start a group theater in Irvington, New York.

Sidney had chosen his law school alma mater as the beneficiary of the award, which had been underwritten by various friends, including twenty-five thousand dollars from Frank Sinatra, because, he explained, Bennington "brought back too many terrible memories."

In his daughter's memory, Sidney also established a series of lectures at Yale. The first one featured film directors

Mike Nichols and Nora Ephron in conversation about everything from films to improvisation, with plenty of theater advice thrown in. Nichols told the audience to look for "what is happening" rather than what is being said in any particular scene. Like life itself, "what is happening is always very complicated and often interesting, while what is being said is not," he reflected.

The second lecture, and what would turn out to be the last because of friction between Sidney and the Yale administration, presented Frank Sinatra in conversation with Sidney. Five hundred people listened to what the *Yale Daily News* described as Sinatra's "rambling" reminiscences and jokes, while student pickets marched outside the auditorium protesting the singer's recent appearance at a concert in South Africa.

Yale officials had been ambivalent about Sinatra's appearance from the very beginning. "They wanted to know if his bodyguards would have guns," Sidney said, because they were apprehensive about the presence of weapons in a crowd. What if there was a riot? Sidney said that Sinatra might have canceled because of all the pressure if he hadn't told the entertainer not to worry about it, although Sidney maintained that he had to almost threaten Yale officials not to cancel the evening. In time, A. Bartlett Giamatti, the president of the university, wrote Sidney that Yale would be in danger of losing its tax exemption if it had someone other than a Yale faculty member deciding the recipient of the Libby Zion fellowship. "I didn't want an award in my baby's name going to something I didn't approve of," Sidney said, so he told Yale "thanks for the memories" when they would no longer allow him to vote. But Yale was not displeased with the outcome because it "didn't really know what to do with this thing that had fallen into their laps, which was sort of *The Sidney Zion Show*," according to a participant.

The Yale evenings were entertaining and eerie at the same time because of their festive touch. It was hard to think of them as memorials, yet as Victor Navasky noted of the Sinatra event, "In a funny way it was appropriate that Sidney had this crooner commemorate Libby, because that's what I thought she wanted to be—she wanted to be a nightclub singer, which was in Sidney's tradition, and that was moving."

But the atmosphere was awkward. Elaborate dinners were served to "the upper class," as Mike Nichols described the select guests. One woman remembered meeting Elsa in the ladies' room as she was changing from street clothes into a sparkling cocktail dress for the Sinatra lecture. "Elsa was crying," the woman recalled, "and I sensed that her tears were because she was dressing up for an occasion that didn't call for celebration. I was so upset after she left the room. Everything just seemed so wrong."

At the two evenings, there was scarcely mention of Libby. Only one person invoked the reality of her. Her younger brother, Jed, not scheduled to speak, nevertheless stood up at the first dinner to say how the evening at Yale had nothing at all to do with his sister. He said that she had picked Bennington College in order to get away from just such things. "Libby wasn't interested in achievement, but in living," Jed protested. The guests were stunned yet relieved to hear the truth so plainly blurted out by a pained and grieving boy. Everyone present, and those who later heard of his statement, were glad to have someone finally speak for Libby. "Why was Sidney setting up something at Yale where Libby had not gone but he had?" a guest asked. "It was the absolute clinching proof, if any were necessary, of how much this was about Sidney, and not about her."

Jed's statement at Yale was "extraordinary," Victor Navasky remembered. He also recalled what happened next. Jed was still struggling with his sobs. "A chorus line of Whiffenpoofs with gray gloves on were poised to come in when the official speeches were over." They had not heard Jed's speech and they assumed that the silence which had suddenly fallen on the audience was their cue to enter. "It was like a film noir," said Navasky. "From out of the west this chorus line of guys started coming in singing 'Goodnight My Coney Island Baby.'" It was not possible to recover the evening as a commemorative occasion. But Mike Nichols did his sensitive best, said Navasky. He opened his and Nora Ephron's conversation by reassuring Jed and the audience that "there's no right way to deal with something like this, and we're all going to be unhappy and uncomfortable—you said something important—and now's the time to move on."

In 1988, the Libby Zion Fellowship was moved to Bennington College, where it is still awarded each year to a performing-arts student. "It's very quiet now," Sidney said.

JUST A FEW short years after Libby's death, a senior doctor at New York Hospital told a reporter that "Sidney has won already; he's the real victor. He's changed the way we do business."

"There is no turning back," pronounced the *Journal of the American Medical Association*, although, as with certain details in Libby's case, controversy over the 405 regulations continues. The words used in these debates are often angry and critical—that the rules create "a time-clock mentality" in medicine, that their implementation is costly to hospitals, that doctors lose their autonomy, that patients don't have continuity of care. Still, among all the words applied to the controversy, the ones that most dramatize the true situation—the *closed order book*—are not used in any discussions.

In February 1987, Sidney told one of the most-watched news programs on television, *60 Minutes*, that "my assumption was, since New York Hospital was a great hospital, that it was an attending doctor" he was dealing with in the emergency room, and it never dawned on him that "my friend Ray Sherman" would have an intern take care of Libby. In fact, he said, he had "no idea he was dealing with interns and residents" until he saw his daughter's hospital and autopsy reports.

Isadore Rosmarin, the associate producer of the segment, "The 36-Hour Day," spoke to a hundred residents in the process of researching the story; most doctors, he said, were afraid to go on record "for fear of their careers." No one from New York Hospital would speak to *60 Minutes*.

The doctors "didn't say they were residents," Sidney told me. "I assumed they were real doctors. I didn't know anything about that world."

Most people still don't.

Few people understand how a teaching hospital works. "No one knows who's in charge in a hospital," said Dr. Robert Gifford, associate dean for education and student affairs at Yale University School of Medicine.

"It's very confusing to the patient," a resident admitted to me. She herself did not know anything about the modus operandi until she became a medical student.

Tom Monahan, the executive director of the New York State Board of Medicine, said, "The public doesn't know who's who. There's a whole battery of people wearing white coats."

* * *

ON MARCH 12, 1987, New York Hospital was fined thirteen thousand dollars by the New York State Department of Health for its "woeful" treatment of Libby. The hospital admitted it failed to give her adequate care. "The rest of the world already had the evidence," blared an editorial in the New York *Daily News:* "The corpse of an eighteen-year-old girl, dead at the hands of blunderers with 'Dr.' in front of their names."

The hospital agreed to a remedial program, a stipulation never before imposed by the state, which had mandated the year before, in 1986, that all hospitals had to report unexpected deaths. (That year, the state also began studying every medical malpractice case on file—closed and pending.)

New York Hospital would have to file a monthly report on the quality of its medical care, as well as an accounting of all deaths that occurred within twenty-four hours of the patient's admission to the hospital. Emergency-room procedures would undergo evaluation, the state of nursing care would be examined, and all doctors would have to submit to a review of their credentials. "That's a start," cautioned the New York *Daily News* editorial. "But only a start." In fact, there had been an even earlier start at New York Hospital. A month before the fine was levied, the hospital asked all its residents to keep a log of their activities for two weeks; on the basis of some of these findings, changes were made in the departments of psychiatry, pathology, and radiology.

Officials of the hospital announced publicly that they paid the fine and agreed to the provisions "solely for the purpose of resolving the administrative dispute" and to "avoid future burdens of time and expense on the hospital and staff." Sidney reacted to the announcement by telling a reporter that the hospital's arrogance was "beyond comprehension." He nevertheless was pleased that the State Department of Health had "forced them to admit everything." Still, the hospital's chief executive officer, Dr. David Thompson, said the fine had been paid to "get out of it." Indeed, privately Sidney said he had been told the hospital paid "so it could get a certificate of occupancy" for a new building.

Dr. Sherman agreed, although he still believed that "it was a mistake for the hospital to admit that anything was done improperly," especially since it was his understanding that it "didn't believe it did anything wrong in the Libby Zion case."

The stipulation contained a clause that specified that New York Hospital's admission of guilt could not be used in any disciplinary hearings or civil or criminal court cases. New York Hospital officials considered what had happened to them as a result of Libby's death to be "standard procedure." Nevertheless, as the malpractice case inched along, the public-relations office conceded that the hospital's attitude was not one of disinterest, and acknowledged that "nerves are still raw around here." In fact, the hospital's lawyers wished that the case "would go away."

But it wouldn't.

Not unlike most medical centers, New York Hospital has a long history of what Sidney calls arrogance and the hospital administrators describe as resistance to mindless attack. It goes back several centuries. On April 13, 1788, a group of inquisitive boys who had been peering into a window at New York Hospital's three-story gray stone building on lower Broadway said they saw doctors dissecting a corpse. The word spread quickly, and a riot ensued. A medical student had made matters worse by dangling an arm from a cadaver out the window. Hundreds of rioters, enraged by rumors of grave robbing—it was actually true, the bodies came from nearby Potter's Field and the Negro Burial Ground—rushed into the hospital building and smashed everything in sight. Half-dissected bodies were carried away and burned. Doctors were dragged out of the building, later to be saved by the sheriff and the mayor. A few doctors managed to get away from the screaming mob, and hid in chimneys, large vats, or escaped altogether to other towns. In time, the mob grew even larger and roamed through the streets of downtown New York. Some of the rioters decided to search out Dr. Samuel Bard, a founder of the hospital. A medical student warned him that the mob was on its way to his house. Dr. Bard stood fast. He threw back the curtains, opened his front door, and waited. While waiting, he read a book, as if he didn't have a care in the world. When the mob entered his house and saw him quietly reading, they were so amazed by his defiance, they retreated.

New York Hospital would perhaps like to think that it has followed the example of Dr. Bard. Its fund-raising efforts, carried on ever since the summer of 1773 when it sponsored the first theater benefit ever at an American hospital, have certainly contributed to its high public prestige. It is one of several hospitals in New York City that regularly treats notables from all parts of the globe: John F. Kennedy, the Shah of Iran, Bob Hope, Andy Warhol, Richard Nixon, Jacqueline Kennedy Onassis.

Yet as often as people praise the hospital, they also denigrate it. A very wealthy, very social, very influential patient, who did not want his name used, told me that he would never set foot in the hospital again; he continues to see its doctors, but at another location. This person not only found the level of care poor, but said the physical surroundings were unkempt. He also remarked that a great deal of time was wasted waiting for busy interns to sign the order book, and that the nurses would not act even in the simplest matters until this was done, attendings or not.

In 1975, Fred J. Cook, the prizewinning investigative author of such books as *The FBI Nobody Knows* in 1964 and *The Nightmare Decade* in 1971, wrote a book about the death of his wife Julia at New York Hospital. "A life had been sacrificed through a stupid, incredible blunder—the failure to take a routine blood test." Cook, who did not sue the hospital, but instead decided to write about what happened as a warning to others, offered New York Hospital "an opportunity to say whatever it might wish." The hospital didn't respond.

It's been an open secret for years that New York Hospital is the place responsible for causing certain errors in the care of a prominent doctor, Harold Lear, as recounted in his widow's 1980 best-selling book, *Heartsounds*. Although Martha Weinman Lear called these errors "abominable," she also had some positive things to say about the hospital. Nevertheless she described how her husband once received twice as much oxygen as he needed, resulting in the burning of the mucous membranes in his nose; how her husband was blamed for being sensitive to a certain medication; how she was told by a nurse, "I can't wake the intern for a Valium, not if I want to keep my job," when Dr. Lear had requested that medication; and how the intern on duty on a Sunday refused to stop reading the sports section of the newspaper to fix her husband's IV needle, which was turning his hand red and causing it to swell. Lear reports that her husband was struck by "how often nurses seemed to be apologizing for doctors. He wondered if nurses had ever apologized for him."

According to a New York State Department of Health veteran, in the year before Libby Zion's death, 1983, an elderly patient at New York Hospital was placed in restraints after suffering a drug reaction. Despite her advanced age, the woman struggled so hard against the restraints that some of her teeth were knocked out. She survived to successfully sue the hospital for her dental expenses. Six months after Libby's death, an intern inserted a breathing tube into a pregnant woman's esophagus. It led to an aspiration pneumonia that killed her.

One doctor at New York Hospital told me that some staff members believe that the Zion case was "sensationalized" because "people are mad at us because we took in the Shah."

Five years before Libby's death, Shah Mohammed Reza Pahlevi, who had been forced to leave Iran in January 1979, when the Ayatollah Khomeini took control of the country, was admitted under another name for treatment of lymphoma. When word of his presence leaked, noisy demonstrators lined the courtyard in front of the hospital's glass entrance doors, as the media blasted Washington for allowing the Shah into the country at so delicate a time. American lives were in jeopardy in all Muslim countries. The Shah's presence in New York precipitated the storming of the American embassy in Teheran on November 4, 1979, when fifty-two hostages were taken. The Shah remained at New York Hospital until December 15. He died in Egypt on July 27, 1980.

ON FEBRUARY 27, 1987, several weeks before the New York State Department of Health stipulation in the Zion case was signed, Andy Warhol, the Pittsburgh-born, celebrity-obsessed craftsman who elevated soda bottles, soup cans, and dollar bills to an art form, died of cardiac arrest at New York Hospital, just one day after successful gallbladder surgery. Hospital officials said he died from a heart-rhythm disturbance; this was confirmed by the medical examiner. Nevertheless, his lawyer said he died from overhydration, which brought on the heart fibrillation, or cardiac arrhythmia.

Two months after Warhol's death, the State Department of Health charged that the Pop Artist—who was afraid of hospitals, and had told his doctor that he knew if he was hospitalized, he would die—was given inadequate care. Absolutely not, hospital officials answered right back; he received "thorough and appropriate care." Yet the state found the hospital guilty of having failed to perform proper presurgical tests, having failed to monitor Warhol's hydration, having failed to determine if he was allergic to an administered antibiotic, and having failed to keep an accurate chart. A private-duty nurse was cited for giving him inadequate care. "Everybody in the hospital dropped the ball," Andy Warhol's lawyer said.

A malpractice suit was filed by Warhol's estate against the artist's private doctor, his surgeon, his private nurse, the intern in charge of his case, and seven other staff members.

The hospital responded with a conciliatory statement that stated "if deficiencies exist, we will correct them." Angela Holder, the lawyer member of the Yale School of Medicine faculty, said that the Andy Warhol suit was actually against the residents, for not checking on the private-duty nurse, who, she said, "fell asleep." This facet of the suit has never been fully brought to the public's attention. The case was settled—for a reported three million dollars—during the course of the trial. According to the settlement agreement, New York Hospital did not admit liability.

Once again, New York Hospital was catapulted into the headlines with another highly publicized death. "People

think, if a guy like Andy Warhol can be treated like that,
how will I be treated?" Sidney Zion told a reporter.

A year after Warhol's death, a patient who had received
"a good outcome" at the hospital's emergency room wrote
a letter to *The New York Times* asking, "Might it not be
possible that what is distinctive about New York Hospital
is the highly publicized nature of its problems?"

That is partially true.

The image of New York Hospital that has been formed
in the public's mind in recent years fosters public scrutiny,
so the good and the bad receive equal time.

In 1988, an emergency-room PGY-2 resident did not
admit a man suffering from a heart attack because the resident believed the patient's pains were muscular; at home
that night, the man died. In 1991, an eighteen-year-old
student received a drug to which she was allergic. As the
New York *Daily News* reported, "Once again, as in the cases
of Libby Zion and Andy Warhol, New York Hospital is
battling charges it neglected a patient and failed to supervise a medical intern."

In 1992, a PGY-2 resident discontinued a crucial medication on a cardiac patient without substituting another.
This mistake, together with other medical-care errors,
eventuated in the patient's death. The family brought suit
against the hospital, asking twelve million dollars in damages. After hearing all the testimony, the jury awarded the
family twice the amount—twenty-four million dollars.

There is every reason to suppose that all, or certainly
most, hospitals in the country have had—and still have—
similar problems. The problems not only involve inexperienced interns and residents, but also inattentive nurses,
aides, and technicians, lack of adequate staff, equipment
errors, and shortage of supplies. Very few incidents are
widely publicized. Most problems are kept quiet because

doctors and hospitals are used to keeping secrets; some are kept concealed because of settlement and/or other agreements.

In general, the public hears about the problems involving well-known people. Yet for every well-known case, there are others of which the public hears nothing. Although there are often complicated factors involved, it has been recognized for years that the majority of problems are created by the house staff.

In 1987, *60 Minutes* interviewed a resident in a Washington, D.C., hospital who told the producers that "writing orders in the wrong chart is a common thing." An intern in a hospital in Harrisburg, Pennsylvania, was asked, "What kinds of errors are you and your colleagues capable of making?" and the answer was "About as many different kinds as there are drugs to give." This exchange was valid three years after Libby's death; it would have been equally valid ten, twenty, or ninety years ago. It is and will remain valid for as long as medicine is practiced.

Yet there are very few formal studies of the problem.

A 1989 survey done by doctors at the University of California, San Francisco Medical School, revealed that 90 percent of the 114 PGY-1s and PGY-2s studied admitted they had made patient errors that brought about complications, longer hospital stays, or death. More than half of these trainees also admitted that they didn't tell supervising doctors about their errors, even though the study's director said, "This is not a paper about 114 incidents of negligence. Some of the house officers described things that were clearly not negligent, things that no one could ever blame them for."

A 1990 survey by a group of Albany, New York, doctors that appeared in the *Journal of the American Medical Association* determined that out of a total of 289,411 medication orders in a single year, 905 contained errors; of these errors, 522 could have been fatal. (The test was set up so that all errors were caught. These patients were luckier than others.) Interns had the highest error rate.

In 1993, a doctor from the University of Florida College of Medicine wrote an article for a medical journal describing the delays in diagnosis and treatment his wife suffered at the hands of an inexperienced house staff. Near death, she was revived by the intervention of attendings, who had not provided any supervision up until that point.

In 1994, an article in the *Journal of the American Medical Association* pointed out that "errors must be accepted as evidence of systems flaws, not character flaws. Until and unless that happens, it is unlikely that any substantial progress will be made in reducing medical errors."

By 1995, the Federation of State Medical Boards would report that although only 0.6 percent of the 615,854 doctors licensed to practice medicine in America were disciplined, still, it was an increase over previous years.

A doctor told me that "you can't defrock residents unless they commit crimes." He explained why: "A hospital is full of uncertainty, and there will be mistakes because there's too much that is unpredictable." This doctor had never "turned back" a resident. In fact, a doctor connected to North Shore University Hospital, one of the many hospitals where Cornell University Medical School offers clinical instruction, told me that doctors there are encouraged to be "lenient" with residents. The unwritten rule is to "be positive," and not to stress the negative.

Still, Angela Holder of Yale told me that "hundreds of residents are sued." She said this isn't clear to the public because the residents are "hospital employees." She added, "The hospital is responsible."

The reason Drs. Leonard, Stone, and Weinstein were

specifically named in the Zion malpractice suit, I learned, was to prevent them from being assimilated into the action against the hospital. Although Sidney wanted to be able to show that Dr. Weinstein "was a victim of the hospital machinery, and exploited financially and physically," he also wanted to make clear that "she was also responsible for not coming to see Libby when she was called three times—plus all the other things she did." He wanted all the doctors named individually. "Nobody's going to be anonymous when they kill my kid," Sidney told me. "I want to say anything I want about them. I want to name them and put their name in the paper. That's why I wanted them in the suit."

Roy Nemerson, a deputy counsel for the New York State Department of Health, said that there are very few cases that he knows of in his office that involve residents. Aside from the Zion case, he could think of only two others. One was a resident who was charged with the fraudulent practice of medicine in 1988 because he used patients to get drugs for himself; his license was revoked. The other case is still pending, and involves misconduct. Mr. Nemerson said that there might be others, but that it was hard to know since records are not classified in such a way as to distinguish residents from regular doctors. When I asked why not, he said that no one had thought of doing it that way. "There are only two distinctions in this office," he said, "fully licensed and not fully licensed."

Fully licensed doctors include PGY-2s and up. "Not fully licensed" is a distinction that refers not to interns, who are exempt from the provisions, but to foreign-trained doctors, who receive a limited permit and are restricted to a particular hospital until they receive full licenses.

"I think patients have a hard time these days," a retired doctor told me. He was referring to everything in the health-care system, from simply going for a doctor's appointment to understanding the categories and distinctions—not of insurance, but of who's in charge of their care in a hospital. What he did not speak of—and what is not being talked about by most doctors—is how the existing hospital system helps attending doctors. The closed order book is their way of having patients taken care of when for one reason or another they judge themselves not to be in a suitable position to do it themselves. "The attendings are getting a benefit because they don't have to come in the middle of the night," pointed out Dr. Emilie Osborn, an associate dean at the University of California, San Francisco School of Medicine. She also added that patients are being cared for by physicians in training programs endorsed by the senior doctors.

The attending doctors are not refusing care of the patient, they're putting the responsibility for this care elsewhere, even though they know in their hearts that the responsibility may not be adequately met. Doctors send their patients to emergency rooms, thus putting them at risk, rather than opening their offices or disturbing their office schedules or visiting the patient at home.

The practice of turning patients over to the house staff "was the way in which things had been done for years and years," Dr. Raymond Sherman declared in deposition.

ON THE CONDITION that I would not identify its participants, I was allowed to sit in on a quality-assurance conference at the University of California, San Francisco School of Medicine. Dr. Homer Boushey, the chief of medical services, and codirector of the medical residency training program, explained that the meeting was extremely confidential, and "not discoverable," that is, not admissible in a court case. He said that because it was off the record, the participants could be totally candid about the circumstances of the event under review.

"The forum is a chance to present mistakes," Dr. Emily Bergsland, the chief medical resident, told me. I was eager to observe if attitudes toward mistakes had changed over the years, since I had read in a book called *Medicine on Trial*, citing a study by Terry Mizrahi, Ph.D., that "novice internists" usually handled mistakes and mishaps in three ways: by denial, by discounting, and by distancing. Residents either managed to forget the mistake or redefined it as a nonmistake. Residents externalized the blame, and "even blamed the disease itself . . . and the patient," and "when they could no longer deny . . . they utilized distancing techniques."

At the quality-assurance session I attended, a PGY-3 resident presented his case in a precise and nondefensive way; plainly he was not embarrassed that a mistake was the focus of interest. He wanted to understand the circumstances. What had been discussed was the situation of a patient who had at first been misdiagnosed because "there are some things you wouldn't know in the emergency room."

There was calm debate about what might have caused the misdiagnosis, and one doctor suggested "lack of feedback from one service to another." Another commented that "the same team should follow the patient," and said that problems arose when they didn't. Someone said it was rare that the same team didn't follow the patient, although the person next to me whispered to no one in particular, "it happens all the time."

Afterward, I complimented the resident on the straightforward manner in which he had handled himself. "We *make* mistakes," he told me in a resolute voice. "Thank goodness we caught it, and I didn't send the patient home." He said that at the least he had learned to keep "better notes."

Dr. Steve Thornquist, the resident at Yale, later told me that since Libby's death there has been a lot more attention paid to what is written on a patient's chart.

"We expect our trainees to make mistakes," Dr. Boushey told me after the quality-assurance conference, explaining that the senior doctors then step in and fix things. Nevertheless, a fourth-year medical student said that one of his teachers told the class, "Get used to the idea that one day you will make a mistake that will kill someone."

A 1989 POSITION paper of the American College of Physicians, an organization formed in 1886 by a group of doctors who thought that the American Medical Association was too political, recommended that "the system governing resident working conditions must reduce preventable medical error to the minimum achievable within the limits dictated by medical uncertainty." The physician-in-chief of New York Hospital at the time of Libby's death, Dr. R. Gordon Douglas, was one of the members who helped write the position paper, which uses six words, *the system governing resident working conditions*, that could be a euphemism—or wiggle words—for the three-word phrase that should be used: *closed order book*. This is the real system that governs resident working conditions and promotes undersupervision and resident-run hospitals.

I became interested in changes in supervision, and contacted the current editor of the *New England Journal of Medicine*, Jerome P. Kassirer, M.D. Some house officers are not adequately supervised, he wrote in reply. But Dr. Kassirer suggested I visit a place "where supervision is done properly," and on his advice I went to the New England

Medical Center in Boston, Massachusetts, affiliated with the Tufts University School of Medicine. Dr. Richard I. Kopelman, director of house staff training there, told me that "the house staff admits patients under the auspices of the attending of the month," and that all patients have "the same attending." But since that attending can't be everywhere at the same time, I still wondered why it was claimed that this system worked. "No house officer works in isolation," Dr. Kopelman explained. "Residents are given a lot of support," he added, and "I don't know" is said a lot. "You can ask whatever you want. It's why it works here," a resident told me. She had turned down a position at Johns Hopkins because it left residents too much on their own.

The residents whom I observed during the day I spent at the New England Medical Center were willing to ask for help at every opportunity. I felt a strong sense of cooperation among the doctors in the meetings I monitored. "We not only teach medicine, but how to reason," Dr. Kopelman commented. Here was a closed order book that appeared to understand "alert hovering." The residents were in charge, but they knew that they were not alone, and they knew they were accountable. The residents told me that bad evaluations were the least of their worries. "We are harder on ourselves than anything else," a resident commented. "No one wants to make a mistake, so if you are unsure, you ask someone."

ON APRIL 30, 1987, Luise Weinstein, M.D., and Gregg Stone, M.D., faced the first of thirty hearings before the New York State Board for Professional Medical Conduct. They were charged with thirty-eight acts of gross negligence and/or gross incompetence. Dr. Maurice Leonard was not charged with any wrongdoing; in fact, his workup of Libby was considered fastidious by many doctors. Dr. Raymond Sherman would be charged later.

These hearings were part of a third campaign against the doctors that Sidney Zion had helped to bring about. He had already begun his first campaign, the civil suit against the hospital and the doctors, by the time the grand jury, which had been his second campaign, failed to bring in criminal indictments. But he still wanted the doctors punished in some official forum other than a courtroom, and now that possibility rested with the New York State Board for Professional Medical Conduct, which had the authority to recommend that the doctors turn in their medical licenses if the hearings determined that they had been grossly negligent in their care of Libby Zion.

Sidney Zion, red-faced and grim, sat in the small third-floor hearing room at 8 East Fortieth Street and watched. This was the first time he had confronted either doctor since the early morning of March 5, 1984, when he had left Libby in their hands. His feelings about seeing them, he said, were "unspeakable."

At the beginning of the hearing, Dr. Stone glanced quickly at Libby's father; Dr. Weinstein did not. She kept her head down as the charges were read by Terrance Sheehan, a lawyer for the New York State Department of Health. "When you see Luise Weinstein around the hospital," a senior doctor said, "it's like seeing a person who lost half her face." Both Dr. Weinstein and Dr. Stone objected to the presence of Libby's father, and wanted him barred from future hearings. Their request was granted in a judicial ruling that reasoned that since he was not a party to New York State's disciplinary proceedings, he couldn't participate in them. Sidney countered that he just wanted to be sure "several private and patently irrelevant" letters Libby had once written to a friend were protected. These were the letters in which she wrote openly about her abuse of cocaine and other drugs. But the court opposed Sidney's request, and the letters were introduced into evidence.

The charges against both doctors ranged from the failure to get Libby's complete medical history to the failure to monitor her condition and vital signs adequately. The most disturbing charge, Sheehan told the three-judge board made up of a retired ophthalmologist, an orthopedic surgeon, and a former medical-school administrator, was that Libby had been given Demerol when the doctors knew she was on Nardil. Mr. Sheehan also spoke out against the "totally incompetent" decision to place restraints on Libby.

But Dr. Weinstein, as the one who mapped Libby's course, defended both her use of restraints and the Demerol, although she conceded that had she been "100 percent sure" that Libby used drugs as she did, she might not have ordered Demerol. She might also have ordered more vital-sign monitoring, she added. She had asked Libby three times about drugs, she said. Libby had insisted that she hadn't taken anything, and then, Dr. Weinstein told the state board, "she turned her back to me."

Had Dr. Weinstein been annoyed by the sick girl's demeanor? "I gave her the benefit of the doubt and believed what she had told me," Dr. Weinstein concluded.

Dr. Stone repeated that he would have considered it "significant" information if he had had proof that Libby was lying about her drug abuse. Both he and Dr. Weinstein believed that "intoxicated" patients could not control their behavior. Libby could.

Dr. Weinstein said the nurses told her they were worried that Libby would fall and injure herself, given the degree of thrashing around they were witnessing, but that there were no changes in her overall medical condition.

Therefore, Dr. Weinstein said, she gave orders for restraints and Haldol over the telephone, instead of in person. "In my judgment, I felt it was appropriate," Dr. Weinstein insisted. "Telephone orders are taken in a hospital. It
is not unusual."

However, the 1984 *New York Hospital Graduate Staff
Manual* emphasizes that "telephone orders are not permitted except when the doctor cannot come to the unit at the
time." Dr. Weinstein explained she "had hoped that with
time, Libby would calm down. When you are taking care of
patients, you can't be in all places at all times and so you
triage. You delegate orders of importance."

Witness after witness testified. New York Hospital spent
more than a million dollars to defend its residents, and by
the time all the judicial proceedings were over, would
spend three million more. In total, both sides would spend
approximately six million dollars in legal expenses.

Witnesses explained that Libby's agitation was considered to be perhaps "a psychiatric manifestation of her reaction to her medical illness"; that a drug screen had been
planned for later on; that Libby looked "very good" when
the Posey restraint was applied; that if Libby's prior illicit
drug use and her abortions weren't obtained in the history,
it wasn't from any "lack of effort" on the doctors' part; that
an emergency psychiatric consultation was not required;
and that there was no report in the whole of medical literature that said that 25 mg of Demerol was contraindicated
with Nardil. One witness said that Dr. Stone's "meticu-
lous" notes, as well as Dr. Weinstein's, were models that
could be used in teaching.

Later, Dr. Stone said, "In retrospect, I wish I had realized at the time that we've got an eighteen-year-old who's
on Nardil. Not a thirty-five-year-old, but an eighteen-year-
old who comes from a good family. It's very unusual for a

young person to be on Nardil, and I haven't seen any young person since who's been on a monoamine oxidase inhibitor. That might have been a clue that something was really wrong with this girl."

On August 6, 1987, the Board for Professional Medical Conduct filed fraud and gross-negligence charges against Dr. Raymond Sherman, alleging that he had been negligent "on more than one occasion." In addition to Libby, referred to as Patient A, there was Patient B, a woman he was covering for another doctor. This patient claimed that Dr. Sherman misdiagnosed a serious condition over the telephone, and that although she did eventually go to the emergency room for treatment, she suffered unnecessary pain and delay because Dr. Sherman never examined her personally.

Overall, Dr. Sherman was cited for failing to obtain medical histories, failing to perform examinations, improperly ordering drugs, failing to supervise "other physicians," rendering an improper diagnosis, and giving false testimony in another New York State Board for Professional Medical Conduct hearing. Dr. Sherman said that these charges—"every single one was false"—were the result of "atypical" procedures. "I was screened by one State Department of Health committee and exonerated. The next thing I heard was that there was going to be another committee," he told me. He believes that Sidney Zion exerted pressure to have this second committee convened.

Dr. Sherman would spend more than $350,000 defending himself, and because his malpractice insurance was not enough to cover all the costs, a defense fund was set up for him by a group of doctors at the hospital. In addition, 380 of his colleagues signed a letter on his behalf protesting the unjustifiable "destruction of his career."

Later, Dr. Sherman said that what happened to him was

definitely "not career enhancing. My life would have been different. I might have done more writing and research." His family felt the pressure too. Dr. Robert Ascheim, an internist from New York Hospital and a colleague of Dr. Sherman's, said that Dr. Sherman is "one of the saints in our business."

Although the establishment of the defense fund was considered unusual when its existence became known, actually it was a practice dating back to the turn of the century.

The medical school and the hospital also contributed to Dr. Sherman's expenses. "Whatever it cost, we were going to fight this battle," he said. "I wasn't going to let this politically connected guy—Sidney Zion—destroy my career without a fight."

The complete charges were never spelled out in the newspaper coverage of Dr. Sherman's case, nor was there mention that he had been accused of furnishing Libby with Valium and Darvocet without examining her and had failed to note those prescriptions in her medical records. The State Board for Professional Medical Conduct had determined that the Darvocet that Libby had taken was first prescribed by Dr. Sherman.

The first of twenty-three hearings on Dr. Sherman's conduct was held on October 7, 1987. None of the hearings for any of the three doctors utilized Associate Medical Examiner Dr. Jon Pearl's description of Libby's condition: "toxic agitation." Dr. Pearl was the first, and seemingly the last, person officially to use the description.

Witnesses reported at the first hearing that only 50 percent of attending doctors come in at the time that a patient is admitted, that there was evidence indicating that admitting Libby to the hospital was not even indicated under the circumstances, that her medical history as presented in the emergency room was adequate, and that there was adequate supervision of both Dr. Stone and Dr. Weinstein. One witness said that had Dr. Sherman gone to the hospital the night of March 4, 1984, he would only have said exactly the same things that he had said on the phone.

The board determined that in 1984 records were not necessarily kept of every single telephone order and that the Valium and Darvocet prescribed to Libby were in "small, innocuous amounts" that would "hardly . . . generate an addiction."

On September 23, 1989, two years after the first Weinstein-Stone hearing, the New York State Board for Professional Medical Conduct—after interviewing thirty-three witnesses, including the former chairman of the American Board of Internal Medicine, six heads of departments of medicine across the nation, and a doctor who was an editor of the standard medical text on pharmacology—reached a unanimous verdict concerning the former intern and resident.

The board agreed to drop all charges.

It presented its findings to the New York State commissioner of health, Dr. David Axelrod, who endorsed their decision.

"I am sad, but not surprised," Sidney said of the board's finding. "It's hard to prove," he later said. "If a judge is loath to hold doctors to the same standards as others, we're not in good shape for gross negligence." He said that the concept "that the doctor didn't mean to do it gets thrown in."

Yet, as Dr. Harvey Klein, a professor of clinical medicine at Cornell University Medical College, and a friend and colleague of Dr. Sherman's at New York Hospital, told some Harvard Medical School alumni in 1991, Dr. Sherman, "like so many other doctors in New York State, was charged with misconduct as a result of misdiagnosis."

A year later, on September 24, 1990, the New York State Board for Professional Medical Conduct also cleared Dr. Sherman of the nineteen charges that had been brought against him.

But it was not over.

Just four months earlier, on May 26, 1990, the New York State Board of Regents, which at the time had the final word on disciplinary actions against doctors—the State Department of Health assumed this responsibility a year later—had overturned the verdict of the State Board for Professional Medical Conduct on Dr. Stone and Dr. Weinstein. The Board of Regents, made up of sixteen members, only one of whom was a doctor, argued that Dr. Weinstein's failure to examine Libby after the nurses summoned her was "totally unacceptable," and therefore found her guilty of gross negligence on this charge.

"It doesn't make any difference whether or not Dr. Weinstein came physically back ten minutes later when you get to a point that an hour later Libby Zion got one mg of Haldol and went to sleep," Dr. Stone told me. "We're talking about a lot of issues that didn't make a lot of difference here." The Regents also found Dr. Stone guilty of gross negligence for diagnosing Libby as having "hysterical symptoms." This working diagnosis, they said, colored the perceptions of those caring for her, and led to her inadequate treatment. In effect, the Regents had come to the official conclusion that most definitely "viral syndrome with hysterical symptoms" was a diagnosis, and not a description.

Still, because the case was a very difficult one to work on, the Regents said, and because Dr. Stone's record had been up to that time unblemished, they decided not to take away his medical license. The Regents concluded that a "censure and reprimand" was a sufficiently serious penalty.

Dr. Weinstein, whose conduct was called both "egregious" and "conspicuously bad," received the same mild penalty because, the Regents said, she was only an intern at the time, just beginning her medical career. They said of Dr. Weinstein that until that point, her career had been unmarred, and that she had been confronted with a very difficult case for a neophyte physician.

"I THINK MUCH worse should have been done to these people," Sidney said of Dr. Weinstein's and Dr. Stone's censures, although he conceded that "wherever Libby is now, she'll be pleased."

On February 5, 1991, the Board of Regents met in closed session to decide whether or not to proceed with any disciplinary action against Dr. Sherman, even though he had been cleared by the New York State Board for Professional Medical Conduct. Two months later, on April 26, they dismissed the case. In essence, the Regents agreed with what one witness had told the State Board for Professional Medical Conduct: nothing could have been done to prevent Libby from dying, and that unless there were an "explanation for her death," no one could postulate what could have been done. Dr. Sherman received no censure or reprimand.

"The last few years have been a strenuous and difficult ordeal," he said at the time. "Even when you know you've done nothing wrong, it's not easy to be subjected to charges of professional misconduct."

"It was a cynical decision," Sidney responded. He said the Regents had reached it "because of tremendous influence from the medical establishment."

Nevertheless, Emlyn Griffith, a member of the Board of Regents, admitted to the Associated Press that while Dr. Sherman's treatment of Libby might have been negligent, it did not represent gross negligence under the law. Dr. Sherman was upset that the very word *negligent* had come up again, and replied, "That may be Mr. Griffith's opinion, but it's not what the Regents' decision said."

Griffith, who had actually voted to find Dr. Sherman guilty of gross negligence, sent Sidney a detailed letter about the situation, a letter that made its way to "Page Six," the gossip section of the *New York Post*. The article included Dr. Sherman's response: "The decision of the full Board was unequivocal . . . I think you should focus on that, rather than how a subcommittee voted."

Dr. Sherman's point of view on the legal definition of negligence is not dissimilar to Sidney's point of view on the legal definition of the presence of cocaine in a body.

There are often two truths, Libby's younger brother, Jed, commented, plainly groping toward a description of what is involved in any legal dispute, the conflict between opposed notions of truth. Emotionally, he said, he sensed what had happened to his sister. But his perception was different from the cold facts. Yet when his feeling on that fateful Sunday that he'd never see his sister alive again was placed alongside the medical facts—and they are presumably more accurate because they are the bare facts—those facts weren't more real to him. "It's bizarre and strange that there are two realities." In the final analysis, he said, it was hard to say which was more real.

BOTH DR. WEINSTEIN and Dr. Stone—the first doctor in his family—appealed the Board of Regents' decision. They were fighting for their medical lives. "The case wasn't about malpractice," Dr. Stone told me. "It was

about a political and personal agenda that one man had."
He strongly believed that Sidney Zion "manipulated the
system to create an emotional and political juggernaut that
turned into the Libby Zion case."

On October 31, 1991, more than eight months after Dr.
Sherman was cleared by the Board of Regents, the New
York State Supreme Court Appellate Division unanimously
voted to overturn the Regents' formal censure of Dr. Stone
and Dr. Weinstein. They, too, were now cleared. They
were no longer part of "a reincarnation of the Holy Inquisi-
tion," which had been Dr. Harvey Klein's description of
the long disciplinary procedure when he spoke to his Harvard Medical School fellow alumni in 1991.

After Dr. Sherman was cleared by the Regents, Sidney
announced that "the whole disciplinary procedure has broken down." In 1991, when the Board of Regents became
the Regents Review Committee of the State Department
of Health, he commented, "It's now doctors judged by
doctors. One layman against two doctors," and, he added
adamantly, "Doctors don't have the capacity to prosecute
themselves."

Some people would say that perhaps what he might
better have said was that doctors have the capacity to prosecute themselves, but not the willingness. "Deny, deny,
deny. The hint is in my chart," Dr. Sherman had said of
Libby Zion. But he could have been talking about himself.

On November 6, 1991, an editorial in the *New York Post*
urged that the Court of Appeals, the state's highest court,
hear the case against the intern and resident. Sidney
avowed, "I'm going to try to get them to appeal it." He
believed that "someone did a lot of work" to bring about
the reversal of the guilty decision. "It was probably Morgenthau . . . the cocaine charges were brought up again.
It was mean-spirited."

He pledged to call Robert Abrams, the attorney general of New York State. When he reached him, "Bobby" told Sidney "that an appeal has to be based on an error of law, not an error of fact." And, Sidney acknowledged, since the decision had been based on fact, no appeal was possible. He became resigned.

But during that first week of November 1991, an ugly incident occurred in the middle of the night at the Zion apartment on West Ninetieth Street. The phone rang, and when Sidney answered, an unfamiliar voice screamed, "Libby was a *w-h-o-r-e.*" Sidney slammed down the receiver.

The phone rang again. This time the voice sang out, "A cheer for the AMA." Sidney was unnerved.

After disconnecting the call, he left the phone off the hook. Was a backlash beginning? he later wondered. How could everything he had fought for have been forgotten? Hadn't Dr. David Axelrod and Governor Mario Cuomo allocated $270 million for the implementation of the Libby Zion regulations in New York State?

Sometime in the middle of October he had been told by "somebody high up" that the word going around was that he had lost the civil case. But how could he lose something that hadn't even been tried yet? Sidney interpreted the rumor to mean that New York Hospital's lawyers were "going around talking about the case." It was seven years since Libby had died. He told his lawyers he wanted to "go public," and write a newspaper column about how the legal system had "ignored, stonewalled, delayed the Libby Zion case."

"I'm not a man of peace, I'm not forgiving," Sidney later said. He wanted *Zion* v. *New York Hospital* to move faster.

Was it pure coincidence, he again wondered, that the

New York Public Library sponsored a talk on November 6, 1991, entitled "Partisan Journalism: The Libby Zion Story and *The New York Times*"? The lecturer was a Long Island high school and college teacher of history named Diana Klebanow.

I attended the talk.

Diana Klebanow had been contacted by the Mid-Manhattan branch of the library system on the recommendation of an unnamed doctor. Klebanow had written an article about the Zion case that she had not been able to publish, even though one magazine editor told her, "Your article changed my opinion of the case." The particular rejection on which she concentrated her talk was that of *The New York Times*.

In 1989, when she had started her research, she had no idea of what she would find, she told the library audience of around fifty people, including Frank Bensel, the lead counsel for New York Hospital. She added that sometimes she regretted what she had found.

She stated that in her opinion, the press had closed ranks, and said that there was a bias in the media concerning the Zion case. She suspected that it was "someone high up" at *The New York Times* who had vetoed her article. "Sidney Zion himself didn't have that kind of clout," she said, "and neither did Andrew Stein." *The New York Times*, she said, had "not only failed to cite the reasons the doctors were exonerated, but never mentioned that Miss Zion had taken cocaine." She explained to her listeners that the newspaper had difficulty accepting the fact that the doctors were not found responsible for Libby's death. "Sidney Zion is more rooted in fiction than fact," she asserted. "Persons using cocaine can die suddenly," she said, going on to explain that "much of the cocaine that is sold is impure, and is often mixed with amphetamines."

How the speaker meant to distribute her blame was hard to understand. Although much of her story was well-reasoned and effective, her presentation was marred by a self-satisfied tone that several people in the audience noted. Some of her listeners felt that she was too anti–*New York Times*, and even too anti-media. In her conclusion she said the story of Libby's death should not have run in the first place. "That was censorship and partisan journalism on her part," a library official observed.

When I later called Klebanow to find out more about her research, background, and motive in the case, and asked for an interview, she was very antagonistic, refusing to discuss anything about the case. "I don't answer questions," she said.

"It's McCarthyite tactics," Sidney raged when he heard about the lecture. "There's no way to connect cocaine to Libby's death, even if there was cocaine," he said, once again uncharacteristically acknowledging the possibility of the drug's presence.

"Is that a death penalty?" he asked. "What kids didn't take drugs? West Side kids do drugs, a friend of mine says. We were talking about it today. It's no big deal."

"THERE IS MORE political intrigue in this case than anything else," Dr. Sherman's colleague, Dr. Robert Ascheim, told me. He was referring to Sidney's conduct, but I discovered that his remark applied to New York Hospital as well. A resident there told me, "One of New York Hospital's goals is to keep things looking good." She meant not only in the Zion case, but in everything else as well.

As the years passed, and the hospital concluded that the case was being tried in the media, an influential New York Hospital doctor paid a visit to an influential *New York Times* editor to ask for fairer coverage of the hospital's side of some of the issues. The newspaper defended its coverage, yet at some point in 1991 when Sidney complained to a former colleague at the paper that a certain article about hospitals hadn't mentioned Libby's case, he said that he was told that his daughter was "no longer a headline name."

12

W HAT COULD HAVE been done differently is part of any adverse outcome," Dr. Raymond Sherman told me, although not specifically about the Zion case. "It is important for a doctor's own education to look for mistakes and make it clear to others what mistakes were made, and how they can be avoided in the future," he added.

However, like all teaching hospitals, New York Hospital had a hard time accepting change, especially change brought on because of a case that embarrassed it and threatened not only its past, but also its future. "The cumulative effect of the 1987 criticism has been devastating," said David Skinner, the hospital's present chief executive officer.

But three years after Libby's death, the medical center experimented with the "night float" system that allowed the intern on duty to get some sleep while another trainee took over for the night. "It was a disaster," said Dr. Joseph

Hayes, vice chairman of medicine in charge of resident training at the hospital. "No intern worth his salt will leave a sick patient," he said, speaking to the belief that night floats create a shift mentality among the residents and don't allow for continuity of care. However, a study in a hospital in New Brunswick, New Jersey, concluded that the night float system boosted the morale of the house staff and had no detrimental effect on patients, although it admitted that miscommunication was a potential problem.

In 1991 Dr. Hayes collaborated on a limited study that, in the words of the Associated Press, suggested "that a hospital patient may be better off with a bone-tired intern who is familiar with the case than a rested one who is not." The authors of the study, published in the *Journal of the American Medical Association* on January 20, 1993, compared two sets of patients—one before the 405 regulations took effect in 1989, and one after the regulations took effect. None of the patients in either group experienced bad outcomes, although the group studied after the 405 regulations were instituted suffered treatment complications and delays in testing.

Conceding that it was still too soon to tell how patients will fare in the future, Dr. Hayes told the Associated Press that instead of "writing little notes," interns whose shifts are ending now use computers. "We are trying to utilize twentieth-century informatics to make the system work," Dr. Hayes said.

Nevertheless, the authors wrote that the medical service they studied was "in full compliance" even before the 405 regulations went into effect. "Our supervision has been unchanged," Dr. Hayes told me. "Everything is the same" at the hospital "except the hours."

This is not entirely true. He said that "years ago on most teaching services there was a ward attending." Ward attendings—senior doctors assigned to remain on a particular floor—no longer exist, as they once did. Now attendings arrive in the morning, or later, and make rounds with the house staff. A study in the *Archives of Internal Medicine* indicated that attendings averaged only twelve minutes of personal exchange daily with interns at a hospital in Detroit, Michigan.

Dr. Hayes said that at New York Hospital the attendings came back after rounds at least once every day. But he pointed out that these responsibilities are totally voluntary, and that most attendings do rounds only once a month, because "it's hard, hard work."

In general, such hospital duties are voluntary. The American Medical Association's *Graduate Medical Education Directory* even states that seeking the "accreditation of residency programs is a voluntary process." Yet Dr. William Ellis, who is medical director of the New York State Bureau of Hospital Service, says that the process may not be formally required, but that it is expected, nevertheless. "It's a cultural issue," he said. "The profession of medicine doesn't like to think anything is mandatory." Indeed, although the licensing procedure for doctors underwent some change a decade after Libby's death, the recommended reexamination for certain specialties every six years is voluntary.

What part did the Zion case actually play in altering hospital conditions? I asked Dr. Emilie Osborn, an associate dean at the University of California, San Francisco School of Medicine. "It increased the pressure to change," she replied. I put these questions to other doctors: Why this case? Was it Sidney's persistence in keeping his daughter's name in the headlines? Virtually every attending with whom I spoke thought that this was so, although most of them also thought that the time was ripe for a change. One doctor said, "A case like Libby's doesn't go away. Rodney King doesn't go away." Dr. Maurice Leonard, the PGY-2 in the ER when Libby arrived, told me that the case "took on a life of its own." Indeed, he agreed that "the changes were good. It's not optimal having junior residents run ERs."

Dr. Joseph Hayes believes that hospital practice becomes more and more difficult for the interns and residents because there is more to learn. There are complicated tests. "They have to deal with DNR, and in a few years it will be euthanasia." He continued, "We had it easy compared to today, even though we had to do our own lab work. Attendings joke that we couldn't get into our own programs today."

In saying that the hospital routine was fundamentally the same before and after the 405 regulations, Dr. Hayes was altogether accurate regarding one critical area: the closed order book. Until the closed order book—placing overmuch authority in the hands of interns and residents—is acknowledged and is itself specifically put on trial, no study will be worth anything, and no amount of twentieth- or twenty-first-century technology will make the system work. The closed order book is built into that system. Even the 1986 grand jury report on Libby had admitted as much. "Senior supervising physicians candidly acknowledged that it was and is the rule, and not the exception, that primary patient care is placed in the hands of interns and junior residents with little or no hospital experience, and that contemporaneous and in-person supervision of these physicians is frequently nonexistent." "The same thing could have happened if I was in the hospital or not," Dr. Sherman acknowledged.

By 1992, according to an article in the January 1992 issue of *M.D.* magazine, the working conditions of interns and residents had become a worldwide concern. The magazine reported that two years earlier, in 1990, house staffs in France went on strike for shorter hours and higher salaries. British Columbia became the first Canadian province to initiate an eighty-hour-week limit for house staffs in all hospitals. "Juniors" in New Zealand, Australia, and the United Kingdom asked for better working conditions, and in 1990 a maximum average of seventy-two hours a week was inaugurated in the United Kingdom. A revolution in medical education was brewing, and the Libby Zion case had its unmistakable importance as a source. In December 1990, the *New York Post* reported that "patients at city-run hospitals are receiving better care as a result of the Libby Zion rules." That same year, an episode of the television series *Law and Order* was based on Libby's death.

In 1991, Andrew Stein held a public hearing, "Code Blue: Emergency Rooms in Crisis." "I can't believe this is still happening," Elsa sighed. She attended the hearing to hear her husband's testimony.

While Sidney was speaking out in public and pursuing his lawsuit, Elsa was trying to understand malpractice. In her capacity as an aide to Stein, she researched and wrote a report on the subject, which appeared in December 1992. She discovered that the year before, in 1991, researchers had found that patient-management mistakes by residents were cited most frequently as related to mistakes leading to negligence. She quoted two doctors who did a study on the quality of house-staff examinations as saying medical educators should be "concerned." This study had been done the year before Libby died. "Resident error is just as true today as it was then," Elsa said somberly.

"They don't care whether we live or die," Sidney told the fifty or so people present at Stein's hearing on emergency rooms. "They continue to spit in the face of the regulations."

But by 1992, twelve states had initiated legislation to improve residency training.

Some medical personnel continued to actively oppose the changes and openly defy the 405 regulations. In 1993, a third-year student at Columbia's College of Physicians and Surgeons told me that "no one pays attention to the Zion regulations" anymore. Some interns and residents even created fake schedules. Doctors talked about being "under attack." In 1994, Mark Green, New York's public advocate, issued a scathing report on the widespread violation of the regulations; in fact, Green's staff discovered that some interns and residents didn't even know what the 405 regulations were. They also discovered that funds specifically designated for increased supervision were not being used for that purpose because they got lost in the general operating budgets of hospitals, and that there was not enough money available to do proper oversight; resources permitted a survey of hospital compliance only once every five or six years. "The major incentive for improvement is bad publicity," Howard Brown, assistant director of systems control at the New York City Department of Health, told Green's staff. YOUNG, TIRED DOCTORS—HAZARDOUS TO YOUR HEALTH, proclaimed a headline in *New York Newsday* on November 17, 1994, after the Green report was made public. "This is a disgrace—my baby died in vain," Sidney lamented.

Yet the report also disclosed that 60 percent of attending doctors and 60 percent of residents in New York endorsed the 405 regulations. But, Dr. Raymond Sherman said, "the jury is still out. We just don't know. There are good things about house officers not being tired, but doctors work late, long hours." And, he added without irony, "doctors should learn early that you've got to be there when people need you."

"No one would trade going back" to the ways things were, a resident said. "Residents love the Bell Commission," a residency director allowed.

Nothing would ever be the same again. As social reformer Wendell Phillips lectured, "Revolutions are not made, they come. A revolution is as natural a growth as an oak. It comes out of the past. Its foundations are laid far back." So it was with what was happening in medicine all around the globe, and the past had as much to do with what was going on as anything else, and nothing could stop it.

''ALL DAY LONG, I sit and wait/watch the clock which holds my fate/all day long I hold myself/till playtime comes around/There can't be/anything else for me/all I want is to get rid of these/boredom blues!" Libby wrote in her journal. "Baby knows I just can't take this fate/sittin' here waitin'/Lord just hesitatin'/can't stay here and I can't go out/I'm gonna split before I flip out/Lord you know I got them/BOREDOM BLUES!"

Libby made up song lyrics that appealed to teen-agers like herself who were struggling with confusion and indecision. She was always reaching out to others to share "my ideas, my dreams, my life." She had written in her application to Bennington College that the songs, poetry, stories, and personal entries in her journal were her most valuable possessions. "Increasing one's self-knowledge," seventeen-year-old Libby wrote in the fall of 1983, "can only increase one's knowledge about the people who surround you, because in order to understand what everyone else is doing, you first have to understand what *you* are doing." Her writing made her feel "content," she said.

Three years after her death, in 1987, there were hints that a million-dollar settlement might somehow be worked out between New York Hospital and Sidney Zion. "Let the chips fall where they may," Adam Zion said. "Because in the end, New York Hospital isn't going to survive the thing. They're not going to win. I don't give a damn about the money. They can't bring me back my sister," he said. "Although I had a dream the other night that she came back to life. I remember saying to her, 'What do you care, you came back to life.' "

Ted Friedman, the Zion family lawyer at the time, took the position that a condition of any settlement must be that the hospital publicly acknowledge its mistakes and the steps it would take to prevent their repetition. But hospitals prefer to restrict what they say. New York Hospital had paid the thirteen-thousand-dollar fine imposed by the New York State Board of Health, and admitted guilt in Libby's death in the March 1987 stipulation, but it was a stipulation that the hospital had signed on the condition that it could never be used in any litigation. Its admission of guilt didn't exist outside the narrow scope of that document. A nationally known medical malpractice jurist, who requested anonymity, spoke of doctors as experts in denial. "The detachment of doctors from the unpleasant realities of their profession is incredible," he said.

New York Hospital wanted the Zion case to be settled because it knew that if there were a trial, and punitive damages were awarded, a settlement might reach as high as ten million dollars. Also, it could no longer afford the negative publicity. Keith Thompson, senior vice president and general counsel for the hospital, believed that "a lot of people probably have used this case for whatever other purposes and horses they wanted to ride." It wasn't just a matter of malpractice.

However, there was no settlement that year. One of the many factors delaying an agreement was the hospital's demand for a gag order. "All kinds of things happen in this case that couldn't happen in any other case," Sidney said. Frank Bensel, the lead counsel for the doctors and New York Hospital, said that it was "a big source of aggravation" to them to pick up a newspaper and read an article about the case that did not contain the facts. The facts, he said, were available but the media didn't do proper research. "There are probably more facts out in the record right now than will probably come out in the trial," Keith Thompson said. "THEY LEFT MY KID ALONE AND KILLED HER was printed over and over again, and that was repeated over and over again on radio talk shows and television until it became written in stone in the minds of many people," Frank Bensel said.

Five more years would pass, years filled with motions, depositions, stalled discovery, delayed conferences, postponements, referees, change of judges, courtroom fines, and bitter clashes among the lawyers, before, in 1992, there was any further discussion of a settlement.

The long delays would place a strain on the Zion family. There were personal and spiritual crises, too. "It wasn't my sister's death that stopped me believing in God," Adam said. No. It was something else, the death of a stranger's pet. "We hit a dog—a golden retriever—and that destroyed my belief," Adam said softly. "That single event made me see it's more nature than anything else."

IN THE SPRING of 1992, private settlement talks were once again arranged by New York Hospital. Sidney said that at the first of several meetings, Ted Friedman announced to the hospital lawyers, "I'm not here to negotiate, I'm here to accept surrender."

And that almost happened.

"They're willing to sell out the doctors on the spot," Sidney said of the hospital's initial agreement in principle to all his conditions. "I never thought they'd do it."

But, in fact, New York Hospital would not agree to all three of Sidney's conditions. Its lawyers were willing to concede that it appeared that there was no cocaine in the case. They were willing to praise the 405 regulations. But they were not willing to accept Sidney's demand that it admit to causing Libby's death. Sidney said his position was not negotiable on that point. But the hospital was not willing to go that far, although it was willing to say, "One could conclude that it caused her death." Sidney said a word like "*conclude* leaves doubt, and gives New York Hospital a way out. I want headlines to read, NEW YORK HOSPITAL ADMITS DOCTORS CAUSED LIBBY ZION'S DEATH."

The nationally known medical malpractice jurist said, "If you dig deep, there's enough of a question of a departure to tell New York Hospital not to risk a trial. But they are very, very firm that they did nothing wrong."

There were several more meetings of the parties. "They came two thirds of the way," Sidney said. Even though he was satisfied that the cocaine issue was basically dead, he was still concerned that the hospital seemed to be "weaseling" by using a word like *appears*, as in "there appears to be no evidence of cocaine." New York Hospital, however, had gone a long way from its 1987 stance that there were "strong possibilities that cocaine may have contributed to Libby Zion's death." The hospital desperately wanted to settle the case.

Sidney also said that officials wanted him to say he regretted calling the doctors criminals. "I said no. I don't even regret trying to indict the doctors." When told by some colleagues that it could amount to a "big problem" if he didn't apologize, he sent word that "there's no fucking way I'll apologize." He was adamant. "I want New York Hospital to bite the bullet, and if they can't or won't, we'll go to trial."

For the next few months he went from saying "I want to see Ray Sherman put under the gun; I want to ruin him" to saying "Maybe right before trial they'll somehow get scared and settle, when they see they'll be on Court TV."

Cheryl Bulbach, a free-lance lawyer hired by Ted Friedman to work full-time on the case, was his secret weapon because she had once been a registered nurse, and had even worked briefly at New York Hospital. She said that "everybody in the medical community knows that the doctors did the wrong things, that everything was screwed up, and that they should have been punished. But the hospital will not admit it." She said that one of her doctor friends suggested that New York Hospital should have opened a Libby Zion memorial wing. "The hospital officials should take their lumps," she said, "and accept what they did that was wrong, and at least, then, they would have done an honorable thing. But they're not going to do that in this case. New York Hospital is going to stonewall all the way through. The Libby Zion case is their Watergate."

ON APRIL 27, 1993, New York Hospital filed for a partial summary judgment, which is the procedural equivalent of a trial. It was asking the Supreme Court of the State of New York to dismiss the Zions' claim for punitive damages, customarily awarded to a plaintiff in order to teach the defendant a lesson for the future. The hospital also wanted the allegations of gross negligence and wanton conduct removed from the lawsuit. "It's a way to poison the mind of the judge," Sidney said of the motion, and he explained that without punitive damages "it would mean my kid's life is only worth a hundred thousand dollars."

New York Hospital asked the new and final judge— Elliott Wilk, who would preside over the Mia Farrow– Woody Allen custody dispute that summer—to make a decision based on the fact that the New York State Board for Professional Medical Conduct as well as the New York State Supreme Court Appellate Division had already found Dr. Stone and Dr. Weinstein innocent of all charges, that the New York State Board for Professional Medical Conduct had cleared Dr. Sherman of all charges, and that Dr. Leonard had never been charged at all in the case. Dr. Leonard was included in the suit because Sidney believed that he had been negligent in admitting Libby to Payson 5 instead of to the intensive care unit.

Dr. Stone, who is licensed to practice medicine in Missouri and California, was being represented by a law firm— Heidell, Pittoni, Murphy, & Bach—other than the hospital's, primarily because of a dispute with Dr. Sherman over whether the giving of Demerol to Libby was discussed in their March 4, 1984, consultation. Dr. Stone had maintained that it was, and that the attending doctor had approved the drug's administration, but Dr. Sherman said that he first learned about the Demerol the morning after Libby's death. "The medicine should not have been given," Dr. Sherman admitted, as did Dr. Leonard. But "there's not major malpractice here," Dr. Leonard believed. "There are no gross departures."

On July 27, 1993, Sidney's lawyers filed an opposition to what they referred to as the hospital's "frivolous" motion. "They hardly ever grant a summary judgment," Sidney said. He wrote the lead for the brief. "If you have any hint of further evidence they'll let you prove it."

There were strong words from all sides. Frank Bensel,

who had called the grand jury report "one-sided" and "necessarily skewed," said that Ted Friedman was "full of sound and fury, signifying nothing." He used "rhetorical hyperbole" and "outrageous publicity stunts." Ted Friedman labeled the hospital "venomous," "stubborn," and "greedy" in its refusal to understand what the "celebrated" case was really about—an attack on the system of neophyte doctors working a hundred hours or more each week. He charged that the hospital had used "conduct reminiscent of the times of Joe McCarthy" in its demand for a written loyalty oath from senior doctors at Lenox Hill Hospital absolving New York Hospital of blame in Libby's death. At the time, New York Hospital and Lenox Hill were contemplating an affiliation, which never came about because Dr. Ira Hoffman, associate chief of medicine at Lenox Hill, had been a witness for the New York State Department of Health at the disciplinary hearings of the doctors. The so-called loyalty oaths were a result of what was perceived as Dr. Hoffman's anti–New York Hospital testimony, especially his sharp words that "Libby had been a throwaway case on a Sunday night of an unpopular style of patient."

"Medicine is in a terrible fix," Dr. Hoffman later commented. "The answers don't lie with doctors, lawyers, or patients."

Noting the 405 regulations, Frank Bensel told the court that "at no time was any involvement with Ms. Zion beyond the new twenty-four-hour limit for 'on-call' treatment of patients." Indeed, as *M.D.* magazine pointed out, one of the ironies in the Zion case is that all the residents had been working for no more than nineteen hours, and Dr. Leonard far less, and all were well within the rules designed by the Bell Commission. But later a sleep expert said that Dr. Weinstein had a sleep "debt" of fourteen and a half hours because she had actually only slept thirty-eight hours that week, whereas the normal amount should have been fifty-two and a half hours.

Ted Friedman charged that Dr. Stone, as a member of New York Hospital's internal medicine residency, had worked in "one of the last remaining 'sweatshops' of the twentieth century." Dr. Stone's lawyer, Luke M. Pittoni, said that such a charge was absolutely unfounded. Dr. Stone signed an affidavit defending the residency program as appropriate. "I chose the New York Hospital–Cornell Medical Center for my residency," he said, "because of its reputation for excellence in patient care and graduate medical education. Of course, I played no role in the design of that program."

On October, 1, 1993, Ted Friedman asked Judge Wilk for a hearing on a motion to exclude the issue of cocaine from any trial proceedings. There were now two motions for the court to consider.

A gossip column in the *New York Post* reported on November 8 that "Ted Friedman will ask that the lawyers for New York Hospital be disciplined for causing key documents to be transferred out of the chief medical examiner's office." The article said that Friedman was also trying to have one of the hospital's experts cited for contempt for allegedly ignoring a subpoena. "But," the column went on, "most seriously of all, Friedman will charge that there is a 'conspiracy of silence' that is denying the Zions access to their own expert witnesses." And the item quoted Friedman as saying, "You could call it an Ivy League Curtain. We had various expert witnesses lined up from Harvard, Yale, Johns Hopkins, and Mount Sinai. The hierarchy has intimidated them into not testifying."

Sidney was incensed that the hospital, without consulting his lawyers, had acquired new slides of Libby's tissues from the medical examiner's office.

"We don't know what part of Libby's body they are from," Cheryl Bulbach said.

"It's an invasion of the crypt," Ted Friedman warned. "There's no excuse for what they did."

But New York Hospital had an explanation.

"Sidney Zion and Ted Friedman don't want the case tried if cocaine is in it," Frank Bensel said, without adding whether or not the slides contained any new details. "They want a pretrial hearing. This is a rarely used procedure," he said. Bensel believed that Sidney was frightened that cocaine might become an issue. Sidney said this wasn't true, even though Alan Dershowitz had informally advised him that cocaine could mess up the whole case.

But Sidney now believed that it didn't matter, and that "we can win with it in. The cocaine is a spurious, fake thing."

ON NOVEMBER 10, 1993, the first of several pretrial hearings was held in the sprawling neoclassical beaux arts Supreme Court building at 60 Centre Street in lower Manhattan. There were very few spectators in the partially wood-paneled courtroom besides the lawyers, their assistants, and Sidney Zion, who would be present at all of the proceedings. Elsa Zion would not attend any of them.

The jury box stood empty, although later at Judge Wilk's invitation, I sat there in order to hear better. Two round clocks were hung on the beige wall facing the bench. One, with large Roman numerals, was not working; the other, similar to the utilitarian ones found in schoolrooms, ticked away. Six-inch metal letters spelling out IN GOD WE TRUST were fastened to the wall over the bench.

There was plenty of debate. Ted Friedman was worried

about the new slides of Libby's tissues. "There are issues of confidentiality," he argued, telling Judge Wilk that the slides were being passed around the medical community. He was concerned that they were becoming the subject of gossip.

"We never bandied these records about," Frank Bensel said. "Mr. Friedman can't say they're privileged. This is a malpractice case where the cause of death is an issue."

Once again impassioned words were exchanged, and in fact there was so much time spent on what Judge Wilk called things that didn't matter that there was no time left to consider the motions before the court.

A month later, on December 17, another hearing was held; this time Judge Wilk announced that there was going to be a "dry run of the trial" before he heard the motions. He wanted "a clearer sense of what's going to happen," and he wanted the lawyers to explain what they had to prove to the jury. "After ten years I assume there aren't many secrets," he remarked.

Two months later, on February 18, 1994, Friedman and Bensel were ready for their dry runs.

"Let's get to business," Judge Wilk said at ten-fifteen in the morning. Ted Friedman went first.

He described Libby, her accomplishments, her depression, her colon problem, and Dr. Greenspan and his bio-feedback-and-Nardil treatment. "Libby demonstrated a strong awareness of Nardil's restrictions," he told Judge Wilk. He listed all the records and transcripts he would put into evidence.

At one point, Judge Wilk asked about the relationship between Libby's pediatrician, Dr. Irene Shapiro, and Dr. Sherman.

"She was in transition," Ted Friedman replied. He said that because of Libby's age, "she was seeing both." Judge

Wilk joked that he knew someone who was still seeing a pediatrician at the age of forty.

"What treatment did Libby Zion receive?" Friedman asked the court after several hours of speaking.

He paused.

There was an eerie silence in the room. A handful of people were spread out over the nine dark-brown wooden benches that faced the counsel's table.

"The court will notice silence," Ted Friedman said to Judge Wilk.

He paused again.

"She didn't get any treatment . . ."

Sidney wept openly.

"They treated her as a girl who didn't need to be cared for," Ted Friedman accused. "There were no grown-up doctors on the scene . . ."

It was a balmy day for February. The temperature was in the fifties. Most of the windows in the courtroom were open. The American flag to the right of Judge Wilk waved softly.

At one a lunch break was called.

"I wish I could have gone deaf in there," Frank Bensel whispered to me as we stood by the elevator waiting to go down to the main floor. We had had two meetings and many phone calls in my effort to gain the cooperation of New York Hospital.

"Don't tempt fate," I answered.

He agreed, and then introduced me to Luke Pittoni, Dr. Stone's lawyer. We all went down in the elevator together. It was a short, tense ride.

When the hearing reconvened, Ted Friedman went on with his "narrative," as he called it. He spoke all afternoon.

He referred to the long hours of residents as "fraternity hazing." He said that he would bring in experts on sleep deprivation. Frank Bensel objected. "It's not admissible," he told Judge Wilk.

"Don't you have to show the doctors had sleep deprivation?" Luke Pittoni asked.

Judge Wilk decided it was a matter for a jury to consider.

After a short break at four, Judge Wilk made a dramatic decision concerning the motion regarding punitive damages.

"What do you want in terms of damages?" he asked Sidney's lawyer.

"Compensatory damages for wrongful death, and punitive damages for conscious pain and suffering," Ted Friedman replied.

"This is an issue for the jury," Judge Wilk said. "New York Hospital's motion for dismissal of punitive damages should be denied."

Sidney gave a tentative smile. It was a victory of sorts. Frank Bensel looked skeptical.

It was too late in the day to decide on the cocaine motion, although Judge Wilk hinted to Frank Bensel that New York Hospital would have to be very specific in its arguments.

"I think the issue is not whether there was cocaine or not," Judge Wilk reasoned. "The real issue is, assuming there was cocaine, did it have anything to do with what she was experiencing? How does it impact on her treatment re the doctors? New York Hospital has to relate the issue of cocaine to Libby's death," he said. "I'd like to know what you have," he told Frank Bensel. "I'd like to avoid a trial about cocaine."

"It's not realistic for the jury to try the issue of cocaine," Ted Friedman spoke up. "It has the smell, the stink, of a skunk in the courtroom," he said. Besides, he went on, "it's not a triable issue of fact."

"If it is not triable, it doesn't come in to the trial," Judge Wilk answered. "If it is triable, it does come in."

Eleven months earlier, Ted Friedman had told me that if cocaine were in the case it would be like "running a race with a ten-pound weight around my waist, and I'd rather not have it."

"Libby Zion used cocaine," Luke Pittoni told Judge Wilk. "The history is important, and would have altered her treatment."

"We'll think about it," Judge Wilk told him as the hearing ended. "We'll think about it."

A HEARING SCHEDULED for March 4, 1994, was canceled, and rescheduled for March 19.

"When can we start the trial?" Judge Wilk asked the assembled group on the appointed day.

There was a brief discussion about "running into summer" and "trouble getting a jury during vacations," and then someone discreetly brought up that a starting date depended on the resolution of certain legal problems that Ted Friedman was having, problems that had jolted the legal community when they first became known in 1990. There were hushed voices in the courtroom. Sidney stared straight ahead. Ted Friedman's prominence was such that it was said that he "all but walked on water," so there was shock when he had been served with a notice and statement of charges which, according to the *New York Law Journal,* "alleged twenty-three separate counts of professional misconduct stretching over a decade and arising out of his representation of personal-injury claimants in three separate matters." The Appellate Division of the New York State Supreme Court was due to make its decision on his punishment that week. Meanwhile, the pretrial hearing in the Zion case would go on. Ted Friedman sat at the counsel's table looking tired and pale.

It was Frank Bensel's turn for a dry run.

He listed his witnesses. "Experts will say that Libby Zion had a preexisting condition before she entered the hospital," he asserted. He said that Libby did not die from an infection or negligence. "Her death was not medically preventable," he argued.

"Cocaine stays in the body a week," Frank Bensel had told me during an exchange in 1992. "Cocaine combined with other drugs and illness such as Libby had can contribute to the syndrome she displayed." He also told me that cocaine in the nose "would indicate that Libby used the drug sometime during the previous few days before her hospitalization," and that the cocaine in her blood "would indicate she used it sometime during the previous week."

Frank Bensel told Judge Wilk that the defense believed that Libby used cocaine in the early evening of March 4. He said that there was a "dramatic deterioration" in her condition at around nine. Bensel pounded away. "Cocaine causes cardiopulmonary collapse," the lawyer said. "We will develop evidence that sudden cocaine death can occur without a large dose. There can be a sudden idiosyncratic reaction. In other words, a safe dose one day can be fatal another."

New York Hospital had come out fighting on the cocaine issue. By not settling the case earlier, Sidney had lost his chance to have the matter of cocaine disappear. Now, in the courtroom, it was not only visible, but in the spotlight.

Luke Pittoni spoke next, on behalf of Dr. Stone. "Libby had a confusing presentation," he told Judge Wilk. Ominously, he claimed that "we will prove that her history was intentionally incorrect, not accidentally so."

Pittoni also pounded away on the cocaine issue. Libby's

rash could have come from cocaine use. The shift to the left in her elevated white blood count could be consistent with cocaine use. There was cocaine in Libby when she arrived at the emergency room.

Sidney looked ill.

After a recess, Luke Pittoni explained that punitive damages had nothing to do with Dr. Stone. "He's told when he's supposed to work. He's a good trooper and does what he is told."

"Punitive damages is not a causative action," Judge Wilk responded. "It will be decided later." The judge went on: "We can talk about gross negligence, but not punitive damages," he said.

"Giving contraindicated drugs is not gross negligence," Luke Pittoni implored.

"It's a jury question," Judge Wilk answered. "Doctors should look in the *PDR*," he said, noting that his own internist always asks him, " 'Are you taking anything?' "

Sidney looked uncomfortable. The afternoon had been draining, he said later.

There was debate about gross negligence. Cocaine came up again. It kept coming up. It had no place to hide in the open courtroom. Sidney seemed close to tears.

"Cocaine is an inflammatory issue," Judge Wilk said, after announcing that he had decided to hold hearings on the reliability of the RIA test for cocaine, and on the chain of custody of the nasal swab.

"I've never heard of a malpractice case where you have to offer proof like this," Frank Bensel said angrily.

"We wanted a hearing," Sidney later said. "Then we could have a witness saying if they thought it was cocaine why didn't they treat her for drugs? Everyone knows not to listen to the patient. New York Hospital doesn't want a hearing because it just wants the jury to hear the word *cocaine*, and then there'll be no punitive damages."

"So you've switched your position?" I asked.

"No," he said firmly. "It's just that if cocaine has to be in, I think we can beat it. I wonder why they are willing to risk being asked that if they suspected drugs, why didn't they act on it? I think they are willing to take that risk because they are so sure the jury will be prejudiced by hearing the word *cocaine* mentioned."

The hearing on cocaine was never held, but Sidney's position had switched, I believed. Two weeks before the March 19 pretrial hearing he had even said "no one thought cocaine was bad in 1984. It wasn't a crime. It was considered a recreational drug."

Eight months later, on November 28, 1994, when I once again asked him if he thought Libby had used cocaine, he answered, "I don't know about that. If she walked into the emergency room with coke, you don't live for more than forty-five minutes." He also admitted, without his characteristic rancor when the subject came up, "I don't know what she was doing."

I wondered if his mother's death in 1993 had brought about this new attitude, for he no longer had to protect Anne Zion from whatever painful truths might emerge from any investigation into Libby's death.

I remembered that Manhattan District Attorney Robert Morgenthau had once said that Sidney accepts as true a sanitized version of Libby's drug use because "he's got to explain it to his mother."

But not any longer.

ON MARCH 22, 1994, Sidney's lawyer, Ted Friedman, was disbarred for thirteen instances of unethical behavior by a panel of five judges from the New York State Supreme Court Appellate Division.

His disbarment, which had nothing to do with Libby's case, was ultimately based on two personal-injury cases. In one, he was accused of inappropriately turning over evidence to a jury and making false statements about the circumstances. And in the other, a private investigator he had hired was accused of bribing a witness, and Ted Friedman was found guilty of not supervising him appropriately. In 1988, Friedman, a distinguished graduate of the Harvard Law School, who was admitted to the bar in 1957, and whose wife of thirty years, Eve Preminger, is a surrogate court judge in New York City, had been indicted for subornation of perjury in that case but had been acquitted. In the 1994 charges, he was found to have paid "unreasonable and excessive sums of money and other benefits to witnesses and prospective witnesses."

"For this court to impose any other sanction would ignore our responsibility to the legal profession and the public," Judge Francis T. Murphy had said about the appellate court's ruling.

"It's a terrible frame-up," Sidney suggested. "You wonder if our case had anything to do with it."

"Some lawyers said he got what he deserved," *The New York Times* reported. "But others, including defense lawyers who openly hated him, said he was hit too hard," the newspaper continued. It was said that he hadn't done anything that other lawyers in New York hadn't done. "And that," *The New York Times* concluded, "was exactly the message the judges were trying to send."

"The appeals court would not hear his case. Ted's out," Sidney said. "I'll have to get another lawyer." Over the summer he hired a husband-and-wife team—Thomas A. Moore and Judith Livingston, of Kramer, Dillof, Tessel,

Duffy & Moore. Moore, an Irish-American graduate of Fordham's law school, who had once studied to become a Catholic priest, had produced million-dollar or higher verdicts in forty-seven malpractice cases. Livingston, a graduate of Hofstra's law school, had won million-dollar or higher verdicts in seventeen malpractice cases.

Judy Livingston would take a backseat in the Zion proceedings. Tom Moore would become the more dominant member of the partnership. Indeed, he had not lost a single case in the last sixteen he had tried.

13

"LIFE WITHOUT DEATH is like stories without deadlines. Nothing ever happens," Sidney Zion wrote to his daughter in the summer of 1982. Five years after Libby's death, in 1989, he ended an op-ed article in *The New York Times* "Once upon a time in America, the finest hospitals were run by the least experienced and most overworked apprentice doctors. Until one Sunday night in New York, a redheaded girl named Libby Zion . . ."

She had made things happen.

An unprecedented grand jury report. The Bell Commission. The Libby Laws.

"Libby Zion's death has changed residency training forever," an editorial in the *Journal of the American Medical Association* declared.

Rightly or wrongly, it often takes a person with a sense of mission, or perhaps even seemingly excessive rage, to bring about significant changes in the way in which an established institution conducts itself. A close family friend said of Sidney Zion that he "needs anger; it fills him up and takes the place of everything else." Another friend commented that "there was no question in my mind that in some way it was a career for Sidney—that having always had trouble producing, having always had trouble really living up to his gifts, which I think are enormous—he found this thing where he didn't have to work. He could crusade, and basically be a lobbyist in some way."

Libby's death, and her family's—and most especially her father's—personal torment had helped make the changes that began to transform medicine. And most important, after a century of tradition, questioning the way doctors are trained became a valid issue.

The final chapter of the Libby Zion case began on November 10, 1994, when the trial of the wrongful-death suit her father brought against New York Hospital and Drs. Sherman, Leonard, Stone, and Weinstein opened in the newly painted room 341 of the Supreme Court building in downtown New York. "There were times when I thought it would never happen," Sidney said.

A great deal would happen over the course of the next three months while the trial lasted, until the verdict was announced. Sidney and Elsa would be present in court every day. But most of what happened during the proceedings seemed to have little to do with the real Libby Zion. Attempts were made to characterize her unusual talent and charismatic personality, and a smiling photograph of her was shown to the jurors, although only two actually looked at it—the others feared it might prejudice their deliberations. But no clear-cut portrait of Libby ever emerged during the trial, and while such an objective is rarely achieved in any court proceeding, still, it seemed a sad commentary that the girl whose death was the reason for the trial was so invisible.

Thomas A. Moore, the Zions' new lawyer, was asking the court to award the plaintiff—the Zion family—two million dollars for Libby's pain and suffering, and one dollar for her wrongful death. "The family doesn't want one penny for the pecuniary loss of their daughter," Moore said. He also asked for punitive damages in an amount to be determined by the jury, and his stirring opening statement—he used no notes at all—laid out all the reasons the doctors and the hospital should be held responsible, and be made to pay heavily, for Libby's death: Dr. Sherman refused to go to the hospital; Libby's fever was ignored; her vital signs were not properly monitored; she was given Demerol, when it was known she was on Nardil; she was placed in restraints. Dr. Weinstein ignored the nurses' pleas to return to the floor.

The defense knew it had to labor hard because both Frank Bensel and Luke Pittoni acknowledged in their opening statements that giving Libby Demerol on Sunday, March 4, 1984, had been a mistake, although it did not cause her death. Frank Bensel emphasized that Libby's agitation and fever were present before the Demerol was injected. Cocaine hung over the defense's argument like a thick cloud. Luke Pittoni emphasized all the other drugs Libby was using and abusing. She hid her history. Libby could not be saved.

"A constellation of errors produced Libby Zion's death," Tom Moore exclaimed to the court, seeming to shout down anyone who suggested that polypharmacy— the use of a number of different drugs—might have killed her. Elsa Zion, out in the third-floor corridor during a break, protested all the effort and time spent on listing her daughter's drug use. "Libby didn't take a *stew* of drugs. She didn't take them *all* at once," she said.

The trial was an ordeal for Elsa. It was said that she suffered more than her husband because she kept her feelings inside. "This is torture," she said sadly. She was eager to put the trial behind her. After hearing Dr. Gregg Stone testify that he had never sent Sidney and her home, she nearly broke down. "He definitely said for us to go," she brooded. "Do you think I would have left otherwise?"

The Zions called eight witnesses: Raymond Sherman, M.D., Luise Weinstein, M.D., Nurse Myrna Balde, Sidney Zion himself, Elsa Zion, an expert in standard of care, an expert in sleep, and an expert in toxicology.

The hospital called eleven witnesses in its effort to convince the jury that Libby's care had been appropriate. In addition to Dr. Maurice Leonard, Dr. Gregg Stone, Dr. Joseph Ruggiero—the chief resident when Libby died—and Nurse Jerylyn Grismer, the defense team called an expert in residency-training programs, an expert in toxicology, an expert in forensic pathology, an expert in standard of care, an expert in sleep, an expert in pharmacology, and an expert in infectious diseases.

In the weeks preceding the trial, the lawyers had picked six jurors and four alternates ranging in age from their early thirties to their mid-fifties, and for the first several weeks of the trial, the jury was composed of four women and two men. On the twenty-second day of the trial, when one of the men was hurt in an accident and could no longer serve, it became five women and one man. "You are the judges of the facts," Judge Elliott Wilk told them on opening day. "We are blessed with extraordinarily capable counsel," he said. He made clear to the jurors that what was important was the quality of the evidence, not the quantity, and he

cautioned them not to harbor prejudices, biases, or feel
sympathy for any of the parties.

The trial was sometimes like soap opera and sometimes
like a Greek tragedy. Tempers flared and there were hostile sidebars. Tom Moore whispered, shouted, and often
appeared close to tears. He periodically sounded like a
philosopher and occasionally like a cabaret performer. "I'm
not sure he respected us," one of the jurors later remarked.
In contrast, Frank Bensel, who had been trying cases for
thirty years, and Peter Crean, who received his law degree
from Fordham's law school in 1981, were steady and detailed, and more formal, displaying emotion only when an-
gered by what they considered excessive theatrics by Tom
Moore. Luke Pittoni, a 1971 graduate of Fordham's law
school and a well-known lecturer on malpractice, was clear
and forceful, and only got derailed from his even course
when he and Tom Moore got into fracases over what Pittoni referred to as Moore's exhibitionism. It was rumored
that theirs was an animosity that went back to their law
school days together. To many, because Pittoni's manner
did not seem at all staged, his overall effect was more
eloquent than Moore's.

Judge Wilk once abruptly ended the day after a particularly hot-tempered bench conference with the five lawyers.
The court reprimanded them—to stop muttering, to stop
whispering, to end snide remarks. Mistrial motions and
requests for sanctions were sought. There were all manner
of questions and answers, attacks on the credibility of the
witnesses, and attempts to trap witnesses, and often the jurors looked anguished and confused. For a while, the arguments presented by both sides threatened to permanently
befog the jury, which comprised a proofreader, an advertising business manager, a retiree from the travel business, a
real-estate lawyer, a supervisor of special education for the

New York City Board of Education, and a graphic-designer job-placement executive. How in the world could these ordinary citizens—could anyone—sort out who was telling the truth and who was not? On Court TV, Harvey Weitz, a civil trial attorney, commented that the case was not typical because there was "a whole raft of claims that are causally related," and "the claim is that every one of these things contributed to the ultimate harm, the death of Libby Zion."

Dr. Harold Osborn, the director of emergency services at Lincoln Hospital in the South Bronx, and the plaintiff's star witness on standard of care, internal medicine, toxicology, and emergency care, said that the doctors did everything wrong. He said that it was the worst case of malpractice he had ever seen. To the doctors, he said, Libby was just "a ditsy redhead with a lot of complaints." She was "perceived as a little girl who cried wolf."

On the seventh day of the trial, Tom Moore had some unexpected difficulty with his star witness. After Frank Bensel requested Dr. Osborn's notes, the doctor slid them out of an eight-by-eleven-inch manila folder, handed them to Frank Bensel, and then bent the folder and placed it in his jacket pocket. Two jurors noticed and brought the action to the attention of the court. Dr. Osborn then took the folder out of his pocket and gave it to Frank Bensel, who announced that it had handwritten notes on it, notes that he claimed were a script for Dr. Osborn's testimony. It was a setback for Tom Moore, and the folder was introduced into evidence.

Dr. Osborn, with his trim bow tie, tinted eyeglasses, and graying ponytail, appeared in stark contrast to most of New York Hospital's expert witnesses, who were for the most part more traditionally tailored, in the image of the kind of male doctor who used to make house calls with a little leather black bag. One juror felt that Tom Moore made a mistake by having Dr. Osborn speak as an expert in so many separate areas of medical care. "The doctor wouldn't concede anything," the juror also commented. "It made me suspicious, because the hospital's experts conceded some things."

There was debate concerning Libby's condition before she entered the emergency room. "The dramatic change in Libby Zion at home is one of the most important aspects of the case," Frank Bensel said. "Libby's agitation was caused by a mix of things," Dr. George Simpson, the hospital's expert in pharmacology, and a professor of psychiatry and director of clinical pharmacology at the University of Southern California, told the jurors. (Later, egged on by Tom Moore, some would insist, Dr. Simpson unintentionally mentioned Libby's past cocaine use in his testimony, and the jury was instructed to disregard his answer.) Tom Moore argued that based on Libby's vital signs and physical exam in the emergency room it should have been clear at once to the doctors how ill Libby really was, and that her condition at home was why her parents brought her to the hospital in the first place.

There was disagreement over Libby's temperature, pulse rate, and blood pressure. Dr. Weinstein said that an intern's and resident's notes are not always exact about time, and that they are sometimes estimates because they are written after the fact. Dr. Weinstein was a studied and determined witness. She did not falter once.

There was a dispute over the extent and origin of Libby's pneumonia. "The doctors couldn't see something that wasn't seeable," Frank Bensel told the jurors. Dr. Charles Wetli, the hospital's expert in forensic pathology, newly appointed chief medical examiner for Suffolk County, New York, and the former deputy chief medical examiner for Dade County, Florida, said there was no pneumonia. Dr. William McCormack, the hospital's expert in infectious diseases, and the director of infectious diseases at the State University of New York Health Science Center at Brooklyn College of Medicine, said there was an early pneumonia that was not picked up because it had not reached the point of any symptoms. Dr. Osborn told the court that pneumonia doesn't always show up in an X ray, and that Libby could have been harboring pneumonia even though she had no cough; he criticized the portable X-ray machine used in the emergency room.

There were differences on whether or not a drug screen had been ordered in the emergency room. It had not, but Tom Moore spoke suggestively about one. "They probably got rid of the drug screen because it showed negative," Sidney speculated, adding, "There's a lot of papers missing in this case." Tom Moore told the jury that Libby's throat culture was missing; one had been scheduled, according to Dr. Stone's notes.

There was debate over whether or not Libby had a viral or bacterial disease, despite the fact that even a member of the plaintiff's legal team acknowledged confidentially that bacterial disease "was affirmably contradicted by the evidence," a judgment that had been officially accepted eleven years earlier by both sides. Libby might have had a viral infection, but she did not have a bacterial one. Still, Dr. Osborn said that Libby's white blood cell count and rigors pointed to bacterial disease, and said that the erythromycin Libby had been taking was the reason there was no bacteria in her urine. "False issues have been created by suggestion alone," Frank Bensel told the jury. One juror said that when Dr. Osborn was on the stand, bacterial disease "seemed obvious," but when the hospital's experts came on, the plaintiff "lost it." Only one juror believed Libby actually had a bacterial disease.

There was lengthy dialogue over whether Libby was comfortable or uncomfortable. Dr. Weinstein said she observed "no acute distress." Dr. Osborn said that Libby was breathing thirty-two times a minute, when the normal rate is twelve. Elsa Zion, of course, had said several times that her daughter was uncomfortable, and remained so when they left her at the hospital. Dr. Sherman admitted that "if she was getting worse, I should have known about it." Tom Moore said that Libby was abandoned by her doctors. Later I learned that New York Hospital has a protocol that permits interns and residents to order constant attendants for a patient. This had not been considered in Libby's case.

There were many clashes concerning Demerol and Nardil, the drug combination that Tom Moore blamed for Libby's death. Dr. George Simpson, the hospital's expert in pharmacology, testified that there had been only twenty reported cases of Demerol-Nardil contraindications since the 1950s. The jury was told that Dr. Greenspan, Libby's psychiatrist, didn't know of the contraindication. Neither did any of Libby's other doctors. Indeed, the majority of doctors in America didn't know about the contraindication in 1984. "No one did," Luke Pittoni said. "Libby's death was the reason that lesson was learned," Tom Moore answered. Dr. Weinstein admitted that she had not noticed the "death can result" phrase when she had checked the *Physicians' Desk Reference.* She even said that the fact that death could result was "not the most important thing" to look for. Dr. Sherman, who testified that in his practice he did not use Demerol for fever, chills, and shaking, also testified to the possibility of a cocaine-Nardil reaction, a much worse contraindication than the Demerol-Nardil one

involving a tiny dose of Demerol. Dr. Sherman had testified earlier, in a deposition, that on Sunday, March 4, 1984,
he had thought cocaine was "unlikely." And Dr. Osborn
said that Libby's presentation at the hospital did not suggest a cocaine-Nardil reaction. Still, Dr. Sherman testified
that if Libby had admitted to ever using cocaine, "it would
have changed the whole picture."

What was a jury to do?

Indeed, shouting matches erupted over the cause of
Libby's death, of which the precise cause would remain
unknown forever. "The medical examiner had trouble
with the cause of death," Tom Moore said, "but he never
concluded that it was Libby Zion—excuse me, that it was
cocaine—that killed Libby Zion." Dr. Osborn announced
that Libby died of nonseasonal heatstroke and serotonin
syndrome, although he conceded that a drug overdose or
toxicity could cause heatstroke, and that death could occur
with a very low dose of cocaine. Luke Pittoni produced
evidence that sudden death from cocaine can occur when
the drug is not found in the blood but only found in the
nasal passages. One juror believed that the hospital
doctored the cocaine evidence. "I call them those 'phan-
tom nasal swabs,' " juror number six, Loretta Andrews,
said. "The events in the hospital are not adequate to explain why she died," testified Dr. Robert Glickman, the
hospital's expert in standard of care, and the chief of the
department of medicine at Boston's Beth Israel Hospital,
affiliated with Harvard Medical School. He said that the
cause of Libby's death "was operative before she entered
the hospital." Indeed, Luke Pittoni believed that Libby
might have suffered a Percodan-Nardil reaction at home
that contributed to her polypharmacy, but he was unable to
pursue that particular contraindication aggressively because there was no documented evidence on the adverse

reaction actually causing death. Dr. Sherman said that Libby died from hyperpyrexia, an exceedingly high fever, although Dr. Wetli, the defense's expert in forensic pathology, said that hyperpyrexia is not a *cause* of death, but a *mechanism* of death. Dr. McCormack, the defense's expert in infectious diseases, didn't speculate as to exactly why Libby died, but he believed that influenza A was a contributing factor. Libby's death had become a hopeless riddle.

The issue of sleep deprivation was vigorously debated.

"It was an interesting experience in this case to get criticized for trying to get two hours of sleep," Dr. Stone commented, referring to the time when his responsibilities to Libby were completed, and he had returned to his apartment to catch up on his sleep.

Dr. Weinstein told the court that she worked the day after Libby's death, and then the following day she took the third part of her national licensing exam. How could she be sleep-deprived if she was able to pass a stressful test with the extraordinary score of 680—the ninety-sixth percentile? A passing grade was 290, and only 50 or 60 percent of the interns taking the test passed. Dr. Michael Thorpe, the defense's sleep expert, and the director of the Sleep Disorder Clinic at Montefiore Hospital in the Bronx, told the jurors that Dr. Weinstein was alert and definitely not sleep-deprived. Nevertheless, Dr. Merrill Mitler, the plaintiff's expert on sleep, and the director of sleep research at the Scripps Clinic in La Jolla, California, told a hushed courtroom that sleep-deprived people occasionally disregard their patients' warning signs and sometimes fail to consult medical literature. Tom Moore said that because Dr. Weinstein was exhausted, she ordered a regular diet for Libby, which illustrated a disregard or lack of knowledge of the food restrictions required of patients on Nardil.

"The Libby Zion case is much larger than Libby Zion,"

Moore preached to the jury. The system in place at New York Hospital was inadequate, irresponsible, unacceptable. An intern should not have been in charge of Libby Zion. An intern! "The madness in hospitals must end," Tom Moore called out. "Libby Zion would have been better off at home."

The jury was not allowed to know about the grand jury report, or the Bell Commission, or the New York State Board for Professional Medical Conduct hearings concerning the doctors. Nor were they told about the changes in hospital rules that had been made since 1984. Still, Frank Bensel defended his hospital. "Resident programs are changing with changing times," he told the court in an attempt to neutralize Tom Moore's assault. "Change comes about in an evolutionary process," Bensel reasoned.

Throughout, Sidney Zion sat somber-faced. The doctors were often in the courtroom. "Look how they all sit together," Sidney remarked. "It's Murderer's Row over there.

"It's real drama, without a script. Gut issues and great journalism," Court TV announced in an advertisement about *Zion* v. *New York Hospital,* one of the most important cases it had covered since its inception in 1991.

"This is a trial of a *case,*" Tom Moore whispered to Sidney during a break. What he meant was that he believed that it wasn't the facts surrounding Libby's death that were on trial, but the controversial issues surrounding her case.

All the major networks covered the proceedings: ABC, CBS, NBC, CNN. The Associated Press, all the New York papers, *The Toronto Star, People* magazine, even the San Francisco–based *Wired* magazine were in attendance as well. Marvin Kitman, *New York Newsday* television critic, placed *Zion* v. *New York Hospital* in the number twelve position on his list of the best shows of 1994. Still, a prominent broadcaster told a group of spectators that his producer didn't want the trial followed on a day-to-day basis, but rather just wanted it covered for "significant" events. On the first day that Dr. Weinstein took the stand, the broadcaster waited in vain to see if Dr. Weinstein would break down and cry. "That would be considered significant," he said.

By the middle of the trial, Tom Moore's face would be seen on the side of most New York City buses as part of a Court TV advertising campaign. "We'll probably have the biggest audience ever," Sidney said proudly.

"SOMETIMES YOU GET people to make admissions they never thought they'd make, by coming in from another direction," Tom Moore told me. He was referring to a dramatic statement made by Dr. Sherman—a skittish and awkward-appearing witness—on the third day of the trial, November 15, 1994. Moore asked Dr. Sherman: If Libby had been placed in an ICU as late as 5:30 A.M., would she have been saved?

"Very likely," Dr. Sherman answered, looking bewildered and shocked at his own reply. He glanced at his lawyers and around the room and very quickly changed his mind. "Possibly," he said. "Possibly."

"The case is over. Negligence has been declared," Tom Moore responded to a standing-room-only courtroom. Later, Moore commented, "It was spectacular. I could have won the case with any of Sherman's answers."

Frank Bensel asked for a mistrial. Tom Moore apologized for saying the case was over.

"Apologizing doesn't always correct the error," Judge Wilk said. But he also denied the motion for a mistrial, and no sanctions were imposed.

During a lunch break, Tom Moore explained that with an admission like Dr. Sherman's, it didn't matter if there was cocaine or not. "She could have been saved."

The jury forewoman, Janet Dubin, later told me that she and some of the other jurors wondered well into the trial why Tom Moore didn't actively pursue Sidney's question, "If they thought it was cocaine why didn't they treat her for drugs?" Dubin thought that not to follow through on such a key point "was a strange way to go."

Dr. Lewis Goldfrank, director of emergency medical services at Bellevue Hospital–New York University Medical Center, and a member of the Bell Commission who had testified before the grand jury, believes that Libby should have been sedated. "Agitation must be sedated, otherwise the patient will die," he told me after the trial. "It doesn't matter to me from a clinical point of view whether a patient has a drug overdose from cocaine or amphetamines or has a drug interaction between over-the-counter drugs and Nardil. It doesn't matter whether a patient is withdrawing from one of the most commonly used drugs in America, Valium, or if the patient has an acute manic episode connected to a manic-depressive illness. We treat these all the same way."

But that hadn't happened the night of March 4, 1984, at New York Hospital. "Residents are not taught to treat symptoms," Dr. Bertrand Bell said, "they are taught to find the exact cause."

And of all the things that had happened at the forty-one-day trial, there remained one thing that didn't happen. Sidney Zion never accused New York Hospital of failing to recognize that his daughter Libby was a drug case. He specifically refused to blame them on this count of negligence, even though at one point an attorney advised him to add such an accusation to his list of charges. But he wouldn't do it. Sidney insisted on staying with the argument that there was no cocaine—or any other drugs—at all. He didn't accuse the hospital of this particular negligence, he later railed, "because she didn't have it. There was nothing, nothing, nothing!" Tom Moore agreed. He told me that he didn't emphasize the hospital's negligence in failing to treat Libby as a drug case because he didn't "want to give credence to cocaine."

Shortly after the trial began, Sidney Zion told Court TV reporter Beth Karas that cocaine "was the biggest lie of all . . . one of the great vicious lies that's ever been told."

Sidney made a decision to base his case on thirty-eight other departures from accepted medical care—such as not putting Libby in the intensive care unit, not ordering arterial blood gases, or not ordering antibiotics—which he believed were sufficient to win punitive damages, his major goal. "The only thing doctors will listen to is a big verdict," Sidney believed. "Then they'll pay attention." Indeed, under New York law, punitive damages are not covered by insurance. But in order to achieve punitive damages, the jury has to find the conduct of the doctors or the hospital wanton and deliberate, and establish that they showed total disregard for the patient. "A jury would have to find some evil motive or reckless indifference on the part of the defendants," Beth Karas said. "Since doctors are rarely, if ever, so evil or indifferent, plaintiffs generally cannot meet the definition, and punitive damages are thus not sought," she added. There are only two known cases in New York State where punitive damages were awarded.

Tom Moore tried to get rid of the cocaine weight around his waist—as Ted Friedman had put it earlier—and aggressively told the packed courtroom that the doctors "killed Libby Zion recklessly and then fraudulently covered it up." He chanted in his often lyrical brogue to a jury that was not allowed to know anything about Libby's past drug use, that "this woman's death has been further marred by the mention of cocaine." He said of New York Hospital, which he called "that citadel of science on the East Side of New York," that "they knew the end of the cocaine story was before it began . . . There is no doubt Libby Zion did not have cocaine in her system before her death." But as in the pretrial hearings, cocaine would not disappear. It was a fog permeating everything. "It was there in the evidence," jury forewoman Janet Dubin said to me. Ironically, she also said that she "never thought it was such an issue. I always thought there were more important issues at stake, but they made cocaine the pivotal point." And so despite Judge Elliott Wilk saying he didn't want a trial about cocaine, that's exactly what he got. Half the time was spent dissecting Libby Zion's toxicological reports. The jurors puzzled over why someone simply didn't put Dr. Jon Pearl, the associate medical examiner, on the stand. Couldn't he settle matters? The answer was yes, but neither side could afford to have him settle matters the way he might have. Had Tom Moore put Dr. Pearl on the stand, the associate medical examiner might have admitted there was indeed a nasal swab and that it had tested positive for benzoyle-cgonine, cocaine's metabolite. There was no way Tom Moore was going to risk that disclosure to the jury. And according to Luke Pittoni, if the defense had put Dr. Pearl on the stand, "we thought he'd do more harm than good," because he "couldn't not say there was a Nardil-Demerol reaction."

Many of the experts spoke of having had a growing awareness of the dangers of cocaine use during the years the case had lingered in the courts. Time had been on the hospital's side. "Based on the evidence and what we've learned over the years," Dr. Gregg Stone testified, "I think cocaine is what killed this poor girl." Even the plaintiff's expert, Dr. Harold Osborn, could not altogether throw out cocaine. He admitted that Libby's urine "is a negative for purposes of the report," that is, calling it a negative was an administrative decision by the medical examiner's office, and did not mean the absence of cocaine.

An inordinate amount of time was spent "smearing"— Sidney's word—Libby, yet it was Sidney who, by not confronting the reality of his daughter's drug use, by making it a mystery, had actually made the issue bigger than ever, so much so that a vast part of the television audience across America that watched the trial on Court TV probably believed his daughter's cocaine use was worse than it actually was.

HOW WERE THE jurors going to understand, interpret, and evaluate the mass of often contradictory evidence they heard? They were going to do it within the framework of a seventeen-page "verdict sheet" that contained a total of forty-eight one-, two-, or three-part questions that would guide them in reaching a fair verdict. Judge Elliott Wilk explained that a verdict sheet, determined by the court and the lawyers for both sides, is almost always used in medical malpractice cases, and that "its intention is to clarify for the court what the jury thinks."

The verdict sheet covered all the alleged departures from accepted medical practice, and asked the jurors to determine that if a certain action was a departure, whether it contributed to Libby's death. Only five out of the six jurors needed to agree on each answer; when the decision was not unanimous, the dissenter's number would be marked on the sheet. That such a complex case could be boiled down as rationally and succinctly as it was in this verdict sheet reflects both the strengths and limitations of the American system of justice.

The jury—all of whom got along so well that they bought weekly lottery tickets together during the long stretch of the proceedings, and once split a twenty-one-hundred-dollar prize—deliberated for four days. In the end, they would answer no to thirty-five of the forty-five yes-or-no questions.

The jury decided that Dr. Sherman did not depart from accepted medical practice by not going to New York Hospital to evaluate and treat Libby, although juror number six, Loretta Andrews, did not agree with the decision. She later wrote that as "the lone dissenting voice on the jury," she "disagreed with the other jurors on many aspects of the case, mainly because of my position that, even though the care the hospital gave was in keeping with accepted medical standards, I found these standards woefully inadequate and inferior." She also said that she had a "huge problem" with Dr. Sherman not coming to the hospital. "It should be a given that he at least show up," she believed, "even if he stays for fifteen minutes. How can he not come?"

Nevertheless, the forewoman, Janet Dubin, commented that "Sidney Zion's testimony is what got Dr. Sherman off." The majority of jurors did not feel that he conveyed the seriousness of Libby's condition at home to Dr. Sherman.

The jury unanimously decided that Dr. Sherman did not depart from accepted medical practice regarding Libby's hydration, by not ordering arterial blood gases for Libby, by making viral syndrome a working diagnosis, by withholding antibiotics, by not including pneumonia in his differential diagnosis, or with respect to the X ray ordered for Libby in the emergency room. The jury also decided he had not departed from accepted medical practice by not ordering Libby's admission to the ICU, although Loretta Andrews dissented. "I said yes only because I thought an attending would have the pull to get her in and make it happen," she said. The jury also did not find Dr. Sherman negligent by ordering Libby's temperature to be monitored every four hours. Again, Loretta Andrews dissented. "It goes back to had he been there, his eyes would have been more experienced," she said, adding that "he probably would have asked more questions of the parents as to what went on at home."

The jury unanimously found that Dr. Leonard—an easygoing and straightforward witness—who had never been charged with any misconduct in Libby's death, did not depart from accepted medical practice with respect to the hydration of Libby or performing a neurological exam on her, nor did he depart by not ordering arterial blood gases for her. His eleven-year ordeal was over.

The jurors said that Dr. Stone—who had been a solid and likable witness—did not depart from accepted medical practice regarding Libby's hydration or by not recommending Libby's admission to the ICU, nor did he depart with respect to the performing of a neurological exam. He also did not depart from accepted medical practice by not ordering arterial blood gases, by not recommending to Dr. Sherman that antibiotics be given to Libby, by not including pneumonia in his differential diagnosis, or by the chest X ray ordered for Libby. The jury also unanimously voted that he did not depart from accepted medical practice by making viral syndrome with hysterical symptoms his working diagnosis.

The jury also decided that Dr. Stone did not depart with respect to the monitoring of Libby's temperature, or by leaving Libby's bedside and the hospital after the completion of his duties. Loretta Andrews dissented on those questions. She said that Dr. Stone "was the only one who articulated Libby's voice in the scenario—she kept telling him she was hot, and he didn't do anything about easing her burning up." She went on, "I have a problem with these people who are doctors and they don't listen to the patients. They all took great notes, but so what? He did his job, but he didn't stress to Dr. Weinstein what Libby's trouble was, and I had a big problem with his leaving."

The jury did not find that Dr. Weinstein departed from accepted medical practice with respect to Libby's hydration, by not ordering Tylenol to be given to her every three hours, or by putting her in restraints, although Loretta Andrews dissented, as she also did on the question of Dr. Weinstein's not ordering Libby's temperature to be monitored more frequently than every four hours, which the rest of the jury agreed was not a departure. "Jesus, Libby was a fever patient," Andrews said. "Temperatures go up and down all the time. She was not a textbook presentation." Loretta Andrews also dissented on the question of Dr. Weinstein ordering Haldol, not coming to see Libby between 4:15 and 4:30 A.M. after she was called to do so by Nurse Balde, and not checking on Libby's status between 4:30 and 6:30 A.M. The majority of jurors decided that these were not departures of accepted medical practice. "My read on this," Andrews said, "is that the residents passed Libby on, and left her in the care of the nurses. So if a nurse says come and have a look, the doctor should make an appearance. If Dr. Weinstein had come, she might have caught what was going on." Later, Andrews wrote in a letter to the editor of *The New York Times* that "the evidence led me to believe that New York Hospital failed in its care of Libby Zion. This jury failed her, too."

The system of training interns and residents that was in place in 1984 received an unexpected boost. The jury said

that New York Hospital's residency program did not impair
the house staff through sleep deprivation, although Loretta
Andrews disagreed. She faulted the system, saying, "If this
is the norm, every American should be out there screaming. If this is the standard, it's not good enough." Yet for
the majority, according to juror number four, Edgar Green,
"there wasn't the kind of proof needed to indict the system."

In what was one of the most important questions concerning the hospital's residency program, the jury decided
that New York Hospital was not negligent in the way the
house staff was supervised. Loretta Andrews dissented. "I
told the other jurors, everyone is in training. There were no
senior eyes on this case. Libby should have survived the
night—even if she had done cocaine—if the doctors had
just done small, compassionate things."

The jury, having reached a negative verdict on thirty-
five of the questions submitted to it, answered yes to the
remaining thirteen questions on the verdict sheet.

It unanimously agreed that Dr. Sherman was not telling
the truth when he denied having a conversation with Dr.
Stone about the order for Demerol, and therefore it found
that he had departed from accepted medical practice by
permitting the use of that drug. The jury also found that
this departure was "a proximate cause of Libby's pain and
suffering or death."

The jury unanimously agreed that Dr. Stone departed
from accepted medical practice by ordering the Demerol,
and said that this departure was a proximate cause of
Libby's pain and suffering or death. "They were an intelligent and well-meaning jury," Dr. Stone commented, "but
they didn't appreciate all the nuances. They weren't
equipped with all the facts."

The jury found that Dr. Weinstein departed from accepted medical practice with respect to Dr. Stone's plan for cool soaks and compresses, although juror number five, Michelle Winfield, dissented. With Winfield dissenting, the jury decided this was a proximate cause of Libby's pain and suffering or death. Winfield explained that because of Judge Wilk's direction that there could be more than one approach to a medical problem, she believed that Dr. Weinstein's decision to use only hydration and Tylenol was a suitable alternate plan that was not negligent. She said that during the deliberations—which were stressful for her because she is the mother of an eighteen-year-old daughter who is a college freshman—she and her fellow jurors had only discussed Libby's suffering as a result of not having cold compresses applied, and because the question included death, she could not agree with the rest of the panel.

The jurors unanimously agreed that Dr. Weinstein departed from accepted medical practice by ordering Demerol for Libby, and that this action was a proximate cause of her pain and suffering or death.

The jurors believed that Dr. Weinstein departed from accepted medical practice by not coming to Libby's bedside after Nurse Grismer's 4:30 A.M. phone call, and said that this contributed to her pain and suffering or death. Michelle Winfield dissented because, she said, she felt that only a "small window" of time had elapsed from when the intern had last seen Libby. "There was no reason for her to come up. I was very clear about that. If they hadn't given the Haldol and Libby hadn't fallen asleep, that would have been a different matter," she said. Another juror, who went along with the decision, nevertheless believed that Dr. Weinstein "was in the wrong place at the wrong time. I don't think she was neglectful, she was young and inexperienced."

In à 1993 interview I had asked Dr. Robert Glickman, the hospital's expert in standard of care, and a favorite of the jurors, "Would it have been better for Dr. Weinstein to have gone up to see Libby?"

"I suppose," he had answered, but he observed that "it was not clear what was going on. It's very humbling." He said that he doubted that the outcome would have been better.

Later, several doctors suggested that interns and residents should have their own insurance for malpractice. Perhaps this is an idea whose time has come.

The jury unanimously found that Dr. Weinstein departed from accepted medical practice by not consulting with more experienced doctors after 4:15 A.M., although on the question of this action actually contributing to Libby's death, juror Edgar Green dissented. He explained that he didn't believe that Dr. Weinstein "did the right thing," but it was "within the scope of a reasonable judgment call," and "under the circumstances her not consulting did not sink to the level of negligence."

It was recommended by one doctor that all relevant medical charts of any given patient be made available to hospitals via a computer network. Some doctors speculate that computer technology will make consultations easier. A television news program reported on "virtual" medicine, and revealed how three-dimensional X rays will be available as a result of advanced technology. *Newsweek* reported on "round-the-clock access to a library of medical information," and described "doc-in-a-box software programs" and on-line databases that are available for "cybercare." There can be no doubt that these are tools whose time has come.

The jurors found that Dr. Weinstein also departed from accepted medical practice by the manner in which she responded to the 6:30 A.M. call. Michelle Winfield dissented. She said that she "didn't hear any evidence that this was an error in judgment."

In another dramatic finding concerning the training of doctors, the jury found New York Hospital negligent with respect to the work load assigned to Dr. Weinstein over the weekend she was in charge of Libby's case. Michelle Winfield dissented. The jury decided, however, that the hospital's negligence on this score was not a proximate cause of Libby's death. Loretta Andrews dissented. She said that she believed that it was built into the system that "someone will drop the ball."

In what was the most controversial finding, the jury decided that Libby had indeed ingested cocaine sometime on March 4, 1984, and that this contributed to her death. Loretta Andrews dissented, later writing to *The New York Times* that "her fellow jurors were swept away by the cocaine theory," a statement that enraged and frustrated her jury colleagues. "This 'theory' was promoted by the media, not by the jurors," Diane DeBellis, juror number two, said. Another juror said, "*Loretta* was swept away by Tom Moore and Sidney Zion!" and added that during the deliberations the dissenter kept repeating, "I just don't *feel* Libby did cocaine." Andrews, who believed that even if Libby had done cocaine, "I don't think the hospital would have treated her any differently," wrote in her letter to the editor that the other jurors made assumptions "that led them to assign partial blame" to Libby for her own death. "They presumed a certain lifestyle," Andrews wrote, in order to prove that she took cocaine. Juror Diane DeBellis said that Andrews's claims are "unfounded" and "demeaning." She said that "the decisions of the majority of five jurors were based on the same evidence made available to the entire panel of six, not preconceived notions or counsel's courtroom demeanor." Juror number three, Judy Jordan, who had not spoken out publicly before, said, "I feel bad that Loretta Andrews feels the way she does." Jordan said that the pressure in the jury room was "horrible" during the deliberations, but she, like the majority of jurors, thinks they did "a good job as far as the decisions were concerned." Sidney Zion fumed that "the only truth you'll hear is from Loretta," to which Judy Jordan commented, "He came looking for justice, and I don't like him now going after the justice system" with his criticisms of the jury.

"This was a very difficult decision to make," Edgar Green pointed out. "The case is bigger than cocaine," Michelle Winfield said, adding that "many other drugs interfered with her." Diane DeBellis said, "We believed that Libby Zion's polypharmacy played a role." But finally, forewoman Janet Dubin said, "There wasn't enough evidence to dispute the fact that she had done cocaine." Nevertheless, the controversy, the burden, and the later back-and-forth letter writing would create a deep chasm among the panel, as well as the alternates, who did not sit in on any of the deliberations. "It made us split as friends," one juror said despairingly.

The jury also found Libby negligent with respect to the history she gave when she went to the hospital, and decided that this, too, contributed to her death. Loretta Andrews dissented. "The history is important," she allowed, but "there are commonsense things to do. Just deal with the fever and keep her comfortable. They put her in restraints!"

The jury unanimously decided that Libby was 50 percent responsible for her death, and that the hospital was 50 percent responsible, although Loretta Andrews has since signed an affidavit stating that she actually was against the split and wanted the hospital to pay 100 percent. She was surprised that her name was not listed as a dissenter. But juror Edgar Green said that every jury member had a copy of the verdict sheet and they went over every question more than once. He did not recall Loretta Andrews either stating a dissent on the 50-50 split, or wanting to be listed as a dissenter. "I think we all came to a compromise on that question," he said. During deliberations, the numbers had ranged from 70 percent for the hospital and 30 percent for Libby, and then 60-40, 55-45, 90-10, and 98-2, until the 50-50 was decided on.

THE HOSPITAL CONSIDERED the decision a victory. Indeed, the former physician-in-chief of New York Hospital, Dr. R. Gordon Douglas—he left that position in 1991 to enter private industry—felt it was a vindication and proved that the training and supervision was "robust and healthy." Dr. Harold Fallon, the hospital's expert in residency-training programs, and a professor of medicine and dean at the University of Alabama School of Medicine, as well as another jury favorite, had testified that in 1982 all of New York Hospital's residency programs received a five-year accreditation, the highest approval rating. Still, necessary changes had occurred and would continue to occur. Jury forewoman Janet Dubin wrote to *The New York Times* that "it is my hope that further changes can be made so that hospitals, specifically teaching institutions, will constantly upgrade the quality of care. It is important to remember that the patient, not the student, is the most important focus of any health care team."

In truth, under the existing system, the supervision of Dr. Leonard and Dr. Stone by Dr. Sherman had been more than satisfactory, and even exceeded what was required of an attending physician in his situation; after all, Dr. Sherman spoke to Dr. Leonard three times, and had a long consultation with Dr. Stone. Dr. Stone had properly supervised Dr. Weinstein, too, and that she did not follow all his advice was her right under the closed order book system. But the system failed. Dr. Stone said that he discussed giving Demerol to Libby with Dr. Sherman, and Dr. Sherman said he remembered no such exchange. This discrepancy was so extreme that they had needed to retain separate lawyers. Still, despite the fact that the jury said that the administration of Demerol was a proximate cause of Libby's death, one juror later commented, "Demerol is not what killed Libby Zion."

"In clinical medicine it would be impossible to have strict, tight control over every patient so no mistake is ever made," Dr. Weinstein told the courtroom on November 17. Sidney Zion buried his head in his hands, close to tears.

Later, Dr. Stone told me, "Doctors are human, and in retrospect we sometimes wish we could change decisions which were made. But most mistakes are minor, and don't result in bad outcomes. Rarely are things black-and-white."

Dr. Glickman admitted that one of the reasons he agreed to testify was "for the cause," to help New York Hospital show the jury that its residency program was in fine shape when Libby was a patient. But in 1993, Dr. Glickman, who had never testified in a malpractice trial before, told me that "it's healthy that people looked at work schedules." He said that the 405 regulations "have sensitized people to balance both service and education," and that the regulations "were a vehicle to talk about improvements. It was suddenly legitimate to talk about that." Indeed, he admitted to me that "the Zion family did a lot of good." Dr. Maurice Leonard later acknowledged that the quality of life is now better for interns and residents.

"There needed to be more supervision," he told me. However, Dr. Stone said that "we need objective evidence whether the Bell regulations change patient care for the better or for the worse."

Dr. Bertrand Bell feels that at the trial the residents "were treated as if they were mature doctors," which they were not. Interns and residents are "graduate medical students," he said. He believes, in fact, that they should not receive their medical licenses until the completion of their residency.

This may be an idea whose time has come.

According to some doctors I spoke to, there was a second casualty on Monday March 5, 1984: the "graduate medical student" in charge of Libby's case. The intern was a victim of the system, and remains a victim of the system, it is said. "Luise Weinstein had the potential to be a superstar, and the Zion case destroyed her. She is the second major tragedy of this case," one doctor told me. "The death of Libby Zion remains the foremost tragedy," he added, "and all the doctors involved in her care mourned her loss. Each of the participants grieved along with the Zion family."

Yet what this doctor left out, many people would later point out, is that while New York Hospital and the doctors clearly regretted Libby's death, no one once said in a personal way: We're sorry. The doctors and the hospital maintained a chilly distance from the beginning of the case to the end.

Although the closed order book was never specifically named as such, Tom Moore had some constructive suggestions regarding it. He told the jurors that "the more experienced doctors should do the ordering and the less experienced ones should do the suggesting." It ought to be the reverse of the current practice, he said.

This, too, may be an idea whose time has come.

In 1993, Dr. Glickman had told me that the closed order book "doesn't disenfranchise anyone," although "there are risks that it's not going to turn out the right way and the patient will die." He had, nevertheless, stressed that "some degree of observed independence is required," and that a modified closed order book can be made to work "in a supervised setting." He believes that most hospitals are coming around to "co-management" between the house staff and attendings.

This may be another idea whose time has come. Yet another is "alert hovering," the term used by Dr. Daniel Federman, dean for medical education at Harvard Medical School.

Interestingly, jury forewoman Janet Dubin stated that if one of the charges against the hospital had been its failure to recognize that Libby was a drug case, it might have made a big difference in the way the jury considered the supervision issue. If the question had been on the verdict sheet—at one point Dubin even talked to the other jurors about asking the court to add it—perhaps the jury might have had a stronger frame for viewing the supervision issue. Perhaps they might have been able to say that doctors with more seniority could have recognized that the signs and symptoms Libby was showing were related to drug use.

IT BEARS UPON Sidney Zion's perhaps prescient awareness of the defects of the system that six years before Libby's death, he reported in the *New York Post* on a confidential state assembly document that revealed that 85 percent of the operations on private patients in the New York area were not performed by licensed, board-certified surgeons, but rather by residents receiving on-the-job training. What was especially scandalous, Sidney wrote on January 20, 1978, was that all this was happening "unbeknownst to patients." He quoted a doctor who said that although there is a consent form, "it's designed to confuse the patient," because if the patient knew a student was going to operate, "a patient would surely say, 'Are you kidding?' "

The few times that as an adult I was a patient in a hospital, before I even understood what was meant by the terms *resident* and *intern*, I remember wondering what it was about their personalities and character that made them choose to work in a hospital, where their time was hardly ever their own, as opposed to a private practice, where they could come and go as they liked. I decided they must be service-oriented—the radicals of their group, the ones who didn't care about making a lot of money in a big practice, but preferred working where there was a lot of action—or perhaps they were more scientifically oriented than "regular" doctors, and wanted to be within easy reach of a wide assortment of illnesses and diseases.

I recall finally asking someone about these doctors who seemed to be everywhere, all over the hospital, coming and going, asking me all sorts of questions night and day. Did all patients get so much attention?

That's the house staff, I was told. The interns are new doctors. How new? Very new, but they have to be very good to work here. The residents look after them. Aha, I thought, the residents reside in the hospital so there's always a doctor available. I felt too foolish to ask if I had figured it out correctly. Besides, it had to be right. The house staff. The residents of the hospital. I remember wondering if these residents minded giving up family life. Why would they want to live in a hospital instead of their own apartments or houses? Perhaps they were like career soldiers. They needed to be on the front line. Maybe they liked the security of a guaranteed paycheck. Or perhaps they were misfits. Good doctors, maybe, but misfits all the same.

I now realize I was not unusual in the extent of my confusion. Beth Karas of Court TV said that she hadn't understood the roles of interns and residents until she covered the Zion case, and others have made identical confessions.

The reason for popular ignorance on this score is surely connected to the closed order book. If patients knew how a hospital worked, they would run out the door. If patients knew that the least experienced person in the vicinity was in charge of their care, they would run even faster. And if patients knew that their private attending doctor—if they have one—was not immediately in charge, they wouldn't go near the hospital in the first place.

The Patient's Bill of Rights, created by the American Hospital Association and which all hospitals display, says that all patients have the right to be told that they are dealing with residents; it specifically states that patients have the right "to be informed of the name and position of the doctor who will be in charge of their care." "The average patient doesn't have the slightest idea what kind of training a resident has," said James Weinlader, Ph.D., the director of resident review activities for the Accreditation Council for Graduate Medical Education, or ACGME, which evaluates all the specialty training programs in the United States.

According to the New York State Department of Health education law, "all health care personnel must wear an identifying badge which shall be conspicuously displayed and legible." Most house staff wear such identification, but these badges are not large enough to be read, especially in an emergency situation; in addition, they generally only say *doctor*, and not *intern* or *resident*. The education law has never been challenged on that issue, and ACGME has no rules about badges at all. Indeed, Sidney Zion remembered that when he first met the residents at New York Hospital in 1984, their badges "didn't say *resident*. They said *doctor*."

Dr. Robert H. Gifford, associate dean for education and student affairs at Yale University School of Medicine—residents at Yale wear a badge that says *resident staff*—believes that "everyone should have a big sign so patients know who's who." He emphasized that "across the board this should be mandatory." Dr. Gifford also emphasized his opinion that residents should be under the purview of medical schools, not hospitals.

These may also be ideas whose time has come.

What about whether a particular residency program is accredited? Although the public can find out which programs are or are not accredited, they have no way of finding out why accreditation has been denied. Still, Dr. Weinlader said, "we have become more open," acknowledging, however, that what may be wrong with any individual institution is kept confidential, adding that it would be "unusual for a major hospital with eighty programs not to have something wrong somewhere."

Such information is not posted. "Patients would only know if they asked," said Dr. William Ellis, medical director of the Bureau of Hospital Service for New York State. And, he added, patients "don't know to ask."

But what if a patient did know to ask about past problems or about the qualifications of interns and residents? "They'll get an answer," Dr. Ellis said, but "whether it's true or not is another matter."

Patients need to take the time not only to read the

Patient's Bill of Rights, but to take it seriously. This, too, may be an idea whose time has come.

"A LOT OF things could have been and aren't," Sidney told *People* magazine. "We could have done something. This could have been a great verdict."

But for the Zions, and three of the doctors, it was a mixed verdict. "We were obligated to deliberate within the framework of the legal system," forewoman Janet Dubin wrote in a letter to *The New York Times*.

Still, it was a landmark decision in what one news account would call "one of the most emotionally wrenching trials in the city's history." It imparted a serious message to patients everywhere: You might be at risk when you go to the hospital, but you and your family must accept some of the responsibility when taking that risk. Many of the jurors agreed with this assessment, juror Edgar Green said. "It's important to realize that patients are ultimately responsible for their own health, and at times for their illnesses," Dr. Maurice Leonard told me after the trial. And Dr. Raymond Sherman said, "You always have to look at the flip side— what's the risk in not going to the hospital?"

The jury awarded $750,000 to the Zions for Libby's pain and suffering, an amount that was cut in half to $375,000 because of the fifty-fifty split in liability. Loretta Andrews dissented. "If I had my way I wanted to double or triple the two million the Zions were asking for," she said. "It seemed clear that for them it was the issues, not the money." During the deliberations, amounts ranging from $100,000 to $6,000,000 were considered, one juror said.

Tom Moore had asked for one dollar for Libby's wrongful death, and his request was granted. Michelle Winfield dissented, voting instead for fifty cents, according to another juror. "I didn't think that's what the parents wanted," Winfield said. "I thought that they wanted punitive damages to say to the world that what happened to Libby was unjust."

The lone dissenter, Loretta Andrews, wanted the hospital held liable for punitive damages, but such damages were not assessed to New York Hospital, Dr. Sherman, Dr. Stone, or Dr. Weinstein by the jury, although Andrews later said that she regretted not dissenting on the doctors. "I don't think they set out to kill Libby, but maybe some people should have been punished, especially Luise Weinstein. She could have done more for Libby." Edgar Green said that "over all, I found that a lot of blame was placed on Dr. Weinstein almost as a sort of compromise. I thought that most of her actions, while perhaps sometimes mistaken, were not really negligent."

Many of the jurors felt that the case had all but taken over their lives. One juror had to be put under the care of a doctor for a locked jaw brought on by tension. One member kept a diary as a way to refrain from talking about the case to anyone; entries described the "calm chatter" of the panel, the "praying hands" of Frank Bensel, and "the piercing eyes" of Tom Moore. Another juror dreamed about the case night after night. Still another said that she never wanted to serve on a jury again.

During the reading of the verdict sheet on February 6, 1995, a cold and cloudy winter day, juror Diane DeBellis said, "I could feel my heart moving my shirt out," and added, "I knew it would not be a popular decision."

And it wasn't.

Tom Moore lashed out that the jury "put the onus on Libby, not the hospital." Luke Pittoni was disappointed at "not getting total vindication," especially since he felt that Nardil-Demerol played no part in Libby's death. But Frank Bensel was at least gratified that the jury had distributed the blame evenly. One of the jurors admitted that some members of the panel wanted the verdict even more on the doctors' side, and felt that Tom Moore "threw in things" meant to confuse them. "It made me cynical," Edgar Green sighed. "The judge said what the lawyers say is not evidence." He believed that when certain testimony was read back to them during the deliberations, the evidence was not there. He speculated that perhaps the dissenters mistakenly gave as much weight to Tom Moore's pleadings as to the evidence. "I just didn't see proof to back up all the plaintiff's allegations," Green said.

Tom Moore would charge, according to the *Manhattan Spirit*, that Libby was "a victim of jury tampering." It was not a useful statement to have made, and Moore later explained to me that the tampering was "indirect," and the result of an anti-malpractice atmosphere in the country, an atmosphere that perhaps caused the jurors to "think cases like the Zion case are meritless."

"Each and every verdict question was dissected," Diane DeBellis said. "In a jury situation it is expected and helpful for there to be differences of opinion."

Juror Michelle Winfield reflected, "I believe the verdict was just because I went on the evidence. Thank God a verdict is final."

"I'm pretty bitter about it," Sidney Zion said. "This is an outrage." After the verdict, he was, in fact, angrier than ever. "I think this jury disgraced themselves, and disgraced justice," he told the press. "The jury stereotyped Libby as a cocaine abuser," he seethed. "They branded her that way because she attended Bennington College and was in a particular social strata." In his weekly column for the *Daily News* he wrote, "So the Big Lie won out, and the city and the country lost out." He called the jurors "subhuman."

"Sidney Zion's been on this crusade too long," commented a juror.

"Sidney Zion should look within," Dr. Stone told me, "and try to live with what was going on in Libby's life. Whether or not he knew any of it, I don't know."

But the girl who died twice—at home, doctors murmured—in the hospital, the Zions cried out—had still changed medicine around the globe.

A reporter approached Elsa Zion to ask her what she thought of the outcome. She mulled over the question, and then looked the man straight in the eye.

"There's nothing left to say."

Shortly after the verdict, Sidney Zion filed a motion for a new trial, and New York Hospital filed a motion for a reduction of the $750,000 award for Libby's pain and suffering.

On May 1, Judge Elliott Wilk issued what would later be referred to by some of the participants as a Solomonic decision. Court TV called it "a significant reversal of the jury's decision."

The monetary award was lowered to $375,000.

The part of the verdict that said Libby's death was caused by cocaine was set aside, and Sidney Zion was granted the right to a new trial on the issue of Libby's culpability in terms of her inaccurate medical history and her use of cocaine. This ruling was not directed at the adequacy of the cocaine evidence. In fact, the judge was not even addressing or questioning the actual cocaine evidence at all. Even though Libby's cocaine use had been proved to the jury's satisfaction, the court was giving the Zions the benefit of the doubt because of a judicial technicality: that the testimony of Dr. George Simpson, the defense witness who inadvertently blurted out Libby's inadmissible cocaine history while he was on the stand, might have tainted the jury's verdict. In other words, just in case the jurors heard what they were told they shouldn't have heard, the court was going to err on the side of caution on Sidney Zion's motion, even though after the trial the jurors told Court TV that this particular testimony had not influenced them at all.

Most legal experts viewed Judge Wilk's ruling as a settlement. "In the interest of justice, the judge came to a determination he thought would end the case," Frank Bensel acknowledged. Luke Pittoni said, "It was an attempt to make an appeal unpalatable for both sides." And it worked, although "we gave up more than the plaintiff gave up," he added.

But neither side wanted either a new trial or a lengthy appeals process. The years and years of turmoil had left their mark on everyone involved.

"In our view, her name is cleared," Sidney said of Libby. Tom Moore said, "Cocaine is out of the case." Sidney added, "We got rid of the ugly stain the hospital tried to put on this kid. And the *issue of her culpable conduct is out. No one can say anymore that Libby Zion used cocaine." He smiled for the first time in months.*

New York Hospital, in a rare show of compassion in a case that seemed as if it would never go away, allowed that the decision was all for the best, especially if it enabled Sidney Zion to preserve his daughter's dignity. "The decision leans toward fathers," Frank Bensel said quietly, "with Mother's Day coming up."

Sidney Zion continues to write a weekly column for the New York Daily News.

Elsa Zion continues to work for the New York City Department for the Aging.

Adam Zion is a lawyer.

Jed Zion is a screenwriter.

Dr. Raymond Sherman continues to have a private practice in internal medicine in New York City, and is still an attending doctor at New York Hospital.

Dr. Maurice Leonard is in a group practice in southern New Jersey, where his specialty is digestive diseases.

Dr. Gregg Stone is part of an eleven-person cardiovascular practice in northern California.

Dr. Luise Weinstein is in an internal-medicine group practice at New York Hospital, and has been a faculty member of the Cornell University Medical College since 1986, where she is involved in creating a new curriculum for the house staff.

ACKNOWLEDGMENTS

CAROLE BARON BELIEVED in this book from the moment she heard I wanted to write it. As my publisher, she never wavered, and coached and coaxed from the beginning to the end. She made me believe in myself more than I ever had before. Her intelligence, intuition, strength, and common sense are wonders to behold.

Tracy Devine's editing skills are everywhere in this book, and I thank her for her talent and wisdom. She is a patient and painstaking craftswoman, and I felt blessed to have her as my working editor.

My husband, Christopher Lehmann-Haupt, is, as always, my toughest and most loving critic. He put off his own deadline to read a draft of this book, and offered penetrating comments and suggestions on that draft and others.

My agent, Lynn Nesbit, as always, served as my reality check.

Fredric Burg, M.D., read this book in its final manuscript stage, and meticulously went over crucial details with me on several occasions. He made a number of suggestions, some of which I accepted, and some of which I rejected.

I listened carefully to all my readers, and I hope I did justice to their ideas. However, any mistakes of any kind are mine, and mine alone.

FOR THEIR TIME, energy, cooperation, and observations, I also thank the following people: the Accreditation

Council for Graduate Medical Education, Mike Alexander, Amy Allina, Marcia Allina, Hans Altibor, Laurie Andrews, Loretta Andrews, Marty Arnold, Robert Ascheim, M.D., Bennett Ashley, Elena Ricocco Bachrach, Myrna Balde, David Bamberger, Richard Baron, Jerry Bauer, Bertrand Bell, M.D., Ben Belitt, Dr. Ruth Bennett, Tina Bennett, Frankie Bensel, Larry Bensky, Noelle Bernstein, Kate Betts, Zerina Bhika, Carol Biondi, June Bingham Birge, Susie Bluestone, Alexandra Boer, M.D., Ellen Borakove, Emily Bergsland, M.D., Lynn Boswell, Mark Bottner, Homer Boushey, M.D., Fredrick Bowman, M.D., Philip Brickner, M.D., Jonathan Brisman, Patricia Taylor Buckley, Cheryl Bulbach, Gerard N. Burrow, M.D., John Burton, the University of California, San Francisco School of Medicine (and especially these students: Angel Khush, Amy Lawrence, Nick Mayper, Ninetta Scott, T. J. Scott, Sylvia Teran), Ina Caro, Chris Carpenter, Rita Charon, M.D. (and some of her students: Don Blair, Thomas Gillespae, Emma Glantz, Jonathan Masoudi, Karen Pilgrim, Jerald Underdahl), Amy Chernoff, M.D., Alan Cheuse, John L. Clowe, M.D., Richard Clurman, Shirley Clurman, Columbia University College of Physicians and Surgeons, Columbia University's medical school library staff, Peter Crean, Peter Crow, Shelly Dattner, Mimi Davidson, Diane DeBellis, Alan DeCherney, M.D., Anna Delaney, R. M. Donaldson, M.D., Michael J. Dontzen, Harriette Dorsen, Janet Dubin, David Duncan, Bonita Eaton, Howard Eder, M.D., Eleanor Eliot, William Ellis, M.D., Nora Ephron, "Paula Este," Jim Fabian, Judy Feiffer, Ruth Fishbach, Herbert Fisher, Rosemary Fisher, M.D., "Barry Fox," "Dale Fox," Bill Freidberger, Eliot Fremont-Smith, Leda Fremont-Smith, Ted Friedman, Arthur Gelb, Alfred Gelhorn, M.D., Robert Gifford, M.D., Steven Glaser, M.D., Diana Golden, Lewis Goldfrank, M.D., Edgar Green, Kenneth Greenspan, M.D., Sharon Griffith, Brita Brown Grover, Sal Guardino, Angie Guirriero, Julie Harston, Harvard Medical School, Joseph Hayes, M.D., Kathleen Healy, Julie Hecht, Laurie Hessen, Dalma Heyn, Kurt Hirschorn, M.D., Angela Holder, Helen Hong, Mort Janklow, Mildred S. Jenkins, Michael E. Johns, M.D., Susan Jonas, Jane Jones, Judy Jordan, Melissa Kamen, D.D.S., Eric Kandel, M.D., Beth Karas, Susan Kartes, Jerome Kassirer, M.D., Christopher Kehew, Katherine Kellogg, Carol Kitman, Marvin Kitman, Richard I. Kopelman, M.D., Laura M. Kosseim, Marnie Krause, Judith Krug, Martha Weinman Lear, Adrienne Legas, Inge Lehmann-Haupt, Noah Lehmann-Haupt, Rachel Lehmann-Haupt, Roxie Lehmann-Haupt, Martin Leib, M.D., Maurice Leonard, M.D., Richard U. Levine, M.D., Marshall A. Lichtman, M.D., Diana Linsky, Judy Livingston, Tamar Luchow, Ivan Lyons, Julia McMillan, M.D., D. Keith Mano, Richard Marek, Esther Margolis, Leo Milonas, Barbara Mohan, Marc Moller, Tom Moore, Robert Morgenthau, Gail Morrison, M.D., Anne Navasky, Victor Navasky, Paul Nelson, M.D., Roy Nemerson, the New England Medical Center and Tufts University School of Medicine, the New York City Police Academy, the Great Almighty New York Public Library, the New York State Council on Graduate Medical Education, the New York State Department of Health, Hugh Nissenson, Marilyn Nissenson, James P. Nolan, M.D., Frances Okun, Louise Ortolevi, Emilie Osborn, M.D. (I would especially like to thank Dr. Osborn for her encouraging and helpful reading of a draft of this book), Kris Oser, Frank Oski, M.D., Sean Pace, Herbert Pardes, M.D., Connie Park, M.D., Tim Patterson, Christopher Pavone, University of Pennsylvania School of Medicine (and especially these students: Rebecca Anderson, Raquel Davila, Peter Kang, Santosh Kesavi, Seth Koss, Resa E.

Lewiss), Gena Tenney Phenix, Luke Pittoni, Tom Pratt, Susan Radocha, Suzanne Rauffenbart, Rupsa Ray, M.D., Pamela Rehak, Laura Richards, Glynne Robinson, Jean Roiphe, M.D., Isadore Rosmarin, David Rothman, Sheila Rothman, Raphael Rudnik, Joanna Chapin Saint, Tim Saint, the St. Lawrence County Historical Society, Elizabeth Saltzman, Herbert Scheinberg, M.D., Lawrence Scherr, M.D., Mary Schilling, Barbara Schuster, Raymond Sherman, M.D., Lori Siegel, Eric Simonoff, Peter Slocum, Stephen R. Smith, M.D., Victor Smith, Benjamin Spencer, Fred Spencer, M.D., Christopher Spina, James Stinnett, M.D., Gregg Stone, M.D., Jane Stone, Donald Tapley, M.D., Suzanne Telsey, Victor Temkin, Joseph Tenenbaum, M.D., Maxie Teninbaum, Keith Thompson, Patsy Thompson, Steve Thornquist, M.D., Daniel C. Tosteson, M.D., Richard Tristman, John Unterborn, M.D., Mildred Vogel, Morris Vogel, Vivian Wallace, Evelyn Walsh, Gary Walters, Paul J. Wang, M.D., Ron Warner, M.D., Alan Wasserman, D.D.S., Nancy Weber, James Weinlader, Stuart Weisman, M.D., Judge Elliott Wilk, Penny Williamson, Michelle Winfield, Sheldon Wolff, M.D., Yale University School of Medicine, Anita Yu, the Zion family, Andrew Zweifler, M.D., Pat Zzop.

One special person connected with New York Hospital, Mrs. John Elliott, Jr., a member of the Board of Governors and its executive committee, remained a steadfast "facilitator"—her term—and when she told me in 1991, "We would like to have a fair story written, too, and whatever is the fair story—let's have it out," I believed her. She added, "I think you're going to be doing a service."

SOURCE NOTES

ABBREVIATIONS USED

SBPMC   The State of New York: Department of Health/State Board for
   Professional Medical Conduct hearing transcripts
NEJM   *The New England Journal of Medicine*
JAMA   *Journal of the American Medical Association*
Depo   Pretrial deposition
Trial trans   *Zion* v. *New York Hospital* trial transcript
CD   court document
Memo   Attorney memorandum
Dr. records   Doctors' records
NYH   New York Hospital
NYT   *The New York Times*
NYP   The *New York Post*
NYDN   The New York *Daily News*
NYN   *New York Newsday*
PDR   *The Physicians' Desk Reference*
SZ   Sidney Zion
EZ   Elsa Zion
AZ   Adam Zion
JZ   Jed Zion

After the trial, Dr. Raymond Sherman, Dr. Maurice Leonard, and Dr. Gregg
Stone agreed to be interviewed. I thank them for their valuable contributions, and
for taking the time to answer all of my questions. The information from these
interviews is incorporated throughout the text.

Dr. Luise Weinstein declined to be interviewed. "I will not talk about the
Zion case, and I will not speak inappropriately about a patient," she told Peter
Crean, her lawyer, who commented, "Luise is a private person."

In general, most of the information and quotations pertaining to the doctors
are from depos, trial trans, SBPMC transcripts, Dr. records, NYH records,
CDs, memos, and newspaper and magazine articles.

AUTHOR'S NOTE

xiii   "Her obituary in *The New York Times* . . ." *NYT*, 3/6/84. p. 10.

xiv   " '. . . a virus that's been going around . . .' " SZ interview and Depo.

PART ONE

CHAPTER ONE

4   Information about Drs. Wasserman and Greenspan from author interviews 9/22/92 and 11/30/92, CD, Dr. records, EZ, and SZ.

4   Additional information on biofeedback in this chapter and others from *Consumer Reports*, 2/93. (See Bibliography—Articles), and author interviews.

4   Additional information on Nardil in this chapter and others from *Overcoming Depression*, by Demetri F. Papolos, M.D., and Janice Papolos, pp. 110–113 (see Bibliography), and *PDR*, 38th ed. (1984) and 44th ed. (1990). (See Bibliography), Depo, memos, trial trans, and author interviews.

5   information about Dr. Irene Shapiro in this chapter and others is from EZ, depo, Dr. records, and trial trans.

5   " 'I think she felt lousy and came back home . . .' " Depo.

5   " 'I think it was 101' . . ." Depo.

6   ". . . Elsa said that 'Libby felt pretty much the same,' . . ." Depo.

6   "Sidney said that his daughter looked 'tired out,' . . ." Depo.

6   ". . . she 'wasn't supervising her.' " Depo.

6   ". . . 'entirely' in charge of taking her Nardil." Depo.

6   "Sidney remembered that Libby 'seemed more upset.' " Depo.

6   "The boyfriend, Ralph Enders, described Libby . . ." SBPMC.

6   "On Sunday, March 4, the day before . . ." Depo.

7   "But by the early afternoon, . . . 'jumpy.' " Depo.

7   "Later on Sunday . . . 'slightly settled down.' " EZ, SZ, and depo.

9   "Sidney remembered Libby as being out of bed . . ." Trial trans.

9   "Adam recalled that Libby . . ." AZ and depo.

10   "Elsa said that she didn't observe anything exceptional . . ." Depo.

10   "However, Elsa did . . ." Depo and EZ.

10   "Libby's 'shoulders were moving,' . . ." Depo and SBPMC.

10   "He recalled that his conversation went something like this . . ." SZ and depo.

12   "Libby, jumpy . . . 'best hospital in the world.' " Depo.

12   Most of the descriptive material about NYH is the result of a three-hour unauthorized tour by NR and writer Hugh Nissenson. I am very grateful for Hugh's unique notes. I am also grateful to a friend of his, who asked for anonymity, who supplied me with a hand-drawn map of the patient area inside the ER. I did manage to see it briefly, but did not stay very long for fear of getting in the way, even though it was relatively calm in there. And to my surprise, no one paid any attention to my presence. Someone did stop me when I wandered over to the pediatric ER, and politely escorted me back to the regular ER waiting area, where I remained for another hour. Hugh and I then toured Payson 5, and I returned there for a second visit a few weeks later. On both trips everyone was warm and friendly, and never once questioned me, even when I sat for a while on a chair opposite the room Libby had been in.

In addition, in 1994 I visited Cornell University Medical College on my own. For over two hours I wandered around the building on York Avenue, reading bulletin boards, peering into doorways, and just generally observing the students and their activities. Again, no one asked me what I was doing there, or questioned my roaming. I had simply walked in the front door and no one stopped me.

13   " 'I remember doing something, saying . . .' " Depo and SBPMC.

14   "Anne Gallagher, an emergency-room nurse . . ." Depo and SBPMC.

17   "Libby's initial blood count . . ." NYH records, depo, and memo.

18   "Anne Gallagher, the emergency-room nurse who first drew Libby's blood . . ." Depo and SBPMC.

19   " 'Can't you give her something to calm her down?' . . ." Depo.

19   ". . . 'looking like something going on inside . . .' " Depo.

19   ". . . 'they didn't ask me.' " Trial trans.

19   " 'I didn't know for certain who . . . "That's that." ' " Depo and SBPMC.

19   ". . . 'Why are you calling me at home? . . .' " Depo and SBPMC.

20   " 'Well, get down here . . . overreacting.' " Depo and SBPMC.

20   " 'What's going on here? . . . happening.' " Depo, SBPMC, and trial trans.

23   "Nurse Anne Gallagher watched . . ." Depo and SBPMC.

24   "Elsa said that she and her husband . . ." Depo.

24   "Sidney said that 'everyone seemed very sympathetic . . .' " Depo.

25   ". . . Myrna Balde said . . ." Depo, SBPMC, and author interview, 2/1/94.

26   "Sidney believes that he 'must have said a few words' . . ." Depo.

28   "Sidney said he would 'drop in the room once . . .' " Depo.

28   "Sidney, however, said that he talked to Dr. Stone . . ." Trial trans.

29   " 'Get Ray Sherman on the phone' . . ." Trial trans.

29   "However, Sidney later said that he had never seen Libby move . . ." Depo.

30   "Nurse Balde agreed." Author interview, 2/1/94.

30   "Still, Sidney said that he told Dr. Stone . . ." Depo, SBPMC, and trial trans.

31   " 'Well, what's the matter with her?' . . ." Depo.

32   "Sidney reassured his wife. '. . . it is,' . . ." Depo and SBPMC.

32   " 'I knew in my heart without any doubt . . .' " Depo and SBPMC.

CHAPTER TWO

40   "As a young girl, Libby often visited her paternal grandparents in Passaic, New Jersey, taking . . ." Information from an article by Judy Voccoli, *Herald News*, 4/85.

41   "Sidney said that his daughter 'never looked depressed' . . ." Depo.

41   "Libby generally did well in school, of which Sidney . . ." Depo.

41   "She had always been a voracious reader . . . weekend visit." Article by Judy Voccoli, *op. cit.*

44   The information about Elsa Zion's background is from interviews with EZ, as well as from material she lent to me, some of which comes via the *New York Genealogy* at the library in Massena, New York. In addition, I am very grateful to Mildred S. Jenkins, the historian of the town of Stockholm, New York, for sending me magazine and newspaper articles.

She also took some photographs. The AAA gave me useful brochures and maps, and I thank them for their help.

49   ". . . 'He was as graceful as they come . . .' " Walter B. Gunnison, *Farm & Garden*, 8/16/86.

51   After the death of Anne Zion, Sidney's mother, I was invited by Sidney to go through a large chest of memorabilia she had kept all her life. The things in it ranged from a palm print of her son's to a lock of Libby's hair. Anne Zion kept every scrap of paper with Sidney's name on it, as well as every mention of his name in columns and articles. It was in this chest that I found the information about Dr. Zion's army career, and the never-posted letter Anne Zion wrote to her son when he got into Yale Law School. Of course, she also kept copies of all the articles and columns he wrote, as well as miscellaneous invitations, records, obituaries, notes—you name it, it was probably in that chest.

52   Throughout this book, the historical background on doctors, hospitals, and medical schools is from *A Pictorial History of Medicine*, by Otto L. Bettmann; *American Medicine and the Public Interest*, by Rosemary Stevens; *Learning to Heal*, by Kenneth M. Ludmerer; *A Doctor's Prescription*, by Kurt Link, M.D.; *The Social Transformation of American Medicine*, by Paul Starr; *The Doctors' Story*, by Thomas Gallagher; *Medical Life Boat*, by Howard H. Hiatt, M.D.; and *I Remember*, by Abraham Flexner. (See Bibliography for details.)

56   "When Sidney was later asked 'What did you do next?' . . ." SBPMC.

61   "Right before he left for Passaic to break the news to his mother . . ." Depo.

61   *Managing Your Doctor*, Freese, p. 154. (See Bibliography.)

62   "Dr. Sherman believes, however, that no matter . . ." Telephone conversation with author, 2/22/95.

CHAPTER THREE

63   "He told a journalist that he 'knew too much' . . ." Jerry Tallmer, "Making Good His Markers," *NYP*.

63   " 'A press card, unlike a lawyer's license . . .' " Sidney Zion, *Read All About It*, p. 12 (see Bibliography). Other quotes are from pp. 29, 51, 54–56, 60, 62, and 64.

64   "His hometown newspaper, *The Record*, noted that he . . ." Article by Laurence Chollet, "Power: An Immorality Tale," 7/9/90, p. B3.

71   *"The National Review* applauded Sidney . . ." Richard Samuelson, 9/19/93, p. 68.

74   Information about the medical examiner's office and Libby's autopsy is from NYH records, CD, memos, and an author visit to the medical examiner's office.

80   " 'He belongs to a fading school of males . . .' " Mary Schilling, interview with author, 6/30/93.

81   "Dr. Sherman hadn't called the Zions . . ." Depo.

81   "Elsa said Dr. Sherman had called her . . ." Depo.

81   *Talking with Patients*, Bird, p. 13. (See Bibliography.)

84   Information on drugs in this chapter and others is from the *Complete Guide to Prescription and Non-Prescription Drugs*, by H. Winter Griffith, M.D. (see Bibliography), as well as the *PDR*, the *Mosby Medical Encyclopedia*, product information material, expert testimony, and author interviews.

CHAPTER FOUR

87   " 'Between the rock and the hard disco . . .' " Sidney Zion, "Outlasting Rock: Sophisticated Melody and Lyrics Make a Comeback," *The New York Times Magazine*, June 1981, p. 16.

96   ". . . the 'most controversial columnist in America' . . ." Jacket copy for *Trust Your Mother but Cut the Cards* by Sidney Zion. (See Bibliography.)

101   Information about Dr. John Lyden is from SBPMC and Depo.

113   "Elsa said that she had several more phone conversations with Dr. Raymond Sherman . . ." Depo.

PART TWO

CHAPTER FIVE

117   In this chapter and others, most of the data on medical schools and interns and residents is from *Medical School Admission Requirements*, 43rd ed. Washington, D.C.: Association of American Medical Colleges (AAMC); the *Graduate Medical Education Directory*, known as the "Green Book," published by the American Medical Association; *Journal of Medical Education:* Physicians for the Twenty-first Century, vol. 59, no. 11, Washington, D.C.: AAMC, 11/84; *Trends in Medical School Applicants and*

Matriculants: 1983–1991, Washington, D.C.: AAMC; the *New York State Council on Graduate Medical Education 4th and 5th Annual Reports;* the *Report of the New York State Commission on Graduate Medical Education, 1/24/86; Essential and Information Items: 1993–1994*, Accreditation Council for Graduate Medical Education (ACGME); *Manual of Policies and Procedures for Graduate Medical Education Review Committees*, ACGME, 2/93; as well as from author interviews, material gleaned from some of the articles and books listed in the Bibliography, depos, SBPMC, trial trans, and memos.

119   "In 1984, residents were the largest group of employees . . ." Depo of Dr. David Thompson.

119   ". . . *Healing the Wounds* . . ." Hilfiker, p. 5. (See Bibliography.)

119   "A doctor who uses the name Dr. X writes . . ." *Intern*, pp. 5–6. (See Bibliography.)

119   "I discovered that most doctors need permission . . ." David Hilfiker, M.D., *Healing the Wounds*, p. 86. (See Bibliography.)

121   The information on NYH interns and residents comes from interviews and confidential documents, the NYH annual report, the bylaws of the medical staff of NYH, SBPMC, and depos of Drs. Sherman, Stone, Weinstein, Carr, Ruggiero, and Douglas.

121   Some background data on Dr. Weinstein is from "Who Killed Libby Zion?" by M. A. Farber, *Vanity Fair*, 12/88.

122   ". . . 'complete and permanent control of the hospital staff . . .' " Nicholas Murray Butler, president of Columbia University, 1910, as quoted in *Learning to Heal*, Ludmerer, p. 165. (See Bibliography.)

125   Information on resident slang in this chapter and others is from "A Glossary of House Officer Slang" in *Becoming a Doctor*, by Melvin Konner, M.D.; *The House of God*, by Samuel Shem, M.D. (see bibliography); and author interviews with medical students, interns, residents, doctors, and administrators.

139   Information concerning Nurse Grismer is from depo and trial trans. Information concerning Nurse Balde is from depo, trial trans, and an author interview. Additional information is also from depos of Dr. Weinstein, Nurse Susan Myerson, and nurse's aide Bronte McKend.

141   "The other patients in Libby's room . . ." The author spoke to one former patient and relatives of the two others; Libby was the fourth.

144   "Later, the Zions would say . . ." CD

146   Some information on codes in this chapter and others is from *The

Patient's Advocate: The Complete Handbook of Patients' Rights, by Barbara Huttman, R.N. (See Bibliography.)

CHAPTER SIX

150   "cocaine . . . remains in the blood for four to six hours . . ." In addition to the references already cited, some information about cocaine in this chapter is from *Cocaine: The Human Danger*, Weiss and Steven, p. 15. (See Bibliography.)

150   ". . . 'dry alcohol' . . ." Author interview with Eliot Fremont-Smith, a drug counselor in Westchester County, New York.

151   Information about cocaine testing from reference books cited, as well as manufacturers' brochures, CD, memo, trial trans, and author interviews.

164   "He said that he believed her." Telephone conversation with author, 2/17/95.

170   "Less than a year later, a panel of lawyers . . ." Joyce Purnick, "Koch Panel Backs Gross in Handling Autopsy Cases," *NYT*, 4/24/85, p. 1.

170   "On Father's Day, Sunday, June 14 . . ." Depo, SBPMC, and author interview.

171   "He told the *San Francisco Examiner* . . ." Warren Hinckle, "Money Won't Do: Dad Wants Doctors Jailed for Daughter's Death," 9/15/85, p. A1.

CHAPTER SEVEN

176   Dr. Bertrand Bell first opened my eyes to the closed order book. He spurred me on, faxed me letters and articles, and offered encouragement, good advice, and helpful suggestions. I am extremely grateful to him.

176   Andrew Zweifler, M.D., letter to author, 3/5/93.

177   Dr. Kurt Hirschorn, interview with author, 1993.

177   Dr. Robert Glickman, telephone interview with author, 5/11/93.

179   ". . . 'the single most potent influence ever' . . ." *Learning to Heal*, Ludmerer, p. 75. (See Bibliography.)

181   "Marshall A. Lichtman, M.D., . . ." Letter to author, 4/2/93.

184   "Even by 1988, an article in *The New England Journal of Medicine* . . ." David A. Asch, M.D., and Ruth M. Parker, M.D., "Sounding Board": "The Libby Zion Case," 3/24/88.

185   " 'Deny, deny, deny,' Dr. Sherman commented . . ." Telephone conversation with author, 2/17/95.

191   "Ruth L. Fishbach . . ." Interview with author, 4/93.

CHAPTER EIGHT

199   " 'There has to be enough supervision on the floor . . .' " Author interview with Dr. Rosemary Fisher, 10/12/93.

201   ". . . the first year of residency training ranks fifth . . ." The American Institute of Stress, 1994. The ten most stressful jobs are: 1. inner-city high school teacher, 2. police officer, 3. miner, 4. air-traffic controller, 5. intern, 6. stockbroker, 7. journalist, 8. customer-service or complaint worker, 9. waiter/waitress, 10. secretary.

201   "One doctor referred to 'the loss of social skills . . .' " The Intern Blues, Marion, p. 284. (See Bibliography.)

201   "After all, they are in what used to be referred to as the fifth . . ." American Medicine and the Public Interest, Stevens, p. 379. (See Bibliography.)

202   "Residents are also prone to what Dr. David Hilfiker . . ." Healing the Wounds, p. 5.

207   "According to the Medical School Admission Requirements Bulletin . . ." p. 226

217   "In his book Becoming a Doctor . . ." Konner, p. 142.

219   "Nevertheless, a study made in Texas the year before Libby . . ." Medicine on Trial, by Charles B. Inlander, Lowell S. Levine, and Ed Weiner, p. 68. (See Bibliography.)

219   "These are 'the facts of life . . .' " Ibid. p. 69.

219   "Another study of 22,112 patients admitted by on-call . . ." Steven D. Hillson, M.D., Bryan Dowd, Ph.D., Eugene C. Rich, M.D., and Michael G. Luxenberg, Ph.D., "Call Nights and Patient Care: Effects on Inpatients at One Teaching Hospital," Journal of General Internal Medicine, vol. 7 (July/August), 1992.

220   "Dr. Stephen R. Smith, associate dean for education . . ." Letter to author, 4/9/93.

220   Dr. Bertrand Bell, Dr. Homer Boushey, Dr. Daniel D. Federman, interviews with author, 1993–1995.

222   "Tradition. As T. S. Eliot wrote . . ." After Strange Gods, 1924.

PART THREE

CHAPTER NINE

225   Most of the information about malpractice is from *A Doctor's Prescription*, by Kurt Link, M.D., Chapter 9 on medical malpractice, by Carolyn Lavecchia, R.N, F.N.P, M.S.J.D., pp. 188–202. (See Bibliography.) Other information and statistics are from *The Malpractitioners*, by John Giunther (see Bibliography); *Consumer Reports*, "The 'Crisis' That Isn't," "Malpractice: A Straw Man," 7/92; *The Patient's Advocate*, by Barbara Huttman, R.N., p. 4 (see Bibliography); *A Measure of Malpractice*, Paul C. Weiler, *et al.*, p. 139 (see Bibliography); "Malpractice Roulette," by Michael J. Saks, *NYT*, op.ed. page, 7/93; *M.D.: Doctors Talk About Themselves*, by John Pekkanen (see Bibliography).

226   "The Eastern Region Alliance of American Insurers . . ." *NYT*, Douglas W. Barnert, Letter to the Editor, 9/3/85.

227   " 'Even the most qualified doctors are frequently sued . . .' " *NYT*, Isadore Rosenfeld, M.D., Letter to the Editor, 9/19/85.

227   "A year after Libby Zion's death . . ." *NEJM*, 3/21/85. "Professional Regulation and the State Medical Boards," by Arnold S. Relman, M.D., pp. 784–785; and "Special Report: The Ethics of Professional Regulation," by Richard Jay Feinstein, M.D., pp. 801–804.

229   "By the end of July . . ." *Ibid.*

230   " 'We are looking into it' . . ." *NYP*, 8/27/85, p. 14.

231   "As Jerry Nachman wrote in . . ." *NYP*, 3/5/89.

231   "A few months later, *New York Times* columnist Tom Wicker . . ." "In the Nation," *NYT*, 12/25/85.

231   " 'I don't care about the civil case,' Sidney said . . ." As quoted by Steve Brill, "Curing Doctors," *American Lawyer*, 9/85.

232   "A Harvard Medical Practice Study . . ." *Patients, Doctors, and Lawyers: Medical Injury, Malpractice Litigation and Patient Compensation in New York*. A Report by the Harvard Medical Practice Study to the State of New York, 1990; copyright, President and Fellows of Harvard College.

233   " 'My goal is to break the madness going on' . . ." SZ as quoted in *New York Newsday*, 8/27/85.

233   Matt Clark, "Libby Z: The Case That Changed House Staff Training," *M.D.* magazine, 1/92.

233   Rutgers University–PBS symposium on "Medical Care: What You Don't Know Can Harm You," 5/27/87. Other information from *NYP*, 8/26/85; Matthew Rose, *New York Newsday;* Warren Hinckle, *San Francisco*

Examiner, 9/25/85; M. A. Farber, "Who Killed Libby Zion?," *Vanity Fair*, 12/88.

237   Testimony regarding Elsa Zion's phone call to Ralph Enders, SBPMC 8/13/87.

241   "During a television appearance in Cupertino, California . . ." "Bay City Limits," Channel 4 program on medical accountability. Pat Van Horn and Jan Rasmussan, hosts, 9/85.

CHAPTER TEN

246   The "other publicized incidents" are from the following sources: Andrew Kirtzman, "More Hospital Hell Cited," NYDN, 12/6/91; Lisa Belkin, "Human and Mechanical Failures Plague Medical Care," NYT, 3/31/92; Linda Wolfe, "A Fatal Error," *New York* magazine, 12/7/92.

248   "Two weeks later, *The New York Times* quoted . . ." Ronald Sullivan, "Grand Jury Assails Hospital in '84 death of 18-year-old," 1/13/87.

249   " 'Evidence showed that junior interns were making life-and-death decisions . . .' " Robert Morgenthau as quoted in *New York Newsday*, "Grand Jury Probe Faults Misuse of City's Interns," by Joe Calderone, 1/13/87.

252   "Two months later . . . the *New England Journal of Medicine* . . ." Vol. 318, no. 12, 3/24/88.

252   "A newspaper editorial referred to the report's 'chilling' revelations" . . . "and not just in New York City . . ." NYP, 1/20/87, and NYDN, 1/17/87. Information also from Deidre Carmody, NYT, 1/15/87; Maralyn Matlick, NYP, 7/1/89.

259   Bruce Elwell, telephone interview with author, 1994.

259   "On September 25, 1987, *The New York Times* . . ." Ronald Sullivan, "New Limits Sought in Medical Studies," 9/20/87, p. 57.

260   Dr. Alfred Gelhorn, interview with author, 1994.

CHAPTER ELEVEN

261   " 'A year to go and do something creative . . .' " Guy Maxtone-Graham, "Fellowship Fosters Creativity," *Yale Daily News*, 2/12/85.

261   ". . . 'taking verbal snapshots' . . ." *Ibid*.

261   ". . . Bennington 'brought back too many . . .' " *Ibid*.

264   "Just a few short years after Libby's death, a senior doctor at . . ." M. A. Farber, "Who Killed Libby Zion?" *Vanity Fair*, 12/88.

264   ". . . 'a time-clock mentality' . . ." Michael I. Cohen, M.D., Joseph Dancis, M.D., Laurence Fineberg, M.D., Kurt Hirschorn, M.D.,

Michael Katz, M.D., and Edward Wasserman, M.D., "Patient Care, Resident Stress, and Government Regulations," 2/19/89.

265   "In February 1987, Sidney told one of the most-watched . . ." *60 Minutes,* "The 36-Hour Day," 2/87.

265   Dr. Robert Gifford, interview with author, 10/12/93.

265   Tom Monahan, telephone interview with author, 9/14/93.

266   " 'The rest of the world already had the evidence' . . ." NY*DN,* 3/28/87.

266   "Officials of the hospital announced publicly . . . new building." *NYP,* 3/24/87.

267   Information on riot from *The Doctors' Story,* Gallagher, Chapters 5 and 6, and *A History of Colonial Medical Education,* Stookey. (See Bibliography.)

269   ". . . the year before Libby Zion's death . . ." M.A. Farber and Lawrence K. Altman, M.D., "A Great Hospital in Crisis," *The New York Times Magazine,* 1/24/88.

270   Information on the shah from *The Shah's Last Ride,* by William Shawcross, pp. 248–256. (See Bibliography.)

270   Information on Andy Warhol from the Associated Press; *NYT*—articles by Ronald Sullivan, Steven Lee Myers, Robert O. Boorstin, M. A. Farber, Lawrence K. Altman, M.D.; *New York Newsday*—articles by Matthew Rose, Jessie Mangaliman; NY*DN*—articles by Serge F. Kovaleski and Andrew Kirtzman; Salvatore Arena, Alex Michelin; *NYP*—articles by Erica Browne and Leo Standora. Also, Claudia Wallis, "A Hospital Stands Accused," reported by Beth Austin in Chicago and Raji Samghabade in New York, *Time,* 4/27/87.

272   Information on hospital problems from Lisa Belkin, "Human and Mechanical Failures Plague Medical Care," *NYT,* 3/3/92; Miriam Shuchman, "When A Young Doctor Errs, Open Discussion Is Advised," *NYT;* Alfred Sacchetti, M.D., Carol Carfraccio, M.D., and Russel H. Harris, M.D., "Resident/Management of Emergency Department Patients: Is Closer Supervision Needed?" *Annals of Emergency Medicine,* 6/92; "Who Was Caring For Mary?", Frederick Southwick, M.D., letter in *Annals of Internal Medicine;* Timothy S. Lesar, Pharm.D., Laurie L. Briceland, Pharm.D., Karen Delcoure, R.P.H., Janet Crilly Parmalee, M.B.A., R.R.A., Vickey Masta-Gornic, and Henry Pohl, M.D, "Medical Prescribing Errors in a Teaching Hospital," *JAMA,* 5/2/90; Lucien L. Leape, M.D., "Error in Medicine," *JAMA,* 12/21/94.

274   "By 1995, the Federation of State Medical Boards . . ." "Punishing of Doctors Increased in 1994," Associated Press; *NYT,* 4/6/95.

275   Roy Nemerson, telephone interview with author, 9/20/93.

277   Discussion about "novice internists" handling mistakes by denial, by discounting, by distancing . . . from *Medicine on Trial,* by Charles B. Inlander, *et al.,* pp. 87–88 (see Bibliography), citing T. Mizrahi, "Managing Medical Mistakes: Ideology, Insularity and Accountability Among Internists-in-Training," *Social Science and Medicine,* vol. 19, no. 2, p. 135.

279   Information on the New York State Board for Professional Medical Conduct is from transcripts, and newspaper articles in *NYP:* Joe Nicholson, 5/1/87; NY*DN:* 5/26/90, 9/25/90, 5/13/91; Associated Press: 11/1/91; *NYT:* Kevin Sack, 11/1/91, Eric Weiner, 9/23/89, Denis Hevesi, 4/28/91, Ronald Sullivan, 8/11/87; NY*DN:* editorial page 11/6/91; *The New York Law Journal:* 2/5/91; and Norton Spritz, M.D., J.D., "Oversight of Physicians' Conduct by State Licensing Agencies: Lessons From New York's Libby Zion Case," *Annals of Internal Medicine,* vol. 1155, no. 3, 8/91.

285   "Yet, as Dr. Harvey Klein, a professor of clinical medicine . . ." *Harvard Medical Alumni Bulletin,* Fall 1991, pp. 42–44.

CHAPTER TWELVE

294   " 'The cumulative effect of the 1987 criticism . . .' " M. A. Farber and Lawrence K. Altman, M.D., "A Great Hospital in Crisis," *The New York Times Magazine,* 1/24/88.

294   " 'It was a disaster,' said Dr. Joseph Hayes . . ." Interview with the author. When Dr. Hayes cowrote the study about restricted resident hours that appeared in the January 1993 *JAMA,* I was allowed to interview him because it was seen as a public-relations opportunity. At our meeting, which was monitored by someone from New York Hospital's public affairs office, I asked Dr. Hayes if I could go on resident rounds with him sometime, and he said sure, he'd call me in a few weeks. He never did.

295   "In 1991 Dr. Hayes collaborated on a limited study . . ." Christine Lane, M.D., Lee Godman, M.D., M.P.H., Jane R. Soukup, M.S., and Joseph G. Hayes, M.D., "The Impact of a Regulation Restricting Medical House Staff Working Hours on the Quality of Patient Care," *JAMA,* 1/30/93.

296   "A study in the *Archives of Internal Medicine* indicated that . . ." David Nerenz, Ph.D., Howard Rosman, M.D., Carol Newcomb, M.H.S.A., Mary Beth Bolton, M.D., Gustavo Heudebert, M.D., Thomas Simmer, M.D., and Sidney Goldstein, M.S., "The On-Call Experiences

of Interns in Internal Medicine," Medical Education Task Force of Henry Ford Hospital, vol. 150, 11/90, p. 2294.

296   The American Medical Association's *Graduate Medical Education Directory*, p. 9.

296   Dr. William Ellis, telephone interview with author, 2/16/93.

297   *M.D.* magazine, *op. cit.* 1/92.

298   "British Columbia became the first . . ." *Ibid.*

298   Information on juniors' hours from an editorial by Bertrand Bell, M.D., "Supervision, Not Regulation of Hours, Is the Key to Improving Quality of Patient Care," *JAMA*, 1/20/93.

298   "In December 1990 . . ." Joe Nicholson, "City Patients Benefit from 'Zion Rules,' " *NYP*, 12/4/90.

299   " 'This is a disgrace . . .' " SZ as quoted in "Scandal of Dozing Docs," by Lucette Lagnado, *NYP*, 10/5/90.

299   Information and some quotations are from "How Hospitals Violate the 'Bell' Regulations Governing Resident Working Conditions," a report by Mark Green, Public Advocate for the City of New York, November 1994.

307   "A gossip column . . ." Neal Travis' New York, *NYP*, 11/8/93, p. 7.

312   "Ted Friedman's prominence was such that it was said that he . . ." Jan Hoffman, "A Warning on the Limits of Aggressive Advocacy," *NYT*, 6/3/93.

315   Information on disbarment from "A Lawyer Is Disbarred for Lapse of Ethics," by Seth Faison, *NYT*, 4/23/94.

316   Information and quotations regarding Judith Livingston and Tom Moore are from Warren St. John, "Best Performance by a Leading Lawyer: Tom Moore Packs Galleries in Zion Case," *The New York Observer*, 12/12/94.

316   Additional information is from Court TV.

CHAPTER THIRTEEN

I attended the trial every day, and took extensive notes. In addition, I am extremely grateful to Beth Karas of Court TV for her considerable guidance.

During the weeks following the trial, I interviewed all six jurors by telephone. In some cases, their comments are from personal interviews held in the courtroom right after the verdict was announced. Unless otherwise noted, their statements are from these interviews.

Information and quotations concerning the lawyers are from author interviews and newspaper, magazine, and television interviews.

Jan Hoffman's articles about the trial that appeared in the *NYT* were helpful. Also helpful were Salvatore Arena's articles in NY*DN*.

318   " 'Once upon a time in America . . .' " Sidney Zion, "Doctors Know Best," *NYT* op-ed page, 5/13/89.

318   "The Libby Laws." In his column in the NY*DN*, "Please Don't Let Libby Have Died in Vain" (3/10/95), Sidney Zion refers to the 405 regulations, or the Bell Regulations, as the Libby Laws. I agree that this is the name that should stick.

318   " 'Libby Zion's death has changed residency training forever' . . ." Timothy B. McCall, M.D., *JAMA*, 1989.

319   " 'There were times when I thought it would never happen' . . ." SZ to author at trial.

325   " 'They probably got rid of the drug screen . . .' " *Ibid.*

329   " 'Look how they all sit together' . . ." *Ibid.*

329   "Marvin Kitman . . ." Marvin Kitman, "Was 1994 the Beginning of TV's 2nd Golden Age?," "The Marvin Kitman Show," *New York Newsday*, 12/30/94.

330   " 'We'll probably have the biggest audience ever' . . ." SZ to author.

331   Dr. Lewis Goldfrank, telephone interview with author, 2/24/95.

331   Dr. Bertrand Bell, telephone interview with author after the trial.

332   "There are only two known cases in New York state . . ." (re: punitive damages) *Gersten* v. *Levine*, 1988, and *Graham* v. *Columbia Presbyterian Medical Center*, 1992. In *Gersten* v. *Levine*, the family of a patient sued a "clinical ecologist" for causing the suicide of the patient by keeping the patient a virtual prisoner in an apartment, and preventing the patient from seeking conventional treatment. In *Graham* v. *CPMC*, a doctor was sued for allowing a postoperative patient to bleed to death.

334   "Judge Elliott Wilk explained . . ." Telephone interview with author, 3/95.

340   Dr. Robert Glickman, telephone interview with author, following my visit to Harvard Medical School, 5/11/93.

340   Computer consultation information from "Virtual Medicine," Channel 7 News, 9/9/94, and Geoffrey Cowley, "The Rise of Cyberdoc," *Newsweek*, 9/26/94.

343   "Indeed, the former physician-in-chief . . ." Letter to the *NYT*, 2/14/95.

343   Janet Dubin and Loretta Andrews both wrote letters to the *NYT*, which were published 2/14/95 and 2/21/95.

346   Ghost surgery scandal exclusive by Sidney Zion, *NYP*, 1/20/78.

348   Dr. James Weinlader, telephone interview with author, 7/27/93.

349   Dr. William Ellis, telephone interview with author, 2/16/93.

350   " 'A lot of things could have been and aren't' . . ." Sidney Zion as quoted in *People* magazine, 2/20/95.

350   ". . . 'one of the most emotionally wrenching trials' . . ." Howard Girsky, "For the Love of His Daughter," New York *Spirit*, 2/95.

SELECTED BIBLIOGRAPHY

BOOKS

Baden, Michael M., M.D., with Judith Adler Hennessee. *Confessions of a Medical Examiner*. New York: Random House, 1989.

Balint, Michael, M.D. *The Doctor, His Patient and the Illness*. New York: International Universities Press, Inc., 1972.

Becker, Howard S., Blanche Geer, Everett C. Hughes, and Anselm L. Straus. *Boys in White: Student Culture in Medical School*. Chicago: University of Chicago Press, 1961.

Bettmann, Otto L. *A Pictorial History of Medicine*. Springfield, Ill.: Charles C. Thomas, Publisher, 1956.

Bigelow, Henry J. *Medical Education in America*. Cambridge, Mass.: Welch, Bigelow, and Co. University Press, 1871.

Bird, Brian, M.D. *Talking with Patients*. Philadelphia: J. B. Lippincott Co., 1973.

Black, David. *Medicine Man: A Young Doctor on the Brink of the 21st Century*. New York: Franklin Watts, 1985.

Blum, Richard H. *The Management of the Doctor-Patient Relationship*. New York: McGraw-Hill, 1960.

Bok, Sissela. *Lying: Moral Choice in Public and Private Life*. New York: Pantheon Books, 1978.

Carver, Cynthia, M.D. *Dealing with Doctors and Other Medical Dilemmas*. Scarborough, Ont.: Prentice-Hall Canada Inc., 1984.

Clark, Edward H., M.D., et al. *A Century of American Medicine*. New York: Burt Franklin/Lenox Hill Publisher and Distribution Co., 1876 and 1971.

Colon, B.D. *O.R.: The True Story of 24 Hours in a Hospital Operating Room*. New York: E. P. Dutton, 1993.

Cook, Fred J. *Julia's Story: The Tragedy of an Unnecessary Death*. New York: Holt, Rinehart & Winston, 1976.

Cousins, Norman. *Anatomy of an Illness*. New York: W. W. Norton & Co., 1979.

Cronin, A. J. *The Citadel*. Boston: Little, Brown & Co., 1937.

Davis, Neil M., Michael R. Cohen, et al. *Medication Errors: Causes and Prevention*. Philadelphia: George F. Stickley Co., 1981.

Doyle, Roger Pirnie. *The Medical Wars: Why the Doctors Disagree*. New York: William Morrow, 1983.

Fishman, Steve. *A Bomb in the Brain: A Heroic Tale of Science, Surgery, and Survival*. New York: Scribner, 1988.

Flexner, Abraham. *I Remember*. New York: Simon & Schuster, 1940.

Fox, Renee C. *The Sociology of Medicine: A Participant Observer's View*. Englewood Cliffs, N.J.: Prentice-Hall, 1989.

Freese, Arthur S., M.D. *Managing Your Doctor*. New York: Stein & Day, 1975.

Gallagher, Thomas. *The Doctors' Story*. New York: Harcourt, Brace & World, 1967.

Giunther, John. *The Malpractitioners*. New York: Doubleday/Anchor Press, 1978.

Glover, Jonathan. *Causing Death and Saving Lives*. New York: Penguin Books, 1977.

Gorovitz, Samuel, M.D. *Doctors' Dilemmas: Moral Conflict and Medical Care*. New York: Macmillan, 1982.

Harrison, Michelle, M.D. *A Woman in Residence*. New York: Random House, 1982.

Hiatt, Howard H., M.D. *Medical Life Boat*. New York: Harper & Row, 1987.

Hilfiker, David, M.D. *Healing the Wounds: A Physician Looks at His Work*. New York: Pantheon Books, 1985

Huttmann, Barbara, R.N. *The Patient's Advocate: The Complete Handbook of Patient Rights*. New York: Viking Press and Penguin Books, 1981.

Illich, Ivan. *Medical Nemesis*. New York: Pantheon Books, 1976.

Inlander, Charles B., Lowell S. Levine, and Ed Weiner. *Medicine on Trial: The Appalling Story of Medical Ineptitude and the Arrogance That Overlooks It*. New York: Prentice-Hall, 1988.

Jones, Steven, M.D. *Medical Mystery: The Training of Doctors in the United States*. New York: W. W. Norton and Co., 1978.

Kassirer, Jerome P., M.D., and Richard I. Kopelman, M.D. *Learning Clinical Reasoning*. Baltimore: Williams & Wilkins, 1991.

Katz, Jay, M.D. *The Silent World of Doctor-Patient*. New York: The Free Press, 1984.

Klass, Perri. *A Not Entirely Benign Procedure: Four Years as a Medical Student*. New York: G. P. Putnam's Sons, 1987.

Klass, Perri. *Baby Doctor: A Pediatrician's Training*. New York: Random House, 1992.

Konner, Melvin, M.D. *Medicine at the Crossroads: The Crisis in Health Care.* New York: Pantheon Books, 1993.

Konner, Melvin, M.D. *Becoming a Doctor: A Journey of Initiation in Medical School.* New York: Viking Press, 1987.

Kraegel, Janet, R.N. and Mary Kachayeanos, R.N. *Just a Nurse.* New York: E. P. Dutton, 1989.

Kramer, Charles, and Daniel Kramer. *Medical Malpractice.* Fifth edition. New York: Practicing Law Institute, 1983.

Kubler-Ross, A. Elisabeth. *Questions and Answers on Death and Dying.* New York: Macmillan, 1974.

Kubler-Ross, A. Elisabeth. *Living with Death and Dying.* New York: Macmillan, 1981.

Lander, Louise. *Defective Medicine: Risk, Anger, and the Malpractice Crisis.* New York: Farrar, Straus & Giroux, 1978.

Lear, Martha Weinman. *Heartsounds: The Story of a Love and a Loss.* New York: Simon & Schuster, 1980.

Levenson, Dorothy. *Montefiore: The Hospital as Social Instrument.* New York: Farrar, Straus & Giroux, 1984.

Levis, Sydney. *Hospital: An Oral History of Cook County Hospital.* New York: The New Press, 1994.

Link, Kurt, M.D. *A Doctor's Prescription: For Getting the Best Medical Care.* New York: Scribner, 1990.

Ludmerer, Kenneth M. *Learning to Heal: The Development of American Medical Education.* New York: Basic Books, 1985.

Macklin, Ruth. *Enemies of Patients: How Doctors Are Losing Their Power and Patients Are Losing Their Rights.* New York: Oxford University Press, 1993.

Marion, Robert, M.D. *The Intern Blues: The Private Ordeals of Three Young Doctors.* New York: William Morrow, 1989.

Merton, Robert K., George G. Reader, M.D., and Patricia L. Kendall. *The Student Physician.* Cambridge, Mass.: Harvard University Press, 1957.

Mizrahi, Terry. *Getting Rid of Patients: Contradictions in the Socialization of Physicians.* New Brunswick, N.J.: Rutgers University Press, 1986.

Mullan, Fitzhugh, M.D. *White Coat, Clenched Fist: The Political Education of an American Physician.* New York: Macmillan, 1976.

Needleman, Jacob. *The Way of the Physician.* New York: Harper & Row, 1985.

Nolen, William A., M.D. *The Making of a Surgeon.* New York: Random House, 1968.

Nuland, Sherwin B., M.D. *Doctors: The Biography of Medicine*. New York: Knopf, 1989.

Nuland, Sherwin B., M.D. *Medicine: The Art of Healing*. New York: Hugh Lauter Levin Associates, Inc., distributed by Macmillan, 1992.

Nuland, Sherwin B., M.D. *How We Die*. New York: Knopf, 1994.

Osler, William, M.D. *Selected Writings*. New York: Dover Publications and Oxford University Press, 1951.

Papolos, Demitri F., M.D., and Janice Papolos. *Overcoming Depression*. New York: Harper, 1987.

Pekkanen, John. *M.D.: Doctors Talk About Themselves*. New York: Delacorte Press, 1988.

Rosenbaum, Edward, M.D. *A Taste of My Own Medicine: When the Doctor Is the Patient*. New York: Random House, 1988.

Rothman, David J. *Strangers at the Bedside*. New York: Basic Books, 1991.

Schiff, Harriet Sarnoff. *The Bereaved Parent*. New York: Crown, 1977.

Seibel, Hugo R., and Kenneth E. Guyer. *How to Prepare for the Medical College Admission Test*. New York: Barron's Educational Series, Inc., fifth edition, 1987.

Shawcross, William. *The Shah's Last Ride: The Fate of an Ally*. New York: Simon & Schuster, 1988.

Shem, Samuel. *The House of God*. New York: Richard Marek, Publisher, 1978.

Siegel, Bernie S., M.D. *Love, Medicine, and Miracles*. New York: Harper & Row, 1986.

Siegel, Bernie S., M.D. *Peace, Loving, and Healing*. New York: Harper & Row, 1989.

Smith, John M., M.D. *Women and Doctors: A Physician's Explosive Account of Women's Medical Treatment—and Mistreatment—in America Today and What You Can Do About It*. Boston: Atlantic Monthly Press, 1992.

Starr, Paul. *The Social Transformation of American Medicine*. New York: Basic Books, 1982.

Stevens, Rosemary. *American Medicine and the Public Interest*. New Haven and London: Yale University Press, 1971.

Stone, John. *In the Country of Hearts: Journeys in the Art of Medicine*. New York. Delacorte Press, 1990.

Stookey Byron, M.D. *A History of Colonial Medical Education*. Springfield, Ill.: Charles C. Thomas, Publisher, 1962.

Walsh, Mary Roth. *Doctors Wanted: No Women Need Apply: Sexual Barriers in the Medical Profession, 1835–1975*. New Haven: Yale University Press, 1977.

Weiler, Paul C., et al. *A Measure of Malpractice: Medical Injury, Malpractice Litigation, and Patient Compensation.* Cambridge, Mass.: Harvard University Press, 1993.

Weiss, Roger D., M.D., and Steven M. Mirin, M.D. *Cocaine: The Human Danger, the Social Costs, the Treatment Alternative.* New York: Ballantine Books, 1988.

Williams, William Carlos. *Doctor Stories,* compiled by Robert Coles. New York: New Directions, 1984.

X, Dr. *Intern.* New York: Harper & Row, 1965.

Yalof, Ina. *Life and Death: The Story of a Hospital.* New York: Random House, 1988.

Zion, Sidney. *Read All About It.* New York: Summit Books, 1982.

Zion, Sidney. *The Autobiography of Roy Cohn.* New York: Lyle Stuart, 1988.

Zion, Sidney. *Markers.* New York: Donald I. Fine, Inc., 1990.

Zion, Sidney. *Trust Your Mother But Cut the Cards.* New York: Barricade Books, 1993.

ARTICLES, BULLETINS, REPORTS, TRANSCRIPTS, REFERENCE BOOKS

Accreditation Council for Graduate Medical Education/ Revision of the General Requirements of the Essentials of Accredited Residencies. Effective July 1, 1992. 4th annual report. New York: New York State Council on Graduate Medical Education, 1991.

Altman, Lawrence K. "Medical Schools Gaining an Unexpected Popularity." *The New York Times,* 5/18/93.

The AMA Family Medical Guide, Revised and Updated. Jeffrey R. M. Kunz, M.D., and Asher J. Finkel, M.D., eds. New York: Random House, 1987.

Anderson, Cerisse. "Judge Dismisses Libel Suit Against New York Hospital." *New York Law Journal,* 8/17/90.

Asch, David A., M.D., and Ruth M. Parker, M.D. "The Libby Zion Case: One Step Forward or Two Steps Backward?" *New England Journal of Medicine,* "Sounding Board."

Bell, Bertrand M., M.D. "Evolutionary Imperatives, Quiet Revolutions: Changing Working Conditions and Supervision of House Officers." *The Pharos,* Spring 1989.

Brill, Steven. "Curing Doctors." *American Lawyer,* 9/85.

Clark, Matt. "The Tragedy That Transformed Training: The Case of Libby Z." *M.D.* magazine, 1/92.

Conigliaro, Joseph, M.D., et al. "Internal Medicine House Staff and Attending Physician Perceptions of the Impact of the New York State Section 405 Regulations on Working Conditions and Supervision of Residents in Two Training Programs." *Journal of General Internal Medicine*, 9/93.

Duncan, David Ewing. "Is This Any Way to Train a Doctor: Medical Residencies, the Next Health-Care Crisis." *Harper's*, 4/93.

Engel, Winslow, M.D., et al. "Clinical Performance of Interns After Being On Call." *Southern Medical Journal*, 6/19/87.

"Enhancing Standards of Excellence in Internal Medicine Training," Federal Council for Internal Medicine, Portland, Oregon. *Annals of Internal Medicine*, 11/87.

Farber, M. A. and Lawrence K. Altman. "A Great Hospital in Crisis." *The New York Times Magazine*, 1/24/88.

Farber, M. A. "Who Killed Libby Zion?" *Vanity Fair*, 12/88.

Featherstone, Harvey J., M.D., et al. "Analysis of Selection Criteria for Medical Residents." *The American Journal of Medicine*, 10/83.

Fiske, Edward B. *The Fiske Guide to Colleges*. New York: Times Books, 1992.

Gifford-Jones, W. "When Will Doctors Require a Law Degree?" *The Evening Times-Globe*, Saint John, New Brunswick, Canada, 3/27/92.

Glickman, Robert M., M.D. "House Staff Training: The Need for Careful Reform." *New England Journal of Medicine*, 4/25/88.

"Graduate Medical Education in New York State During an Era of Change: The 405 Regulations and Beyond," A Joint Proposal by The Johns Hopkins University, The University of Pennsylvania, and Harvard University. September, 1994.

Griffith, H. Winter, M.D. *Complete Guide to Prescription & Non-Prescription Drugs*. 9th ed. New York: The Putnam Publishing Group/The Body Press. Perigee Books, 1992.

Grun, Bernard. *The Timetables of History*. New York: Simon & Schuster, 1975.

Harvard Medical Alumni Bulletin, Winter 1989, Fall 1991, Spring 1992, Winter 1992–93.

Hentoff, Nat. "Are You Trying to Tell Me My Daughter Is Dead?" *The Village Voice*, 4/1/86.

Hillson, Steven D., M.D., et al. "Call Nights and Patient Care: Effects on

Inpatients at One Teaching Hospital." *Journal of General Internal Medicine*, July/August, 1992.

Hinckle, Warren. "Money Won't Do: Dad Wants Doctors Jailed for Daughter's Death." *San Francisco Examiner*, 9/15/85.

Holder, Angela R., and Hughes, John S. "Professional Responsibility" course booklet. Yale Medical School, 9/92.

"How Hospitals Violate the 'Bell' Regulations Governing Resident Working Conditions," a report by Mark Green, Public Advocate for the City of New York, 1994.

"How Safe Are Our Hospitals?" Hearing on Medical Malpractice. City Council/City of New York, Before Andrew Stein, Chairman, March 3, 1986.

The Johns Hopkins Medical Handbook, Simeon Margolis, M.D., and Hamilton Moses, III, M.D., medical eds. New York: Rebus, Inc., distributed by Random House, 1992.

Journal of Medical Education: Physicians for the Twenty-first Century. November 1984. Washington, D.C., and Baltimore: Association of American Medical Colleges.

Kubovy, Itamar. "Sleep Deprivation: A Brief Review of the Research." A booklet prepared for Theodore Friedman, 1992.

Leape, Lucian L., M.D. "Error in Medicine." *Journal of the American Medical Association*, 12/21/94.

Lofgren, Richard P., M.D., et al. "Post-call Transfer of Resident Responsibility: Its Effect on Patient Care." *Journal of Internal Medicine*, November/December, 1990.

Lurie, Nicolo, M.D., et al. "How Do House Officers Spend Their Nights?: A Time Study of Internal Medicine House Staff On Call." *New England Journal of Medicine*, 6/22/89.

Mayo Clinic Family Health Book. David E. Larson, M.D., editor in chief. New York: William Morrow & Company, 1990.

McCuje, Jack D., M.D. "The Distress of Internship." *New England Journal of Medicine*, 2/14/85.

Medical Malpractice Hearing. City Council/City of New York. Andrew Stein, Chairman. 1/21/86.

Medical School Admission Requirements: U.S. and Canada. 40th ed.—1990–91, and 43rd ed.—1993–94. Washington, D.C.: Association of American Medical Colleges.

The Mosby Medical Encyclopedia, rev. ed. New York: Penguin Books, 1992.

Nachman, Jerry. "Bitterness Lingers on Anniversary of Libby Zion's Death." *New York Post*, 5/5/89.

Nerenz, David, Ph.D., et al. "The On-Call Experience of Interns In Internal Medicine." *Archives of Internal Medicine*, 11/90.

Orey, Michael. "Zion Up-Date: Trouble for New York Hospital." *American Lawyer*, 4/87.

Patients, Doctors, and Lawyers: *Medical Injury, Malpractice Litigation, and Patient Compensation in New York:* A Report by the Harvard Medical Practice Study to the State of New York, 1990. Copyright/President and Fellows of Harvard College.

Peabody, Francis W., M.D. "The Care of the Patient." *Journal of the American Medical Association*, 3/9/27.

Physicians' Desk Reference, 44th ed. Oradell, New Jersey: Medical Economics Company, Inc., 1990.

Reports of the New York State Commission on Graduate Medical Education, February 1986. Albany, New York: New York State Commission on Graduate Medical Education.

"Risk Management Guidelines." *Diagnosis*, the Newsletter of the Medical Staff of the Presbyterian Hospital, 7/92.

Rosenthal, Elisabeth. "Elite Hospitals in New York City in Financial Bind." *The New York Times*, 2/13/95.

Schroeder, Steven A., M.D., et al. "Residency Training in Internal Medicine: Time for a Change." *Annals of Internal Medicine*, 4/86.

Schwartz, Robert and Janet Freedman. "Letter to the Editor." *New York Newsday*, 5/16/89.

Smith, Jay W., M.D., et al. "Emotional Impairment in Internal Medicine House Staff." *Journal of the American Medical Association*, 3/7/86.

Spritz, Norton, M.D. "Oversight of Physicians' Conduct by State Licensing Agencies: Lessons from New York's Libby Zion Case." *Annals of Internal Medicine*, 8/91.

Stone, Michael. "New York Hospital on the Spot." *New York*, 6/22/87.

Tanne, Janice Hopkins. "The Best Hospitals in New York." *New York*, 11/18/91.

Trends in Medical School Applications and Matriculants, 1989–1992. Washington, D.C.: Association of American Medical Colleges.

Wallis, Claudia, et al. "A Hospital Stands Accused." *Time*, 4/27/87.

Weiler, Paul C., et al. "Proposal for Medical Liability Reform." *Journal of the American Medical Association*, 5/6/92. As reprinted in the Yale Medical School course book.

Wicker, Tom. "In the Nation: 'Blaming the System.'" *The New York Times*, 2/4/87.

Yedidia, Michael J., et al. "Doctors as Workers." *Journal of General Internal Medicine*, 8/93.

Zion, Sidney. "Doctors Know Best?" *The New York Times*, 5/13/89.

Zion, Sidney. "Ghost Surgery Scandal." *New York Post*, 1/30/78, p. 3.

APPENDIX I
Medical Documents

PATIENT'S BILL OF RIGHTS

As a patient in a hospital in New York State, you have the right consistent with law, to:

- Understand and use these rights. If for any reason you do not understand or you need help, the hospital MUST provide you with assistance, including an interpreter.

- Receive treatment without discrimination as to race, color, religion, sex, national origin, disability, sexual orientation or source of payment.

- Receive considerate and respectful care in a clean and safe environment free of unnecessary restraints.

- Receive emergency care if you need it.

- Be informed of the name and position of the doctor who will be in charge of your care in the hospital.

- Know the names, positions and functions of any hospital staff involved in your care and refuse their treatment, examination or observation.

- A no smoking room

- Receive complete information about your diagnosis, treatment and prognosis.

- Receive all information that you need to give informed consent for any proposed procedure or treatment. This information shall include the possible risks and benefits of the procedure or treatment.

- Receive all the information you need to give informed consent for an order not to resuscitate. You also have the right to designate an individual to give this consent for you if you are too ill to do so. If you would like additional information, please ask for a copy of the pamphlet "Do Not Resuscitate Orders—A Guide for Patients and Families."

- Refuse treatment and be told what effect this may have on your health.

- Refuse to take part in research. In deciding whether or not to participate, you have the right to a full explanation.

- Privacy while in the hospital and confidentiality of all information and records regarding your care.

- Participate in all decisions about your treatment and discharge from the hospital. The hospital must provide you with a written discharge plan and written description of how you can appeal your discharge.

- Review your medical record without charge. Obtain a copy of your medical record for which the hospital can charge a reasonable fee. You cannot be denied a copy solely because you cannot afford to pay.

- Receive an itemized bill and explanation of all charges.

- Complain without fear of reprisals about the care and services you are receiving and to have the hospital respond to you and if you request it, a written response. If you are not satisfied with the hospital's response, you can complain to the New York State Health Department. The hospital must provide you with the Health Department telephone number.

Source: New York State Department of Health

DATE (MO., DY., YR.)		LOCATION	SERVICE		**F 172 03 32**	
18					**ZION, LIBBY**	
AGE	DOCTOR				IF NO PLATE, PRINT NAME, SEX, AND HISTORY NO.	

ORDERED		DOCTOR'S ORDER	Single Executed Time By Whom	Standing "Noted" Time By Whom	Orig. Discontinued
Date	Time				
3/5/84	3 AM	Admit to P5 – P3 boarder			
		Diagnosis – Fever			
		Cond – Fair			
		VS – Per routine			
		Allergies – None known		D. Gismar RN 3:20 AM	
		Diet – Regular			
		Act – OOB as tolerated		3/5	
		IV – D5 ½ NS @ 150 cc/hr			
		Meds – Tylenol 650 mg po Q 4h ATC			
		Demerol 25 mg IM x 1 Now			
		Am bloods – CBC c̄ diff, ANA, ESR,			
		heterophile antibody, EBV titer,			
		CMV titer.	R.W. 3/5 4 AM		
		Urine for C+S.		D. Gismar RN 3:20 AM	
		Throat culture.		3/5	
		Weinstein			
3/5					
					19

45166 THE NEW YORK HOSPITAL DOCTOR'S ORDER SHEET

Dr. Luise Weinstein's "closed order book," written at 3:00 A.M. on March 5, 1984.

"I suspect this is just a viral syndrome with hysterical symptoms," from Dr. Gregg Stone's note, March 5, 1984; detail enlarged.

DATE & TIME	NURSING PROGRESS RECORD (CONTINUED) (SIGN ALL ENTRIES WITH NAME AND TITLE)	DATE & TIME	NURSING PROGRESS RECORD (SIGN ALL ENTRIES WITH NAME AND TITLE)
3/5 5ᴬ	Pt c̄ visible shaking, thrashing across bed, trying to climb over siderails, nurse called Dr. Weinstein – intern on P3 @ 415ᴬ Pt promptly put on bed jacket restraint c̄ noted effectiveness; nurse restrained pt further c̄ 4-point restraint c̄ noted effectiveness – pt still thrashing herself across bed Dr. Weinstein called again @ 430 and asked to come up and see pt as pt needs some sort of sedation we are afraid she will hurt herself. Dr. Weinstein prescribed 1mg Haldol Sq for sedation. Chart checked for allergy – none noted. Pt given 1mg Haldol @ 430ᴬ	640ᴬ	hard to assess. Cardiac team called to P-5 nurses began CPR on pt immediately before calling code response prompt.
	J. Grismer, RN	730ᴬ	After working on pt for 50 minutes of care pronounced pt dead.
			J. Grismer, RN
600ᴬ	Pt c̄ noted T-118° – Dr. Weinstein called ordered stat cooling blanket and cold compresses. nurses and aides sponged pt down noted ↓ color, called code p̄ ↓ resp and pulse tingling ↓ pulse and resp – both weak,		25

43460

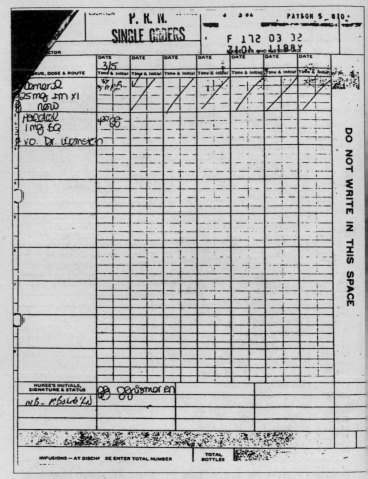

Order sheet signed by nurses showing dispensing of Demerol and Haldol to Libby Zion.

(facing page) Handwritten note by Dr. Jon Pearl on the last page of Libby's autopsy report. The term "toxic agitation" at the bottom is used for the first and only time.

AUTOPSY

Approximate A[...]   Approximate Weight

Height

Identified by

Stenographer[...]

   I he[...]

the body of

6th

and said aut[...]

M84-1921   -3-

TOXICOLOGY:

Sent for toxicology: Blood, bile, brain, liver, stomach, urine.

CAUSE OF DEATH:

BILATERAL BRONCHOPNEUMONIA PENDING FURTHER STUDY.

ANATOMICAL FINDINGS:

Reddish Discoloration of Face and Lower Extremities.
Consolidation of Right Upper and Left Lower Lobes.
Tracheobronchitis.
Status Post Dental Extraction, Left Lower Jaw.

Report of Toxicology reviewed. Report of hospital noted.

Clinically the patient had signs & symptoms of sepsis,
and of antigen free of pneumonitis were seen grossly & microscopic.
Although a small area histodid 5 days before death. The deceased was
treated with erythromycin, & the site of extraction was not probed
due to her sedation during two brief hospitalization meperidine
and butorphenol were administered within a few hours of death.
These drugs were not recovered in good amount toxicology due to
the small amount given & the sensitivity of the testing under
further she had been treated with phenalgine.

In view of the above the cause of death is:

acute pneumonitis 4 days following dental shock
and in course of treatment with an erythromycin. (hypoxemia?)
Pyrexia and sudden collapse shock following injection
of meperidine & butorphenol while in restraint for
toxic agitation. History of therapeutic phenalgine
injection.

     unclassified

             [signature]
             5/18/84

3/21/84/prs

84-1921

utopsy
the p[...]

M84-1921

CARDIOVASCU[...]
Heart weig[...]
with no c[...]
markable[...]

PULMO[...]
rig[...]
co[...]

Face[...]
the e[...]
reas[...]
simila[...]
of the[...]
of the[...]
with s[...]
There[...]
genit[...]
Rigid[...]

CENTR[...]

Head[...]
Ther[...]
of t[...]
injur[...]
There is no evide[...]

The mouth is examin[...]
or significant patho[...]
where the first left[...]
or edema here. It i[...]
small piece of tissue[...]
because there is no exp[...]

ENDOCRINE and adren[...]
Thyroid and adren[...]

SKELETO-MUSCULAR SYSTEM:
Unremarkable.

R-E SYSTEM:
Spleen weighs about 150 grams and has dark re[...]
prominence to malpighian corpuscles.[...]

[...]ows
[...]hou
[...]ind
[...]ridi
[...]hiti
left
the
[...]rkab

traum[...]
empty socket
little inflamma[...]
tion alone. A
ifficult to get tissue
ue.

5/8/89

From Borough of .... MO........-1921

Case of .... Libby Zion .... Address .... 215 West 90th

Autopsy by Dr. .... Pearl .... Date .... March 6, 84

Information Desired by Medical Examiner:

Examine for .... SANDA

Organs sent for Analysis .... Blood 60cc, Bile 6cc, Urine 30cc, Stomach 50cc, Brain, Liver

History:

18 (White, Female) .... 7 cc of URINE rec. from Dr. Pearl (3/9/84)

Age .... New York Hospital .... Occupation

Place of Death .... Date of Death .... March 5, 84 .... 2.45 pm

Time in Hospital .... 6 hours

Medication ....

Symptoms .... The dec. developed a fever following a tooth extraction (5

State by what means death occurred .... days prior to admission at the hospital) and later also an ear ache.

The dec. had a history of a drug abuser (amphetamines and marijuana)

Pathological Findings: .... Bronchopneumonia. .... PFS

Condition of Body .... On 3/16/84 at 2.30 ...

Delivered by ....

SAVE

Medical Examiner

March 9, 1984, Office of Chief Medical Examiner/Division of Laboratories report stating that Libby "had a history of a drug abuser (amphetamines and marijuana)." This description appears in no other official documents.

THE CITY OF NEW YORK
OFFICE OF CHIEF MEDICAL EXAMINER
520 FIRST AVENUE
NEW YORK, N.Y. 10016

1. - 3/:

TOXICOLOGY LABORATORY

DECEASED	LAB. NO.	M.E. CASE NO.
LIBBY ZION	1303/84	M84-1921

AUTOPSY BY DR.	LOCATION OF AUTOPSY	DATE OF AUTOPSY	TIME OF AUTOPSY
Pearl	Manhattan	3/6/84	

SPECIMENS SUBMITTED:

XX BLOOD XX BILE XX URINE XX STOMACH CONTENTS XX BRAIN XX LIVER ☐ KIDNEY

☐ OTHER, SPECIFY:

SPECIMENS RECEIVED IN LABORATORY BY	DATE RECEIVED	TIME RECEIVED
Dr. Nalini Valanju	3/7/84	10 am

RESULTS: EQUIVALENTS: 1 mag/ml=1.0mg/L=0.1mg%; 1mag/gm=1.0mg/kg=0.1mg%

SAMPLES RECEIVED FROM THE HOSPITAL

BLOOD: (culture media, dilution 1: 10) - Meperidine & other basic
drugs - not detected- gas chromatography (GC),
Cocaine - detected by Radioimmunoassay, but not detected by (GC)
Opiates not detected by (RI)
Barbiturates not detected by liquid chromatography (LC)
Salicylates detected- 2.8 mg % by Fluorometry (FLU)

URINE: Amphetamines, Barbiturates, Benzoylecgonine, Cannabinoids &
Opiates - not detected by Enzyme Immunoassay (EI)

SAMPLES COLLECTED AT THE AUTOPSY

BLOOD: Ethanol - not detected- by Conway Diffusion
Cocaine & Opiates - not detected - by (RI)
Meperidine & other basic drugs - not detected by (GC)
Barbiturates- not detected by (LC)
Salicylates detected, 20.6 mg % by (FLU)

URINE: Basic, Acidic drugs & Opiates- not detected by thin-layer chromatography (TLC)
/Amphetamines, Benzoylecgonine & Cannabinoids- not detected by (EI)

LIVER: (100g) Pheniramine derivative detected by (TLC) & Spectrophotometry (S)
Pheniramine, Haloperidol & other basic drugs not detected by (TLC)

BILE: Cocaine & Opiates not detected by (RI)

STOMACH CONTENT: Salicylates not detected by Chemical Test (CT)
Trace of Acetaminophen detected by (TLC)
Basic drugs not detected by (TLC)"

SWABS: Trace of Cocaine detected by (RI)-not enough material for confirmation
by (TLC)

SIGNED _____ DATE 5/8/84
DIRECTOR OF LABORATORY
Prof. Milton L. Bastos

May 8, 1984, toxicological report on Libby Zion. Note that cocaine
was detected in her hospital blood by RIA, and that a trace of cocaine was detected in a nasal swab. Also note high level of a salicy-
late, aspirin, in autopsy blood. Aspirin is found in Percodan.
Pheniramine, an antihistamine, was detected in her liver. A trace of
acetaminophen, or Tylenol, was detected in her stomach.

TOXICOLOGY LABORATORY

DECEASED		LAB. NO.	M.E. CASE NO.
LIBBY ZION		1303/84	M84-1921

AUTOPSY BY DR.	LOCATION OF AUTOPSY	DATE OF AUTOPSY	TIME OF AUTOPSY
P. rl	Manhattan	3/6/84	

SPECIMENS SUBMITTED:

☑ BLOOD   ☐ BILE   ☑ URINE   ☑ STOMACH CONTENTS   ☐ BRAIN   ☐ LIVER   ☐ KIDNEY

Culture blood received from Hospital

☐ OTHER, SPECIFY:

SPECIMENS RECEIVED IN LABORATORY BY	DATE RECEIVED	TIME RECEIVED
Dr. Nalini Valanju	3/7/84	10 am

RESULTS: EQUIVALENTS: 1 mg/ml=1.5mg/g=0.1mg%;   1mg/g=1.5mg/g=0.1mg%

SUPPLEMENTARY REPORT

BLOOD (culture media, dilution 1:10) bottle number 1,
date Feb, 29, used for the analysis described
in th original report.
Cocaine not det cted by Radioimmunoassay on august, 24.

BLOOD (Culture media, dilution 1:10) bottle number 2,
no date, not used for analysis.
Cocaine not detected by Radioimmunoassay on August, 24 .

Refer to original report issued o 5/8/84.

SIGNED: _____ DATE 8/27/87
DIRECTOR OF LABORATORY

1) CASE FILE

August 27, 1984, "highly unusual" supplementary toxicological report showing no cocaine in Libby's hospital blood.

APPENDIX II
Verdict Sheet

Sample Instruction Sheet used by jury to reach a verdict in *Zion* v. *New York Hospital*. Check marks indicate the consensus reached by jurors, with dissenting jurors noted.

SUPREME COURT OF THE STATE OF NEW YORK
COUNTY OF NEW YORK

.... X

SIDNEY E. ZION, as Administrator
of the estate of LIBBY ZION,
deceased,

Plaintiff, Index No. 15353/85

-against-

THE NEW YORK HOSPITAL, RAYMOND SHERMAN, M.D., MAURICE LEONARD, M.D., LUISE WEINSTEIN, M.D., and GREGG STONE, M.D.,

Defendants.

.... X

VERDICT SHEET

1. (a) Did Dr. Leonard depart from accepted medical practice with respect to the hydration of Libby Zion?

Yes_____ No__✓__

Dissenting Juror, if any   Number_____

(b) If "yes," was that departure a proximate cause of Libby Zion's pain and suffering or death?

Yes_____ No_____

Dissenting Juror, if any   Number_____

2. (a) Did Dr. Leonard depart from accepted medical practice with respect to the performing of a neurologic examination on Libby Zion?

Yes_____ No__✓__

Dissenting Juror, if any   Number_____

(b) If "yes," was that departure a proximate cause of Libby Zion's pain and suffering or death?

Yes_____ No_____

Dissenting Juror, if any   Number_____

3. (a) Did Dr. Leonard depart from accepted medical practice by not ordering arterial blood gases for Libby Zion?

Yes_____ No ✔____

Dissenting Juror, if any   Number_____

(b) If "yes," was that departure a proximate cause of Libby Zion's pain and suffering or death?

Yes_____ No_____

Dissenting Juror, if any   Number_____

4. (a) Did Dr. Sherman depart from accepted medical practice by not going to New York Hospital to evaluate and treat Libby Zion?

Yes_____ No ✔____

Dissenting Juror, if any   Number 6___

(b) If "yes," was that departure a proximate cause of Libby Zion's pain and suffering or death?

Yes_____ No_____

Dissenting Juror, if any   Number_____

5. (a) Did Dr. Sherman depart from accepted medical practice with respect to the hydration of Libby Zion?

Yes_____ No ✔____

Dissenting Juror, if any   Number_____

(b) If "yes," was that departure a proximate cause of Libby Zion's pain and suffering or death?

Yes_____ No_____

Dissenting Juror, if any   Number_____

6.   (a) Did Dr. Sherman depart from accepted medical practice by not ordering Libby Zion's admission to an Intensive Care Unit?

Yes_____   No ✓_____

Dissenting Juror, if any   Number **6**

(b) If "yes," was that departure a proximate cause of Libby Zion's pain and suffering or death?

Yes_____   No_____

Dissenting Juror, if any   Number_____

7.   (a) Did Dr. Sherman depart from accepted medical practice by not ordering arterial blood gases for Libby Zion?

Yes_____   No ✓_____

Dissenting Juror, if any   Number_____

(b) If "yes," was that departure a proximate cause of Libby Zion's pain and suffering or death?

Yes_____   No_____

Dissenting Juror, if any   Number_____

8.   (a) Did Dr. Sherman depart from accepted medical practice by making viral syndrome the working diagnosis for Libby Zion?

Yes_____   No ✓_____

Dissenting Juror, if any   Number_____

(b) If "yes," was that departure a proximate cause of Libby Zion's pain and suffering or death?

Yes_____   No_____

Dissenting Juror, if any   Number_____

9.   (a) Did Dr. Sherman depart from accepted medical practice by withholding antibiotics from Libby Zion?

Yes_____   No ✓_____

Dissenting Juror, if any   Number_____

(b) If "yes," was that departure a proximate cause of Libby Zion's pain and suffering or death?

Yes_____ No_____

Dissenting Juror, if any   Number_____

10. (a) Did Dr. Sherman depart from accepted medical practice by not including pneumonia in the differential diagnoses for Libby Zion?

Yes_____ No✔_____

Dissenting Juror, if any   Number_____

(b) If "yes," was that departure a proximate cause of Libby Zion's pain and suffering or death?

Yes_____ No_____

Dissenting Juror, if any   Number_____

11. (a) Did Dr. Sherman depart from accepted medical practice with respect to the chest X ray ordered for Libby Zion?

Yes_____ No✔_____

Dissenting Juror, if any   Number_____

(b) If "yes," was that departure a proximate cause of Libby Zion's pain and suffering or death?

Yes_____ No_____

Dissenting Juror, if any   Number_____

12. (a) Did Dr. Sherman depart from accepted medical practice by ordering Libby Zion's temperature to be monitored every four hours?

Yes_____ No✔_____

Dissenting Juror, if any   Number **6**

(b) If "yes," was that departure a proximate cause of Libby Zion's pain and suffering or death?

Yes_____ No_____

Dissenting Juror, if any   Number_____

13. (a) Did Dr. Sherman know that Dr. Stone intended to administer Demerol to Libby Zion?

Yes ✓____   No____

Dissenting Juror, if any   Number____

(b) If "yes," did Dr. Sherman depart from accepted medical practice by permitting the administration of Demerol to Libby Zion?

Yes ✓____   No____

Dissenting Juror, if any   Number____

(c) If "yes," was that departure a proximate cause of Libby Zion's pain and suffering or death?

Yes ✓____   No____

Dissenting Juror, if any   Number____

14. (a) Did Dr. Stone depart from accepted medical practice with respect to the hydration of Libby Zion?

Yes____   No ✓____

Dissenting Juror, if any   Number____

(b) If "yes," was that departure a proximate cause of Libby Zion's pain and suffering or death?

Yes____   No____

Dissenting Juror, if any   Number____

15. (a) Did Dr. Stone depart from accepted medical practice by not recommending Libby Zion's admission to an Intensive Care Unit?

Yes____   No ✓____

Dissenting Juror, if any   Number____

(b) If "yes," was that departure a proximate cause of Libby Zion's pain and suffering or death?

Yes____   No____

Dissenting Juror, if any   Number____

16. (a) Did Dr. Stone depart from accepted medical practice with respect to the performing of a neurologic examination on Libby Zion?

Yes_____ No ✓_____

Dissenting Juror, if any   Number_____

(b) If "yes," was that departure a proximate cause of Libby Zion's pain and suffering or death?

Yes_____ No_____

Dissenting Juror, if any   Number_____

17. (a) Did Dr. Stone depart from accepted medical practice by not ordering arterial blood gases for Libby Zion?

Yes_____ No ✓_____

Dissenting Juror, if any   Number_____

(b) If "yes," was that departure a proximate cause of Libby Zion's pain and suffering or death?

Yes_____ No_____

Dissenting Juror, if any   Number_____

18. (a) Did Dr. Stone depart from accepted medical practice by making viral syndrome with hysterical symptoms the working diagnosis for Libby Zion?

Yes_____ No ✓_____

Dissenting Juror, if any   Number_____

(b) If "yes," was that departure a proximate cause of Libby Zion's pain and suffering or death?

Yes_____ No_____

Dissenting Juror, if any   Number_____

19. (a) Did Dr. Stone depart from accepted medical practice by not recommending to Dr. Sherman that antibiotics be administered to Libby Zion?

Yes_____ No ✓_____

Dissenting Juror, if any   Number_____

(b) If "yes," was that departure a proximate cause of Libby Zion's pain and suffering or death?

Yes_____ No_____

Dissenting Juror, if any   Number_____

20. (a) Did Dr. Stone depart from accepted medical practice by not including pneumonia in the differential diagnoses for Libby Zion?

Yes_____ No✓_____

Dissenting Juror, if any   Number_____

(b) If "yes," was that departure a proximate cause of Libby Zion's pain and suffering or death?

Yes_____ No_____

Dissenting Juror, if any   Number_____

21. (a) Did Dr. Stone depart from accepted medical practice with respect to the chest X ray ordered for Libby Zion?

Yes_____ No✓_____

Dissenting Juror, if any   Number_____

(b) If "yes," was that departure a proximate cause of Libby Zion's pain and suffering or death?

Yes_____ No_____

Dissenting Juror, if any   Number_____

22. (a) Did Dr. Stone depart from accepted medical practice with respect to the monitoring of Libby Zion's temperature?

Yes_____ No✓_____

Dissenting Juror, if any   Number 6

(b) If "yes," was that departure a proximate cause of Libby Zion's pain and suffering or death?

Yes_____ No_____

Dissenting Juror, if any   Number_____

23. (a) Did Dr. Stone depart from accepted medical practice by ordering the administration of Demerol to Libby Zion?

Yes ✔ No____

Dissenting Juror, if any   Number____

(b) If "yes," was that departure a proximate cause of Libby Zion's pain and suffering or death?

Yes ✔ No____

Dissenting Juror, if any   Number____

24. (a) Did Dr. Stone depart from accepted medical practice by leaving Libby Zion and New York Hospital on the morning of March 5, 1984?

Yes____ No ✔

Dissenting Juror, if any   Number **6**

(b) If "yes," was that departure a proximate cause of Libby Zion's pain and suffering or death?

Yes____ No____

Dissenting Juror, if any   Number____

25. (a) Did Dr. Weinstein depart from accepted medical practice with respect to the hydration of Libby Zion?

Yes____ No ✔

Dissenting Juror, if any   Number____

(b) If "yes," was that departure a proximate cause of Libby Zion's pain and suffering or death?

Yes____ No____

Dissenting Juror, if any   Number____

26. (a) Did Dr. Weinstein depart from accepted medical practice with respect to Dr. Stone's plan for "cool soaks/compresses"?

Yes ✔ No____

Dissenting Juror, if any   Number **5**

(b) If "yes," was that departure a proximate cause of Libby Zion's pain and suffering or death?

Yes ✓   No _____

Dissenting Juror, if any   Number **5**

27. (a) Did Dr. Weinstein depart from accepted medical practice by not ordering Tylenol every three hours for a temperature greater than 38 degrees Celsius?

Yes _____   No ✓

Dissenting Juror, if any   Number _____

(b) If "yes," was that departure a proximate cause of Libby Zion's pain and suffering or death?

Yes _____   No _____

Dissenting Juror, if any   Number _____

28. (a) Did Dr. Weinstein depart from accepted medical practice by ordering Demerol for Libby Zion?

Yes ✓   No _____

Dissenting Juror, if any   Number _____

(b) If "yes," was that departure a proximate cause of Libby Zion's pain and suffering or death?

Yes ✓   No _____

Dissenting Juror, if any   Number _____

29. (a) Did Dr. Weinstein depart from accepted medical practice by not ordering Libby Zion's temperature to be monitored more frequently than every four hours?

Yes _____   No ✓

Dissenting Juror, if any   Number **6**

(b) If "yes," was that departure a proximate cause of Libby Zion's pain and suffering or death?

Yes_____ No_____

Dissenting Juror, if any   Number_____

30. (a) Did Dr. Weinstein depart from accepted medical practice by ordering that Libby Zion be placed in restraints?

Yes_____ No **✓**

Dissenting Juror, if any   Number **6**

(b) If "yes," was that departure a proximate cause of Libby Zion's pain and suffering or death?

Yes_____ No_____

Dissenting Juror, if any   Number_____

31. (a) Did Dr. Weinstein depart from accepted medical practice by not attending at Libby Zion's bedside when called by Nurse Balde between 4:15 A.M. and 4:30 A.M.?

Yes_____ No **✓**

Dissenting Juror, if any   Number **6**

(b) If "yes," was that departure a proximate cause of Libby Zion's pain and suffering or death?

Yes_____ No_____

Dissenting Juror, if any   Number_____

32. (a) Did Dr. Weinstein depart from accepted medical practice by not attending at Libby Zion's bedside when called by Nurse Grismer at 4:30 A.M.?

Yes **✓** No_____

Dissenting Juror, if any   Number **5**

(b) If "yes," was that departure a proximate cause of Libby Zion's pain and suffering or death?

Yes ✓____   No_____

Dissenting Juror, if any   Number **5**

33. (a) Did Dr. Weinstein depart from accepted medical practice in ordering the administration of Haldol to Libby Zion?

Yes_____   No ✓____

Dissenting Juror, if any   Number **6**

(b) If "yes," was that departure a proximate cause of Libby Zion's pain and suffering or death?

Yes_____   No_____

Dissenting Juror, if any   Number_____

34. (a) Did Dr. Weinstein depart from accepted medical practice by not checking on Libby Zion's status between 4:30 A.M. and 6:30 A.M.?

Yes_____   No ✓____

Dissenting Juror, if any   Number **6**

(b) If "yes," was that departure a proximate cause of Libby Zion's pain and suffering or death?

Yes_____   No_____

Dissenting Juror, if any   Number_____

35. (a) Did Dr. Weinstein depart from accepted medical practice by not consulting with more experienced physician(s) after 4:15 A.M.?

Yes ✓____   No_____

Dissenting Juror, if any   Number_____

(b) If "yes," was that departure a proximate cause of Libby Zion's pain and suffering or death?

Yes ✓____   No_____

Dissenting Juror, if any   Number **4**

36. (a) Did Dr. Weinstein depart from accepted medical practice by the manner in which she responded to the call at 6:30 A.M.?

Yes ✔   No _____

Dissenting Juror, if any   Number **5**

(b) If "yes," was that departure a proximate cause of Libby Zion's pain and suffering or death?

Yes _____   No ✔

Dissenting Juror, if any   Number _____

37. (a) Was New York Hospital negligent with respect to the manner in which its interns or residents were supervised?

Yes _____   No ✔

Dissenting Juror, if any   Number **6**

(b) If "yes," was that negligence a proximate cause of Libby Zion's pain and suffering or death?

Yes _____   No _____

Dissenting Juror, if any   Number _____

38. (a) Was New York Hospital negligent with respect to the work load assigned to Dr. Weinstein on March 4–5, 1984?

Yes ✔   No _____

Dissenting Juror, if any   Number **5**

(b) If "yes," was that negligence a proximate cause of Libby Zion's pain and suffering or death?

Yes _____   No ✔

Dissenting Juror, if any   Number **6**

39. (a) Did New York Hospital maintain a residency program which impaired the ability of its interns or residents to treat Libby Zion because they were sleep-deprived?

Yes_____ No ✓_____

Dissenting Juror, if any   Number **6**

(b) If "yes," was that negligent conduct?

Yes_____ No_____

Dissenting Juror, if any   Number_____

(c) If "yes," was that negligence a proximate cause of Libby Zion's pain and suffering or death?

Yes_____ No_____

Dissenting Juror, if any   Number_____

If you have not answered "yes" to *any* of the above questions regarding proximate cause, you have found in favor of defendants and need go no further. If you answered "yes" to *any one* of the above questions regarding proximate cause, consider the remaining questions.

40. (a) Did Libby Zion ingest cocaine on March 4, 1984?

Yes ✓_____ No_____

Dissenting Juror, if any   Number **6**

(b) If "yes," was that a proximate cause of Libby Zion's pain and suffering or death?

Yes ✓_____ No_____

Dissenting Juror, if any   Number **6**

41. (a) Was Libby Zion negligent with respect to the medical history she gave when she went to New York Hospital?

Yes ✓_____ No_____

Dissenting Juror, if any   Number **6**

(b) If "yes," was that negligence a proximate cause of Libby Zion's pain and suffering or death?

Yes ✓   No_____

Dissenting Juror, if any   Number **6**

42. If your answer to 40(b) or 41(b) is "yes," what is the percentage of fault of

Defendants **50**%
Libby Zion **50**%

TOTAL 100%

Dissenting Juror, if any   Number_____

DAMAGES

1. What damages do you award to plaintiff for Libby Zion's pain and suffering?

$ **750,000.00**

Dissenting Juror, if any   Number **6**

2. What damages do you award to plaintiff for Libby Zion's wrongful death?

$ **1.00**

Dissenting Juror, if any   Number **5**

Punitive Damages

1. Should New York Hospital be held liable for punitive damages?

   Yes_____ No ✓_____

Dissenting Juror, if any   Number **6**

2. Should Dr. Sherman be held liable for punitive damages?

   Yes_____ No ✓_____

Dissenting Juror, if any   Number_____

3. Should Dr. Weinstein be held liable for punitive damages?

   Yes_____ No ✓_____

Dissenting Juror, if any   Number_____

4. Should Dr. Stone be held liable for punitive damages?

   Yes_____ No ✓_____

Dissenting Juror, if any   Number_____

INDEX